Asian Canadian Writing
Beyond Autoethnography

Asian Canadian Writing
Beyond Autoethnography

Eleanor Ty and Christl Verduyn,
editors

Wilfrid Laurier University Press

This book has been published with the help of a grant from the Canadian Federation for the Humanities and Social Sciences, through the Aid to Scholarly Publications Programme, using funds provided by the Social Sciences and Humanities Research Council of Canada. We acknowledge the financial support of the Government of Canada through the Book Publishing Industry Development Program for our publishing activities.

Library and Archives Canada Cataloguing in Publication

Asian Canadian writing beyond autoethnography / Eleanor Ty and Christl Verduyn, editors

Includes bibliographical references and index.
ISBN 978-1-55458-023-1

    1. Canadian literature—Asian-Canadian authors—History and criticism. 2. Asian Canadians in literature. I. Ty, Eleanor, 1958– II. Verduyn, Christl, 1953–

PS8089.5.A8A84 2008   C810.9'895   C2008-901648-3

Cover design by Blakeley Words+Pictures. Cover image: *Eternal Spirit 2*, intaglio/relief print by Gloria Kagawa, www.gloriakagawa.com. Text design by Catharine Bonas-Taylor.

© 2008 Wilfrid Laurier University Press
Waterloo, Ontario, Canada
www.wlupress.wlu.ca

This book is printed on Ancient Forest Friendly paper (100% post-consumer recycled).

Printed in Canada

Every reasonable effort has been made to acquire permission for copyright material used in this text, and to acknowledge all such indebtedness accurately. Any errors and omissions called to the publisher's attention will be corrected in future printings.

[contents]

[part 4] Global Affiliations

[acknowledgements]

We would like to acknowledge and express thanks to the various individuals, institutions, and organizations that helped make this book possible. First and foremost, sincere thanks to the contributors for their insightful work and generous collaboration. Some of the essays developed from papers they delivered, along with many other presenters, at the conference "Beyond Autoethnography: Writing Race and Ethnicity in Canada," which we organized and held at Wilfrid Laurier University in the spring of 2005. For funding support of the conference, many thanks to the Social Sciences and Humanities Research Council (Aid to Scholarly Conferences) and to the Department of English and Film Studies, the Canadian Studies Program, and the offices of the Dean of Arts and the Vice-President Academic at Wilfrid Laurier University. The success of the conference was assured by all those who presented their work at it, and by organizational assistance from our students and colleagues: Denise Handlarski, Marci Prescott, Miriam Raethel, Kristen Lautenbach, Jenny Wills, Sylvia Terzian, and Paul Tiessen. We thank them all. Preparation of the manuscript was facilitated by funding from our respective Social Sciences and Humanities Research Council grants. Jenny Wills helped enormously with bibliographic, endnote, indexing, and other textual details. We are very grateful to the Director of Wilfrid Laurier University Press, Brian Henderson, for his commitment to publication of the volume, and to Jacqueline Larson, Lisa Quinn and Leslie Macredie on the Press's editorial and marketing teams, for their assistance with its production. Anonymous readers provided valuable feedback and suggestions and the Aid to Scholarly Publication Program granted valuable funding support. Finally, to our families for their ongoing support and good humour as we pursued this and other research projects, our heartfelt thanks and deep appreciation.

Eleanor Ty and Christl Verduyn

[introduction]

Eleanor Ty and Christl Verduyn

*A*sian Canadian Writing Beyond Autoethnography explores some of the latest developments in the literary and cultural practices of Canadians of Asian heritage. The focus of the volume is on works by writers, artists, and intellectuals published in the last ten years that have shifted noticeably and even dramatically in style, genre, and subject matter from those produced some twenty or thirty years ago under the broad rubrics of ethnic or racial "minority writing"[1] or multicultural production. Research and writing on multiculturalism, race, and ethnicity have developed and changed considerably in Canada in recent years, as they have in the United States. The advent of postcolonial literary theory and anti-racist cultural practice during the 1980s in Canada generated intense investigation and interrogation, including of terminology itself. The term minority writing, for example, has been analyzed as a construct and expression of the power and literary politics of a given time and context.[2] Canadian critic and author Smaro Kamboureli has argued powerfully that "multicultural writing is not minority writing for it does not raise issues that are of minor interest to Canadians. Nor is it, by any standard, of lesser quality than the established literary tradition. Its thematic concerns are of such a diverse range that they show the binary structure of 'centre' and 'margins,' which has for so long informed discussions of Canadian literature, to be a paradigm of the history of political and cultural affairs in Canada."[3] Writing from the United States in the late 1980s, Abdul JanMohamed and David Lloyd observed that "Western humanism still considers us [minority cultures] barbarians beyond the pale of civilization; we are forever consigned to play the role of the ontological, political, economic, and cultural

1

Other according to the schema of a Manichaean allegory that seems the central trope not only of colonialist discourse but also of Western humanism."[4] Today, commentators are more circumspect with regard to such sweeping statements about Western humanism, and more cautious about making such clear divisions between the West and the non-West, between the civilized and the savage. A racially minoritized writer in North America, for example, may no longer necessarily be associated mainly with the marginal, minor, or Other the way JanMohamed and Lloyd asserted. In 2000, Sri Lankan–born Canadian Michael Ondaatje was awarded the Kiriyama Pacific Rim Book Prize, the Prix Médicis, the Governor General's Award, and the Giller Prize for his novel *Anil's Ghost*, set in the civil war landscape of Sri Lanka in the late twentieth century.[5] While Ondaatje's success does not negate a history of political, economic, and cultural colonialization and othering of non-Western subjects, there are strong indications that ethnic and racially minoritized authors in Canada and in the United States have made gains in their effort to claim Canadian or American subjectivity and to "return the gaze," to echo a phrase used by Himani Bannerji.[6]

In his major survey, *A History of Canadian Literature* (1989), W.H. New noted how ethnicity, region, and gender marked the literature of the quarter century between 1960 and 1985.[7] In the fiction and poetry of the 1970s, New observed, realist accounts were the dominant mode of representation: "historical realism in fiction or drama; social themes and authenticity of detail were paramount, vocabulary and rhythm drew on vernacular speech, the presence of a recording 'I' as observer or participant in political and social issues reinforced the immediacy of the literary work."[8] New described the typical tendencies of the novel of this period:

> There emerged among writers concerned to declare the experience of a particular ethnic group a series of semi-documentary works that in fiction most characteristically took the form of the *Bildungsroman* or novel-of-growing-up. One typical premise results in integration and success. A more common one involves a child of immigrant parents who adapts to the new land more readily than the parents do but who never seems quite to belong; the impulse to reject old values (or the desire to retain them) recurrently stands between the individual and the majority.[9]

Among the poets New included were Marilyn Bowering, Erin Mouré, Lorna Crozier, Sharon Thesen, Mary di Michele, Eli Mandel, George Ryga, Joy Kogawa, and others. Some of the novelists listed included Rudy Wiebe, Marika Robert, Jan Drabek, Austin Clarke, Myrna Kostash, Harold Sonny Ladoo, Frank Paci, and Joy Kogawa.[10] Though there are inevitably exceptions to this kind of generalization, New's observations about the type of work being produced in that earlier period provide a useful point of departure for our discussion of the expansion of modes of writing about race and ethnicity in the last decade.

While earlier work by ethnic writers was often concerned with immigration, the moment of arrival, issues of assimilation, and conflicts between the first and second generation, literary and cultural production in the new millennium is not solely focused on the conflict between the Old World and the New World or the clashes between culture of origin and adopted Western culture. Recent works by ethnic, multicultural, or minority writers in Canada have become more diverse and experimental in form, theme, focus, and technique. No longer are minority authors identifying simply with their ethnic or racial cultural background in opposition to dominant culture. Many authors consciously attempt to question or problematize the link between ethnic identity and literary production, while still recognizing the racialized context in which they write. Globalization, rapid shifts in technology and communication, cross-cultural and intra-community networks, and racial and cultural hybridization have affected and challenged representations of the Other in contemporary novels, plays, poems, and films. Questions of sexuality and gender have further complicated the assumptions about the ethnic subject and its representation—in particular, its autoethnographic representation. The essays in this collection explore ways in which Asian Canadian authors have gone beyond what Françoise Lionnet calls autoethnography, or ethnographic autobiography[11] and how the representations of race and ethnicity, particularly in works by Asian Canadians, have changed in Canada in the last decade.

The term "autoethnography," according to Deborah Reed-Danahay, "synthesizes both a postmodern ethnography, in which the realist conventions and objective observer position of standard ethnography have been called into question, and a postmodern autobiography, in which the notion of the coherent, individual self has been similarly called into question.[12] Reed-Danahay notes that "the term has a double sense—referring either to the ethnography of one's own group or to autobiographical writing that has ethnographic interest."[13] Similarly, James Buzard defines autoethnography as "the study, representation, or knowledge of a culture by one or more of its members," but he notes that the term is "currently occupying the curious position of appearing at once the obvious successor to discredited ethnographic modes and, as yet, a far from universally adopted term in contemporary discourse on culture."[14] Buzard points out that the term has been used "at the junction of Sociology, Communication Studies, and Education," but it is still relatively under-used "by critical humanities and social-science scholars over the past several decades" who are clustered into two tropes of "voice and place—those of 'Letting the Silenced Speak,' 'Telling Our Own Story,' or 'Speaking for Ourselves,' on the one hand, and those of 'Situated Knowledges,' 'the Politics of Location,' or 'Standpoint Epistemologies.'"[15] Underlying both definitions of the term is the belief in the "essentialness" of a particular group, an implication of the special "insider" status of a group member. Even Mary Louise Pratt's reformulation of the term to focus on "contact zones," where "colonized subjects undertake to represent themselves in ways that *engage with* the colonizer's own terms," is still predicated on an "authentic" other.[16] This essentialist notion is problematic when applied to a heterogeneous group of pan-Asian Canadians who are, in many ways, still in the formative stages of developing hybridized group identities. To put it another way, Smaro Kamboureli observes in her essay that the term autoethnography, with its implication of a native informant, is "marked by the condition of complicity" (Section 11).

We use the term "beyond autoethnography" not so much to "discredit" ethnography, as suggested by Buzard, because ethnography, too, has been in the process of "personalizing, politicizing, and socializing its praxis," and reinventing itself, particularly as "critical ethnography."[17] Practitioners of "critical ethnography," such as D. Soyini Madison, emphasize its "ethical responsibility to address processes of unfairness or injustice within a particular *lived* domain."[18] The goals of critical ethnography, as defined by Madison, are similar to the politics of Asian Canadian Studies: "The critical ethnographer also takes us beneath surface appearances, disrupts the *status quo*, and unsettles both neutrality and taken-for-granted assumptions by bringing to light underlying and obscure operations of power and control."[19] Nor are we suggesting that autoethnography itself is no longer useful, because so much of what Asian Canadians are today has been the product of the situatedness and the politics of voice that was the empowering feature of the feminist and postcolonial discourses of the 1980s and early 1990s. Instead, we are using "beyond autoethnography" to characterize and highlight texts that refuse to be contained simply by their ethnic markers. We are not signalling the end of the trend of autoethnography, the practice in which a member of a marginalized group studies, examines, and speaks on behalf of that group, but suggesting that new possibilities in creative expression and writing by Asian Canadians are not necessarily predicated on the exposition of one's ethnic identity. Going "beyond" autoethnography or critical ethnography means moving away from questions of "authenticity," essentialist identity politics, and a view of a cultural group that is static, rather than evolving. In addition, as Paul Lai perceptively notes, going "beyond autoethnography" also raises questions about the way literary critics approach ethnographic texts, about the ways we highlight certain features and not others of works by ethnic or minority writers. The terms "beyond" and "autoethnography" are more fully theorized, philosophized, and explicated by Smaro Kamboureli in the first essay of this collection.

Multiculturalism and Ethnic and "Minority" Writing in Canada: Historical Overview

In a review of thirty years of multicultural policy and Canadian literature, Judy Young recalled the difficulty, during the early years of the Multiculturalism Program subventions for studies on writers and writing activities of Canada's "minority" communities, to find researchers and research on work from the Chinese, Japanese, and other Asian communities.[20] Language presented an early obstacle until English and French began to replace writing in languages from the Asian continent. This situation was not unique to Asian Canadian artistic communities; other minority groups in Canada faced similar linguistic hurdles. Other groups, too, confronted a history of marginalization from mainstream Canadian society and culture.[21] For Canadians of Asian descent this is a particularly painful history. Chinese Canadians, for example, suffered the indignity of the 1923 Chinese Immigration Act, designed to prevent the arrival of their families and relatives. Japanese Canadians were treated as enemies of Canada during World War II,[22] dispossessed of their homes and interned in camps, a history that many Canadians have come to know through Joy Kogawa's powerful 1981 novel, *Obasan*.[23] Canadians of Asian background in general have had to contend with the "identification of the North with the superiority of white northern races and its concomitant denigration (and exclusion from immigration) of the so-called southern races, particularly Asians."[24] Some scholars see the socio-political inequities continuing in present-day Canadian society. Anti-racist critic Himani Bannerji points out that Asian Canadians and other visible minorities cannot as readily be assimilated into white Canada the way other ethnicities, such as Eastern European, Scottish, or Irish have been assimilated. Visible minorities remain "an ambiguous presence," Bannerji states, "our existence a question mark in the side of the nation, with the potential to disclose much about the political unconscious and consciousness of Canada as an 'imagined community.' Disclosures accumulate slowly while we continue to live here as outsider-insiders of the nation which offers a proudly multicultural profile to the international community."[25] Resistance to such obstacles and to ideological constructions of belonging and nationhood have underwritten much of Asian Canadian literary and cultural work. Yet, despite such challenges, Asian Canadian writing emerged to critical attention by the late 1980s. In addition to individual authors, such as Joy Kogawa, Michael Ondaatje, Neil Bissoondath, Bharati Mukherjee, Rohinton Mistry, Rienzi Crusz, M. Lakshmi Gill, Sunita Namjoshi, Cyril Dabydeen, M.G. Vassanji, Fred Wah, Roy Miki, Roy Kiyooka, and Richard Fung, who were producing work in this period, several anthologies featuring Asian Canadian writers and artists appeared: Gerry Shikatani and David Aylward's *Paper Doors: An Anthology of Japanese Canadian Poetry* (1981); M.G. Vassanji's *A Meeting of Streams: South Asian Canadian Literature* (1985); Cyril Dabydeen's *A Shapely Fire: Changing the Literary Landscape* (1987); Paul Wong's multimedia *Yellow Peril Reconsidered* (1990); and Cyril Dabydeen's *Another Way to Dance: Asian Canadian Poetry* (1990).[26] Today, Asian Canadian writing is one of the most vibrant, exciting, and prominent areas of literary publication and criticism in Canada, as the essays collected here indicate.

A mere three decades ago, the literary landscape in Canada looked significantly different. British-Canadian writers and critics dominated the fields of literature and literary criticism in English Canada, with a handful of exceptions from a small number of Canadian ethnic minority groups such as the Icelandic, Jewish, Ukrainian, and later, the Italian communities.[27] This was not for want of work from minority cultural communities in the country. Research by George Elliott Clarke, for example, has amply illustrated the existence in Canada of a rich and important literary production in Canada by Africadians.[28] Pierre Anctil is uncovering a vast body of writing in Yiddish by Jewish immigrants to Montreal in the first half of the twentieth century.[29] Similar recuperative work on native literature was done by Penny Petrone, by Jeanne Perreault and Sylvia Vance, and subsequently by a generation of aboriginal scholars.[30] Language of expression has not been the only obstacle to the dissemination and appreciation of minority writing in Canada. A suitable critical framework was required in order to recognize, receive, and evaluate the writing of minority Canadians. In the 1970s, feminist and postmodern literary criticism widened the boundaries of Canadian literature considerably to include a great deal more work by women and experimental writers.[31] The development of postcolonial literary theory and anti-racist cultural practice during the 1980s and 1990s, and more recently of diaspora studies, has had a similar expansive impact on Canadian literature. So, too, have changing demographics in postwar Canadian society[32] and a number of influential cultural events during the last decade of the twentieth century.

Canada's demographic profile changed significantly in the last quarter of the twentieth century as a result of complex global and national economic, social, and political factors. Post-war immigration policies and the development of multiculturalism in Canada were major contributing elements in the ethnic and racial diversification of the population. Both have been the focus of extensive analysis, critique, debate, and publication in recent decades that together have provided the context in which Asian Canadian writing has emerged and taken its place on the Canadian literary scene. Multiculturalism as official federal policy was introduced by the Trudeau government in 1971; it was broadened and legislated as the Canadian Multiculturalism Act in 1988. Over time the policy has become a "directional beacon" for Canadians, as James Frideres has put it, one that has both provoked and confused its supporters and critics alike. These differing responses arise in part from multiculturalism's ties to two opposing philosophies, Frideres points out, referring to Charles Taylor's reading of multiculturalism: "the politics of equal recognition, which is constructed out of the principle of universalism, according to which social attributes such as religion, ethnicity, and the race of individuals are irrelevant, and the principle of difference, which recognizes and values distinct dissecting social characteristics such as ethnicity and race."[33] Complicating the discussion is the fact that multiculturalism is also integrally linked to other policies and legislative acts in Canada, including the Canadian Charter of Rights and Freedoms, the Constitution Act, and immigration policy. Shifts in Canadian immigration policies following World War II have been a major contributing factor in the development and experience of the multicultural Canada envisioned by the policy initiative as well as in a shift from the ideology of Anglo-conformity that dominated before 1940 to an ideology of cultural pluralism.[34] Prior to 1962, immigration policy discerned "preferred" and "non-preferred" countries from which to encourage immigration. Preference lay with northern European countries, whose populations were considered better suited to "northern" Canada.

New policies in the early 1960s de-emphasized country of origin in favour of immigrant skill sets and their match with Canada's labour needs. The flow of immigrants to Canada shifted from northern to southern Europe and the proportion of "visible minorities," defined by Employment and Immigration Canada (1987, B-3) as "persons, other than Aboriginal peoples, who are non-Caucasian in race or non-white in colour," began to increase in Canadian society. The shift continued and extended beyond

Europe through the 1970s, and by the 1980s over half of Canada's immigration population came from South Asia, China, South America, and the Caribbean. In 1991, Balakrishnan and Hou report, "68 per cent of new arrivals to Canada were visible minority immigrants, about two-thirds of whom were blacks, Chinese, and South Asians (Statistics Canada 1996b)."[35] In Toronto and Vancouver, the two largest centres of immigrant population in Canada, visible minorities currently make up 37 and 36 percent of the population respectively.[36] "With each census, the proportion of immigrants from Europe has decreased. The greatest proportion now comes from Asia and the Middle East.... The numbers of South Asian and Chinese immigrants are increasing rapidly."[37] Between 1991 and 2001, for example, the countries that sent the largest groups of immigrants to Canada were the People's Republic of China, India, and the Philippines, whereas between 1961 and 1970 they were the British Isles, Italy, and the United States.[38]

Further to the changes in Canada's demographics of the preceding two decades, during the 1990s, broader public awareness of and attention to questions of race and ethnicity in Canada were generated by a number of galvanizing cultural events such as the 1994 Writing Thru Race conference. Controversy was sparked by criticism of the organizers' decision to limit daytime sessions and discussions to writers from Canada's aboriginal and minority communities. Sides were taken and positions defended and attacked in Canadian newspapers and magazines for months. The same year, Neil Bissoondath's *Selling Illusions: The Cult of Multiculturalism* (1994) elevated the already intense ongoing discussions about Canada's Multiculturalism Policy to widespread public attention. Bissoondath's critique of the policy garnered a great deal of media coverage and debate on radio and television as well as in newspapers and magazines. These discussions were buttressed by further debate and controversy over cultural representation and appropriation. Described in 1992 by the Racial Minority Writers' Committee, advisory to the Writers' Union of Canada, as the "misrepresentation of cultures and the silencing of their peoples," appropriation and its debates asked questions about voice, who speaks for whom, and the appropriation of another's culture. Of concern across Canada's minority cultural communities, these issues were particularly intense for writers and artists in Canada's aboriginal communities who had already made appeals to white writers "to refrain from telling stories involving Indians so as to enable Native peoples to tell their own stories and claim their own history."[39] The controversy over cultural appropriation, Rosemary Coombe has explained, "is founded upon particular premises about authorship, culture, property, and identity that are products of a history of colonial appropriation and define the persistent parameters of a European legal imaginary."[40] For Roy Miki as well, cultural appropriation was another consequence of colonialism, racial oppression, and exploitation, and like writers from Canada's aboriginal communities, Asian Canadian writers too, Miki observed, began "to interrogate and undermine representations of their communities manufactured by outsiders, often liberal and sympathetic white writers, artists, and film-makers whose intentions may be sincere but who fail to account for differences based on subjectivity, language, history, and the problematics of appropriation. Instead of assisting Canadians of Asian ancestry, these products of white assumptions and biases have all too often confirmed and reinforced the systemic racialization process through which privilege and power has been maintained."[41]

Attention to issues of race and ethnicity added layers of complexity and nuance to the more gender-focused analysis of the 1970s and 1980s. This development had resonance in the publishing domain. At the outset of the 1990s, Linda Hutcheon and Marion Richmond's *Other Solitudes: Canadian Multicultural Fictions* (1990) heralded a decade of active publication of multicultural writing including new anthologies of writing from the Asian Canadian communities, such as *Shakti's Words: An Anthology of South Asian Canadian Women's Poetry* (1990) and *Many-Mouthed Birds: Contemporary Writing by Chinese Canadians* (1991) and Lien Chao's *Beyond Silence: Chinese Canadian Literature in English* (1997).[42] *Shakti's Words* is a TSAR publication, a press responsible for the addition of many new works by Canadian writers of Asian background. From its beginnings as a literary magazine, *The Toronto South Asian Review*, in 1981, TSAR has become a successful and important publisher whose achievements include the first anthologies of South Asian Canadian literature, South Asian Canadian women's poetry, and South Asian Canadian and American women's fiction, as well as crucial critical studies, such as Arun Mukherjee's important *Oppositional Aesthetics: Readings from a Hyphenated Space* (1994), and the first historical and critical study of Chinese Canadian writing in English, Lien Chao's *Beyond Silence: Chinese Canadian Literature in English* (1997).[43] TSAR publishes all the literary genres, including poetry, anthologies, and critical essays, by writers such as Cyril Dabydeen, Rienzi Crusz, Lakshmi Gill, Suniti Namjosi, Nurjehan Aziz, Chelva Kanaganayakam, among others. The work is ongoing, with new names and publications appearing steadily. With Jim Wong-Chu, Lien Chao, for example, recently completed *Strike the Wok: An Anthology of Contemporary Canadian Chinese Fiction* (2003).[44] Anthologies such as this and parallel publications by other presses such as Guernica or The Mercury Press[45] that publish other "cultural minority" writers in Canada clearly demonstrate the "multicultural" nature of contemporary Canadian literature. Smaro Kamboureli's 1996 anthology, *Making a Difference*, makes it plain that this is not a recent phenomenon, even if sustained critical attention to multicultural writing in Canada dates from the end of the twentieth century. Indeed, in her second edition of the anthology (2006), Kamboureli writes critically of Canadian literary criticism's belated recognition of previously ignored writers, particularly those from Canada's aboriginal and cultural minority communities. "The belatedness of Canadian literature's overhaul" constitutes Canadian literary criticism's "trauma" today, she argues, commenting on current anxiety, even obsession, within "CanLit as an institution" regarding the realization that colonialism is not a thing of the past nor "a mere spectral presence haunting Canadian literature and criticism" but rather "a condition that is still present in institutional and critical practices today."[46] The second edition of *Making a Difference* seeks to address the cultural and political implications of this condition by reaching further back and further forward than the anthology of ten years earlier. Kamboureli's historical overview of Canadian multicultural literature in 1996, with selections organized by author birthdate, traced back to work by Frederick Philip Grove (1879–1948)[47] and Laura Goodman Salverson (1890–1970),[48] both of whom were publishing during the first two decades of the twentieth century. Many other authors followed whose work dated from well before the official multicultural era of 1970s Canada. Authors Roy Kiyooka (1926–94), Fred Wah (b. 1939), and Roy Miki (b. 1942), appear in the first half of Kamboureli's 1996 anthology, while authors SKY Lee (b. 1952) and Hiromi Goto (b. 1966) appear in the second half. In the second edition published in 2006, Kamouboureli's historical view extends from slave narratives to post-millennium publications. "Multicultural writing" in Canada clearly is longstanding and deep-rooted despite the minority status it has been assigned until recent years.

Two collections of essays, Winfried Siemerling's *Writing Ethnicity: Cross-Cultural Consciousness in Canadian and Québécois Literature* (1996) and Christl Verduyn's *Literary Pluralities* (1998) examined questions of race and ethnicity in both Canadian and Québécois literatures and cultural criticism at the end of the twentieth century. Contributors addressed race and ethnicity in relation to factors of class, gender, and generation, and national and international contexts and debates about multiculturalism, language politics, and cultural identity. A relatively late institutionalization of Canadian and Québécois literatures, Siemerling noted, contributed to a delayed impact of ethnicity in literary studies in the country, as "a national literary discourse could be seen as a prerequisite for a discourse of ethnicity in literary studies."[49] Work on ethnicity, Siemerling observed, offered an innovation role for literary studies.[50] In her introduction, Verduyn identified the search for new models and concepts of critical analysis and writing indicated by many of the essayists. Sneja Gunew, for example, posited the potential for new possibilities of representation in the disjunction of voice and body illustrated by opera, karaoke, and ventriloquism. Hiromi Goto explored popular fascination with notions of extraterrestrials and alien abduction to point out parallels with the ways in which Canadian society views "foreigners" and to point toward possibilities of new representations beyond the stereotypical. These and other essays in *Literary Pluralities* prefigure the concerns of the present volume.

An important aspect of literary politics that has been consequential for multicultural writing is its generic categorization by the literary institution. The work of Canada's multicultural writers has often been regarded as autobiographical and thus of secondary literary status. Alternatively, it has been critiqued as "stuck in the convention of literary realism,"[51] noted by New above. As Joseph Pivato has pointed out, "in the not-too-distant past ethnic minority writing was dismissed as work of low literary value because it was perceived as too sociological [and] criticized as poor realism or naturalism. In general, ethnic minority writing was reduced to the oral history of immigrants or to the sociology of new settlement in ethnic neighbourhoods."[52] For his part, Pivato chose to turn such criticism around and to argue that the biographical dimension of multicultural writing increases rather than diminishes the literary value of the work. For Pivato, the conventions of literary realism, in particular the use of the first-person narrative, offer a form of agency and "freedom to act in conformance with, in opposition to, or without regard for biological or social determinants."[53] Pivato acknowledges, however, that narratives of minority experience, "even innocent biographical narratives," are textualized representations, mediated by language and discourse. Thus, if autobiographical narrative constituted an important stage in the development of multicultural writing, it contained within it as well the potential for moving beyond, as the title of this volume suggests.

Emergence of "Asian Canadian"

While Asian Canadians such as the Eaton sisters[54] were writing as early as 1910, the term Asian Canadian did not come into general use until the late 1970s, with the parallel emergence of the Asian American movement in the United States. An early documented use of the term can be found in 1978 in the title of *The Asianadian: An Asian Canadian Magazine,* a journal founded by Tony Chan, Cheuk Kwan, and Paul Levine (Lai Bo).[55] During the late 1970s and through the 1980s, K. Victor Ujimoto and fellow sociologists Gordon Hirabayashi and Josephine Naidoo organised a series of symposia on the social conditions of "Asian Canadians."[56] The term was also used by video artist Richard Fung in the early 1980s to refer to the pan-ethnic alliances of Canadians of mainly Chinese and Japanese origins at the time. Fung recalls how he grew up "thinking of myself as 'racially' Chinese, since in Trinidad there aren't other East or Southeast Asian communities, and the Indians and Chinese don't co-identify as coming from Asia. When I came to Canada, however I found myself redefined as Asian, and I began to seek connections with other people who looked like me and were similarly racialized.... So for me Asian pan-ethnicity has always been about the social and is always a response to a racialized context."[57] Until the 1980s, however, most Canadians of Asian origin did not use the term Asian Canadian. They were more accustomed to calling themselves Chinese Canadians, Japanese Canadians, Canadians of Filipino, Korean, or South Asian origin, and even Caribbean Canadians. Even when Asian Canadians worked together on a project, such as the collaborative effort of *Inalienable Rice: A Chinese and Japanese Canadian Anthology* (1979) they still used distinct nationally-based racial categories to designate their work in the title.[58]

Issues of terminology and categorization have been a vital part of the development of minority writing in Canadian literature and literary criticism. Resistance to the label *ethnic,* rejection of the construct of race, challenges to the notion of "hyphenated Canadian"—such phrases and usages of language have been subjected to intense scrutiny by scholars and writers alike. "Asian Canadian" is no exception. Many Canadians of Asian ancestry, Roy Miki has pointed out, "would not relate to the generalization of commonalities implied, and would perhaps react negatively to such an alignment of communities from diverse source countries.[59] Yet, like other combinations of cultural labelling and "Canadian," Asian Canadian has gained currency, albeit tentative and provisional, in critical and creative writing by and about Canadians of Asian background. "The term has assumed more theoretical importance," Roy Miki explains, "amongst writers and cultural workers of Asian ancestry as a means of forging alliances necessary to develop a politics of cultural difference."[60] Himani Bannerji has written about the importance of naming in the formation of identity. She asserts the need for self-naming in order to combat the violence of misnaming, terms such as "Pakis," "Coons," "Chinks," and "niggers" as well as "colonial subject," "the native," "the negro," "the coolie," and the "Oriental."[61] She argues that "both the need for an identity, which negates the imposed one, as well as the character of the emerging forms, depend on the specific history of domination and dispossession.... It is also important to remember that the task is always more than one of simple negation."[62] Bannerji suggests that identity involves integrating difference and class, historicizing difference, avoiding the creation of mythologies, and having an open-ended notion of social-self definition."[63] It is in this combined pragmatic, political, and theoretical, but ongoing critical vein that Asian Canadian is discussed here.

Donald Goellnicht's "A Long Labour: The Protracted Birth of Asian Canadian Literature" presents a cogent account of the reasons why Asian Canadian literature developed so slowly compared to Asian American literature. According to Goellnicht, despite the fact that there have been several anthologies and special journal issues on Asian Canadian creative writing since the 1970s, Asian Canadian literature, that is, the "clear identification of an ethnic minority literary tradition in English and the academic study of it as such," has taken "twenty to twenty-five years to be 'born.'"[64] Some of the reasons Goellnicht cites include the relatively small population of Asian and Black Canadians during the 1960s, a time when the Civil Rights and Black Power Movement in the U.S. helped to create strong pan-African and pan-Asian ethnic movements; the absence in Canada of the anti–Vietnam War movement; and the adoption of Trudeau's "official multiculturalism" and "bilingualism" policies which "produced an illusion of equality of opportunity" at the same time as it positioned French Canadians as the "persecuted or privileged minority—depending on one's perspective."[65] Terry Watada has noted that "in 1969, there was no such thing as Asian Canadian writing, at least not as a genre,"[66] but even by the late 1990s, the category of Asian Canadian Literature was still not widely in use. Nina Aquino, the artistic director of Fu-GEN, a Toronto-based Asian Canadian theatre company, recalls her surprise when she started doing her research on Asian Canadian theatre that the John P. Robarts Library at the University of Toronto did not have a category for it.[67]

Today, there are several Asian Canadian theatre groups in Toronto and Vancouver which make it their mandate to showcase Asian Canadian actors, producers, directors, and writers.[68] Film festivals such as the *Toronto Reel Asian International Film Festival* and *The Vancouver Asian Film Festival* feature work by Asian artists, frequently including independent Asian Canadian artists.[69] While there is at present no equivalent to the interdisciplinary

Journal of Asian American Studies in Canada, there are several scholarly and creative journals that have devoted special issues or sections to Asian Canadian literature and culture. For example, in 1999, *Canadian Literature* published a special issue on *Asian Canadian Writing*, edited by Glenn Deer. *Canadian Theatre Review* had a special issue on "Chinese Canadian Theatre" edited by Jennifer Kay Chan in the spring 2002 issue which featured scripts by Marty Chan, Bobby Del Rio, John Ng, and Yung Luu. Recently, *Amerasia* published a special issue, *Pacific Canada: Beyond the 49th Parallel*, guest edited by Henry Yu and Guy Beauregard and featuring twenty Canadian scholars, writers, and artists, to commemorate the 1907 Pacific coast race riots against Asians in San Francisco, Bellingham, Wash., and Vancouver, B.C. *Essays in Canadian Writing* had a special interdisciplinary issue called "Asian Canadian Studies," which was edited by Guy Beauregard and Yiu-Nam Leung (Volume 85, 2005).

The Asian Canadian Writers' Workshop publishes *Ricepaper*, "a national literary and arts magazine committed to providing perspectives on contemporary Pacific Asian Canadian identity and culture and profiles on emerging and accomplished Pacific Asian Canadians. The magazine showcases diverse works by writers, artists, performers, filmmakers, and cultural producers of Hapa, East Asian, and Southeast Asian descent" (http://www.ricepaper.ca). Although *West Coast Line: A Journal of Contemporary Writing and Criticism*, does not have an exclusively "Asian Canadian" mandate, it has featured a large number of Asian Canadian contributors, especially in the 1990s, with Roy Miki as editor. Several special issues, such as one called "Colour: An Issue" (Spring 1994) and one called "Transporting the Emporium: Hong Kong Art and Writing Through the Ends of Time" (no. 21, 1997) presented many Asian Canadian writers and scholars. The Winter 2000 (33, no. 3) issue included interviews with Rita Wong, Rajinderpal Pal, Ashok Mathur, and Tamai Kobayashi, among others. Several libraries, such as Ryerson University Library, the Vancouver Public Library, and the Halifax Public Library also make a point of featuring Asian Canadian works on their websites, especially in May, which has been designated as Asian Heritage Month.[70] There are also websites, such as www.asiancanadian.net and www.asian.ca, dedicated to providing bibliographies, history, news, and events of interest to Asian Canadians.

Once we name the group, however, we are already also creating boundaries and delimiting possibilities. As Karlyn Koh points out: "Ironically, while the concept of community is premised on the gesture of inclusion, whereby individuals who share something in common are invited to come together, the very lines that are drawn around a community compel an exclusion of others. Between exclusion and inclusion, it seems to me, is precisely where community emerges—not as a place but as a spacing of finite figures crossing, shattering the mirror that grounds community as experience that is shared."[71] Currently, the most widely accepted definition of Asian Canadian includes Chinese, Japanese, Indian, Pakistani, Filipino, Korean, Vietnamese, Thai, etc. Canadians, that is, people from East, South, and Southeast Asia. Canadians of Afghan, Arab, Iranian, Armenian, Assyrian, Iraqi, Lebanese, and Syrian descent, that is, people from West Asia, are traditionally classified as Middle-Eastern or Arab Canadian.[72] There are debates about who should be included in such a group, the advantages of such a pan-ethnic Asian definition, and whether Asian Canadian has more in common with postcolonial studies in Canada or with Asian American Studies in the U.S.[73] Some U.S. critics have claimed, or simply incorporated, Asian Canadian Joy Kogawa's *Obasan* as part of Asian American literature.[74] Donald Goellnicht has meticulously traced the way Asian Canadian literature has evolved differently from Asian American literature. He notes that in Canada, literature by South Asian Canadians "was classified as 'Commonwealth literature,' a term that gave way in the late 1980s to 'postcolonial literature.'"[75] South Asian Canadians are sometimes studied under the larger rubric of Indo-Anglian literature, as in Chelvanayakam Kanaganayakam's *Counterrealism and Indo-Anglian Fiction*, or even as South Asian American literature.[76] More common is the inclusion of Asian Canadian work among that of other minorities, anti-racist groups, and coalitions. For example, Himani Bannerji's *Returning the Gaze* is a collection of essays by Asian, native, and black women. *Telling It* by the Telling It Book Collective features native, Asian Canadian, and lesbian writers, while *Our Words, Our Revolutions*, edited by G. Sophie Harding, includes poems, stories, and essays by black, First Nations, and other women of colour in Canada.[77] *Adjacencies*, which began as a conference at the University of Montreal in 1998 called "The Third Solitude: Canadian Minority Writing," contains thirteen essays on various aspects of minority culture on topics such as the works of Austin Clarke, Robert Majzels, Michael Ondaatje, Marguerite-A. Primeau, Aritha van Herk, and Sheila Watson, and on Icelandic-Canadian, Italian-Canadian, and Doukhobor writing.[78] More recently, works by Asian Canadians have been studied in the framework of Asian North American literature, as in Eleanor Ty and Donald Goellnicht's *Asian North American Identities Beyond the Hyphen* and Eleanor Ty's *The Politics of the Visible in Asian North American Narratives*.[79]

In his article "The Emergence of 'Asian Canadian' Literature," Guy Beauregard provocatively asks whether Asian Canadian literature functions merely as "Can lit's supplement."[80] Using Slavoj [Ži]ek's terms, he wonders whether Asian Canadian is simply a kind of regulated transgression or "obscene supplement" that does not participate enough in an ongoing critique of 'Canada' as it has been narrated in Canadian literary history.[81] However, in Derrida's use of the term *supplement* is both that which is "added on and that which substitutes for and supplants."[82] We suggest that Asian Canadian literature as it has developed functions in both senses of the word *supplement*, that is, as an addition, like a supplementary volume of a dictionary, whereby the original is not longer sufficient without supplement, and as a substitute for the original. In this sense, Joy Kogawa, Rohinton Mistry, SKY Lee, Wayson Choy, and others represent what it means to be Asian Canadian at the same time as they rewrite what it means to be Canadian, showing us the contradictions, omissions, and fissures in specific historical moments in Canadian history and culture. Though the essays in this collection do not deal in depth with the works of these and other important Asian Canadian writers, they form the necessary backdrop for more recently published books. Many of the texts studied are in dialogue with or revise earlier works by Asian Canadian and Asian American authors. *Asian Canadian Writing Beyond Autoethnography* is not intended to be a comprehensive study or survey of contemporary Asian Canadian literature, nor to deal with all genres. The essays examine creative works that engage with one or more of the following concerns and questions: the impact of globalization and transnationality, the reconfiguration and play of textual and generic conventions, the questioning of our understanding of sexuality and gender, the claiming of a subjectivity not necessarily linked to ethnic culture, and the potential of hybridity and hybrid identities. Many of the works the essayists consider are particularly conscious of redefining "Asian," no longer seeing it as a geographical point of origin, but as a space of mobility and of becoming. Together the essays and the works analyzed reveal the ways Asian Canadians are "in transit," to use Glenn Deer's phrase, and moving "beyond the constraints of racial categories and into the ongoing assertions of identity in borrowed or invented voices" of their own.[83]

Critical Readings

We begin with three essays that look at some of the theoretical challenges in the writing of autoethnography and at ways some Asian Canadian authors have negotiated with these issues. Smaro Kamboureli's essay on "The Politics of the Beyond" meditates on the two key words that form the title of our volume and examines the genealogy of autoethnography. For Kamboureli, among many things, autoethnography is inscribed by paradox, has a legacy of complicity, and is both genre and method. This provocative piece provides an excellent starting point for many of the essays which examine the ways in which Asian Canadian authors attempt to go beyond the ethnographic impulse. Kamboureli issues a useful caution against too rapid or unreflective a move "beyond," a preposition which expresses an optimism that she finds as yet unwarranted, given the "belatedness" of Canadian literature discussed above. Accordingly, Kamboureli first directs her attention to "*how* autoethnography has come about, and what it signifies," observing that not so long ago it was thought to represent a radical shift, one "intended to demystify the construction and representation of otherness." Promises of transparency and veracity notwithstanding, autoethnography's "self-reflexiveness as genre and method ... pronounces its complicity in articulating otherness for the difference it offers," Kamboureli states, reflecting Du Bois's "double-consciousness." Even though autoethnography renegotiates disciplinary boundaries, challenges orthodoxies, and questions notions of home, belonging, displacement, and reterritorialization as it probes the relationship of subject and community, it fails for all this to make up the shortcomings of the study of the other. "For it perpetuates the dialectic of normative and othered subjectivities," Kamboureli explains; "autoethnography can worry the concept of community all it wants," she states, "but it continues to speak from the perspective of and about the subject's extended 'family' by employing sameness as its benchmark." Hence, we have the desire among many minority writers today to move "beyond." To do so requires coming to terms with the complicity inherent in autoethnography, an act with the potential to inaugurate new critical directions, Kamboureli contends. The new critical directions do not lead to some future time and place, however; rather, they find us wandering back over the terminological terrain of problematic concepts of ethnicity, diaspora, citizenship, and the writings that represent these concepts—this time with awareness of the provisionality of our critical acts. Acutely expressed in Kamboureli's opening essay, this critical awareness informs all the essays that follow.

In "Autoethnography Otherwise," Paul Lai asks us to imagine and perform autoethnography otherwise, which shifts the understanding of the other by emphasizing the literary critic, and literary studies as a field, rather than simply the texts themselves. Lai asks that we acknowledge the crucial and conflicted relationship of literary studies to anthropology as well as other social science and humanities disciplines. Taking up Fred Wah's prose work, Paul Lai argues that Wah forces us to tackle autoethnography otherwise because there is no straightforward account of "ethnic" truth in his experiences. Similarly, Kristina Kyser shows in "Tides of Belonging: Reconfiguring the Autoethnographic Paradigm in Shani Mootoo's *He Drown She in the Sea*" that the novel suggests alternatives to the link presumed to exist between "minority writers" and the culture(s) represented in their texts. Kyser offers a compelling investigation of the role of dreams and the unconscious in the novel. She also examines the part played by the dominant spatial metaphor in the novel—the sea—in disconnecting the self-culture relationship and questioning autoethnographic authority. *He Drown She in the Sea*, Kyser concludes, depicts the connection between identity and culture as far more volatile and less portable than has been assumed. Indeed, belonging may be more comparable to the tides, which rise and fall according to context and location and in so doing represent the blend of beliefs, values, traditions, and practices that make up ethnicity. This is a powerful comparison because, Kyser observes, no body is free of tidal influence. "The shifting and competing nature of tides parallels the range of influences on the self," Kyser writes, "from unconscious projections to significant historical events." The tides of belonging are in flux and ebb with physical distance, Kyser finds. The loosened ties of self and culture suggested in Mootoo's novel represent a radical challenge to autoethnography.

The second section of our book, "Generic Transformations," draws attention to a number of ways in which Asian Canadian writers and artists are mobilizing genre and form in their challenge to essentialist representations of Asianness. In "Strategizing the Body of History: Anxious Writing, Absent Subjects, and Marketing the Nation," Larissa Lai examines the ways in which Asian Canadian writers such as Evelyn Lau and Wayson Choy complicate the familiar genres of the diary, the memoir, and auto(ethnobio)graphy itself. Of Lau's *Runaway*, Lai asks to what extent autobiographical writing can be a liberatory practice if it covers rather than uncovers a fundamental void. Under the circumstances, autoethnography actually reproduces stereotype and status quo, Lai argues. Only insofar as autobiographical writing becomes novel-like or literary can it produce the unified national subject, and even then, the production is only apparitional. The marginalized body is not in fact drawn into the fold of the nation. "It is the text, not the body or the history from which it emerges," Lai states, that enjoys this privilege but "only in the sense that it is put into the service of the same capitalist white supremacist hegemony under which we still live." This would seem to be a strong argument for moving "beyond" autoethnography.

As creative writers, Hiromi Goto and Larissa Lai each turn to speculative fiction, in combination with elements of myth, history, science fiction, dystopia, and even pioneer writing, to present a hybrid literary form that disrupts "realist" ethnographic representations of Asianness. In Goto's *The Kappa Child* (2001), the mythical water creature, the Kappa, and in Lai's *Salt Fish Girl* (2002), the shapeshifter Nu Wa, throw "reality" into question and open up new ways of seeing and being. Pilar Cuder-Domínguez brings an analysis of speculative fiction together with Joshua Fishman's definition of ethnicity as being, doing, and knowing, to address the politics of representation in Goto's and Lai's work. She draws on the critique by feminist critics Jenny Wolmark and Jane Donaworth of the status of minority women as aliens in speculative fiction to show how Goto and Lai overturn this status in their novels. As suggested in Paul Lai's essay, Fred Wah combines and "hybridizes" genres in his exploration of Asian Canadian identity. Continuing critical discussions on Wah, Joanne Saul explores Wah's creative-critical poetics of "the hyphen between image and text." Wah has created a wide variety of signature forms that transgress traditional generic boundaries of criticism, autobiography, poetry, and prose, such as strangles, rambles, biotexts, biofictions, photo-texts, as well as, Charles Bernstein adds, essays in poetic lines, prose with poetic motifs, interviews that mime speech, speeches that turn into song[84]—all amounting to what Wah himself describes as "poetics of equivocation, of betweenness, of hybridity."[85] Transforming literary genre is an intensely political act for Wah, who asserts that race disrupts genre. His innovations with genre point the way beyond "autoethnography," his refusal of generic boundaries mirroring his resistance to a fixed, ethnic, raced, or national identity such as Asian Canadian.

The third section, "Artistic/ Textual/ Bodily Politics," consists of three essays that examine the effects of an author's physical relocation across national borders, as well as the effects of locating texts in a space outside the mainstream. The three essays see parallels between the condition of multiple uprootings and boundary crossings with textual and artistic transgressions. The connections between the marketing and reception of a book and the ethnic identity of its author are explored in Christine Kim's study of feminist small presses and their role in the formation of Canadian literature. Contemporary authors Shani Mootoo and Larissa Lai, both Asian Canadians, have received very different critical receptions for their novels published within a year of one another. While both *Cereus Blooms at Night* (1996) and *When Fox Is a Thousand* (1995) attempt to complicate the relationship between the individual and cultural identity, Kim, borrowing Pierre Bourdieu's vocabulary, argues that economic interests and academic discourses shape the reaction and treatment of the works. In Kim's view, Mootoo's novel "travelled" better across a postcolonial international community eager and ready for works that opened up questions of hybridity and gendered identities. In contrast, Lai's work, positioned as multicultural literature, has not achieved the same kind of success because it critiques the dominant representations of Asian Canadians while being marketed as an Asian Canadian work. Kim draws a further parallel between the relationship of small and large presses and the relationship between colonized and colonizer countries. She quotes Gareth Griffiths, who argues that "the colonies produced the raw material (the literary text) and the metropolitan societies added the value (critical judgement, evaluation, and commentary) and, of course, took most of the profit." Kim's essay reminds us of the important work of feminist small presses which make an effort to introduce new ways of thinking about and beyond ethnicity, gender, and culture.

Ming Tiampo's piece, using the works of artists Ken Lum and Paul Wong, urges us to look more broadly at the way works of art by so-called others are being perceived, received, and understood. Both Chinese-Canadian artists actively resist the temptation to focus only on Chinese-Canadian issues without ignoring them, and think instead about their larger imagined community—the nation. For Tiampo, it is essential to disassociate the terms "white" and "mainstream," refiguring the entire texture of discourse and dislocating the authority of the hegemonic voice rather than making measured interventions and insertions.

The third essay of this section looks at an Asian Canadian artist who has travelled across many borders. Born in Harare, Zimbabwe, of Chinese parents, Laiwan moved to Canada in 1977. Tara Lee maintains that Laiwan's border-crossing subjectivity is reflected in her textual use of different kinds of media. Laiwan is an artist, poet, writer, and filmmaker whose "cyborg poetics" highlights the fragmentation of bodies in a global and technoscientific context. In order to remind society of the fissures caused by alienation, by violence, and by dislocation, Laiwan intersperses her work with technoscience images such as x-rays and ultrasounds. What was interior becomes exterior, breaking down the boundaries and binaries of private/public and self/other. Lee contends that through this cyborg poetic performance, Laiwan propels us further towards the exploration of our multiple and complex identities.

The last section, "Global Affiliations," is an extension of the resistance to one national identity expressed in the work of many of the writers included in this volume. Suniti Namjoshi's work, for instance, occupies an "elsewhere" territory, Eva Karpinski explains in her contribution to the collection, on a map of contemporary, postcolonial, transnational literature. Karpinski reads Namjoshi as a cosmopolitan, border subject whose experimental work *Goja: An Autobiographical Myth* (2000) ("funded by an arts grant from the Canada Council, written in England, and published in Australia," Karpinski adds, making her point), moves "beyond autoethnography." Combining Western and Asian traditions, and Christian, Hindu, and Greek symbolism, Namjoshi experiments with mythopoiesis and discursive heteroglossia to project herself into radical otherness and forge an ethics of connection and connectedness that rejects the logic of polarities which forces the autoethnographic subject into complicity. In refusing the distinction between "East" and "West," *Goja* deflects ethnographic expectations and outlines an ethical system that Karpinski calls "conjunctural ethics." This is an ethics of respect for life and refusal to exploit other people, as indicated by Karpinski in her essay's title: "'Do not exploit me again and again': Queering Autoethnography in Suniti Namjoshi's *Goja: An Autobiographical Myth*." Namjoshi, Karpinski shows, embraces hybridity and "outsiderism" as ways and means to critique racist and heterosexist elements of society globally.

Shani Mootoo also delineates an ethics for global belonging in her work. Mariam Pirbhai examines Mootoo's ethics of global citizenship as a praxis of inclusion that posits community as a vehicle of affiliation for multiply identified individuals and collective identities. In Mootoo's ethical vision, community broadens beyond the "ethnos" or nation to encompass the human community. Without denying ethnic and cultural autonomies or specificities, Mootoo calls for a concept of community that perceives difference as a vital, life-giving part of the whole. Pirbhai sees in *Cereus Blooms at Night* Mootoo's conviction that difference does not mean opposition but rather empathy; not instability but coherence; not the mechanical preservation of self but the compassionate triumph of survival. As such, the novel expresses "a new poetics and praxis of inclusion, one that situates the local community within the wider frame of the global community." Mootoo writes beyond the limits of autoethnography, Pirbhai concludes, by presenting individuals as members of a complex, diasporic, globalized "ethno-scape."

Shanghai-born writer Ying Chen is one of the few Asian North American authors to write in French. Christine Lorre examines her oeuvre, noting that Ying Chen stages a "poetic rebellion" by refusing to be a spokesperson for China or the Chinese, or for Quebec's Chinese minority. Lorre observes that Chen moves increasingly to the space beyond the ethnographic, as her last three novels, in contrast to her first three works, become increasingly devoid of any ethnic markers. Interrogating the position of an ethnic writer once race and ethnicity have been erased, Lorre notes that Chen looks for new ways of writing that draw not only from Chinese but also from French and Anglophone traditions.

In/Conclusions

In the first essay of this volume, Smaro Kamboureli points out that the trope of the beyond does not provide a straight and certain path by which to come to terms with the complexities of identity and concepts of race and ethnicity, or the written expressions of these in autoethnography. *Beyond* is a double signifier, Kamboureli notes, that signals both an impasse and a desire to get to the other side. Believing that it is possible to move beyond impasse, however, is no small accomplishment, Kamboureli comments, for as Rey Chow has written, it means recognizing the "tyranny of the given"[86] and how to rise above it. The writers and artists whose works are examined by the contributors to *Asian Canadian Writing Beyond Autoethnography* show how it is possible to go beyond the given toward new expressions and representations of identity and difference. We see our volume of essays as a way to highlight some of the innovations in recent works by Asian Canadians and to continue the discussion begun by other critics about the links between the individual, cultural identity, and artistic production. We hope that our collective enterprise contributes to the ongoing lively debates about these and other complex issues relevant to our understanding of Canadian writing within a global context.

NOTES

1 Quotation marks around the first appearance in this essay of the words "minority writing" signal the problematic nature of the term. Subsequent use in the essay will dispense with the quotation marks but not with the understanding of the problematic nature of the term.

2 Smaro Kamboureli, "Introduction," in *Making a Difference: Canadian Multicultural Literature* (Toronto: Oxford UP, 1996), 3.

3 Ibid., 3.

4 Abdul R. JanMohamed and David Lloyd, "Introduction: Toward a Theory of Minority Discourse: What Is To Be Done?" in *The Nature and Context of Minority Discourse*, ed. Abdul R. JanMohamed and David Lloyd (New York: Oxford UP, 1990), 2.

5 It is worth noting that Ondaatje considers himself more of an international, rather than an ethnic, writer. His works, even in the 1970s, do not conform to W.H. New's observations about the period. He has not written a bildungsroman in the realist style, though *Running in the Family* is semi-autobiographical.

6 Himani Bannerji, ed. *Returning the Gaze: Essays on Racism, Feminism and Politics* (Toronto: Sister Vision Press, 1993).

7 W.H. New, *A History of Canadian Literature*, 2nd ed. (Montreal: McGill-Queen's UP, 2003), 204.

8 Ibid., 226.

9 Ibid., 228–29.

10 Ibid., 226–30.

11 Françoise Lionnet, *Autobiographical Voices: Race, Gender, Self-Portraiture* (Ithaca, NY: Cornell UP, 1989), 99.

12 Deborah E. Reed-Danahay, "Introduction," *Auto/Ethnography: Rewriting the Self and the Social*, ed. Deborah Reed-Danahay (Oxford: Berg, 1997), 2.

13 Ibid.

14 James Buzard, "On Auto-Ethnographic Authority," *The Yale Journal of Criticism* 16, no. 1 (Spring 2003): 61.

15 Ibid.

16 Mary Louise Pratt, *Imperial Eyes: Travel Writing and Transculturation* (New York: Routledge, 1992), 7.

17 Stephen Gilbert Brown and Sidney Dobrin, "Introduction," *Ethnography Unbound: From Theory Shock to Critical Praxis* (Albany: State U of New York P, 2004), 2. See also Jim Thomas, *Doing Critical Ethnography* (Newbury Park, CA: Sage, 1993).

18 D. Soyini Madison, *Critical Ethnography: Method, Ethics, and Performance* (Thousand Oaks, CA: Sage Publications, 2005), 5.

19 Ibid.

20 Judy Young, "No Longer 'Apart'? Multiculturalism Policy and Canadian Literature," *Canadian Ethnic Studies* 33, no. 2 (2001): 88–116. Young writes in her endnotes, "We had great difficulty finding researchers to do Chinese and Japanese because there were no researchers with adequate knowledge of the language to be able to review the existing body of work. By the late 1980s the situation had changed so much that there began to develop a whole identifiable literary and artistic community of Chinese, Japanese and other Asian origins—though working almost entirely in the official languages [English and French]," note 11.

21 In addition to Asian groups, Italian and Ukrainian immigrants, among many others, also experienced marginalization from mainstream "Anglo-Saxon" Canadian society.

22 See important historical and sociological accounts of Asian Canadians in Ken Adachi's *The Enemy That Never Was: A History of the Japanese Canadians* (Toronto: McClelland and Stewart, 1976) and Peter S. Li's *The Chinese in Canada*, 2nd ed. (Don Mills: Oxford UP, 1998).

23 Joy Kogawa, *Obasan* (Toronto: Penguin, 1981).

24 Cameron, Elspeth, ed., *Multiculturalism and Immigration in Canada: An Introductory Reader* (Toronto: Canadian Scholars' Press, 2004), xvii.

25 Himani Bannerji, *The Dark Side of the Nation: Essays on Multiculturalism, Nationalism and Gender* (Toronto: Canadian Scholars' Press, 2000), 91, 113.

26 Gerry Shikatani and David Aylward, eds., *Paper Doors: An Anthlogy of Japanese Canadian Poetry* (Toronto: Coach House, 1981); M.G. Vassanji, ed., *A Meeting of Streams: South Asian Canadian Literature* (Toronto: TSAR, 1985); Cyril Dabydeen, ed., *A Shapely Fire: Changing the Literary Landscape* (Oakville, ON: Mosaic Press, 1987); Paul Wong, ed., *Yellow Peril Reconsidered* (Vancouver: On Edge, 1990); and Cyril Dabydeen's *Another Way to Dance: Asian Canadian Poetry* (Stratford, ON: Williams-Wallace, 1990).

27 For more on ethnic population in Canada, see Enoch Padolsky in *Ethnicity and Culture in Canada: The Research Landscape*, eds. J.W. Berry and J.A. Laponce (Toronto: U of Toronto P, 1994), 361–86.

28 Africadian is George Elliott Clarke's preferred term for Canadians of African descent. See George Elliott Clarke, "Embarkation: Discovering African-Canadian Literature," in *Odysseys Home: Mapping African-Canadian Literature* (Toronto: U of Toronto P, 2002), 3–23.

29 Pierre Anctil, ed., *Through the Eyes of the Eagle: The Early Montreal Yiddish Press (1907–1916)*, trans. David Rome (Montreal: Véhicule Press, 2001).

30 Penny Petrone, *Native Literature in Canada: From the Oral Tradition to the Present* (Toronto: Oxford UP, 1990); Jeanne Perreault and Sylvia Vance, *Writing the Circle: Native Women of Western Canada* (Edmonton: NeWest, 1990).

31 As Roy Miki commented in "The Future's Tense: Editing, Canadian Style," even Frank Davey's seminal challenge to "thematic criticism" in "Surviving the Paraphrase" (1974), "still fell short of proposing a theory of textuality to account for the contextual relationship of literary works to social, cultural, historical, and linguistic constraints—constraints which, on the one hand, make them possible, and on the other, assign them value in literary institutions" (*Broken Entries*, 37–38). "Of all the 'isms' that have surfaced in the past fifteen years," Miki states, "perhaps feminism and post-structuralism together have been the most instrumental theoretical positions to resist and critique the power of patriarchic nationalist forms and the normative ahistoricism of humanist beliefs in universality." See "Asiancy: Making Space for Asian Canadian Writing," in *Broken Entries: Race, Subjectivity, Writing* (Toronto: Mercury Press, 1998) 104.

32 As related to immigration, the change in Canadian demographics following World War II was in fact the fourth "phase" distinguished by the "Report of the Royal Commission on Bilingualism and Biculturalism, Book IV." The previous three periods were (1) prior to 1901, (2) 1901 to the outbreak of WWI, and (3) 1920s to the outbreak of WWII. Phase 1 ended with a decision taken by Clifford Sifton, Minister of the Interior, to develop the West. Phase 2 was halted by WWI. Phase 3 came up against both the outbreak of WWII and the Depression.

33 James S. Frideres, "Managing Immigrant Social Transformations," in *Immigrant Canada: Demographic, Economic and Social Challenges*, ed. Shiva S. Halli and Leo Dreidger (Toronto: U of Toronto P, 1999), 70.

34 See Howard Palmer, "Social Adjustment," in *Immigration and the Rise of Multiculturalism* (Toronto: Copp Clark, 1975), 44–53.

35 T.R. Balakrishnan and Feng Hou, 1999, in Cameron, *Multiculturalism and Immigration*, 173.

36 Statistics Canada, "Visible Minority Population by Census Metropolitan Areas (2001 Census)." (19 March 2008), http://www40.statcan.ca/l01/cst01/demo53e .htm and http://www40.statcan.ca/l01/cst01/demo53c.htm.

37 Statistics Canada, "Canada's Visible Minority Population in 2017" *The Daily* (22 March 2005). (19 March 2008), http://www.statcan.ca/Daily/English/050322/ d050322b.htm

38 Statistics Canada, "100 Years of Immigration to Canada (1901–2001)," (26 January 2004) http://www12.statcan.ca/english/census01/products/analytic/ multimedia.cfm.

39 Rosemary Coombe (1994) in Cameron, *Multiculturalism and Immigration*, 138.

40 Rosemary Coombe (1994) in Cameron, *Multiculturalism and Immigration*, 134.

41 Roy Miki, "Asiancy: Making Space for Asian Canadian Writing," in *Broken Entries: Race, Subjectivity, Writing*, 104.

42 For a critique of *Many-Mouthed Birds*, see Roy Miki, "Asiancy: Making Space for Asian Canadian Writing" (*Broken Entries* 101–24). Miki writes: "For *Many-Mouthed Birds* the selection policy fails to contradict the implications of 'orientalism' on the cover, and instead retreats to aesthetic values that skirt constraints placed on writers of colour.... The compromising bridge between the (potential) disruptiveness of the anthology and the commodificatory assumptions of 'surprise, enlighten and entertain' misrepresents the texts of writers who resist, even reject, transparent aesthetic norms" (121).

43 As announced in its website, TSAR has "played a role in the formulation of the Indo-Caribbean identity through the publication of several ground-breaking titles ... kept in print books by major Caribbean writers Sam Selvon, Ismith Khan, and John Stewart ... published provocative and perceptive social and literary critical works by Arnold Itwaru, Arun Prabha Mukherjee, and Himani Bannerji ... [and introduced] the important Zimbabwean writer Yvonne Vera."

44 Lien Chao and Jim Wong-Chu, eds., *Strike the Wok: An Anthology of Contemporary Canadian Chinese Fiction* (Toronto: TSAR, 2003).

45 Guernica, for example, has published many Italian Canadian writers, but has also brought out anthologies of Arabic Canadian writing.

46 Smaro Kamboureli, *Making a Difference: Canadian Multicultural Literatures in English*, 2nd ed. (Don Mills, ON: Oxford UP, 2006), xiii.

47 Born Felix Paul Greve in Radomno, Prussia, in 1879, Grove immigrated to Canada from America after faking suicide in 1909. Grove wrote poetry, drama, and novels in German and in English, but is best known for his autobiography, *In Search of Myself* (1946).

48 Daughter of immigrants from Iceland, and author of *Confessions of an Immigrant Daughter*, Laura Goodman Salverson has been credited with having written one of Canada's first autobiographical works.

49 Winfried Siemerling, *Writing Ethnicity* (Toronto: ECW Press, 1996), 10. See also Winfried Siemerling, *Discoveries of the Other: Alterity in the Work of Leonard Cohen, Hubert Aquin, Michael Ondaatje, and Nicole Brossard* (Toronto: U of Toronto P, 1994) and Winfried Siemerling, *The New North American Studies: Culture, Writing and the Politics of Re/Cognition* (New York: Routledge, 2005).

50 Winfried Siemerling, *Writing Ethnicity* (Toronto: ECW Press, 1996), 10.

51 Joseph Pivato, in "Representation of Ethnicity as a Problem: Essence or Construction," in *Literary Pluralities*, ed. Christl Verduyn (Peterborough, ON: Broadview Press, 1998), 158.

52 Ibid.

53 Joseph F. Rychlak, "Morality in a Mediating Mechanism? A Logical Learning Theorist Looks at Social Constructionism," 44–60, in *Social Discourse and Moral Judgement*, ed. Daniel N. Robinson (San Diego, CA: Academic Press, 1992), 50, as paraphrased by Joseph Pivato, "Representation of Ethnicity," 159.

54 Edith Eaton, pseudonym Sui Sin Far (1867–1914) and her sister Winnifred Reeve Eaton, pseudonym Onoto Watanna (1877–1954).

55 According to Tony Chan, "The concept for *Asianadian* was inspired by the Asian American movement, which was spreading across university campuses in America during the late 1960s and early 1970s. The founders of *Asianadian* had set out to create a similar sense of cultural identity and political consciousness among Asian Canadians through this magazine, which would give the Asian community an opportunity to speak out." *The Asianadian*, http://faculty.washington.edu/chanant/asianadian/addendum/collective.html (accessed February 2, 2006).

56 Selected papers from these symposia were published. See *Asian Canadians in a Multicultural Society*, ed. K. Victor Ujimoto and Gordon Hirabayashi (Saskatoon: U of Saskatchewan, 1979); *Asian Canadians, Regional Perspectives: Selections from the Proceedings, Asian Canadian Symposium*, ed. K. Victor Ujimoto and Gordon Hirabayashi (Halifax: Mt. Saint Vincent U, 1981); *Asian Canadians: Aspects of Social Change: Selections from Proceedings*, ed. K. Victor Ujimoto and Josephine Naidoo (Guelph, ON: U of Guelph, 1984); *Asian Canadians: Contemporary Issues: Selections from the Proceedings, Asian Canadian Symposium VII* (Winnipeg: U of Manitoba, 1986).

57 Monika Kin Gagnon and Richard Fung, "(Can) Asian Trajectories," *13 Conversations about Art and Cultural Race Politics* (Montreal: Artextes Editions, 2002), 98.

58 According to Larissa Lai and Jean Lum, *Inalienable Rice: A Chinese and Japanese Canadian Anthology* (Vancouver: Powell Street Review, 1979) was the result of writers and artists, like Jim Wong-Chu, Sean Gunn, Sharon (Sky) Lee, and Paul Yee, who were part of the Asian Canadian Writers' Group. See Larissa Lai and Jean Lum, "Neither Guests Nor Strangers," *Yellow Peril Reconsidered*, ed. Paul Wong (Vancouver: On Edge, 2000), 21.

59 Roy Miki, "Asiancy: Making Space for Asian Canadian Writing," in *Broken Entries: Race, Subjectivity, Writing*, 124.

60 Ibid., 124.

61 Himani Bannerji, "The Passion of Naming: Identity, Difference and Politics of Class," in *Thinking Through: Essays on Feminism, Marxism, and Anti-Racism* (Toronto: Women's Press, 1995), 23, 29.

62 Ibid., 28.

63 Ibid., 37.

64 Donald C. Goellnicht, "A Long Labour: The Protracted Birth of Asian Canadian Literature," *Essays on Canadian Writing* 72 (Winter 2000), 2.

65 Ibid., 4, 6, 8, 9.

66 Terry Watada, "To Go for Broke: The Spirit of the 70s," *Canadian Literature* 163 (1999): 80.

67 Sydnia Yu, in an interview with Nina Aquino, "Asian Canadian Theatre Group Looks to Future," *Young People's Press* (11 February 2003), http://www.ypp.net/fullarticle.asp?ID=154 (accessed 17 February 2006).

68 In addition to Fu-Gen in Toronto, Loud Mouth Asian Babes and the Filipino theatre company The Carlos Bulosan Cultural Workshop feature works by Asian artists. In Vancouver, the Vancouver Asian Canadian Theatre is trying to take theatre to new directions (Sydnia Yu, "Asian Canadian Theatre Group").

69 The Toronto Reel Asian International Film Festival is usually held in November and showcases films, documentaries, and videos by Asians from around the world. The Vancouver Asian Film Festival is also held in November and features independent North American Asian filmmakers.

70 May was designated Asian Heritage Month in 2001 through a Senate motion introduced by Senator Vivian Poy. Large cities such as Vancouver, Toronto, Halifax, Montreal, Edmonton, and Calgary have celebrated Asian Heritage Month since 1993. See Multiculturalism, "Asian Heritage Month" (22 February 2006), http://www.pch.gc.ca/progs/multi/asian-asiatique/index_e.cfm.

71 Karlyn Koh, "At the Edge of a Shattered Mirror, Community?" *Asian North American Identities Beyond the Hyphen*, ed. Eleanor Ty and Donald Goellnicht (Bloomington: Indiana UP, 2004), 150.

72 The community of Asian Canadians is still developing and very much in flux. For example, the definition of "Asian Canadian" in the Wikipedia encyclopedia does include West Asians, but it lists the largest Asian groups in Canada as Chinese, Indo, Filipino, Vietnamese, Korean, Japanese, and Pakistani (22 February 2006), http://en.wikipedia.org/wiki/Asian_Canadian.

73 In recent sessions of the conference of the Modern Language Association and the Association for Asian American Studies, there have been several papers on the links and alliances between Asian American Studies and Arab American Studies, between Asian American and Muslim American literatures. These developments have been precipitated by the events of September 11, 2001.

74 For example, King-Kok Cheung, *Articulate Silences: Hisaye Yamamoto, Maxine Hong Kingson, Joy Kogawa* (Ithaca, NY: Cornell UP, 1993) and Sau-ling Cynthia Wong, *Reading Asian American Literature: From Necessity to Extravagance* (Princeton, NJ: Princeton UP, 1993).

75 Goellnicht, "A Long Labour," 15.

76 Chelvanayakam Kanaganayakam's *Counterrealism and Indo-Anglian Fiction* (Waterloo, ON: Wilfrid Laurier UP, 2002) examines Suniti Namjoshi along with R.K. Narayan, G.V. Desani, Anita Desai, and Zulfikar Ghose. Rajini Srikanth's *The World Next Door: South Asian American Literature and the Idea of America* (Philadelphia, PA: Temple UP, 2004) includes sections on Michael Ondaatje and on Shani Mootoo.

77 Himani Bannerji, ed., *Returning the Gaze: Essays on Racism, Feminism and Politics* (Toronto: Sister Vision Press, 1993); Telling It Book Collective, *Telling It: Women and Language Across Cultures: The Transformation of a Conference* (Vancouver: Press Gang, 1990); Sophie G. Harding, *Our Words, Our Revolutions: Di/Verse Voices of Black Women, First Nations Women, and Women of Colour in Canada* (Toronto: Inanna Publications, 2000).

78 Domenic A. Beneventi, Licia Canton, and Lianne Moyes, eds. *Adjacencies: Minority Writing in Canada* (Toronto: Guernica, 2004).

79 Eleanor Ty and Donald C. Goellnicht, eds., *Asian North American Identities Beyond the Hyphen* (Bloomington: Indiana UP, 2004) and Eleanor Ty, *The Politics of the Visible in Asian North American Narratives* (Toronto: U of Toronto P, 2004). Recently, Winfried Siemerling has also done a comparative study of black and native writers in North America. See *The New North American Studies: Culture, Writing and the Politics of Re/Cognition* (New York: Routledge, 2005).

80 Guy Beauregard, "The Emergence of 'Asian Canadian Literature'": Can Lit's Obscene Supplement?" http://www.ucalgary.ca/UofC/eduweb/engl392/492/beauregard.html (accessed 2 February 2006).

81 Ibid., footnote 13.

82 Jacques Derrida, *A Derrida Reader Between the Blinds*, ed. Peggy Kamuf (New York: Columbia UP, 1991), 33.

83 Glenn Deer, "Asian North America in Transit," *Canadian Literature* 163 (Winter 1999): 15.

84 Charles Bernstein, *My Way: Speeches and Poems* (Chicago: U of Chicago Press, 1999), xi.

85 Fred Wah and Frank Davey, "Meandering Interview," *Open Letter* 12, no. 3 (Summer 2004): 102.

86 Kamboureli, quoting Rey Chow, "The Secrets of Ethnic Abjection," in *"Race" Panic and the Memory of Migration*, ed. Meaghan Morris and Brett de Bary (Hong Kong: Hong Kong UP, 2001), 60.

part one

Theoretical Challenges and Praxis

[chapter one]

The Politics of the Beyond
43 Theses on Autoethnography
and Complicity

Smaro Kamboureli

> Before I even begin to follow in fact a tortuous itinerary, here is the thesis, in direct and broadly simple terms, that I am submitting to you for discussion. It will be distributed among a series of propositions. In truth, it will be less a thesis, or even a hypothesis, than a declarative engagement, an appeal in the form of a profession of faith: faith in the university and, within the university, faith in the Humanities of tomorrow. —Jacques Derrida[1]

1. It is a commonplace thesis that the critical act is nearly always complicit with its object of criticism.

"Beyond Autoethnography," my subject here—that is, how or why "recent cultural productions" have "moved beyond the politics of identity, beyond what Françoise Lionnet has termed 'autoethnography,' or ethnographic autobiography"—resonates with complicity.[2] Two premises are implicit in this statement—at least as I hear it: that "ethnic, multicultural, and minority writers in Canada"[3] have so far written in an autoethnographic manner; and that critical discourse has displayed a tendency to read these writers as autoethnographers, irrespective of whether or not they have written directly in this mode.[4]

Even though the paratactic structure of this phrase implies that "ethnic, multicultural, and minority" literatures are distinct categories, it is not immediately apparent what the differences between them are; nor is it possible to identify readily which Canadian writers belong to each of these categories—if they are indeed as distinct as the syntax of the phrase suggests.[5]

For example, are Roy Kiyooka's *Mothertalk: Life Stories of Mary Kiyoshi Kiyooka* and *Pacific Rim Letters* autoethnographies? Is Wayson Choy's *Paper Shadows: A Chinatown Childhood* an "ethnic" or a "multicultural" example of autoethnography, if it is indeed that? And could we read Himani Bannerji's collection *Returning the Gaze: Essays of Feminism, Race, and Politics*, Arun Mukherjee's *Oppositional Aesthetics: Readings from a Hyphenated Space*, and Roy Miki's *Redress: Inside the Japanese Canadian Call for Justice* as critical instances of autoethnography? Such questions, though worthy of note, do not necessarily address the most urgent questions posed today by or about writers of the diaspora or texts like the ones I mention here.

What is evident, however, is that these "ethnic, multicultural, and minority" labels—including, of course, my preferred one, diasporic—point to a triage that derives not so much from the literature in question, but from the various entanglements and politics of critical discourse and methodology, hence the need to address the issue.

2. Autoethnography has reached its limits.

"Beyond autoethnography" seems to have a deictic and spatial function, pointing to a field that lies ahead of autoethnography. I hear "beyond autoethnography," then, as a thesis that asserts—perhaps inadvertently so—the end of autoethnography, that autoethnography has reached its limits. But as Wittgenstein says, "If someone is merely ahead of his time, it will catch him up one day."[6] So, though certainly an enticing proposition, I am less interested in seeing what lies "beyond autoethnography," than I am in investigating *how* autoethnography has come about, and what it signifies.

3. *Beyond* implies a purposeful gesture, but it is *how* that shows the way.

Beyond suggests a crossing over that assumes there is already some unspecified critical space awaiting us. The future tense it embodies is the kind relying on presumed knowledge, for this preposition is marked by optimism—perhaps even faith, given the function of *beyond* as a noun—that there is a (better?) space we can reach and inhabit as critics.

In comparison, the adverb *how* is more modest; it doesn't assume there is a beyond. Instead, it points to the means we can employ to explore knowledge and ways of knowing. *How* has an instrumentalism that is key to the critical act, fundamental to the ways and methods in which we produce knowledge. Hence the beauty of its modesty—and my having opted here to employ it as the means through which to respond to the exhortation "beyond autoethnography."

4. Autoethnography is a compensatory gesture.

This may indeed be the right time to consider moving beyond autoethnography, but there was a time when the advent of autoethnography was thought to be a radical shift, especially in the field of anthropology, signalling major methodological and ideological changes in relation to both personal narratives by minority subjects and the narratives produced about them by cultural anthropologists. Autoethnography appeared, with gradual but considerable force, as a compensatory response to the various anxieties that arose from the politics of representation. It was intended to demystify the construction and representation of otherness, to offer, what Michael M.J. Fischer calls, "authentic anchorages,"[7] reference points and methodological turns that would account for the contingencies that informed at once the self-articulation of minority subjects from the position as native informants or as authors of their own narratives and the ethnographer's fieldwork account. "Polyvocality," as James Clifford says, "was restrained and orchestrated in traditional ethnographies by giving to one voice a pervasive authorial function and to others the role of sources, 'informants,' to be quoted or paraphrased."[8] Autoethnography offered a release from these restraints. It promised transparency—greater veracity regarding the experience of otherness and the process of narrativizing it, a materialist, we could say, representation of personal and cultural histories.[9]

5. Autoethnography is a praxis rather than an epistemology.

Since its inception about thirty years ago, autoethnography has emerged as a slippery concept. Despite its relatively short history—be it defined or employed as method, genre, or discourse—it has already accrued, as Deborah E. Reed-Danahay writes, "multiple meanings." A fluid concept, autoethnography "can be traced through two veins—that concerned primarily with ethnography and that with life history."[10] Because the life histories autoethnography is related with are almost invariably those of groups that attract the critical attention of the ethnographic gaze, the double condition of being an other and being othered shows autoethnography to be a response to the complicity characterizing representations of otherness. A recurring feature of autoethnography, this double condition renders autoethnography as a historiography that declares the demise of the progressive linear narrative and its attendant ideologies. Autoethnography, then, posits itself as a praxis rather than an epistemology.

Understood this way, autoethnography is akin to what D. Soyini Madison calls "'new,'" "critical," or "postcritical ethnography."[11] Interestingly, what characterizes the critical shift she is concerned with is also a gesture designed to take ethnographers "beyond [their] individual ... selves"[12] and "beneath surface appearances" in order to "resist domestication," that is, to be better able "to penetrate the borders and break through the confines in defense of ... the voices and experiences of subject whose stories are otherwise restrained and out of reach."[13] While her intention is to "take ethical responsibility" and to expose, as well as "contextualize," the "power positions" of ethnographers, "thereby making [their positionality] accessible, transparent, and vulnerable to judgment and evaluation,"[14] as her prepositional adverbs suggest critical ethnography not only remains correlative to the assumption that the condition of otherness is transparent and therefore assimilable, but also privileges the critical ethnographer's subject position. Hers is a praxis that aspires to bring greater epistemological clarity to the ethnographer's position. Critical ethnography is "grounded in the empirical world of the Other."[15] Nevertheless, even though she stresses that "our subjectivity is an inherent part of research, but in critical ethnography it is not my *exclusive* experience—that is autobiography, travel writing, or memoir (or what some people call *autoethnography*),"[16] it is the ethnographer's subjectivity that the methodological shifts she is calling for reveal, in all its good intentions. What marks the apotheosis of critical ethnography, as Madison rhapsodizes, is its ability to grant the ethnographer with greater self-awareness. As she writes, "it is through dialogue and meeting with the Other that I am most fully myself. The wonderful paradox in the ethnographic moment of dialogue and Otherness is that communion with an Other brings the self more fully into being and, in doing so, opens you to know the Other more fully."[17] How that "communion" (a word Madison uses rather frequently) is to be achieved when the "Other" remains other is not entirely clear. What the transparency of Madison's method makes clear, instead, is that this communion is a one-way dialogue. In this praxis of dealing with the Other, the other operates as an instrument that facilitates the ethnographer's "contribut[ion] to emancipatory knowledge,"[18] an "emancipatory knowledge" that remains invested in, and therefore sanctions, traditional notions of humanism.

6. The cultural logic of autoethnography is not symptomatic of the postmodern condition.

"Whether the autoethnographer is the anthropologist studying his or her own kind, the native telling his or her life story, or the native anthropologist," Reed-Danahay sees "displacement" as being at the core of autoethnographic discourse, an aspect that, as she states, reflects "the postmodern condition."[19] She does not distinguish between diverse kinds of displacement. In attributing the cultural logic of the autoethnographic act to the postmodern condition, she fails to consider that the social and cultural contingencies, as well as the material conditions, that influence the production of culturally specific autoethnographic texts may be dramatically different, if not entirely at opposite ends, from the kinds of fragmentation and ephemerality postmodernism revels in. It seems that the postmodern slant of her definition allows the relativism often pervading postmodern interpretation to translate the autoethnographic act into a universal impulse: irrespective of their differences, all autoethnographers appear to exist in homogeneous time.

7. Autoethnography is a discourse of paradoxes.

Autoethnography is inscribed by paradox: it sets outs to thematize and avert tactics of appropriation and unreflected accounts of otherness, thus operating as a discourse of empathy toward the other, but it cannot fully sunder itself from the regime of Western progress. Its self-reflexiveness as genre and method, rather than diffusing complicity, pronounces its complicity in articulating otherness for the difference it offers. In seeking to expose the previously occulted processes of mediation in the interpretation of the other, autoethnography has delivered its promise to bring about a different form of relations, and has done so by enacting the commerce between intention and complicity.

8. Autoethnography is the result of slippage from the "auto" in autochthonous to the "auto" in autobiography.

In one of the earliest recorded instances of autoethnography, Karl Heider links the "auto" of autoethnography to that of autochthonous.[20] As the practice of autoethnography became more widely employed, however, the "auto" of the term has gradually become associated with the "auto" in autobiography and life-writing. Notwithstanding its persistent emphasis on the self of the writing subject, autoethnography is invariably characterized by the cross-disciplinary alignment between cultural anthropology and literature, in that life-writing is mostly the object of the latter. This is certainly a productive cross-fertilization, but it is precisely this alliance that draws attention to autoethnography's complicity with its need for "authentic anchorages."[21]

9. Autoethnography has a legacy of complicity.

When cultural anthropologists such as Clifford began to refer to ethnographers as "novelists manqué,"[22] when they started theorizing and practicing ethnography by employing interdisciplinary methods, notably methods heavily dependent on literary discourses, they were not simply responding to the advent of postmodern aesthetics. Similarly, while they stopped short of calling "ethnographies fictions,"[23] by calling attention to the fictionality of ethnography "in the sense [that it is] 'something made or fashioned,'" they were not simply acknowledging "the partiality of cultural and historical truths," what Clifford refers to as "the banal claim that all truths are constructed."[24] They were also acknowledging the complicity of the ethnographic act and of anthropological fieldwork research methods with hegemonic and imperial practices. While "anti-colonial pressures, colonial discourse analysis, and critical race theory have decentered the predominantly Western, and white, traditional fieldworker"[25] and his or her research and writing methods, they have also released ethnographic discourses from the normative curtailment of emotions and measured affection toward the object of the ethnographic gaze.

10. Autoethnography provides a record of the ethnographer's conversion process.

Initially seen as an instance of "the self-reflexive 'fieldwork account,'"[26] autoethnography is symptomatic of the release of the ethnographer's affect. It marks the ethnographer's passage from repression to conversion, conversion understood in Patrick Riley's definition of the term. As Riley writes, conversion, historically understood as an experience of change in Western theistic discourses, signifies the "experience of change" and "transformation of character" through structures and tropes that "lend coherence and continuity" to narratives of the self.[27] As a process that causes the "self's dissolution into alterity,"[28] conversion posits a "cogent challenge to essentialist conceptions of subjectivity and representation."[29]

The genealogy of autoethnography archives the concern with the sublimation of the ethnographer's affect and methodological anxiety. In traditional ethnography, as Clifford writes, "[e]xpressions of overt enthusiasm and love were circumscribed"; "[a]nger, frustration, judgments on individuals, desire, and ambivalence went into private diaries."[30] This circumvention of the personal was at once disguised and signalled by the ethnographic act's rhetoric of objectivity and critical distance. While the ethnographer's conversion was both a matter of affect and method, autoethnography also provided a solution to the growing unease of liberally-minded anthropologists about the political implications of their fieldwork methods and strategies of representation.

Early examples of what we call autoethnography today, like Michel Leiris's *L'Afrique fantôme* (1934), may have preceded the poetics and politics of postmodernism and the debates of cultural appropriation, but, interestingly enough, were at the same time accompanied by such essays as

Leiris's "L'ethnographe devant de colonialisme" (1950) or his three-part autobiography, *Manhood* (1946), texts that might not offer a justification of interventionist tactics or the fetishization of the other but which, nevertheless, accounted for the contingencies and complicities of ethnographic practices.

Autoethnography, then, reflects, if I can appropriate Du Bois's expression, a "double-consciousness": the release of affect, as well as of the taboos that have shaped the work of cultural anthropologists, and the confrontation with the complicities embedded in the conventional methods and practices of ethnography.

11. Autoethnography appeases certain kinds of complicity, but it is never fully released from complicity.

Autoethnography signals a renegotiation of disciplinary boundaries and methods, a re-mapping of spatial practices and professional etiquette, a questioning of orthodoxies. If "[m]ovement in and out … discretion, absorption, and the 'view from afar'"[31] were the principles that have traditionally defined the ethnographic act, autoethnography sets out to deconstruct these principles. In doing so, it also realigns the notions of community and native informant. Clifford wonders whether anthropology has "adequately confronted the problem of doing sanctioned, 'real' fieldwork in a community one wants *not* to leave." The question he raises, along with his point that "North American minorities are entering the field in relatively small numbers,"[32] exposes, among other things, the fact that, even though the advent of autoethnography has helped to revitalize the field, it has not shifted radically its foundational value system. Thus, autoethnography may have a remedial function, for it operates as a kind of (self-)writing cure for some fieldworkers, but it also raises a host of questions about the notion of home, and its attendant notions of return, reterritorialization, belonging, filiation, affiliation, and displacement. In other words, as a critical and methodological response to various kinds of complicities, autoethnography is itself indelibly marked by the condition of complicity.

12. Autoethnography realigns the relationship between autoethnographer and community.

If "the hallmark of modern autobiography," as Patrick Riley writes, "is the drama of authorship itself,"[33] the drama of autoethnography constitutes the relationship between the writing subject and his or her community. To put this otherwise, the drama in autoethnography emerges from the political tensions between an autoethnographer and the community she or he writes about by writing about herself or himself. Virtually all attempts to define autoethnography, and its many variants, are informed by the quandary of insider/outsider, and by the related question as to whether or not the autoethnographer is or acts as a native informant.[34]

13. Autoethnography is (not) the prevalent discourse of the other.

Postmodern autoethnography, ethnic autobiography, confessional ethnography, native anthropology, autobiographical ethnography, auto-ethnology, auto-anthropology, self-reflexive field account, postethnography—these are all variants of autoethnography. Each of these terms privileges a certain element of the writing project in question but, considered together, they show that autoethnography moved quickly beyond cultural anthropology to infiltrate literary production. Reed-Danahay explains that these variants are defined in terms of the autoethnographic subject's position in relation to a given community. No matter what their generic, aesthetic, or methodological differences, these autoethnographic discourses share, as Reed-Danahay's account reveals but does not thematize, one common denominator: they are all concerned with ethnicized and racialized subjects, or with peasants or working-class subjects. As a critical gesture that attempts to resolve the shortcomings of the study of the other, autoethnography founders, for it perpetuates the dialectic of normative and othered subjectivities.

14. In literary studies, autoethnography manifests itself as both genre and method.

The desire in cultural anthropology to reconstitute the representation of otherness parallels the practice of literary critics to read the writing of diasporic authors as a reflection of their communities' social realities and histories. In this case, autoethnography is manifested both as genre—life-writing narratives—and method—the trend of reading a text, whether a novel or personal account, through the author's ethnic community. Notwithstanding the fact that reading autoethnographically in this context may reflect, at a certain level, a desire to effect social change, the autoethnographic method as practised by literary critics is, as is the case with autoethnography in cultural anthropology, often complicitous with the process of othering and fetishizing diasporic subjects.

15. Autoethnography stresses a subject's relationality to his or her community, but does not necessarily question what constitutes community.

Even though the autoethnographic method does not always reduce the writers in question to the position of native informants, it proceeds on the assumption that there is an inexorable affinity between them and their respective cultures and communities. This relationality is certainly there, but it is not always addressed in ways that question the foundationalism of Western concepts of community, as well as the affect (or lack of) that determines a subject's community affiliations. The premise that one is born into a community, that community, therefore, pre-exists the subject's formation, refutes the "elasticity of community."[35] While inherited notions of community assume that it gives shape to a collective will by managing internal differences, that it is a regulatory institution a subject inherits by means, mostly, of filiation, community is best understood at this point as belonging "to the economy of discourse and articulation."[36]

16. Autoethnography is an alibi for complicity.

Given its genealogy, how to move beyond autoethnography immediately signals the difficulties of methodology and of the politics of representation it is laden with, difficulties that pivot around the condition of complicity. How to move beyond autoethnography means coming to terms with complicity as an integral element of the autoethnographic method.

17. Definition of complicity.

The condition of complicity entails at once opacity and disclosure, invisibility and visibility, discomfort and accountability. According to its dictionary definition, it signifies being an accomplice in something that is at best wrongful, at worst criminal.

18. The double act of naming complicity.

When, on the one hand, we declare our own complicity as critics, complicity denotes a sense of anxiety and guilt. While our declaration may be sincere and well intended—as is the case, more often than not, with the practice of self-location in postcolonial criticism—it may also be a strategy designed to foreclose disapproval of our critical discourse by others. Alternatively, this same declaration may be an assertion of the difficulty, if not impossibility, of extricating ourselves from practices we set out to critique, what Leela Ghandi calls "the always-already complicity of Western knowledges with the operative interests of Western power."[37]

When, on the other hand, we identify complicity as a condition that marks someone else's work, we frown upon that critic's undeclared ideological affiliation, and expose the collusion we perceive between the critic's intentionality and his or her method. Indeed, outing a critic's complicity or outing a particular theory's or method's complicity with certain ideologies—for example, those revolving around structures of knowledge/power, cultural appropriation, racialization, and racism—not only speaks to the political unconscious characterizing all critical praxis, but has the potential to mark the inaugural moment of new critical directions, of more nuanced—if not new—methodologies.[38]

19. Naming complicity can be productive.

Complicity is as fluid and paradoxical a concept as is autoethnography. It is a negative condition whose meanings and effects depend on how and why it is manifested, and who deploys it as a strategy or trope. Thus, while complicity implies wrongdoing and guilt, identifying an act as complicitous has the potential to generate a certain productive agency.

20. We can spot complicity, but there is no guarantee we can move beyond it.

Declarations of complicity involve ethical and political questions: they are guided by the desire to expose the constructedness and mediation of value systems but are also engaged in a hermeneutics of suspicion, and therefore they cast doubt on the existence of solid ontological or epistemological grounds for locating truth once and for all. For example, while poststructuralism is credited for having exposed the complicity of subjectivity to power structures, it has also been found guilty of masculinist and bourgeois ideologies. Similarly, as Vicki Kirby writes,

> feminist ethnography, like all ethnography, is caught and empowered by unacknowledged complicities with masculinism and, indeed, with imperialism. [...] [F]eminist scholarship that attends to this bind is effectively censored when difference is conflated with pluralism. This explains why what norms itself as feminism within anthropology is increasingly impatient with other feminisms that engage poststructuralism and postmodern scholarship.[39]

Thus, even when we attempt to foreclose the dangers of complicity by practising a non-disinterested criticism by means of self-location or by rigorously unmasking the ideological premises underlying our critical methods, there is no guarantee that we can move beyond the ethical, political, or methodological problems underlying our complicity.

21. We never speak for ourselves. We speak at the limit.

The condition of complicity is revelatory, but its disclosures result in "partial truths"—"partial" in that they are "inherently [...] committed and incomplete."[40] Complicity, then, is the symmetrical opposite of sovereign subjectivity, of unalloyed agency.

We never speak for ourselves; we speak, instead, through the networks of meaning and value that impel us to act—for or against them. The partiality and incompleteness complicity embodies reveal that the critical act is constantly at a state of crisis, at the limit between knowing and unknowing. We kid ourselves if we think that taking another critic's complicity to task makes us, by default, more politically committed, more genuinely ethical, than her or him. We all inhabit the same prison house of language and disciplinary practices. "Writing," as Jean-Luc Nancy says, may be "the gesture which obeys the sole necessity of exposing the limit—not the limit of communication, *but the limit on which communication takes place*."[41]

22. Complicity is about being on the limit.

Complicity denotes the liminality of the critical act, being on the limit. If identifying complicity implies a desire to address the impropriety of speech acts, or that of other actions, we cannot expose the "proper" without "appropriation." The concept of the proper, Peggy Kamuf argues, "caves in, indeed its collapse has already occurred before we can utter its name, but also *so that* we can utter its name: the proper name and the name of the proper is always *in memoriam*."[42]

23. Identification of complicity does (not) signal a turn to ethics.

Identifying complicity declares the critic's self-interest in politics and ethics, but it is not necessarily clear "[w]hat kind of a turn ... [this] turn to ethics [is]. A Right turn? A Left turn? A wrong turn? A U-turn? Whose turn?"[43] John Guillory says, "[t]he turn to ethics is a turn away from the political," a "reduction of politics to morality, to the spectacle of a morality play."[44] But then he turns around himself to posit that "a turn to ethics is desirable and even inevitable for literary study at the present time."[45] He warns us not to "indulge" in what he calls "a political fantasy, the fantasy of transforming the world to a degree vastly greater than can reasonably be expected of perhaps any disciplinary practice." Instead, because there is "as yet no credible way to assess" the "effects" of our discipline, any "political effects" we may want to achieve "in the world must be achieved through a practice of reading." Like Kamuf, he, too, draws attention to the liminality of the reading practice that defines our profession: "The limits of this reading practice," he states, "constitute the limits of disciplinary power."[46]

24. Acknowledging complicity should be a categorical imperative.

The condition of complicity—being complicitous and dis/identifying complicity—is about the incommensurability of the critical act. To appropriate some of the terms Kamuf's argument revolves around: What do we expose when we expose complicity? In the name of whom or what do we expose complicity? And to what is complicity exposed by exposing itself?

25. Complicity is/as Negative Capability.

At this particular juncture of global times, as a condition that produces partial truths, complicity is at the core of postcolonial and diaspora studies and their shared ethical and political goals. Roy Miki identifies this problematic by calling attention to "the nation's complicity with corporate actions that give rise to the flow of migrant bodies, while simultaneously shoring up its territorial borders to prevent those bodies—all too often racialized—from becoming 'citizens.'"[47] What brings the nation's complicity "into relief"[48] is another complicity, namely, "the constructedness of the norms," the "historical narratives," that grant "coherence" to the "Canadian nation-formation." The result of this double complicity, Miki goes on to say, is that "the nation's identitarian discourses are not 'natural,' a given that both precedes and supercedes its 'individuated' subjects; rather, they are the extension of historical trajectories through which its subjects were marked and translated from the signs of colonial invasion and territorialization into the abstract language of 'citizenship.'"[49] If one of the mutual goals of postcolonial and diaspora studies is, as Miki puts it, to "disarticulate"[50] these trajectories, then identifying complicity in this context can be synonymous with what Miki calls a "moment of alteration,"[51] a moment that promises to take us beyond autoethnography and toward an understanding of diasporic literatures as "no longer … 'other.'"[52] Complicity, in this light, does not merely lie in the nation's appropriation of its citizens; complicity also articulates the negative capability of diaspora and postcolonial studies.

Being on the limit, yet again.

26. We cannot move *beyond*—we can only reside *beside*—complicity.

Declarations of complicity are at once constantive and performative enunciations, and thus can perpetuate complicity by naming it—a rehearsal act—or make a difference by trying to move beyond the political and intellectual crises complicity brings to the fore. It behooves us, then, to pay attention to what is involved in declarations of complicity as interpretative acts.

27. Complicity is situated between a hermeneutics of suspicion and a hermeneutics of trust.

Paul Ricoeur makes a fundamental, albeit controversial, distinction in his book, *Freud and Philosophy*. On the one pole, Ricoeur says, there is a hermeneutics "conceived as the unmasking, demystification, or reduction of illusions," a hermeneutics of suspicion; on the other, there is "interpretation conceived as the recollection or restoration of meaning,"[53] what Richard J. Bernstein calls "a hermeneutics of trust."[54] "Three masters, [...] Marx, Nietzsche, and Freud," according to Ricoeur, "dominate the school of suspicion."[55] This polarity, which Ricoeur considers to be "the truest expression of our 'modernity,'" is what "animate[s]" hermeneutics.[56] Ironically, however, theories interested in recuperating these three masters from "suspicion"—Brian Leiter's edited volume, *The Future for Philosophy*, is one recent example—fail to notice that "there is a subtle dialectical relation between these extremes," that "they are mutually dependent,"[57] indeed complicitous with each other.

28. Identifying complicity is not about moralizing, but about the possibility of creating productive sites.

If a declaration of complicity is going to have any efficacy, we ought to remain alert to the danger of being caught in a hermeneutic circle, to the need to strike a balance between suspicion and trust. This does not inevitably mean adopting a Habermasian politics of consensus. Whereas the act of identifying complicity has the potential to serve as its own teleology, a trope that can turn us into what Brian Leiter calls "moralizing interpreters"[58] or into morally self-satisfied agents, it can also make a difference by eliciting accountability, by translating the quandary of subject/power relations into a productive site.

29. Complicity is always relational.

The act of naming complicity—a performative act—confers agency on the speaking subject. Furthermore, it asserts the paradox that, though a negative condition, complicity can also play an effective role either because it may be employed as a heuristic strategy that mimics (and therefore distorts) our desire to move beyond a complicitous act, or because it functions as a site that elicits a counter-discourse. But this counter-discourse does not necessarily mean that we're moving beyond what it responds to. Complicity is always relational and at the limit.

30. We must not employ complicity as a trope of rehearsal.

Identifying complicity can initiate a process of disidentification and differentiation, a process that can involve, as Christopher Kutz argues in *Complicity: Ethics and Law for a Collective Age*, the "individual difference principle" and the "control principle."[59] Integral to the condition and structure of complicity according to Kutz, these principles can help us move beyond the hermeneutics of suspicion, and toward a critical practice that can translate complicity from a trope of rehearsal to an object of inquiry.

31. The identification of complicity cannot in itself effect radical change.

As a condition of relationality, complicity alerts us to the fact that, even though meaning is socially constructed, there are value systems and principles that have long attained a naturalness, a naturalness that constitutes the various communities we belong to—either through affiliation or filiation. Because a community, as Emmanuel Melissaris states, "can be as oppressive as it can be liberating,"[60] a declaration of complicity can articulate and mediate our relationship to it, but the acknowledgement of complicity alone does not effect a radical change in how we configure the concept of community.

32. Autoethnography both exposes and brackets the complicity involved in the construction and representation of otherness.

Even when the critical act is wary of essentialisms, it still yields to the tendency to read autoethnography and community through each other.

Françoise Lionnet does not directly problematize autoethnography and community, but her close reading of Zora Neale Hurston in "Autoethnography: The An-Archic Style of *Dust Tracks on a Road*," certainly avoids the perils of identifying Hurston with her black culture. Autoethnography, as Lionnet states, is "the defining of one's subjective ethnicity as mediated through language, history, and ethnographical analysis."[61] It has a "contextual frame of reference," and "there is no 'essential' quality to be isolated in the content of [...] [the] tales" it consists of.[62] Reading Hurston's book as an instance of "'figural anthropology' of the self,"[63] she takes note of "the textual mechanism that generates the journey of ethnic self-scrutiny, the slippage between the particular and the universal, individual and collective" elements of Hurston's book.[64] She thus demonstrates that what characterizes *Dust Tracks on a Road* as autoethnography is that it "create[s] its own genealogy by simultaneously appealing to and debunking the cultural traditions it helps to redefine." Hence Lionnet calls this book "an orphan text."[65]

33. Autoethnography is (not) an orphan text.

The condition of being an orphan attests to a sense of belonging but also loss; it speaks of close ties that have been severed. But even when it is configured to articulate an orphaned condition, autoethnography is not entirely devoid of the kind of attachments that essentialist notions of community evoke. The social and cultural history of being an orphan, along with the narratives of illegitimacy, abandonment, and abjection that often accompany it, makes it apparent that the orphaned condition is far from being desirable.

An orphan autoethnographic text, then, does not necessarily reconceptualize community in ways that demystify its inherited essentialisms. If anything, it evokes regret for the loss of an immanent relationship that is translated into an attempt to replace what is lost with a surrogate family, be it an adopted family or nation-state.

34. Autoethnography originates in displacement, but it is after similitude.

The old caveat that a nation is structured like a family demonstrates that the essentialisms characterizing our inherited notions of community are so thoroughly embedded in our social structures that any attempt to reconfigure community would require persistent effort and a highly creative project. As Georges Van Den Abbeele argues, such attempts

> are belied by the Western philosophical tradition's apparent inability to think beyond the subject as its organizing category. [...] The one who stands for the multitude is the familiar formula behind a host of authoritarianisms, from the absolutism of classical France through a plethora of modern forms of statism and totalitarianism. [...] In other words, [...] theories of social contract have a hard time explaining from where and how these freely engaged subjectivities are constituted. This is because [...] the social is thought from the standpoint of the individual who *then* encounters "others." As such, both organicist and contractual theories of community conceal the essentialism of a subject immanent to itself, which speaks either for and as a whole that would precede the parts (*com-unus*) or as a part that is itself already a whole before its encounter with other "parts" (*communis*).[66]

Precisely because it is closely aligned with the formation of subjectivity in relation to community, autoethnography cannot by itself reconfigure the essentialist legacies of community. Orphan textuality or not, autoethnography can worry the concept of community all it wants, but it continues to speak from the perspective of and about the subject's extended "family" by employing sameness as its benchmark. Hence its complicity.

35. Autoethnography is in dialogue with representations of otherness.

Mary Louise Pratt's definition of autoethnography shows the complicities inscribed in the autoethnographical act in sharp relief. Pratt writes that autoethnography is a text in which people undertake to describe themselves in ways that engage with representations others have made of them. [...] Autoethnographic texts are not, then, what are usually thought of as autochthonous or "authentic" forms of self-representation. [...] Rather they involve a selective collaboration with and appropriation of idioms of the metropolis or conqueror. They are merged or infiltrated to varying degrees with indigenous idioms to create self-representations intended to intervene in metropolitan modes of understanding.[67]

Though Pratt does not rely exclusively on literary texts, the differences her definition of autoethnography entails foreground the reasons why some critics tend to read the literary productions of "ethnic, multicultural, and minority writers" as autoethnographies.

36. Reading autoethnographically translates autoethnography back into ethnography.

Azade Seyhan argues that diasporic "writers become chroniclers of the histories of the displaced whose stories will otherwise go unrecorded."[68] Though certainly true in many cases, this statement should not be confused with the deployment of autoethnography as critical method. There is a fundamental difference between a writer wanting to record his or her own experience of displacement through life-writing or fiction and the overdetermination of the critical act to read diasporic authors autoethnographically, whether they write in that mode or not—what is implied in Seyhan's statement that "modern immigrant writing is almost exclusively autobiographical in nature."[69]

Rey Chow, who, like Seyhan, also notes that a large number of diasporic writers favour the autobiographical mode, reads this literature neither (auto)ethnographically nor sociologically. Seeing narcissism not in its conventional meaning as excessive selfishness, but in its Freudian sense as an instinctual mechanism of self-preservation that we have to give up at an early point in our lives, she accounts for the recurrence of the autobiographical mode in immigrant writing in a highly nuanced way. Because immigrant writers find no corresponding image or reflection of themselves[70] in dominant society, they suffer from a "lost or wounded narcissism—a narcissism that is not allowed to take its course, that has become inaccessible"; thus "felt by an entire group of people, narcissism becomes a transindividual issue of attachment and belonging."[71] Chow, then, considers the autobiographies of immigrant writers as being a "symptomatic attempt to (re)gain access to a transindividual narcissism, to grope for a self-regard that has not yet existed."[72] This self-regard is accomplished through the permeability of the transindividual subject. Such life-writing texts reveal the ethos of the writing subject's community without being reduced to sociological transcripts or turning the autobiographer into an unambiguous native informant.

37. What lies beyond autoethnography is already here.

Chow's reading of life-writing discourse demonstrates that ethnography is not intrinsic to diasporic literary texts; instead, it signals that we have already moved *beyond* autoethnography. Even when they write autobiographically, diasporic subjects, understood as transindividual, do not necessarily set out to reproduce a benign or beleaguered image of their communities.

Reading "ethnic, multicultural, and minority" writing autoethnographically, then, not only reflects a tendency to totalize the intents and meanings of diasporic discourse, but also reveals the complicities that mobilize such critical inclinations. If reading diasporic authors autoethnographically implies a critic's desire to instrumentalize their writing in order to facilitate the desire to change society—surely a tendency reflecting a liberalist ethos—then the critical desire to move beyond autoethnography should, ideally, entail a critique of liberalism.

38. *Beyond* is not about the future it allegedly points to. It is "an archive of confession."

Beyond the hermeneutics of suspicion, beyond pluralism, beyond the binary of subject/object, beyond complicity, beyond autoethnography. There seems to be something about this preposition—*beyond*—that makes us call upon it so often, something that makes it recur, with remarkable consistency, at every turning point of our critical enterprise.

Beyond is a double signifier, a trope that at once signals an impasse that we must overcome, a stalemate we have to resolve, and a desire, a willingness, to move away from such deadlocks. *Beyond*, then, signifies process, but its directionality, though indeterminate, activates a progressivist logic. There may be no specific telos inscribed in the *beyond*, but, as soon as we become engaged in its troping, we run the risk of adopting the fallacy of emancipation, a progress away from what lies before it. Giorgio Agamben reminds us that progressivism always entails "compromising":

> One has to yield on everything, one has to reconcile everything with its opposite, intelligence with television and advertisement, the working class with capital, freedom of speech with the state of the spectacle, the environment with industrial development, science with opinion, democracy with the electoral machine, bad conscience and abjuration with memory and loyalty.[73]

Believing, then, that we can move *beyond* a certain critical or political impasse implies that we have already accomplished something important, namely, that we have recognized the "tyranny of the given"[74] and that we can now rise above it to engage productively with the effects and affects of this tyranny, be it the tyranny of the professoriat as a community or that of thinking of community as having an essence. It is, to invoke Derrida, "an archive of confession, a genealogy of confessions."[75]

39. *Beyond* professes the incommensurability of our critical act.

The trope of the beyond cannot provide any answers as to how we can come to terms with the incommensurabilities of such difficult concepts as ethnicity, diaspora, citizenship, and the writing, such as autoethnography, that often represents them. In this context, the invitation to move beyond autoethnography points not so much toward anticipatory solutions but toward the liminality as much of autoethnography as of other discourses by and about diasporic subjects.

40. *Beyond* is haunted by the spectre of complicity.

The trope of the beyond makes no promises that we can disengage ourselves from the complicities tying together the creative and critical acts. Beyond is forward looking, but what we try to move beyond remains haunted by the spectrality of complicity. It carries along with it a disjunctive temporality. No matter the kind of impasse we try to move beyond, what comes after is already hybridized by what precedes it.

41. The after is complicitous with the before.

If Pheng Cheah is right when he suggests that the euphoria characterizing hybridity theorists—and his primary examples are Homi Bhabha and James Clifford—grants to culture an emancipatory function as opposed to various forms of oppression, then the trope of the beyond, especially in relation to autoethnography, is complicit with the same kind of "closet idealism"[76] that inspires certain theories of hybridity.

42. Declaring complicity is *"like* a profession of faith."[77]

Similar to the trope of the beyond, complicity stands at the crossroads of archeology and teleology: archaeology, because complicity is traceable to, and brings into relief, the contingencies, along with their histories, that construct our positions and discourses; teleology, because in every declaration of complicity there is the desire, be it clearly articulated or subliminally operating, to reach a telos, a site where we will be liberated from the troubling legacies that produce complicity.

43. Autoethnography is a symptom of errancy.

If complicity is an ineluctable element of the human condition in general and of critical discourses in particular, as I believe it is, we have to come to terms with the fact that we cannot fully disentangle ourselves from the burdens of affiliation, filiation, and responsibility. As an aleatory figure, complicity haunts our critical discourse, but it is not a spectre we want to do without. Keeping us on our toes, this spectre is a reminder of the errancy that marks our critical acts. It is the awareness, albeit not always inscribed in our discourse, of the provisionality of our critical acts that has given rise to autoethnography.

Anne Norton's *95 Theses on Politics, Culture, and Method* inspired the form of this essay. I would like to thank Eleanor Ty and Chrystl Verduyn for providing me with the opportunity to reflect on this topic. The Canada Research Chair Program has provided the resources and time to pursue this writing project.

NOTES

1 Jacques Derrida, *Without Alibi*, ed., trans. Peggy Kamuf (Stanford, CA: Stanford UP, 2002), 202.

2 See the objectives of "Beyond Autoethnography," as outlined by the conference co-organizers Christl Verduyn and Eleanor Ty: http://info.wlu.ca/~wwweng/ety/Ethnicity-conference.htm.

3 See the call for papers issued for the above conference.

4 There are far too many examples of the kind of criticism in which the critic tends to read literature by diasporic authors as social commentary on the authors' ethnic communities or society at large, although, as Ty and Verduyn state in their call for papers, "[n]o longer are ethnic and minority authors identifying simply with their ethnic and racial groups in opposition to dominant culture. Many authors consciously attempt to question or problematize the link between ethnic identity and literary production, while still recognizing the racialized context in which they write" (see website in note 2). Denise Chong, who wrote *The Concubine's Children: Portrait of a Family Divided* (Toronto: Viking, 1994), and Evelyn Lau, author of, among other texts, *Other Women* (Toronto: Random House of Canada, 1995) and *You Are Not Who You Claim* (Victoria: Porcepic, 1990), would be two examples of such authors. See also Charlotte Sturgess, special issue of *Commonwealth Essays and Studies* 24, no. 1 (2001): 73–78, as well as Eleanor Ty's "Writing Historiographic Autoeuthnography: Denise Chong's *The Concubine's Children*," in her recent book, *The Politics of the Visible in Asian North American Narratives* (Toronto: U of Toronto P, 2004).

5 Although important, a discussion of how these terms operate as synonyms, have overlapping meanings, are marked by distinct genealogies, or signify different constituencies at particular moments in given nation-states, though relevant to my argument, is not an integral part of it. Such terms, even though they help advance

our understanding of certain subjects, tend to operate as heuristic critical devices and legislative gestures that say more about the power systems attempting to define and curtail the subjects in question than about the subjects themselves. Their significance must always be measured in relation to the times and particular contingencies that give rise to them.

6   Ludwig Wittgenstein, *Culture and Value*, ed. G.H. von Wright, trans. Peter Winch (Chicago: U of Chicago P, 1980), 8e.

7   Michael M.J. Fischer, "Ethnicity and the Post-Modern Arts of Memory," in *Writing Culture: The Poetics and Politics of Ethnography* (Berkley: U of California P, 1986), 200.

8   James Clifford, "Introduction: Partial Truths," in *Writing Culture: The Poetics and Politics of Ethnography*, ed. James Clifford and George E. Marcus (Berkeley: U of California P, 1986), 15.

9   Different aspects of this methodological (and aesthetic) shift are thematized in most of the contributions to Clifford and Marcus's *Writing Culture*. See especially Mary Louise Pratt (27–50), Stephen A. Tyler (122–40), and Marcus (165–93 and 262–66). See also Clifford's *The Predicament of Culture: Twentieth-Century Ethnography, Literature, and Art* (Cambridge, MA: Harvard UP, 1988); George E. Marcus and Michael M.J. Fischer, *Anthropology as Cultural Critique: an Experimental Moment in the Human Sciences* (Chicago: U of Chicago P, 1986); and Clifford Geertz, *Local Knowledge: Further Essays on Interpretive Anthropology* (New York: Columbia UP, 1989). Ivan Karp and Steven D. Lavine's edited volume, *Exhibiting Cultures: The Poetics and Politics of Museum Display* (Washington: Smithsonian Institute Press, 1991), though it deals with cultural objects as opposed to cultural narratives, also addresses pertinent issues.

10 Deborah E. Reed-Danahay, ed., *Auto/Ethnography: Rewriting the Self and the Social* (Oxford: Berg, 1997), 4.

11 D. Soyini Madison, *Critical Ethnography: Method, Ethics, and Performance* (Thousand Oaks, CA: Sage, 2005), 8. Despite the fact that she refers to, and employs, George N. Noblit, Susana Y. Flores, and Enrique G. Murillo Jr.'s notion of "'postcritical ethnography,'" and its pronounced emphasis on "positionality," Madison's terminology is inconsistent. Thus, while her argument revolves around "postcritical ethnography" as a "critique" of "traditional notions of critical ethnography" (7), she still prefers, as the title of her book suggests, the term "critical" as a qualifier of ethnography. See also George N. Noblit, Susana Y. Flores, and Enrique G. Murillo Jr., *Postcritical Ethnography: An Introduction* (Cresskill, NJ: Hampton, 2004).

12 Ibid., 9.

13 Ibid., 5.

14 Ibid., 8.

15 Ibid., 8.

16 Ibid., 9.

17 Ibid., 9.

18 Ibid., 5.

19 Reed-Danahay, 4.

20 See Karl Heider, "What Do People Do? Dani Auto-ethnography," *Journal of Anthropological Research*, 31 (1975): 3–17.

21 The relationship between autoethnography and autobiography raises very important, but also highly problematic, issues; nevertheless, because I am interested here in exploring the ways in which complicity forms part of the genealogy of

autoethnography vis à vis anthropology, I am not pursuing its links with the auto-biographical act as such. For three examples of the many excellent studies of autobiography that focus on the life-narratives of diasporic or other minority subjects that are akin to autoethnography, see Joanne E. Baxton, *Black Women Writing Autobiography: A Tradition within a Tradition* (Philadelphia, PA: Temple UP, 1989), Doris Sommer, "'Not Just a Personal Story': Women's *Testimonios* and the Plural Self" in *Life/Lines: Theorizing Women's Autobiography*, ed. Bella Brodzki and Celeste Schenck (Ithaca, NY: Cornell UP, 1988), and Julie Rak, *Doukhobor Autobiographical Discourse: Negotiated Memory* (Vancouver: U of British Columbia P, 2004).

22 Clifford in Clifford and Marcus, "Introduction: Partial Truths," 4. Carolyn Ellis's *The Ethnographic I: A Methodological Novel about Autoethnography* (Walnut Creek, CA: Altamira, 2004) is an excellent example of theorizing the self-reflexiveness, ethics, and methodological questions raised by autoethnography in a first-person narrative cast as a novel.

23 Clifford in Clifford and Marcus, "Introduction: Partial Truths," 4.

24 Ibid., 6.

25 James Clifford, *Routes: Travel and Translation in the Late Twentieth Century* (Cambridge, MA: Harvard UP, 1997), 69.

26 Clifford in Clifford and Marcus, "Introduction: Partial Truths," 14.

27 Patrick Riley, *Character and Conversion in Autobiography: Augustine, Montaigne, Descartes, Rousseau, and Sartre* (Charlottesville: U of Virginia P, 2004), 1.

28 Ibid., 9.

29 Ibid., 10.

30 Clifford, *Routes: Travel and Translation in the Late Twentieth Century*, 69. One early turning point in the containment of the personal in ethnographic work was the release of Bronislaw Malinowski's *A Diary in the Strict Sense of the Term* (London: Routledge and Kegan Paul, 1967), which shattered, among others, the taboo of sex in the field. See *Taboo: Sex, Identity, and Erotic Subjectivity in Anthropological Fieldwork*, eds. Don Kulick and Margaret Willson (London: Routledge, 1995) as an example of how ethnographers theorize and narrativize their breach of professional etiquette or the ambivalence of situations they find themselves in.

31 Ibid., 84.

32 Ibid., 84.

33 Riley, *Character and Conversion*, 5.

34 There is no shortage of studies about the construction and/or role of the native informant in the fields of anthropology and postcolonial theory and literary criticism. I consider Rey Chow's "Where Have All the Natives Gone?" in her *Writing Diaspora: Tactics of Intervention in Contemporary Cultural Studies* (Bloomington: Indiana UP, 1993) one of the most insightful treatments of the topic. See also *Thunder Through My Veins* by Gregory Scofield (Toronto: Harper, 1999) and Warren Cariou's *Lake of the Prairies* (Toronto: Random, 2003), examples, possibly, of Métis autoethnography where the "native informant" is at once inside and outside his various communities.

35 Linda Singer, "Recalling a Community at Loose Ends," in *Community at Loose Ends*, ed. Miami Theory Collective (Minneapolis: U of Minnesota P, 1991), 125.

36 Ibid., 125. Alfonso Lingis's *The Community of Those Who Have Nothing in Common* (Bloomington: Indiana UP, 1994), offers a radically different concept of community by considering the community of the living with that of those who are dying.

37   Leela Ghandi, *Postcolonial Theory: A Critical Introduction* (New York: Columbia UP, 1998), 5.
38   I think of the politics of cultural appropriation both in Canada and the U.S.A. as representing one of the most important recent cases where cultural and racial politics and methodology were debated through the prism of complicity. For an insightful critique of the so-called culture wars in Canada, see Michael Keefer's *Lunar Perspectives: Field Notes from the Culture Wars* (Toronto: Anansi, 1996), which includes references to most other relevant sources in the Canadian context.
39   Vicki Kirby, "'Feminisms, Reading, Postmodernisms': Rethinking Complicity," in *Feminism and the Politics of Difference*, ed. Sneja Gunew and Anna Yeatman (Halifax: Fernwood Publishing, 1993), 30.
40   Clifford in Clifford and Marcus, "Introduction: Partial Truths," 7.
41   Cited in Peggy Kamuf, "On the Limit," in *Community at Loose Ends*, ed. Miami Theory Collective (Minneapolis: U of Minnesota P, 1991), 14.
42   Ibid., 16.
43   Marjorie Garber, Beatrice Hanssen, and Rebecca L. Walkowitz, "Introduction," to *The Turn to Ethics*, ed. Marjorie Garber, Beatrice Hanssen, and Rebecca L. Walkowitz (New York: Routledge, 2000), vii.
44   John Guillory, "The Ethical Practice of Modernity: The Example of Reading," in *The Turn to Ethics*, ed. Marjorie Garber, Beatrice Hanssen, and Rebecca L. Walkowitz (New York: Routledge, 2000), 29.
45   Ibid., 30.
46   Ibid., 31. I offer a more detailed reading of the ethics of reading in my article "The Limits of the Ethical Turn: Troping towards the Other, Yann Martel, and Self," *University of Toronto Quarterly* 76, no. 3 (Summer 2007): 937–61.
47   Roy Miki, "Altered States: Global Currents, the Spectral Nation, and the Production of 'Asian Canadian,'" *Journal of Canadian Studies* 35, no. 3 (2000): 47.
48   Ibid., 48.
49   Ibid., 48.
50   Ibid., 53.
51   Ibid., 53.
52   Ibid., 56.
53   Paul Ricoeur, *Freud and Philosophy: An Essay on Interpretation*, trans. Denis Savage (New Haven, CT: Yale UP, 1970), 9.
54   Richard J. Bernstein, *Freud and the Legacy of Moses* (Cambridge: Cambridge UP, 1998), 15.
55   Ricoeur, *Freud and Philosophy*, 32.
56   Ibid., 27.
57   Bernstein, *Freud and the Legacy of Moses*, 16.
58   Brian Leiter, "The Hermeneutics of Suspicion: Recovering Marx, Nietzsche, and Freud," in *The Future for Philosophy*, ed. Brian Leiter (Oxford: Clarendon Press, 2004), 75.
59   Christopher Kutz, *Complicity: Ethics and Law for a Collective Age* (Cambridge: Cambridge UP, 2000), 117–18.
60   Emmanuel Melissaris, "Review of *Complicity: Ethics and Law for a Collective Age*, by Christopher Kutz," *Law and Politics Book Review* 14, no. 6 (2004): 423.
61   Françoise Lionnet, *Autobiographical Voices: Race, Gender, Self-Portraiture* (Ithaca, NY: Cornell UP, 1989), 99.
62   Ibid., 101.
63   Ibid., 99.

64 Ibid., 115.

65 Ibid., 101.

66 Georges Van Den Abbeele, "Introduction," to *Community at Loose Ends*, ed. Miami Theory Collective (Minneapolis: U of Minnesota P, 1991), xi, xii.

67 Mary Louise Pratt, "Transculturation and Autoethnography: Peru 1615/1980," in *Colonial Discourse/ Postcolonial Theory*, ed. Frances Baker, Peter Holme, and Margaret Iverson (Manchester: Manchester UP, 1994), 28.

68 Azade Seyhan, *Writing Outside the Nation* (Princeton, NJ: Princeton UP, 2001), 12.

69 Cited in Rey Chow, "The Secrets of Ethnic Abjection," in *"Race" Panic and the Memory of Migration* (Hong Kong: Hong Kong UP, 2001), 76.

70 Ibid., 64.

71 Ibid., 65.

72 Ibid., 66.

73 Giorgio Agamben, *Means without End: Notes on Politics*, trans. Vincenzo Binetti and Cesare Casarino (Minneapolis: U of Minnesota P, 2000), 137.

74 Chow, "The Secrets of Ethnic Abjection," 60.

75 Derrida, *Without Alibi*, 80.

76 Pheng Cheah, "Given Culture: Rethinking Cosmopolitical Freedom in Transnationalism," in *Cosmopolitics: Thinking and Feeling Beyond the Nation*, ed. Pheng Cheah and Bruce Robbins (Minneapolis: U of Minnesota P, 1998), 299.

77 Part 1 of the Catechism of the Catholic Church deals with the Profession of Faith, including the Apostles' Creed.

chapter two

Autoethnography Otherwise

Paul Lai

Reading ethnic literatures *as* ethnic literatures is a practice embedded in a variety of discourses, including publishing and academic ones. Literary critics sometimes attend to the former discourses in analyzing the creation of niche markets and audiences. We understand the material conditions of book publishing as constitutive of how the reading public at large receives books labelled as novels, autobiographies, non-fiction, memoirs, and so on. However, when addressing the latter discourses, we often focus on how texts push against academic sites, disciplinary boundaries, and institutional expectations of multicultural knowledge without also considering how criticism itself functions as a technology for making sense of and defining ethnic literatures. As a practice, North American literary criticism has a decades-long tradition of considering ethnic literatures as autoethnography, legitimizing certain texts over others for their adherence to conceptions of cultural representation.

The particular problematic (or discursive terrain by which we understand and think about objects) sketched out by the phrase "autoethnographic fiction" has been central to studies of ethnic literatures, but it is nevertheless one that deserves renewed attention precisely because the questions it raises seem so readily anticipated and naturalized. Thinking of ethnic literatures through the rubric of autoethnography—both what fiction is autoethnographic and what fiction is beyond (or not) autoethnographic—is one way that criticism functions as a technology of recognition. That is, we understand certain kinds of texts to be "Asian North American," for example, because of a set of criteria we elaborate. While it has been important to focus on the autoethnographic qualities of ethnic literatures, the move to consider such literatures beyond autoethnography should also raise concerns about the function and the character of literary criticism.

This essay considers how to examine texts "beyond autoethnography" in two sections: the first discusses how anthropology and literary studies as modes of cultural critique and disciplinary practice understand autoethnographic fiction, and the second takes up Canadian poet-critic Fred Wah in an attempt to perform a kind of autoethnographic criticism otherwise, one that highlights how Wah's writing moves at odds against the usual genres of ethnic writing but focuses less on whether Wah's texts are themselves beyond autoethnography and more on why we as literary critics are invested in claiming those texts as such. These comments are speculative and meant to bring together different critical vocabularies in the consideration of autoethnography.

Autoethnography Otherwise

For our purposes, autoethnography is the kind of writing that non-white, non-mainstream authors use to give us an account of their experiences in Canada. The idea is that autoethnography as a writing style participates in certain assumptions of objectivity, truth, and authority that we associate with the human sciences. In other words, the autoethnographer is what the native informant became. We invest in autoethnography the ability to tell us something about another culture in a truthful manner.

For literary studies at large, autoethnographic fiction carries a veneer of the unsophisticated. It is the underdeveloped cousin of serious literary fiction or experimental writing; it is fiction that mimetically produces the cultural experiences of the author's ethnic group (usually in non-white or off-white understandings of "ethnic"), writing that strives for unquestioning verisimilitude. It is autobiographical fiction or fictionalized memoir, writing that ultimately is *about* the author and, by extension, her cultural group. Particularly for non-white or non-Anglophone writers in Canada and the U.S., this slide from autobiography to autoethnography, from individual history to group history, is a function of multiculturalism and its need to make sense of minority peoples against a normative mainstream (ostensibly "white," but always already constructed as such in ways that also efface important particularities of white individuals and ethnic groups). Histories of the academic study of many ethnic literatures often begin with this understanding of autoethnographic fiction, a cultural nationalist model of ethnic awareness, because it serves an important legitimizing function for both the fiction and the experiences it conveys in telling stories heretofore untold.

Some critics within fields of ethnic literary studies have usefully expanded this singular understanding of autobiography and memoir as mimetic writing by examining the representational strategies that ethnic writers employ. In turn, some critics have also argued that autobiography and memoir are important genres in themselves, offering especially for studies of ethnic writers (and women) new perspectives on the relationship between experiences and writing.[1] For example, Eleanor Ty explains the conceptual framework for her analysis of Denise Chong's text:

> I use the term "historiographic autoethnography" to emphasize a consciousness of the act of writing history and to highlight the complexity of ethnic self-representation. [...] The term historiographic autoethnography, then, questions the way in which history has been narrated; what, and from whose viewpoint, it has been told; and, at the same time, it articulates an awareness of the useful terms of Euro-American-dominated ethnography that reverberate in one's act of self-representation.[2]

While these literary critics still study fiction that is ostensibly about the author and her cultural group (though often about other matters as well), they complicate the text, the medium through which authors transform and transmit experiences to readers. What matters is the text as mediation, as language that transforms and engages in productively disruptive ways what we consider to be reality.

In this sense, such critics perform a sort of "autoethnography otherwise," borrowing from Kandice Chuh's useful formulation of the act of Asian Americanist critique as "imagining otherwise," or imagining the Other in different ways than previously available, especially against the grain of hegemonic discourse.[3] The shift here is in placing the burden of autoethnographic *reading* onto the literary critic, onto the formations of literary studies as a field, rather than on the texts themselves. Such a shift emphasizes the importance of the critic and the academy in bringing to visibility certain writing over others, and points to the political impulses behind such criticism guiding the selection of writing.[4]

The work of examining the limits of autoethnography in literary studies, then, hinges not so much on texts that are or are not about the author's cultural group, but rather lies in considering how we take up, within various institutional contexts, these writers and their texts as representing their cultural group. Instead of reading the texts thematically or content-wise as non-autoethnographic, we might accept the impossibility of escaping any notion of the autoethnographic subject in ethnic literary studies. Indeed, it may be just as useful to consider how a text written by an ethnic writer, ostensibly *not* about her cultural group, still gives us insight into sociological issues relevant to that group. Consider, for example, the well-known case of African American writer James Baldwin's second novel *Giovanni's Room*.[5] Written explicitly to challenge the notion that African American writers could only truthfully write African American characters, the novel is a hauntingly beautiful journey into the mind of a gay white male expatriate American in France. And though some may argue that Baldwin's own sexuality allowed him to represent his character David's homosexuality so artfully, what is most striking about the novel and its reception in African American literary studies is how it has been seen alternately as something not quite African American and something that remarkably points to racial questions in America precisely because of the absence of African American characters. The palpable whiteness of David thus becomes a way to think about race and therefore about African Americans' place in America. And to cite another example, Japanese British writer Kazuo Ishiguro's *The Remains of the Day*, set in England during WWII and revolving around white characters, serves as another reminder that ethnic writers who write non-ethnic characters offer stimulating opportunities for literary critics to consider the place of the autoethnographic subject.[6] Is this text still undeniably one written by a Japanese British author? Likewise, Michael Ondaatje's *The English Patient* treads similar ground in focusing on a story about Europe during World War II, but since it is written by a mixed-race Asian Canadian, does it ultimately have something to tell us about "Asian Canadian" culture?[7] What do we make of Kevin Chong's *Baroque-a-Nova*, a novel by a Chinese Canadian that is about an 18-year-old young man's coming of age after the death of his folk-singing mother in a story that is visibly not about Chinese Canadian history or culture?[8] Is this text one we can still consider as autoethnography? Does Chong's narrative still give us something to discuss about the politics of representation for a Chinese Canadian writer?

Another way to perform autoethnography otherwise would be to consider the institutional and cultural sites that help reinforce the problematic of reading ethnic writers autoethnographically. We could look at publishing houses and their decisions to take on certain kinds of books rather than others, at the marketing of writing by ethnic writers, or at how reviews in literary magazines and major newspapers characterize ethnic writing. We could consider, too, how the authors themselves conceive of their work in relationship to their cultures. Is there an explicit political or cultural commitment on the part of the author? What goals does the author imagine accomplishing in her writing? These questions and approaches to thinking about the movement of texts through institutions and from authorial intentions foreground the importance of articulating the work of autoethnography to particular locations and projects. In other words, the autoethnographic text, even if it is identifiable by content and form, still must circulate in certain ways to function as autoethnography.

To perform autoethnography otherwise in literary studies, finally, would be to acknowledge the crucial and conflicted relationship of literary studies to anthropology as well as other social science and humanities disciplines. Within anthropology, ethnography carries different valences and is weighted with a different sense of critical tradition. Postmodernist-influenced anthropologists and those invested in self-reflexive critical writing who understand the importance of the critical act in creating a sense of the culture studied have argued that the ethnography of the past—when white, Western men went "out there" to Oceania and other foreign lands to study objectively and detachedly some bounded, static, primitive cultures—has been superseded by a much more nuanced, reflective ethnography. This updated ethnography questions the division between insider and outsider, between subject and observer. Anthropologists have developed a range of different ideas and methods to do ethnography differently, from participant observation to co-ethnic ethnography and autoethnography. Explicitly and implicitly, they draw on literary studies' work in questioning the link between writing and reality.[9]

In a collection of essays on the importance of ethnography for Asian American Studies, cultural anthropologist Martin Manalansan writes of these new ethnographers,

> [i]n many instances, the "researchers" are themselves "natives" or members of the community in which they are conducting research. This situation complicates relationships in the field and transforms the ethnographic enterprise. Ethnographers are no longer the distant omniscient strangers that they have traditionally been constructed to be. They have acquired a new role in viewing and representing communities and peoples. Subjects of ethnographies are no longer the ignorant natives who passively accept intrusion but are continuously asking "Why?" and "What for?" These subjects are now apprehended as producers as well as products of history, and shapers and builders of culture.[10]

The knowledge that ethnographers produce is always embedded in particular frameworks of knowing shaped by academic work and the personal lives of the researchers. For Asian North American (auto)ethnographers and other ethnic anthropologists, too, this knowledge often has a politicized, community-activist purpose or commitment. Unlike the old ethnographers who meant to document objectively some static foreign culture, these autoethnographers live in and participate in the cultures they study. Their academic work, in turn, helps to transform, critique, and validate those cultures.

Some of the other contributors to Manalansan's volume note the specific importance of the relationship between the ethnographer and her subjects. This is a relationship that must be sustained and negotiated in complex and distinct ways in each situation. Ethnography as co-ethnics, for example, means studying those with whom you share an ethnic identity, whether or not you belong to their particular community. Miliann Kang's essay "Researching One's Own: Negotiating Co-ethnicity in the Field" points out the difficulties of this kind of ethnography but also how much such work helps point out the differences within cultural groups as indexed by race, profession, generations, and so on.[11]

Given this anthropological orientation towards and embrace of critical autoethnography, how can literary critics approach the study of autoethnography in literary texts? This kind of autoethnography otherwise would consider fiction writers as autoethnographers, and to do so would require thinking of the author, her text, and the culture in the same kind of conflicted relationships noted in anthropological work. It would require an acknowledgement of the multiple layers of autoethnographic criticism in literary studies since, if fiction writers are themselves autoethnographers, literary critics are a second order of critical inquiry. What are the dynamics that result from this multi-layered cultural critique? What status does a literary critic claim in terms of being an observer? All of these questions should help make the practice of autoethnography more self-critical, more open to an examination of the various institutional sites through which the discourse of autoethnography circulates. Rather than give up on autoethnography, too, these approaches to "autoethnography otherwise" challenge the bleak perspective that cultural critic Rey Chow brings to the study of ethnicity when she argues that all ethnic cultural production is inescapably bound up in a "coercive mimeticism," the incessant and necessary performing of an ethnic self for a mainstream audience as well as one's own ethnic group that only serves to circumscribe any revolutionary potential of such productions.[12] Autoethnography otherwise, concerned with complicating the perceived simplicity of ethnic writing as mimetic, pushes us to read across genres, across cultures, across disciplines, across media, and across other expectations of ethnic literatures.

With all of these considerations of autoethnography otherwise, I would like to add that for literary studies, it might be most useful to ask if it is possible to claim poetics as autoethnography. If we think of poetics as the conscious attention to the mediating and productive qualities of language, especially as it challenges expectations of mimeticism or transparency that haunt ethnic autoethography, we can foreground the critical practice of reading poetics autoethnographically without burdening the text itself with the need to be autoethnographic. Also, what is the function of poetics in cultural critique, and what is the function of academic criticism in bringing to light poetics as autoethnography? The following section, far from providing answers to these questions, takes them up tentatively through the work of Fred Wah.

Fred Wah's Challenging Poetics and the Re-Meaning of Race

Having raised the spectre of incommensurability between writing (fiction) and criticism, I would now like to consider what it means to do both together in the work of Fred Wah. I focus on Fred Wah's prose writing— his biofictions and critical essays—rather than his poetry because while his strategies of disrupting expectations in language communication might be readily accepted in poetry—especially what we see as "experimental," "avant-garde," or "language poetry"—they take on a more challenging or disruptive cast in prose. In the "Contexts and Acknowledgements" section of *Faking It*, his collection of critical writing, Wah notes,

> I admit to a certain pretense in the formal essay because I find it a struggle to let logic and argument have control. For a variety of reasons, social and cultural, I want to undercut the hegemony of such forms. The "Strangle" pieces here serve some of that desire to intervent and push at the boundaries of more intentional compositions. They are, to an extent, sealed from easy understanding in order to play out the possible and sustaining blur around book reviews and other gestures like the critical biotext "Was Eight." I've used these sections as a way of keeping open my own thinking, by play, dissonance, and juxtaposition.[13]

It is in this spirit of disrupting our expectations of the formal essay—the thesis, the argument—that I present the following comments. And not to be outdone by Wah, in many ways, I note that I am also "faking" this very move to move beyond the critical essay form. But I think it is a worthwhile move to consider, and one that others have taken in various venues, such as the performative writing of queer theorist Eve Sedgwick and the critical-poetic writing of contemporary American poets like John Yau and Nathaniel Mackey.[14] I hope that these observations, and a greater than usual (in the traditional academic essay) reliance on excerpts of Wah's writing, create the space for critical thinking and reflection about the uses of criticism and writing. I have chosen to take on Wah's work precisely because he already challenges the divide and the compatibility between criticism and other writing (on which criticism might be seen as parasitic), but I ultimately consider how literary critics can perform an autoethnography otherwise in reading texts for the ways they disrupt our expectations of ethnic autoethnography.[15]

Of the particular form that "faking it" takes for his work, Wah explains in a published interview:

> The term "faking it" comes from improvisation. In music, particularly in trumpet playing, you fake it. In fact, one of the big books of music for jazz musicians is *The Fake Book*. You see, there's the Real Book and then there's the Fake Book. I'm beginning the book with a little essay called "Faking It" that explains that when you're faking it you're doing it out of necessity, you're not doing it just to have fun. There's a pressure, a force there. It's the same as when you're playing jazz.[16]

As the trumpet player performing in tandem with other musicians within the improvisational space of jazz must adhere to the various logics of musicality, Wah feels a "pressure" to fake his writing against the conventions of the essay, of writing more generally, and of ethnic writing as understood by a reading public, mainstream critics, and academic critics. What is interesting about Wah as a figure through which we can explore "autoethnography otherwise" as well as the faking of a different kind of essay is that he *both* so readily eludes usual understandings of ethnic writers *and* allows for an ethnographic recuperation. He is both the prime example for the need to perform autoethnography otherwise and a mundane example of how to read ethnic literatures ethnographically in the first place. His writing forces us to tackle autoethnography otherwise because there is no straightforward account of "ethnic" truth in his experiences. However, because he claims himself as an ethnic writer of sorts, hybrid though his body is, he opens himself to reading his body against his work autoethnographically— that is, critics can make arguments about how his writing reflects reflexively (if not uncritically) the complicated intersections of his body.

Wah is consistently concerned with what Susan Rudy describes as "an improvisational, disjunctive poetics." Even so, Rudy characterizes Wah's lengthy writing career in two major phases—early work focusing on "personal geography and history" (1965–1980) and later work dealing with "the articulation of a racialized poetics in North America" (1981–present).[17] Such a bifurcation suggests that his later work is more amenable to the (auto)ethnographic rubric of reading ethnic writing. Indeed, before Wah's

own more self-reflective turn towards themes of racialization, he was read
by poets and critics as a figure within circles of Canadian poets interested
in disrupting the transparency of language and meaning.[18] Since his 1981
work *Breathin' My Name with a Sigh*, however, critics have taken up Wah's
writing under the rubrics of race as troubled by Wah's poetics.[19] More
recently, critics have pressed Wah's writing to the service of postcolonial and
diasporic literary studies, using his work to break open Canada's borders
and CanLit's canon.[20] Within this emerging body of criticism about Wah's
work more recently, too, we see a shift in terms of poets and writers with
whom he is connected. Much of the later criticism tends to link him to
such Asian Canadian writers as Michael Ondaatje, Roy Miki, and Hiromi
Goto rather than to non-Asian writers invested in language play such as
Robert Creeley or bp Nichol.

In his biotext *Diamond Grill*, Fred Wah recounts a story of his father's
initiation into the Lions Club.[21] A version of the same passage shows up in
the first selection of critical essays in the collection *Faking It*. He writes,

> [w]hen he joins the Lions Club and has to give an initiation speech, he gets
> my mother to help him write something up. She says he's very nervous about
> this event; worried that he might flub it, make a fool of himself, the only
> Chinaman at an all-white dinner meeting. But there he is, with his little
> speech on a piece of paper in front of all these Baker Street nickel million-
> aires in the Hume Hotel dining room, thanking these guys for inviting him
> to join their club, thanking them for making Nelson such a wonderful place
> to live and raise his family, and then thanking them for this meal with the won-
> derful *sloup*. We always kid around at home when he says *sloup* and he laughs
> and, we suspect, even says it that way intentionally just to horse around with
> us. But here such a slip just turns him copper red (the colour you get when
> you mix yellow with either embarrassment or liquor). So when he hears him-
> self say *sloup* for soup he stops suddenly and looks out at the expected embar-
> rassed and patronizing smiles from the crowd. Then he does what he has
> learned to do so well in such instances, he turns it into a joke, a kind of self
> put-down that he knows these white guys like to hear: he bluffs that China-
> men call soup *sloup* because, as you all know, the Chinese make their café soup
> from the slop water they wash their underwear and socks in, and besides, it's
> just like when you hear me eating my soup, Chinamen like to slurp and make
> a lot of noise. That's a compliment to the cook!
>
> So he fakes it, and I guess I pick up on that sense of faking it from him,
> that English can be faked. But I quickly learn that when you fake language
> you see, as well, how everything else is a fake.[22]

This is a wonderful passage for those of us interested in language, culture,
and meaning. And it is clearly one that Wah himself has embraced as an

important anecdote marking self-realization. But even as this story tells us that we fake our way through life and meaning, the genre of the anecdote and the life story tell us that this is still writing about one's culture. It might be one built of faked notions of language and culture, but it is nonetheless writing about culture; it is autoethnography. This is not to say simply that Wah concedes to the pressures of explaining his culture in his writing. Instead, it is to suggest a different question about autoethnography. Where is the truth in autoethnography? And if there is no truth in autoethnography, is it still useful? How can we think of Wah as an autoethnographer?

Wah's biofictions thoughtfully place himself at the centre of a piece of writing that dares its readers to understand him as an ethnic Other, part Chinese in a white Canadian space. But like the critical (auto)ethnographers of today's cultural anthropology, he is unwilling to let his words stand for themselves and for his culture. His words are opaque; they resist giving us a clear and untroubled view of his past and the histories of his family and the Chinese in Canada. The fakery of his posture, though, is not a dead end. He does not lament the impossibility of knowing "Fred Wah" or the complicated intersections of lives that led to his presence and his poetic career. He celebrates the devilish possibilities that erupt upon recognizing how his father has faked his way to acceptance by his white peers—accepted as a Chinaman *and* as a Lion's Club member, an oddly contradictory juxtaposition sutured by the fake "sloup."

Linguistic philosophy (such as in the work of Donald Davidson[23]) helps us distinguish between a language or speech act's truth claims and its success or take-up. The father's truth claim that the Chinese make *sloup* from slop water is patently false. Not even the white audience is meant to think this claim true, even as it plays on their stereotypes of dirty Chinese. What is interesting in this anecdote is how the claim gets taken up in the moment of communication. It is a success. It becomes a joke. It is a nod towards the moment of autoethnography, the moment of ethnic confession, the moment of autobiographical expression. But it lies. It makes of the father and the audience conspirators in a ruse to re-articulate the Chinaman's place in the white Lion's Club. It re-means what the men in the room know about race, about the Chinese, about the father's understanding of the English language and Canadian culture.

Fred Wah's *Faking It: Poetics & Hybridity* is a challenging book, one that does not go down easy—nor is it meant to. What caught my attention, however, was how Wah's essays worked in a mode of theorization and argumentation that mirrored language poetry more than literary criticism.

As I quoted earlier, Wah notes that many of these essays work through "play, dissonance, and juxtaposition." His essays read as a series of related comments on a topic or theme that help open up possible meanings rather than a directed, singular argument about that topic. This interest in juxtaposition as a way of generating meaning without fixing it—indeed, generating meaning and "sustaining blur" or ambiguity—seems crucial to shifting what we literary critics do in writing about writing. What is so generative about literary criticism—why we can write incessantly about the same text—is precisely what makes any full-faithed attempt also a failure. We can never pin down what a text means, or even a full range of what it might mean. Creative writing creates the space for understanding how we make meaning in the world at large through language. And in the work of critical creative writers like Wah, their writing creates a space for re-articulating that meaning—that is, a space to re-mean, to change the meaning of—by not simply replicating how meaning functions in the world, but by making visible to us the constructed-ness, the fictionality, the fakeness of meaning. This is what can take writing "beyond autoethnography."

With this understanding of poetics and criticism, I will ask again, is it useful to claim poetics and criticism—rather than the narratives of novels—as autoethnography? Does Wah's prose writing tell us about his culture, about his people, about himself? And if it does, is that all it does, and is it what is ultimately most interesting about his prose? At the beginning of his essay, "A Poetics of Ethnicity," Wah explains,

> I use the term "poetics" here not in the theoretical sense of the study of or theory about literature, but in its practical and applied sense, as the tools designed or located by writers and artists to initiate movement and change. That is, [following Charles Bernstein] "poetics as a sort of *applied poetic*, in the sense that engineering is a form of applied mathematics." The culturally marginalized writer will engineer approaches to language and form that enable a particular residue (genetic, cultural, biographical) to become kinetic and valorized. For Canadian writers like Joy Kogawa and Rohinton Mistry, the stance is to operate within a colonized and inherited formal awareness while investigating their respective enactments of internment and migration. But others, such as Roy Kiyooka and Marlene Nourbese Philip, operating from spatial allocation similar to those of Kogawa and Mistry, have chosen to utilize more formal innovative possibilities. This second group of writers seems to me to embody an approach that might properly be called something like "alienethnic" poetics. This poetics, while often used for its ethnic imprint and frequently originating from the necessity to complicated difference, is certainly not limited to an ethnic "project"; the same tactics could as well be used

for other goals. Feminist poetics, for example, have arguably contributed some of the most useful means to compose ethnic intention.[24]

Wah's sense of ethnic writing seems to be that it *does* deal with the experience and fictions of race. In that sense, it is autoethnographic. But what is most interesting or challenging for him is writing that does so through different kinds of structures and styles. Again, it is this sense of writing culture beyond scientific objectivity, beyond the ethnographic gaze of truth and authority, that moves Wah's poetics.

Wah's *Diamond Grill* is interesting as biofiction in part because of its incorporation of non-autobiographical discourses. Again, it is the juxtaposition of genres, of different modes of making meaning and asserting authority, that collides and brings forth the possibilities of meaning. Some of the pages in *Diamond Grill* consist of excerpts from local histories, early twentieth-century cultural texts about racial difference, and even footnoting of academic criticism. In one section, Wah writes,

> Whenever I hear grampa talk like that, high muckamuck, sitkum dollah, I think he's sliding Chinese words into English words just to have a little fun. He has fun alright, but I now realize he also enjoys mouthing the dissonance of encounter, the resonance of clashing tongues, his own membership in the diasporic and nomadic intersections that have occurred in the northwest North America over the past one hundred and fifty years.
>
> I don't know then, that he's using Chinook jargon, the pidgin vocabulary of colonial interaction, the code-switching talkee-talkee of the contact zone.[25]

At this moment in the text, Wah cites Mary Louise Pratt's work in *Imperial Eyes* for her discussion of the practice of "code-switching" as a linguistic practice laying claim to cultural power by subjugated peoples and her discussion of "the contact zone" as the space of colonial encounter that foregrounds interactive and improvisational dimensions rather than simple imperial domination. Pratt's work has been central to anthropological discussions of autoethnography because she defines it in a particularly engaging way. "[A]utoethnographic texts are not ... 'authentic' or autochthonous forms of self-representation [but rather involve] partial collaboration with and appropriation of the idioms of the conqueror."[26] We can see in this definition a distancing from the ideas of an essential ethnic self and a move towards the hybrid colonial subject. Insert Homi Bhabha here, add colonial mimicry, and stir.

But is this enough? James Buzard writes in "On Auto-Ethnographic Authority" that what we miss in this definition of the autoethnographic text is how we judge the cultural authenticity of the hybrid text or the writer.[27] And what we are left with is an absence of discussing who gets to speak on behalf of a culture, as the person who is best suited, from within the culture, to translate for outsiders what the culture is. On whose authority are you an autoethnographer? While Buzard seeks the reimposition of a distance between scholar and studied culture, Wah and his creative critical writing that mixes genres seeks not just to collapse that distance between scholar and culture but the distance between the ways of knowing that separate the two. To tell truths of one's self is not a simple claim of self-representation. Such truths swim in larger representational fields, weave with the literature and criticism of other people. In Wah's work, the autoethnographic impulse, the faking it of Chinese Canadian identity and culture, is always about complicated hybridity.

Other scholars also worry over the authority of the autoethnographer, or the "credibility" of field notes, in Elaine Bass Jenks's term. Jenks wonders,

> To be perfectly honest, I'm not sure if my field notes are any good. I'm not sure I wrote down the right things. Are my notes filled with others' experiences and void of my own? Or is the other way around? Did I write too much about my experiences and not enough about others'? And speaking of others' experiences, I'm not sure I had the right to write down what I did. Not everything I wrote is complimentary; should I edit out the negative comments before I write up my study? Further, I'm not sure how many of my notes are useless. What am I going to do with the lists of who helped pass out dessert each day? Will the names of the swimming groups turn out to be important observations? How will I judge my field notes?[28]

Consider Jenks's concerns about how field notes might capture adequately the kind of culture or experience she writes. Wah's writing, in contrast, is remarkably free of any anxieties about truthful representation. As Wah notes repeatedly, his writing is meant to make up meaning, to remake meaning about things we think we know. It is the act of "faking it" that characterizes his approach to writing identity and culture—a very different one from autoethnography proper, perhaps, but one that still yearns for the same kind of ability to understand and construct a culture in words.

Because his mixed-race background makes his body such a useful one for thinking through how meaning circulates in embodied and linguistic forms, Wah often references himself in his writing about race. But in a collection of critical essays about poetics and hybridity, is Wah writing about his culture? Or is perhaps criticism about other writing not appropriately ethnographic or autoethnographic? By way of conclusion, a quote from the end of Wah's essay, "Faking It":

But the more I wrote the more I discovered that faking it is a continual the-atre of necessity. No other way to be in language, but to bluff your way through it, stalling for more time. And when I get it, that little gap of renewal, I see the accent not in my own little voice, but there in the mouth of the word within the word, there in the "land only of what is," right there at the tips of our fingers, in the "sniff" of the pen as it hunts the page.[29]

NOTES

1 Feminist literary critics in particular have been at the centre of critical efforts to revalue autobiographical writings and memoirs, especially those by women who have been associated with the "private" sphere and notions of the self as opposed to public and social discourses. For critical work, see Sidonie Smith, *A Poetics of Women's Autobiography: Marginality and the Fictions of Self-Representation* (Bloom-ington: Indiana UP, 1987). For a creative approach to these issues, consider Audre Lorde, *Zami: A New Spelling of My Name* (Berkeley, CA: Crossing Press, 1983). Lorde describes her project as "biomythography," a blend of genres that contributes to new forms of self-representation.

2 Eleanor Ty, *The Politics of the Visible in Asian North American Narratives* (Toronto: U of Toronto P, 2004), 36.

3 Kandice Chuh, *Imagine Otherwise: On Asian Americanist Critique* (Durham, NC: Duke UP, 2003). In turn, Chuh borrows the phrase and concept of "imagining otherwise" from Avery Gordon, whose work pushes sociological inquiry to take on the complexities of what it studies. Let me also note that in the interests of full disclosure, my citational practice will show an investment and training in Asian American, meaning United States-based, Studies.

4 The reception of Theresa Hak Kyung Cha's *Dictee* (New York: Tanam Press, 1982) within Asian American Studies is an important example of how such political commitments guide the reading and availability of texts. In the volume of essays edited by Elaine H. Kim and Norma Alarcón, *Writing Self, Writing Nation: Essays on Theresa Hak Kyung Cha's* Dictee (Berkeley, CA: Third Woman Press, 1994), Elaine Kim, Lisa Lowe, and others take up Cha's difficult art book text as challeng-ing for Asian American literary studies precisely because it eludes usual autoethno-graphic readings of texts transparently documenting experience.

5 James Baldwin, *Giovanni's Room* (New York: Dell, 1988; copyright 1956).

6 Kazuo Ishiguro, *The Remains of the Day* (New York: Knopf, 1989).

7 Michael Ondaatje, *The English Patient* (New York: Knopf, 1992). Ondaatje is per-haps most similar to Wah of other Canadian writers with a literary reputation that in many ways first arises from poetry communities rather than ethnic writ-ing communities. His later novel, *Anil's Ghost* (New York: Knopf, 2000), treads ground that might be more easily considered "autoethnographic fiction" since it features a Sri Lankan–born character who grows up abroad and returns to her birth land during civil war.

8 Kevin Chong, *Baroque-a-Nova* (Toronto: Penguin, 2001). Saul St. Pierre, the pro-tagonist, is mixed-race white and Native. The novel features other Asian Cana-dian characters such as Navi, Saul's best friend, who is Sikh; Anders Wong, the suburb's only homeless man, who is Chinese Canadian; and Nathan Shaw, a for-mer lover of Helena St. Pierre and a Chinese Canadian whose forefathers helped build the country's transcontinental railroad.

9 For example, one of the foundational texts for the poststructuralist, rhetorical, constructivist turn in (cultural) anthropology is James Clifford and George E. Marcus, eds., *Writing Culture: The Poetics and Politics of Ethnography* (Berkeley: U of California P, 1986).

10 Martin F. Manalansan IV, "Introduction: The Ethnography of Asian America: Notes towards a Thick Description," in *Cultural Compass: Ethnographic Explorations of Asian America* (Philadelphia, PA: Temple UP, 2000), 3.

11 Ibid., 38–48.

12 Rey Chow, *The Protestant Ethnic and the Spirit of Capitalism* (New York: Columbia UP, 2002).

13 Fred Wah, *Faking It: Poetics & Hybridity, Critical Writing 1984–1999* (Edmonton, AB: NeWest Press, 2000), 1.

14 See Eve Sedgwick, "Teaching Experimental Critical Writing," in *The Ends of Performance,* ed. Peggy Phelan and Jill Lane (New York: New York UP, 1998); John Yau, *Radiant Silhouette: New & Selected Work, 1974–1988* (Santa Rosa, CA: Black Sparrow Press, 1989); and Nathaniel Mackey, *Discrepant Engagement: Dissonance, Cross-culturality, and Experimental Writing* (New York: Cambridge UP, 1993).

15 Viet Thanh Nguyen's argument in *Race and Resistance: Literature and Politics in Asian America* (New York: Oxford UP, 2002) also considers academic criticism has taken Asian North American literary texts and placed them in a binary tension between accommodation and resistance. His call to critics is to read the texts more closely for the ambiguous and multiple ways that they represent the world. While he credits texts with an expansiveness unrecognized, and to some extent unrecognizable within the ideological framework of ethnic literary studies, by critics, my approach is to push further attention on criticism's investments in making claims about ethnic literary texts.

16 Fred Wah and Susan Rudy, "Fred Wah on Hybridity and Asianicity in Canada," in *Poets Talk: Conversations with Robert Kroetsch, Daphne Marlatt, Erin Mouré, Dionne Brand, Marie Annharte Baker, Jeff Derksen and Fred Wah*, ed. Paula Butling and Susan Rudy (Edmonton: U of Alberta P, 2005), 158. Wah is hardly the only Asian North American writer to take up the jazz improvisational ethos of "faking" in his writing. The poet Lawson Fusao Inada has incorporated jazz and improvisation into his poetry in collections such as *Legends from Camp* (Minneapolis, MN: Coffee House Press, 1993). Maxine Hong Kingston, too, takes up the critically productive possibilities of improvisation in the subtitle of her novel *Tripmaster Monkey: His Fake Book* (New York: Knopf, 1989). David Leiwei Li discusses Kingston's play with the "fake book" and Frank Chin's polemical essay on Asian American writers who are "real" versus "fake" in his book *Imagining the Nation: Asian American Literature and Cultural Consent* (Stanford, CA: Stanford UP, 1998).

17 Wah and Rudy, "Fred Wah on Hybridity and Asianicity in Canada," 144.

18 For a brief sense of how Wah's work was received earlier in his writing career, see George Bowering, "The Poems of Fred Wah," *Concerning Poetry* 12, no. 2 (1979): 3–13.

19 Some important criticism that engages with how Wah's writing makes race an alienating concept by way of disrupting language meaning includes Jeff Derksen, "Making Race Opaque: Fred Wah's Poetics of Opposition and Differentiation," *West Coast Line* 29, no. 3 (1995–1996): 63–76; Pamela Banting, *Body, Inc.: A Theory of Translation Poetics* (Winnipeg: Turnstone Press, 1995); Susanne Hilf, "'Hybridize or Disappear': Exploring the Hyphen in Fred Wah's *Diamond Grill*," in *Towards a Transcultural Future: Literature and Society in a 'Post'-Colonial World,*

ed. Geoffrey Davis, Peter Marsden, Bénédicte Ledent, and Marc Delrez (New York: Rodopi, 2005), 239–47; Charlene Diehl-Jones, "Fred Wah and the Radical Long Poem," in *Bolder Flights: Essays on the Canadian Long Poem*, ed. Frank Tierney and Angela Robbeson (Ottawa: U of Ottawa P, 1998), 139–49; and Susan Rudy Dorscht, "'mother/father things I am also': Fred(,) Wah, Breathin' His Name with a Sigh," in *Inside the Poem: Essays and Poems in Honour of Donald Stephens*, ed. W.H. New (Toronto: Oxford UP, 1992), 216–24.

20   Some criticism along these lines includes Cynthia Sugars, "'The Negative Capability of Camoflage': Fleeing Diaspora in Fred Wah's *Diamond Grill*," *Studies in Canadian Literature* 26, no. 1 (2001): 27–45; Smaro Kamboureli, "Faking It: Fred Wah and the Postcolonial Imaginary," *Études canadiennes/Canadian Studies: revue interdisciplinaire des etudes canadiennes en France* 54 (2003): 115–32; Robert Budde, "After Postcolonialism: Migrant Lines and the Politics of Form in Fred Wah, M. Nourbese Philip, and Roy Miki," in *Is Canada Postcolonial? Unsettling Canadian Literature*, ed. Laura Moss (Waterloo, ON: Wilfrid Laurier UP, 2003), 282–94; Joanne Saul, "Displacement and Self-Representation: Theorizing Contemporary Canadian Biotexts," *Biography: An Interdisciplinary Quarterly* 24, no. 1 (2001): 259–72; and Guy Beauregard, "Asian Canadian Literature: Diasporic Interventions in the Work of SKY Lee, Joy Kogawa, Hiromi Goto, and Fred Wah," Ph.D. diss., U of Alberta, 2000. It is important to note that the various authors here make substantively different arguments about Wah and postcoloniality or diaspora; some are also in strong disagreement over how Wah engages with the paradigms of postcoloniality or diaspora.

21   Fred Wah, *Diamond Grill* (Edmonton, AB: NeWest, 1996).

22   Wah, *Diamond Grill*, 66.

23   Donald Davidson, *Inquiries into Truth and Interpretation* (Oxford: Oxford UP, 1984).

24   Wah, *Faking It*, 51–52.

25   Wah, *Diamond Grill*, 68.

26   Cited in James Buzard, "On Auto-Ethnographic Authority," *Yale Journal of Criticism* 16, no. 1 (2003): 67.

27   Ibid.

28   Elaine Bass Jenks, "Searching for Autoethnographic Credibility: Reflections from a Mom with a Notepad," in *Ethnographically Speaking: Autoethnography, Literature, and Aesthetics*, ed. Arthur P. Bochner and Carolyn Ellis (Walnut Creek, CA: AltaMira Press, 2002), 171.

29   Wah, *Faking It*, 16.

[chapter three]

Tides of Belonging
Reconfiguring the Autoethnographic Paradigm in Shani Mootoo's *He Drown She in the Sea*

Kristina Kyser

In Shani Mootoo's latest novel, *He Drown She in the Sea*, the similarities between the author's and the protagonist's social identities—both are Indo-Caribbean immigrants to Canada—and the realistic detail with which the racial and class tensions in both of these places are portrayed suggest that the novel might offer readers outside this cultural context access to a privileged, "insider" perspective: the connection between the personal and the cultural that is promised by autoethnography. However, while Mootoo's novel does reflect the racialized context out of which she writes, it also resists the manner in which the autoethnographic paradigm configures its three constitutive elements: the self (*auto*), culture (*ethno*), and the connection between them that is asserted through writing (*graphy*). Specifically, the novel complicates the presumed link between writer and culture that often underlies readings of minority texts, thereby challenging the assumption that ethnic writers are representative of their cultures and impeding the means by which ethnic writing is often classified and interpreted.

Autoethnography—a term now widely used in reference to literature as well as social science—is perhaps best understood as a reaction to traditional ethnography. Its practice is based in what Arthur Bochner calls "the narrative turn" in the human sciences and the recognition that "we are inside what we are studying [and the] reflexive qualities of human communication should not be bracketed 'in the name of science.'"[1] In turning to narrative "as a mode of inquiry,"[2] autoethnographers seek to forfeit traditional ethnography's claim to objectivity—what Carolyn Ellis refers to as the tendency to present accounts of other cultures "as if they were written from nowhere by nobody."[3] This foregrounding of subjectivity is motivated partly by an ongoing quest to locate the authentic insider perspectives of silenced peoples for whom traditional ethnographers presumed to speak. The primary characteristic of autoethnography is the connection it asserts between the personal and the cultural, and autoethnographic texts often "attempt to demonstrate the lived experience and humanity of authors and their people to outside audiences."[4]

Although it has some obvious advantages over traditional ethnography, there are a number of problems with the autoethnographic paradigm. Despite wariness among cultural theorists about concepts of "pure" or "authentic" culture, autoethnography still depends on a related form of essentialist thinking. As James Buzard notes in his article "On Auto-Ethnographic Authority," "perceiving the transcultural or hybrid nature of a text *does not* protect us from concepts like authenticity: in order to label the text correctly (as autoethnography), we must know that the author of the text really was a member of a [particular] group."[5] To label a work autoethnography is also to foreground its genesis in the author's culture at the expense of other relevant aspects of his or her subjectivity. This approach is akin to what Paul Gilroy refers to as "cultural insiderism," and it involves "an absolute sense of ethnic difference" maximized to the point that it "acquires an incontestable priority" over all other aspects of social and historical experience and identities.[6] Problematic assumptions about the authenticity and priority of ethnic identity are compounded by the fact that, as Buzard points out, "our established metaphors for conceptualizing cultures and the authoritative or responsible manner of relating oneself to them—mainly those of place and movement—have become quite mixed up."[7] For example, authoritative knowledge of a culture had to be proven (in however flawed a manner) by ethnographers, while it is assumed in the case of autoethnographers. This is partly because autoethnography has retained the use of problematic spatial metaphors that are conducive to essentialism: the use of the insider-outsider binary, for example, often implies that "one common culture lies across every inch of a people's land like an evenly applied coat of paint" and that every "insider" enjoys equal access to it and is capable of enunciating it.[8] According to Buzard, even recent ethnological approaches that emphasize the mobility of their subjects—such as James Clifford's *Routes*—depend on the equally problematic conceptions of "culture-as-steamer-trunk" or of an ethnographic Table of Elements: namely, culture as a portable unit that is still capable of containing those who are its "insiders," and that remains undissolved in mixture to the point that an infinite number of combinations are possible.[9] All metaphors of this nature, no matter how much they appeal to concepts like hybridity and diaspora, rely on the assumption of a self that is fundamentally defined by a culture or cultures and whose authority as a spokesperson derives from this essential connection.

Any such connection between Shani Mootoo and a culture of which she is an insider is troubled as much as revealed by *He Drown She in the Sea*. In particular, the novel resists the priority, uniform distribution, and portability of ethnicity as a determinant of identity. In place of culture as the primary origin of subjectivity and text, the novel implicitly offers alternatives such as the unconscious. Instead of following the coat of paint or steamer trunk model, the novel destabilizes the self-culture relationship through its dominant spatial metaphor, the sea, with the result that the basis for autoethnographic authority is questioned along with Mootoo's status as a representative Indo-Caribbean writer. In beginning and ending with dreams, the novel emphasizes that not all aspects of the self are mediated by a culture of origin: unconscious projections, an unusual familial legacy, and transcultural influences are all revealed by Harry's framing dreams in a manner that discourages the autoethnographic tendency to extrapolate from the individual back to culture—a tendency based on the implied causal relationship from originary ethnicity through subjectivity to text, which is illustrated by the coat-of-paint metaphor. Similarly, the sea voyages in the novel raise questions about how spatial conceptions of culture can accommodate migration and whether insider status is as portable as the steamer-trunk analogy suggests. The novel as a whole portrays the connection between self and culture as more volatile and contingent than the autoethnographic paradigm allows for: a "tide of belonging" that ebbs and flows according to circumstance. The implications of this reconfiguration include the need to reassess how insider authority is assigned and valued, how ethnic texts are classified—particularly in relation to the social and political realities they are deemed to reflect—and what kind of access to this reality is granted to "outside" audiences by autoethnographic writing.

Inside the Insider: Sea Dreams

He Drown She in the Sea begins with an account of Harry St. George's recurring dream: "Almost a decade after he left Guanagaspar, a dream he used to have recurs. Though he lives by the sea now, the sea in this dream is invariably the other one, that of his earliest childhood."[10] In beginning the novel this way, Mootoo in some sense takes up the autoethnographic imperative to speak from inside a particular subjectivity. By prefacing the narrative with a voyage into the protagonist's unconscious, however, she takes this movement inside to such an extreme that the next step—extrapolating from the personal to the cultural—is not really viable. On the one hand, the dream includes unconscious projections and familial idiosyncrasies that belie the notion of the self as completely "coated in," or representative of, a particular culture. On the other hand, the novel begins in such a way that an autoethnographic approach to it is immediately established in competition with a psychoanalytic dream interpretation: readers are faced with a text (the "manifest dream") stemming from a particular subjectivity (the dreamer), the origin of which is an inferred abstraction (the unconscious) that will aid in determining the text's significance or "latent" meaning. A similar configuration is implied when the primary substance and meaning of a minority text is derived from another abstraction: the writer's ethnicity.[11] Given the alternative of the psychoanalytic approach, the primacy of culture as the origin of the text is challenged.

A psychoanalytic interpretation of Harry's dream might read as follows: his childhood nightmare—recurring during a time in his adult life when he is feeling neglected and powerless—reveals in its personification of the sea the extent to which Harry's feelings are externalized and projected (or "displaced") onto his surroundings. The entire sequence of the dream is coloured by the frustration that Harry feels as a child who knows something important and yet is not granted any authority. He notices the sea gather itself into an enormous tsunami off shore but no one will heed his warnings: "He runs up and down the beach screaming to people. They see only a little boy, too young to know anything, too young to pay him attention. When they ignore him, he begins forcibly pushing them off the beach, trying to sound like a reasonable adult, a big man begging them to get back inside. [...] But he is too small, too young, for them to take seriously" (2). Although Harry is able to convince his mother to take refuge with him in their house, everyone else is drowned, and the dream ends with the two of them walking along the beach amidst the corpses: "the boy and his mother sigh and shrug and say to each other, 'If only, if only'" (4). The dream tsunami that obliterates everyone who does not listen to Harry is a manifestation of the rage that arises out of his position as a child with limited agency and authority; the wave itself a displacement of his own painfully thwarted omnipotence. This is supported by Harry's curious lack of affect in the dream: "he knows that everyone else will be swept away by the sea, but it is more a feeling of regret that this will happen than one of panic" (3); it is also consistent with the emotions of a child. This interpretation of the dream points to the aspects of subjectivity that are not culturally mediated. Put another way, the psychoanalytic reading severs the novel from its Indo-Caribbean context, thereby troubling any essential connection between self and culture.

In addition to belying the primacy of culture as origin for the text, the dream can also be read in a manner that undermines autoethnographic assumptions about cultural uniformity; the ethnic coat of paint that determines insider authority. Specifically, Harry's dream is intimately tied to the familial legacy of drowning that his mother fears will be passed from his father, Seudath, to him (271). This is problematic for the autoethnographic paradigm because the St. George family is a cultural anomaly: Seudath is a "strange more-African-than-Indian Indian" whose occupation as a fisherman is a result of his adoption by Mako and Eugenie and actually sets him apart from the majority of Indo-Caribbean men (102). The significance of the sea in the dream is thus not representative of Harry's Indo-Caribbean roots but of his family's idiosyncratic amalgam of cultures and experiences, including Seudath's death. The sea in the dream is associated with this family legacy through its personification as a devouring being, akin to the waves that "stretched up like ravenous mouths" to eat Seudath (105). In Harry's dream the sea is bulging, "inhaling and exhaling painfully" and swelling to the point that "it is bound to split its plastic-like surface, emptying it of its intestines and all that it has swallowed" (1–2). The promise of this imminent expulsion suggests the ejection of Seudath's remains, his being one of those bodies that, "once snatched by the sea," was never returned (329). Seudath's death is also evoked by the way in which Dolly and Harry's house survives the dream tsunami: "There is one final surge, coming at them so high now that it crashes at half height of the house. But the house is like a rock in the ocean. The sea rises around it and then passes by" (3–4). The fact that the house is "like a rock" connects it to the boat, named *St. Peter,* on which Seudath died (107).[12] The contrast between the doomed boat and the miraculously saved house could be a reflection of Harry's wonder and guilt at having survived when his father perished— emotions that reflect Harry's particular family legacy in contrast to the larger Indo-Caribbean culture. As in the psychoanalytic reading above, this interpretation of the dream throws into question both Harry's status as a cultural representative and the efficacy of narrative in conveying an essential connection between self and ethnicity.

The similarities between the opening dream and the one that ends the novel are also significant, as they highlight aspects of both nightmares that encourage transcultural or mythical readings, further undermining the autoethnographic extrapolation from text to singular cultural origin. The novel's concluding dream not only reflects the plight of Harry and Rose as they depart Guanagaspar, but also plays upon the significance of Harry's last name. In this dream, as in the previous one, Harry perceives the sea's sudden menace and rescues a woman from the tsunami—although now Harry is a man, not a child, and the woman involved is not his mother but his lifelong love, Rose. The similarities between the two rescue dreams are of more than passing significance, since Harry's last name links him to a saint famous for rescuing a princess from a dragon—a story descended, according to Frazer's *Golden Bough*, from the ritual drowning of virgins to appease a water spirit.[13] A Jungian reading of the dreams would likely parse them in terms of three archetypes: the hero (or ego) fighting the dragon (the shadow or instinct) to rescue the maiden (purity or innocence). Jung, of course, was not an advocate of cultural particularity but rather of the collective unconscious that connected all of humanity and that occasionally left coded hints in dreams in the form of archetypes. A Jungian reading, like a psychoanalytic approach, runs in contradistinction to the autoethnographic paradigm. Beyond being a hero of legendary status, St. George is relevant to Mootoo's novel in several additional ways: he is dedicated to watching over those in peril at sea;[14] he is the patron saint of agricultural workers and field hands, Canada, and England,[15] which links him to Harry (as landscaper) and his Indo-Caribbean ancestors through their cultivation of the earth and through the influence of English empire on their lives. The intertwining of such transcultural riches in Harry's dreams does not support the kind of exclusivity of cultural origin that autoethnography seems to require. Furthermore, the name St. George does not come to Harry via a clear lineage but from a series of contingencies: his father is abandoned as a child in Raleigh and adopted by Mako and Eugenie, to whom he says "in between heaving sobs, 'I name Seudath'" (103). The origin of his surname is never explained but it is presumably taken by Seudath's adoptive parents from Raleigh's western parish of St. George (103). The interweaving of colonial and personal history, place, and chance in Seudath's naming—in addition to his subsequent life as a man who is culturally more African than Indian—point to the contingent and variable nature of identity formation. Seudath's experience as a cultural orphan reinforces the problems with using a text to infer an absent (and abstract) origin, since he is severed from the ethnic lineage central to the autoethnographic paradigm.

In some ways, Harry's final dream (346–47) appears more positive than his first one: there are no unbelieving or scornful onlookers to be killed by the wave and there is no house that must withstand it like a rock. Instead, Harry is a self-assured adult who "knows beyond any doubt that if [Rose] does precisely as he tells her, they will survive" and they do—they cling to each other and to the bottom of the ocean until the two tidal waves clash and disperse above them. The chapter is entitled "Air" and it concludes the book with the lines "the sea is calm again [...] the sun shines as brazenly as before, and the sounds of the people continue, as if uninterrupted, and they, he and she, have broken the water's surface" (347). Harry and Rose's escape in the dream from the clashing tidal waves and the menacing uprooted seaweed that wraps itself around them corresponds to the escape they have just managed from their former lives and the constraints of family and class that have kept them apart since they were children. The fact that they break the surface of the water at the end of the dream and the novel suggests that they have succeeded, against all odds, in freeing themselves from the limitations of their social identities—or at least Harry dreams it to be so. The similarities and differences between this dream and the one that opens the novel reinforce the sea's personal and cumulative significance in Harry's unconscious: by the close of the novel he has outgrown his childish rage and seems to have escaped his familial legacy. To the extent that this final dream has cultural significance, it hints not at an indissoluble connection between the self and ethnicity but at the radical break from their previous lives and identities that Rose and Harry are hoping to achieve.

Culture in Transit: Sea Voyages

Although the outcome of Rose and Harry's escape to Honduras is left open in the novel, readers are not left to consider the significance of their voyage in an interpretive vacuum. Throughout the text, the impact of migration on cultural insider status is constantly in the foreground because virtually every character has been transplanted: Tante Eugenie and Uncle Mako are the descendents of Afro-Caribbean slaves, Dolly and Rose's ancestors were brought as indentured labourers from India, and Harry has amplified his displacement by immigrating to Canada. The cultural significance of the lovers' sea journey is tied up with the other voyages that are so significant to the rest of the novel—the transatlantic passages to the New World made by Europeans, Africans, and Indians. This connection is emphasized by the fact that Harry and Rose take Uncle Mako's boat for their voyage—the same boat that he had always hoped to use for his "return" to Africa. The possibility that the lovers have engineered an escape from the confines of culture thus invites juxtaposition against the hopes, expectations, and historical outcomes associated with those other voyages, each of which has different implications for the relationship between self and culture in transit.

As Carl Pedersen notes, Euro-Americans tended to view the Atlantic Ocean as Thoreau did: as a "Lethean stream" that allowed them to forget the Old World and start afresh.[16] Such a vision of the sea voyage as fresh start is hinted at in the novel by Rose's preparations for her escape with Harry: from the beginning of the novel she drops hints about "another chance," a "fresh start," and her "next life" (7, 8, 10, 314, 338). This notion of Rose and Harry's voyage as a clean break is emphasized by Christian imagery that links Rose's escape to the crucifixion and resurrection. Rose's signal to Harry that her drowning is a deception is the gold crucifix that she removes before entering the ocean and tells Piyari to hold for him. When the pair are reunited, she frames her decision to escape Guanagaspar with the statement, "'In this place I am dead, Harry'" (338). Rose's disappearance is also linked to Seudath's death by the sea's refusal to return their bodies; the connection between Rose and Christ is thus further emphasized by the fact that Dolly begins mourning Seudath after three days (106)—the period between the crucifixion and the resurrection—whereas Harry receives the cross, guesses that Rose is alive, and the two of them prepare for their own sea voyage; significantly, one that will take three days (341).[17] This sequence, combined with Harry's closing dream about "breaking the surface," could be read as indication that Rose and Harry have escaped their previous identities and will be reborn at sea, where the metaphorical coat of cultural paint will presumably be washed away.

Of course, readers need not take the novel's Christian imagery at surface value. To return to Thoreau's Lethean stream analogy, his use of an Old World allusion to express the fresh start offered by the New World is no accident—the Americas could be seen as "new" only with the aid of imposed European ideas such as the Christian Eden and of subsequent amnesia about the treatment of indigenous peoples.[18] The European perception of the settlement of the Americas in this sense parallels the ethnographic dream of objectivity: people freed from their cultural and conceptual roots voyage to new lands for a fresh start untainted by origins.[19] The fact that both of these paradigms rely heavily on the projection of religious and cultural ideals and the suppression of other versions is made obvious only when different accounts, such as the Afro-American perspective, are considered. To return to Rose and Harry, it is no accident that they leave Guanagaspar on a boat once intended to return a descendant of slaves to

Africa—a symbol of cultural roots that still pull at Mako generations after being severed.

In contrast to the Lethean stream, Pedersen explains that the Atlantic was, for Afro-Americans, "a transformative Middle Passage where an African past and an American future, one in danger of fading from memory, the other imposing its hegemonic will, were constantly in conflict over contested spheres of power," and while Euro-Americans strove to forget their origins "the slave imagination was articulating an alternative discourse rooted in memory and yearning for a return."[20] This alternative discourse is to the European account of the transatlantic voyage what autoethnography is to traditional ethnography: a reminder of the fact that all knowledge is situated, that the experiences and perceptions of all individuals are coloured by their cultural origins. Rose and Harry may escape the confines of class and family in Guanagaspar, but their mutual attraction can also be viewed in the context of their common cultural roots in India. As Dolly tells Harry of their ancestors and the Sanghas':

> They cross them terrible waters—let me tell you—in the same stinking boats. All of we lie down side by side, catch head lice, cough, and cold, chew betel leaf together, and spit blood. They enter this country through the same procedures. They did have to line up for placement, answer the same questions, and do daily hard labour under estate boss and the hot sun in cane field. Everybody get treat the same way. (219)

Dolly's narrative about the voyage of Indian indentured servants emphasizes their commonalities irrespective of their current, divergent positions in Guanagasparian society, and the lifelong bond between Harry and Rose that forms in childhood and survives both of their separate marriages similarly reinforces the power of origins. In another passage describing the transatlantic voyage, Dolly even uses a kind of religious or mythic idiom that gives her account of common origins increased metaphysical weight:

> All of we cross Black Water, sometimes six and sometimes seven months side by side in the same stinking boat, to come here. Same-same. All of we. One set leaving something unsavoury behind, another set looking for a fresh start. How, child, how out of those beginnings some end up higher than others and some end up lower, tell me this? Well, God alone know. (192)

Of course Dolly's creation myths are told to ease Harry's pain at the very real class divisions that exist between him and Rose, and, far from supporting the sanctity of cultural origins, the novel is filled with examples of people who identify across racial and cultural boundaries instead of within them. For instance, Rose sees a group of women from India while she is in

Canada and notes, "Maybe they were from Pakistan. Or maybe they were from Sri Lanka. I can't tell these things" (53)—so much for her ongoing identification as "Indian." Later in the novel, in a conversation with Kay, Harry notices her lack of class pretension and realizes to his surprise that "although this woman is from up here and, well, white-skinned is the best way he could put it, she is perhaps more like he is than he is like his Indo-Guanagasparian Rose" (76), thus undermining any sense of close identification based on his and Rose's cultural roots. Harry's connections to race and place are further troubled by his elation at being an "insider" in Canada when he goes canoeing, combined with his later recognition that he would, "more than likely, never have achieved the status of insider" in the upper-class circles of Guanagaspar (42, 87). Finally, at the pivotal moment of their longed-for reunion, Harry looks at the new, confident Rose and registers that she "feels foreign to him" (341).

The pull of origins is also counterbalanced in the novel by an undermining of the nostalgia for home. When Mako dreams of returning to Africa, Eugenie chastises him, saying, "'Ey, old man, keep up with the times, na, man. What family you have over there, pray tell? We ent going "there," you hear? Them days dead and gone. Them people "there," you making up stories about them in your head; you think they even have time for we? They bound to laugh at you in your face, old man'" (198). The European dream of the transatlantic voyage as the way to a new beginning reveals the impossibility of denying origins, but the failure of the back-to-Africa movement also reveals the danger of viewing them in essentialist terms. Pedersen notes about Afro-Americans Richard Wright and Eddy Harris that they "returned from their reverse Middle Passages to Africa with any racial fantasies about the continent largely dispelled. As Harris concluded at the end of his journey of self-discovery: 'Africa is the birth of mankind. Africa is the land of my ancestors. But Africa is not home.'"[21] It is the conceptual equivalent of this physical return—the ever-accessible arc from self back to culture of origin—that Buzard locates in autoethnography and criticizes through his steamer-trunk analogy. As interactions in the novel show, neither the ethnographer's amnesia nor the autoethnographer's essentialism properly accounts for what occurs when individuals cross cultural borders.

Writing the Self-Culture Connection: Tides of Belonging

Mootoo's *He Drown She in the Sea* resists the autoethnographic paradigm by depicting how elastic and volatile the connection between self and culture is. When Harry returns to Guanagaspar at the end of the novel, he smells the air that is saturated with the sea's odours and a "tide of belonging" washes over him: "Elderberry Bay and all that he has accomplished in that part of the world seem in an instant like a dream, a good dream, but very far away" (291). Just as Guanagaspar had receded into a dreamscape when Harry was in Canada, the inverse is now true on the island, so that the influence of place is depicted as relative and shifting. Unlike the metaphors of culture as coat of paint or steamer trunk, the version of cultural identity that best accounts for the shifting allegiances of the characters in Mootoo's novel is not of an essential or portable connection but of an oscillating force: a tide of belonging that rises and falls according to context and location.

Tides are a result of the competing gravitational pulls exerted on water and earth particles by the larger bodies of the earth, sun, and moon, and they shift according to complex factors including the elliptical orbits of these bodies and variations in the earth's topography. What is less commonly known is that every body in the universe has some tidal effect, however small, on every other body.[22] The shifting and competing nature of tides parallels the range of influences on the self—from unconscious projections to significant historical events—in a way that the uniformity of culture-as-paint does not. If the connection between self and culture is reflected in writing, then tides more accurately represent the protean mix of beliefs, values, customs, and behaviours that constitute ethnicity and the impossibility of keeping different cultures discrete. The interpenetration of cultures accounts for the repeated sense of being both inside and outside that Mootoo's characters experience: like the "off-colour moral justifications" that Harry's friends invent to avoid consuming Old World wines, boundaries between cultures never stay in place for long: most people ingest a combination as mixed as Mrs. Sangha's breakfast of New Brunswick sardines, sweet Ceylon tea, and "God Save the Queen" (39, 119). Harry is a Canadian "insider" but he is also in "unfamiliar waters," because the insider-outsider binary is an oversimplification of the multiple tides of belonging to which he is subject (42, 44). In his work on the Black Atlantic, Paul Gilroy explains that "the reflexive cultures and consciousness of the European settlers and those of the Africans they enslaved, the 'Indians' they slaughtered, and the Asians they indentured were not, even in situations of the most extreme brutality, sealed off hermetically from each other."[23] Gilroy argues that the historic encounters between these cultures that occurred as a result of transatlantic voyages constitute "a counterculture to modernity" and are of great significance not only to people of the Caribbean but also for Europe, Africa, and America. Studying the significance of the Black Atlantic offers the possibility of nothing less than "a different sense of where modernity might itself be thought to begin in the constitutive relationships with outsiders that both found and temper a self-conscious sense of Western civilization."[24] Gilroy's mention of the transatlantic voyages of indentured Asians provides useful context for Mootoo's depiction of Indo-Caribbean people and suggests that a far more complex and fluid conception of culture and its origins is necessary than the kind of essentialism fostered by autoethnography.

The voyages in *He Drown She in the Sea* bear out that nobody is ever free of tidal influence: there is no "new world" available either physically or conceptually and no capacity to speak "as if from nowhere." Neither, however, does the steamer trunk of culture remain with the migrant as an ever-redeemable ticket home—a guarantee of perpetual insider status. The tides of belonging are always in flux and they ebb with physical distance. Just as Mootoo takes the autoethnographic movement "inside" to its logical end in her depiction of the unconscious, she also takes the movement away from her culture further than the autoethnographic paradigm allows, emphasizing the tenuous nature of the connection that her writing traces between herself and Indo-Caribbean culture. Most notably, the fact that Mootoo chooses to write fiction and to set her novel on a fictional island (as opposed to her native Trinidad, for example) emphasizes the constructed, subjective aspects of her depiction of the Caribbean and undermines her own insider status by making the island a product of her memories, desires, and imagination, as opposed to a real country. This self-positioning implies an acknowledgement that the author has put enough physical and psychological distance between herself and the Caribbean that, for her, its pull has lessened and her status as insider has changed. Unlike European voyagers to the New World, Mootoo has no illusions of a fresh start, but, aware of the pitfalls that accompany the dream of a return, she also avoids essentializing home. Her fictional islands—Lantanacamara in *Cereus Blooms* and Guanagaspar in *He Drown She*—foreground the nature of her writing as a nexus of experience, subjectivity, and representation. Their fictiveness is a cutting-loose of the "real" Caribbean—a gesture that releases that place and its culture from the author's possession as surely as it forecloses her readers' ability to claim them through her texts. In removing the concrete link between herself and other Indo-Caribbean people, Mootoo also implies that the relationship between *auto*, *ethno*, and *graphy* is one in which the alchemy of self and writing transmit culture in a way that is as deeply personal and idiosyncratic as it is representative.

NOTES

1 Carolyn Ellis and Arthur P. Bochner, "Autoethnography, Personal Narrative, Reflex-ivity," in *Handbook of Qualitative Research*, ed. Norman K. Denzin and Yvonna S. Lincoln (London: Sage, 2000), 743.

2 Ibid., 743.

3 Ibid., 734.

4 Ibid., 742.

5 James Buzard, "On Auto-Ethnographic Authority," *The Yale Journal of Criticism* 16, no. 1 (2003): 68.

6 Paul Gilroy, "The Black Atlantic as a Counterculture of Modernity," in *Theorizing Diaspora: A Reader*, ed. Jana Evans Braziel and Anita Mannur (Oxford: Black-well, 2003), 52.

7 Buzard, "Authority," 62.

8 Buzard, "Authority," 63.

9 Buzard, "Authority," 70.

10 Shani Mootoo, *He Drown She in the Sea* (Toronto: McClelland and Stewart, 2005), 1. All parenthetical references will be hereafter referencing Mootoo's *He Drown She in the Sea*.

11 For a description of dream processes and interpretation, see Ian Craib, *Psychoanaly-sis: A Critical Introduction* (Cambridge: Polity, 2001). Craib describes four kinds of "dream work" via which the dream material is encoded: condensation, dis-placement, symbolization, and secondary revision. It is the analyst's job to help the patient, through free association, to decode the dream and find its latent meaning (28–29).

12 Peter—from the Greek *petros*, or "piece of rock"—was the name given by Christ to the fisherman Simon, and it relates to Christ's vision of this disciple as the rock upon which he would build his church (Matt. 16:18).

13 John Heath-Stubbs, "The Hero as a Saint: St. George," in *The Hero in Tradition and Folklore*, ed. H.R.E. Davidson (London: Folklore Society, 1984), 10.

14 Ibid., 1.

15 "Saint George," *Patron Saints Index*, Catholic Forum Online, http://www.catholic-forum.com/saints/saintg05.htm.

16 Carl Pedersen, "Sea Change: The Middle Passage and the Transatlantic Imagina-tion," in *The Black Columbiad: Defining Moments in African American Literature and Culture*, ed. Werner Sollors and Maria Diedrich (Cambridge, MA: Harvard UP, 1994), 42.

17 The comparison between Seudath and Rose can be taken further by considering the fact that St. Peter (after whom Seudath's boat is named) was also crucified but, unlike Christ, was not resurrected.

18 For an assessment of the significance of Eden in Mootoo's first novel, *Cereus Blooms at Night*, see Sarah Phillips Casteel's paper, "New World Pastoral: The Caribbean Garden and Emplacement in Gisele Pineau and Shani Mootoo," *Inter-ventions* 5, no.1 (2003): 12–28.

19 For an exploration of other misconceptions of travel as revealed in Mootoo's ear-lier work, see Susan Billingham's article, "Out on Main Street" in *Identity, Com-munity, Nation: Essays on Canadian Writing*, ed. Danielle Schaub and Christl Verduyn (Jerusalem: Hebrew U Magnes P, 2002), 74–88, and how it undermines the idealism of Rosi Braidotti's "nomadic subjectivity."

20 Pedersen, "Sea Change," 43.

21 Pedersen, "Sea Change," 50.
22 McGraw-Hill Encyclopedia of Science and Technology, 5th ed., s.v. "Tide," http://www.answers.com/topic/tide.
23 Gilroy, "Black Atlantic," 51.
24 Gilroy, "Black Atlantic," 64.

[part two]

Generic Transformations

[chapter four]

Strategizing the Body of History
Anxious Writing, Absent Subjects,
and Marketing the Nation

Larissa Lai

Writing the self, in autobiographies and memoirs, is often seen as a way to "break the silence," especially for marginalized subjects and those people who have been rendered invisible through racist exclusion from Canadian cultural life. I want to argue in this chapter, however, that self-writing, autobiography in particular, can produce ambivalent results. In some cases, writing the self can deepen oppression, not just by reiterating it, but by driving deeper underground aspects of marginalized subjectivity that do not fit into conventions of autobiography. This is not to deny autobiography its liberatory power, but only to show that because of generic conventions combined with racist stereotypes, and perhaps because of the problem of articulation itself, there is a contradiction; in other words, the liberatory power of autobiography is not pure. There is a tension between generic trope and experience. Important silences can be broken, but others can also be more deeply encrypted. Further, the circulation of the text in the aftermath of "breaking the silence" does work that is partially, but not fully, liberatory, and may have the unfortunate effect of retrospectively folding the marginalized subject back into a discourse of national belonging, while actually covering over the violent history of exclusion it was supposed to have expiated.

I want to be very clear that I am not advocating the uselessness or apoliticalness of autobiography. What I do want to do is push the question of how the marginalized subject might productively write herself into presence—personal, social, cultural, national, and political. I recognize the writing of self as important, but not as a complete liberation or a complete presencing. This chapter offers that critique.

The anti-racist movements of the late 1980s and early 1990s were largely predicated on the notion of "breaking the silence," that is, making space for the articulation of histories that until that point had been kept from the official record. Working in an oppositional mode, self-identified anti-racist thinkers and activists noted that official histories tended to privilege the already privileged, that is, the white, male, heterosexual ruling class. Anti-oppression cultural workers sought the articulation of marginalized histories as a first step in liberating subjects excluded from official histories. Under the aegis of "the universal" the histories of racialized peoples had not only been silenced but also made invisible. Collective texts in particular, such as the remarkable lesbian of colour anthology *Piece of My Heart*, mark an important turning point in the materialization of marginalized histories—to frame it in psychoanalytic terms, the "bringing to light" of "that which ought to remain hidden."[1] A considerable number of Asian North American texts employed the strategy of breaking the silence as a mode of empowerment. Asian Canadian examples include Wayson Choy's *The Jade Peony*, Denise Chong's *The Concubine's Children*, and Evelyn Lau's troubling *Runaway*, among others.

A second, very significant recognition of that moment was the importance of the question "who speaks?" as Himani Bannerji has articulated in *Thinking Through*.[2] Emerging, at least in the academic world, from Foucault's recognition of regimes of power, the notion that the marginalized body articulates her or his own history differently from the way a privileged expert, however liberal and open-minded, might articulate it, may not have been a new idea, but the extent to which it circulated and was put into action in the late 1980s was extremely important. Bannerji writes:

> A text which is coherent with my experience as a non-white woman, for example, when inserted into the tentacles of an alienating interpretive device, loses its original reference points and meaning, and becomes inert and inverted. Thus, *The Wretched of the Earth* in the light of O. Manoni's *Prospero and Caliban* becomes an example of Oedipal counterphobia of the colonized, or Angela Davis' *Women, Race and Class* an example of "black feminism," no more than just a "different" perspective in feminism.[3]

Bannerji is critical of psychoanalysis and feminism in this context because she recognizes them as oppressive impositions on the experiences of women of colour. A politic focused on the body insists that "we the marginalized" must speak for ourselves in our own voices. It also refuses to make nomenclatural equivalences of speaking voices, such that, as Bannerji describes above, one voice becomes substitutable for another, like in valence, and different only in style. It matters who speaks. What is said, moreover, must be heard differently depending on the body speaking and on that body's history. To recognize the radical incommensurability of marginalized difference in relation to hegemonic power opened liberatory possibilities that were enormously productive but also potentially stultifying in terms of the pressure they put on marginalized writers to speak and (accurately and comprehensively) represent.[4]

A feminism focused on the body became, in the 1980s and 1990s, a productive strategy for the writing of a very particular kind of liberatory text. Bannerji writes:

> Feminism ideally rests on a transformative cognitive approach which validates subjectivity and direct agency. It is disinterested in "expertise," which reduces women to outsiders and operators of the machinery of the status quo knowledge. Thus beginning from ourselves, with a project of self and social transformation (encoded in the slogan "the personal is political") does not require an apology but, on the contrary, becomes a basic imperative.[5]

While Bannerji adamantly refuses "apology," the articulation of such a notion in this otherwise determinedly "right on" stance recognizes the potential for backlash. The reactionary reading is contained in the call for social transformation. There is already the expectation that one will not be heard, which might in fact help produce an unhearing audience (in addition, of course, to audiences that do hear). I would suggest that Bannerji recognizes the problem of identity formation in reaction to hegemonic naming, that is, that it is always both a refusal and a reiteration. Later, Bannerji does indeed say, "[...] knowledge cannot be produced in the context of ruling but only in conscious resistance to it."[6] Furthermore:

> It must retain the integrity of our concrete subject positions within its very project and its present-day method of investigation, in so far as it searches the history of social relations to trace the reasons for and the forms of our oppression.[7]

By recognizing the historical situatedness of this body-based strategy, Bannerji does, in some measure, recognize its contingency, though perhaps not as adamantly here as she does later. Her recognition of contingency is more forcefully expressed, however, precisely in her articulation of the political use of speech:

> "You can't speak my reality" has been a strong demand of ours. But in real political terms, are these the only options that face us—those of mutually exclusive agencies? Or must we begin to use my previously suggested integrative and reflexive analysis to work out a political position which allows anyone to speak for/from the experiences of individuals and groups, while leaving

room to speak "socially" from other locations, along the lines of relations that (in)form our/my own experience?[8]

In my mind, these are the crisis questions of the political historical moment of the 1980s and 1990s. To phrase it in Marxist terms, this is the turning point of the dialectic. Roy Miki deepens the problem by posing it as an ontological one with serious implications for the subjectivity of the marginalized other:

> A one-dimensional oppositional positioning is hardly an adequate basis for new cultural forms which can represent the localized subjectivities of writers of colour. While such contests of will and confrontation may be a pragmatic strategy for certain instances requiring immediate interventionist action, they do not instigate the internal transformations necessary for moving beyond the constraints of racialization to make spaces where difference and diversity are constantly being (re)negotiated. For Canadian writers of colour— and here I speak in (personal) terms of Japanese Canadians—the internal "battle" to overcome the powerful effects of racialization may, finally, be the most formidable.[9]

This interior space that Miki describes is so radically under siege that "breaking the silence" cannot articulate it. Noting the pressures that assimilationist assumptions exert on the marginalized other, Miki remarks that simple subjectivity is no easy matter:

> Historically and even at present, the strain of a domineering exterior on the interior of those in the state of exclusion created/creates complicated networks of ambiguities, repressions, and compromises that infiltrate the language and geography of their subjectivity. [...] [T]he experience of inner and outer is not merely an instance of decontextualized, abstract binary, but vitally connected to community-based positioning vis à vis—or contained by, or surrounded by—an overriding white majority from which it is estranged either by language, or by sociocultural values, or by the phenomenon of physicality, i.e., the appearance of the semiotic body inscribed with the constructed signs of "race."[10]

He suggests further that the pressure on Japanese Canadians in the aftermath of internment is so extreme that any kind of interiority for the "JC" subject is "erased, rendered speechless, or so devoid of content that the subject does not or cannot even recognize its absence."[11] Instead, "dominant values outside come to censor, repress, or otherwise propagandize the inside."[12]

The political strategy of breaking the silence has necessitated an engagement with an already established tradition of autobiography. Indeed, as

Sidonie Smith and Julia Watson have noted, since the 1970s women's autobiography (and that of other marginalized categories, I would suggest)
has risen from a status with little respect to a site of privilege for thinking
about contemporary issues at the intersection of feminism, postcolonialism,
and postmodernism.[13] It is thus important to recognize both what it does
and does not do, what the possibilities and pitfalls of its writing and circulation are. The drive to "break the silence" layers over autobiographical
tradition in interesting and contradictory ways that sometimes foil the
intent behind breaking the silence, and sometimes adds to the practice of
autobiography to make it work differently from how it has historically.

The French structuralist Philippe Lejeune suggests that the true subject
of autobiography is the name of author.[14] He argues that there exists a
pact between reader and writer that promises that the person named as
author on the cover of the book is the person whose story the autobiography will tell: "Le pacte autobiographique, c'est l'affirmation dans le texte
de cette identité, renvoyant en dernier ressort au *nom* de l'auteur sur la cou-
verture."[15] However, he also notes that as readers, we tend to find the
"truth" of autobiographical texts not in what they tell us directly, but in the
moments of rupture, when something more profound and more literary
leaks through:

> En face d'un récit d'aspect autobiographique, le lecteur a souvent tendance
> à se prendre pour un limier, c'est-à-dire à chercher les ruptures du contrat (quel
> que soit let contrat). C'est de là qu'est né le mythe du roman "plus vrai" que
> l'autobiographie: on trouve toujours plus vrai et plus profond ce qu'on a cru
> découvrir à travers le texte, malgré l'auteur.[16]

If autobiography is a completely transparent practice that leaves little room
for an unconscious of any kind, then there is even less room for an unconscious of the kind Miki describes, an unconscious with indeterminate content, so unformed that it cannot even leak. I suggest that there is a logic
of partialness at work here, that the work of autobiography, in spite of its
apparent power, does metonymic work. Something of experience is articulated, but the articulation of partial experience drives deeper into repression that which is not, or perhaps, cannot, be articulated. Something may
be given between the lines, but there is more beneath the lines that does
not appear. Further, the appearance of articulation furnishes the autobiographical subject in her/his social context with a kind of solidity, and perhaps even national belonging, that is in fact illusory because of the
fundamental absence that does not make it to the light of day.

Miki valorizes writing as a mode of self-knowledge, a way in which the
propagandized "inside" can begin to take shape. He does not stipulate

whether this shaping might occur transparently or "à travers le texte." But because he emphasizes the act of writing, between the lines or beneath them, the question of knowledge produced in spite of the author is beside the point.

But how to write is no easy question. The silence is complicated. It does not have certain content. Miki theorizes the emergence of the subject as beginning with interchange between inside and outside that is interrupted by doubt:

> [...] the passageway between inside/outside (suddenly) transforms into a place of static, of noise, of perceptual destabilizations. [...] [T]he disturbed subject/writer [is] set adrift in a shifting space of vertiginous pluralities that awaken the desire to speak, to write. But where to begin?[17]

Miki quotes Gail Scott, who frames a similar problematic in feminist terms. Scott asks, "What if the surfacing unconscious stream finds void instead of code?"[18]

This is a key question in attempting to make sense of writing projects that emerge from the moment of the body politic. As Miki's analysis of Joy Kogawa's *Obasan* suggests, the retrieval of history is not as easy as it might appear on the surface. It is certainly not nearly as simple as an (autobiographical) recounting of "what happened." The content of the silence, if it can ever be materialized, is almost certainly more (and less) than mere reportage. Miki notes that, in the apparently redemptive close of the novel, the speaking voice of the Japanese-Canadian subject is absent, papered over by the signatures of three white men.[19]

The notion of breaking the silence requires silence to have content. In this historical moment, it seems there are two possibilities for what that content can be—trauma or the void. If it is trauma, the trauma needs to be reconstructed and redeemed. This is indeed what *Obasan* appears to do. But it cannot do so without contradiction. If, as Scott suggests, it is emptiness, what are the consequences of confronting this emptiness? Is this the same emptiness that the deconstructionists would suggest lies at the heart of any attempt at representation? If the play of signifiers is truly endless, does it matter what history is called into play? Or, to frame the problem psychoanalytically, if we can know history only through traumatic repetition, and can never know the original event, does it matter what gets repeated? These are problems I shall attempt to explore through two apparently transparent autobiographic texts, specifically those of Evelyn Lau and Wayson Choy.

Before I enter into this discussion, however, I want to raise a second problematic, that of the relationship between the writing subject and the ethnographic tradition, particularly for those who have traditionally been the objects rather than the experts of ethnographic research. Through the ideals that emerged from the question "who speaks?" autobiography became an obvious and important strategy for countering hegemonic white texts that spoke authoritatively and categorically for the other. As a discipline of the other, anthropology in particular underwent massive shifts. Clifford and Marcus's *Writing Culture: The Poetics and Politics of Ethnography* was very important for this reason. A major feature of this shift is the recognition that "literary procedures pervade any work of cultural representation."[20] This recognition takes place, however, at a historical moment when cultural critics are themselves arguing that literature is a transient category.[21] The concerns of both disciplines overlap in the sense that they recognize the instability of narrative and narrative meaning. Clifford also notes the rise of the "indigenous ethnographer" as one who is able to study her own culture from "new angles and depths of understanding,"[22] though he does note that these are not necessarily better than the depths and angles non-indigenous ethnographers are capable of, only different, and perhaps useful for that reason. It is the repositioning of anthropology with regard to those it studies that Clifford thinks is significant.[23] Its authority is no longer automatic. Further, it is not only the object of study who is constructed by the discipline; the ethnographer herself or himself is also constructed through her or his own writing practice.[24] Self-reflexivity becomes a necessary injection into the ethographic method.

Soyini Madison notes a shift from the practice of conventional ethnography to a critical ethnography that "begins with an ethical responsibility to address processes of unfairness or injustice within a particular *lived* domain."[25] Further, she insists on a particular politicized relation to ethnographic practice: "Critical ethnography must further its goals from simply politics to the politics of positionality. The question becomes, How do we begin to discuss our positionality as ethnographers and those who represent Others?"[26]

Further, what happens when the subject and object of ethnographic or literary discourse are identical? Clifford notes that in classical ethnography, while the authorial voice of the ethnographer is clear, there is always a firm separation between the subjectivity of the author and the object of her or his study.[27] Of the confident, consistent voice of the ethnographer, Clifford asks: "What desires and confusions was it smoothing over? How was 'objectivity' textually constructed?"[28] The new, self-reflexive ethnography allows discussion of previously unacknowledged concerns including violence, desire, confusion, struggle, and economic transactions with informants.[29] I might ask further, if the "ethnographer" and his "object" are identical, are one and the same person, what happens to these fraught power relations? One might think of them as the impossible struggle between inside and outside, ego and superego, that Miki articulates in "Asiancy." One might look to the poststructuralists and the "death of the author" to suggest that the object remains the object, written by a language that allows only a narrow range of discourse, regardless of who speaks it.

In one of the autobiographical interruptions to his theoretical text, Miki recounts a moment as a young student in 1950s Winnipeg, when he had to read aloud from Ann Marriott's Depression-era prairie poem "The Wind Our Enemy." The class reads the poem aloud, one line per student, down the aisles. Coincidence places the line "Japs bomb China" in Miki's mouth. Years later, as a professor, poet, and theorist, he writes: "No one exposed, except for the chuckle chuckle, this moment of linguistic anguish. The match between the word and 'me' struck a chord but the unspoken fluttered out the (open) window. Even 'i' was numbed by the evacuated words."[30]

What if it doesn't matter who the writer is? What if, as postmodern theory suggests, all language is quotation? What I am trying to suggest here is that the coincidence of the marginalized writer with her autobiography can function not unlike the accidental "moment of linguistic anguish" that Miki describes. Without the tools to counter this effect, the subaltern can be left numbed by the emptiness of her own words. Without anyone to expose the anguish, the void that the words were meant to fill is only deepened.

This might help illuminate, in some measure, what is so discomfiting about certain autobiographical texts of that moment. The most discomfiting of these, in my mind, is *Runaway*, the teenage diary of Evelyn Lau. The coincidence of both text and body with a range of abject signifiers—Asian, woman, child, model daughter, prostitute, drug addict—places both, as objects, within a history and economy of the worst Western stereotypes of the Oriental. As a confessional, lucidly written in a "quality" authorial voice, it verifies for the racist reader (or the racist in every reader) the truth of what that reader always suspected about not these kinds of texts, but certainly these kinds of bodies. I want to be careful here. To blame the text, or its young writer, seems suspiciously like blaming the victim of what was, without a doubt, a miserable and harrowing childhood. What I want to do in the aftermath of not just the writing but also the circulation of the text is to consider the way in which it works, as a small step in beginning to imagine writing strategies that resist such oppressive consumption.

Reading Descartes' *Discourse,* Marc Eli Blanchard suggests that the moment of writing autobiographically is not identical with the moment in which a fiction of the coherent self is delivered to the reader through the autobiography.[31] Instead, if I read him correctly, what occurs is a process something like this:

> I doubt myself.
> I write autobiography, attempting to know myself.
> In so doing, I convince others of coherence precisely at the site where I doubt.
> When I see their certainty, I think I know myself, though never completely.
> I doubt myself.
> I write more autobiography, attempting to know myself etc.

For the marginalized subject, particularly for a child with no reflection of herself to look to in order to know herself, this process can border on the obsessive. Blanchard indeed remarks that autobiography aims to recreate a primal mirror stage.[32] I might argue that this is precisely what Lau is doing in *Runaway*. Certainly, she makes no claims to be producing a liberatory text, except in so far as she sees reading as escape:

> By that age [six], I had already become an avid reader—reading was like living in a fantasy world; it had become my form of escape. I thought that by writing I could give that same feeling to other people, that they could open one of my books and disappear for awhile. Even then, it was important for me not to stay rooted in reality.[33]

Interestingly, however, the very next paragraph consists of nothing but truth claims about "reality":

> I was born in Vancouver to Chinese immigrants. I was a shy and introspective child, exceedingly sensitive to the tensions and emotions around me. My parents were strict, overprotective and suspicious of the unknown society around them. By kindergarten, I was already expected to excel in class, as the first step in my pre-planned career as a doctor or lawyer. I wasn't allowed to spend much time with the neighbourhood children; consequently I always had my nose in a book.[34]

What I am suggesting here is that these truth claims are actually the construction of a fantasy about race and childhood.[35] One might argue that, by writing, Lau constructs a kind of escape from reality. And that the problem with her reality is that it is not articulable, that it is, instead, precisely the void that both Scott and Miki point to. By returning, at the paragraph's end, to the book, Lau textually enacts the escape she claims to have anxiously carried out over and over again, when, under her mother's nervous, watchful eye, she was supposed to have been studying:

They forbade me to write unless I brought home straight A's from school, and right up until I left home at fourteen I was not allowed out of the house except to attend school and take piano lessons—not on weekends, not after school. I went submissively to my bedroom and stayed there descending into months of depression alleviated only by the fact that I would continue to write secretly under my math textbook. My mother would sneak into the room very quietly to check if I were doing my homework; I would hold the textbook tilted upwards with one hand and write with the other, slamming the book down when I heard her footsteps. As a result, I was in a constant panic; a kind of fight or flight reaction to all that went on.[36]

The illusion of reality thus blossoms for a moment only to be pulled down into writing or reading, which Blanchard says for the autobiographer are one and the same. Blanchard suggests that the autobiographer is attracted "by the mirage of his own vision." S/he wants to see herself looking at the spectacle of herself in order to freeze her own actions in the moment of recollection. S/he is looking for the feeling of being tangential to herself and the world.[37] Blanchard writes:

By simply looking at *how it was*, or rather *how it might have been*, he may with impunity fulfill his desire and by the sheer magic of memory, substitute for the reality of a time past a scene, a tableau, where implicitly, indefinitely repeatable acts are no longer those of a subject upon an object but rather the scheme of a voyeur constantly reenacting a fragmentary scenario.[38]

For Lau, I argue, writing produces a profound state of non-being, a state of obliteration. In many ways it functions in the same way drugs function, as Lau's psychiatrist Dr. Hightower, in fact, observes.

I talked speedily about the deepest, darkest things with Dr. Hightower, but like he said, echoing disappointment through me, "You're just relating them. You're recording these experiences, not feeling them, not reliving them. The drugs are a protective barrier. You can't start real work until you stop doing them." And God, more than ever I need to resolve what's happened in my childhood or else I can't go on.[39]

The substitutability of the word "them" in this passage suggests a substitutability between living and doing drugs, experience and its obliteration. There is also, I would argue, a substitutability between experience and writing. They are one and the same, and yet profoundly separate from one another. The writer inhabits what Kristeva, in *The Powers of Horror*, calls the abject—that pre-subjective state in which the psychoanalytic child does not know the difference between itself and the world, or itself and its own excrement.

The horror of this book is that it uses void-producing text to cover over a deeper void for which there is no language. It emerges from a profoundly abject state. Kristeva describes this state as the "non-separation of the subject/object, on which language has no hold but one woven of fright and repulsion."[40]

In her family bathroom, the mirror does not provide her the moment of recognition that Lacan tells us it ought. Instead, it provides only another image of her own obliteration where even writing, which perhaps holds the possibility for differentiation, for entry into subjecthood, is not possible: "It was all falling apart. Those visits with my parents, me in their bathroom watching a reflection in the mirror gulping pills, the writing meaning nothing, not wanting to ever write again, the drugs that were my world and my death."[41]

In *The Threshold of the Visible World*, Kaja Silverman has noted that the non-identical mirror may produce a fantasy that can be a tremendous relief for those whose subjectivity is too difficult to uphold. She calls this the fantasy of the body in bits and pieces. For Silverman, however, this is a fantasy she associates with the masculine subject, which tends to be overdetermined as whole, perfect and unitary in a way that is highly constructed and requires great effort on the part of the masculine subject.[42] For Lau, no such socially sanctioned subjectivity is offered. However, if one is to take her at her word, the pressure that her parents exert upon her to perform the "model daughter" is excessive, and certainly more than she can bear. The Lau of this text is both more and less than a full subject. Held together on the one hand by unrealistic parental expectation, torn apart on the other by the most destructive of Althusserian hailings—"junkie whore"— she oscillates between the sublime and the abject: "Not at all short of but always with and through perception and words, the sublime is a *something added* that expands us, overstrains us, and causes us to be both *here*, as dejects, and there, as others and sparkling."[43]

But which is which? Lau states repeatedly that she would rather be living drugged out on the streets than return to the stifling entrapment of her parent's home. She is caught in that abject space of non-differentiation, the inability to distinguish between self and society, inside and outside, in spite of the constant, narcissistic assertion of the "I." It appears that no subjectivity is produced here, but only a deepening of the void. What is produced for public consumption is a doubly virulent stereotype of the Asian woman as innocent and childlike on the one hand and excessive and sexually deviant on the other, given new lease and new power by its packaging as a diary, as an autobiography. To deepen this study, one might examine

Lau's poetic and fictional works, particularly *Other Women* and *You Are Not Who You Claim* to question who the "other" of the former might refer to. If, as I have argued, the writing persona of these texts has not emerged as a fully formed subject, but rather inhabits that unformed, fear-ridden site of the abject, then it appears doomed to repetition, circling around the formation of the "I" until it is able to separate itself from fear-laden not-yet-objects that swirl around it. I argue that in the case of *Runaway*, the incommensurable gap between inside and outside that Miki discusses is widened rather than narrowed, and it is made all the less articulate because of the appearance of articulation. Autobiography, as a truth regime, has become a kind of camouflage papering over an ever-deepening, ever more desperate void.

The obvious question to ask at this juncture is whether or not this problematic holds true for all autobiography, or whether there is something particular about *Runaway* that produces these effects. Writing about Doukhobor autobiography, Julie Rak (citing Sidonie Smith and Judith Butler) considers interiority to be a performative effect of autobiography rather than its "originating centre":

> ... [P]erformativity ... can still operate as an effect of language, but one which does not have to work within an economy of interiority and exteriority. This version of performativity can work within an economy of exteriority and event, as a communication of identity issues which does not tell the self to the self, or heal the split between the lonely points of enunciation and utterance, so much as recover the fractured memories of a community, or operate as a means of telling the community story to itself and to other communities. The place of witness narrative here is that it suggests how subjectivity can be constructed to recount a traumatic event so that the community can work through it. Instead of a dependency on temporary identifications which can be unfixed, the event itself stands for interiority and performs the work of identification for those who do not have an individuated subjectivity to unfix.[44]

Two problems emerge from this critique. First of all, if the work of autobiography is primarily "exterior," in other words social, then the ideological labour of the text matters. As Rita Wong has noted, the way in which Lau's work is marketed functions to reproduce stereotypes. Regardless, unfortunately, of Lau's own agency, desire, or action, it is difficult for her work to escape culturally overdetermined readings. Wong writes:

> Sometimes I have the disturbing feeling that, if Lau had not come along, the machine would have found someone else because it needs to have a bit of "colour" (but not too much) mirroring or serving the symbolic order so that

it can disavow its historical and systemic racist tendencies. Luckily for those in the book business who have benefitted from her labour, Lau's literary fixation with Old White Daddies seems to fit the bill. This narrative, only one of many possible narratives, is not to minimize Lau's talent as a writer but to remind us of the many ways in which social relations can influence reader reception.[45]

Though Wong is writing about the social labour of Lau's fiction, I would like to recognize here that the work of autobiography is also social. As indeed Robert Stepto, writing of the politics of slave narrative in the American South, tells us, autobiography and its circulation is highly subject to "race ritual," in which certain elements must be offered in order for the text to be received as "real." In the case of the slave narrative, the onus is upon the freed slave to prove not the truth of escape and freedom, but in fact, his literacy.[46] Further, a white guarantor is required,[47] as well as the whole marketing and circulation machinery of the white publishing establishment. Stepto notes further that the social labour of the text affects its reception:

> Slave narratives were often most successful when they were subtly pro-abolition and they were overtly anti-slavery—a condition which could only have exacerbated the former slave's already sizeable problems with telling his tale in such a way that he, and not his editors or guarantors, controlled it.[48]

The important thing to be aware of here is the extent to which the partial truth of autobiography reinforces already-received social and political knowledge functioning in the service of the status quo. I would suggest that this knowledge is a complicated mix of both apprehension and misapprehension. Even, for instance, Elly Danica's agonizing *Don't: A Woman's Word*, in spite of the productive feminist work it does, repeats violence against women in its accounting of that very violence. This is the contradiction of reclaiming the name of the other, that Hegel discovered long ago, and that Franz Fanon so eloquently elaborates in *Black Skins, White Masks*. In readerly terms, it seems to be important, then, to read autobiography as critically as one reads any other kind of text.

This is not to deny its power as witness for both self and community, as Rak notes. The second, perhaps deeper question that emerges from Rak's observations about performance is the extent to which one considers selves and communities as pure effects of enacted language. If the autobiographical work, as Rak suggests, "stands in for interiority" and "performs the work of identification," then there is no access to language.[49] Butler herself is less certain about this. Reading *Discipline and Punish*, she imagines the work of language to produce "the soul" as a kind of exterior, one which obliterates the (interior) body in order to bring the subject into existence. She writes:

> Here it is precisely at the expense of the body that the subject appears, an appearance which is conditioned in an inverse relation to the disappearance of the body, and appearance of a subject which not only effectively takes the place of the body, but acts as the very soul which frames and forms the body in captivity.... The bodily remainder, I would suggest, survives such a subject in the mode of already, if not always, having been destroyed, a kind of constitutive loss.[50]

First of all, it seems important to ask if there are other ways to produce the subject that are less violent. Butler has in mind the subject production of "the prisoner" as Foucault imagines him, named, contained, and made by the law. In an Althusserian sense, she acknowledges, we can respond to our hailing, or resist it. Butler places liberatory possibility there. In the act of autobiographical writing, in which one is essentially self-hailing, surely there must be some kind of room for give. When the writer actively works to maintain the body against such a "constitutive loss," I would argue, surely there is the possibility for some kind of interiority. If the writer chooses not to do this, then the loss or obliteration of the interior (however one might choose to name it) remains a melancholy possibility.

In a bleakly optimistic way (in the sense that it still allows much possibility for Bannerji's formulation), it might be worth remarking that Lau's intention is not to "break the silence" in the sense that Bannerji seems to mean. In her thorough critique of *Runaway*, Lien Chao remarks: "Lau's 'I' speaks the voice of a strong ego wanting to be one of the top writers in Canada instead of just a third prize or youth competition winner."[51] At least temporarily, Lau obliterates herself in the passage Chao quotes:

> Evelyn isn't alive at all, it's always her writing, her writing.... She's floundering in some kind of murky half-life, some kind of swamp where she still spins fantasies about seeing her books on shelves and people actually reading them, books that would make people think and feel.[52]

Here again, the text empties the writer. Lau produces absence for herself, in precisely the same move as she produces powerful self-representation for her readers' consumption. I suggest that Lau fills a Malinche-like position for both white and racialized Canadian society, both debased and empowered by exoticized, heterosexual femininity. As such, she, or rather, her representation of self, is unacceptable in polite Chinese Canadian society. And yet the mirage she offers holds great fascination for uncritical white or white-identified Canadian readers for whom her self-representation confirms all the most virulent stereotypes of the Oriental woman. The position is a deeply archetypical one that does unsettling political work I cannot support, however much compassion I might feel for the evacuated subject who produces it.

In a troubling but compelling article questioning the validity of False Memory Syndrome, Janice Haaken asks why we tend to assume that the recovery of trauma is necessarily the path to healing in women's autobiographical narrative.

> The trauma/dissociation model has been important in bridging feminist clinical and political practice and in holding onto a conception of women both as rational agents and as damaged victims. At the same time, this model reinforces traditional constructions of feminine experience that can be debilitating. One problem involves the centering of female disturbances on trauma memories, and of recovery on the retrieval of those memories. The therapeutic preoccupation with the recovery of trauma memory engages women, paradoxically, in a quest that reaffirms their fragility and position of nonrecognition. Both therapist and patient assume that women's untold stories are more important than the remembered ones, and that the unrevealed drama provides the key to the kingdom.[53]

She suggests that repressed trauma has been a very useful "container" into which we can project the many unsettling, unresolvable aspects of women's experience, and further suggests that in fact childhood neglect might be just as significant a factor as trauma in the formation of the female subject, but that it gets overlooked because it is more difficult to theorize.[54] These ideas echo what I have suggested with regard to *Runaway*. If autobiographical writing, rather than elucidating a trauma, can, in fact cover over or even produce a fundamental void, to what extent is it a liberatory practice? It has the power to reproduce stereotypes and the status quo, but does it have to? I think I would argue here that there are times when self-narrativizing does in fact "work through" and resolve repression (to speak in psychoanalytic terms) but that this is not a guarantee, and that it is possible for it, in fact, to compound violence in the form of "traumatic repetition." Or, to complicate matters further, it might do a bit of both. As in the reappropriation of the racist name, the subject in question is both freed and reinjured in a single move.

Homi Bhabha's work on the uncanny has been productive as a tool for thinking through the ways in which histories of the marginalized can be retrieved. Freud originally formulates the uncanny as "everything that ought to have remained hidden but has suddenly come to light."[55] For him the uncanny emerges when we recognize the familiar in the unfamiliar, which he conceives as a return of the repressed, the expression of something forgotten that presses unexpectedly on consciousness and makes our skin crawl. In his conception of "the beyond" Bhabha reformulates Freud's uncanny as model of history for the marginalized—those whose histories are broken and fragmented through war, dislocation, slavery, or the loss of language. The uncanny becomes a useful model of memory for those living on the interstices of society, in doubled time/spaces that can be imagined in various ways. He provides examples from the work of contemporary artists of colour—stairwells, radio waves, borderlands of any kind. These sites call up a history different from the linear patriarchal monolithic histories of nation states:

> For the demography of the new internationalism is the history of postcolonial migration, the narratives of cultural and political diaspora, the major social displacements of peasant and aboriginal communities, the poetics of exile, the grim prose of political and economic refugees. It is in this sense that the boundary becomes the place from which *something begins its presencing* in a movement not dissimilar to ambulant, ambivalent articulation of the beyond that I have drawn out: "Always and ever differently the bridge escorts the lingering and hastening ways of men to and fro, so that they may get to other banks [...] The bridge gathers as a passage that crosses."[56]

While both Haaken and Bhabha theorize a "something" beneath consciousness that may or may not be useful in understanding the psychic life of the marginalized subject, Haaken's is a stable core, where Bhabha's is a more mobile thing—always moving "to and fro," here and there and back again—as he says, ambulant, and ambivalent.

In her relentless drive towards a specified trauma, in the iterations of misery, Lau misses something that may be fundamentally inarticulable. In attempting to write the core that Haaken is so suspicious of, she comes up repeatedly with void, at precisely the site where she needs matter. It may be that it is not so much the act of writing per se that papers over the void, but only a misstep in the directions the writing probes. Wayson Choy, on the other hand, in his autobiographical text *Paper Shadows*, is aware of his ghosts from the outset. The generic descriptor on the cover of the book indeed points to them: "A haunting memoir from the bestselling author of *The Jade Peony*."

The opening conundrum with which Choy hooks his reader is that of the appearance of his mother eighteen years after her death. An uncanny stranger, someone from his childhood whom he has forgotten, calls to tell him she saw his mother on the street. Although the story turns out not to be true, Choy's receipt of the message is the instigating incident in a series of incidents that results in Choy discovering that he is adopted.

What Choy seems to strive for, which Lau does not, is a kind of doubleness in language—what might simply be called metaphoricity. By giving ground to these uncanny, unstable hauntings, Choy acknowledges the presence of the unknowable. It may or may not be traumatic, but that is not what is important. By making space for that which evades language, paradoxically, he makes space for language to matter. It is a kind of feeding of hungry ghosts, in which the void is given a nod in order that it not infiltrate and traumatize the entire work.

After the introduction of the reanimated mother, Choy presents us with three more hauntings. They present themselves narratively as mysteries. Poetically, they work as linguistic parapraxes. The first haunting takes place when the Choy of the narrative is four years old. He presents us with a sound:

> I woke up, disturbed by the sound of a distant clanging, and lifted my head high above the flannelled embankment that was my mother's back to see if a ghost had entered the room. Mother rolled her head, mouth partially open, sound asleep. I rubbed the sleep from my eyes to survey the near darkness. What I saw, reflected in the oval mirror above the dresser, was the buoyant gloom alive with winking and sparks. A cloud of fireflies.[57]

There is both a wonder—the fireflies—and a terror—the clanging sound—contained in the moment, with the body of the mother there to cleave the two together. The body of the mother looms large. Her back is a "flannelled embankment." The content of the haunting that Choy describes here is highly feminized, and highly ambivalent, wonder and terror rolled into one, redeemable only through story: "I remembered how fireflies came together to rescue lost children in the caves of Old China."[58]

The young Choy imagines the bedroom he shares with his mother also as a cave, one which is both safe and fraught with danger:

> My mind conjured a wild, hairy creature, eyes like fire, heaving itself, and the chains it was dragging, towards our bedroom cave. I turned to stone. / My child's wisdom said that Mah-ma and I had to lie perfectly still, or the monster would veer towards our bed, open its hideous wet mouth and devour us.[59]

The child requires the mother to protect him from feminine horrors—of the cave, and the "hideous wet mouth." But as a thing of the feminine, the mother can never protect him completely. Interestingly, it is the presence of the aural uncanny, in the form of the clanging noise, that keeps the sensation of spine-tingling chill in place.

In the daylight world, the clanging turns out to be the chains of the milkman's horse—yet another figure of wet, feminine openings.[60] On one occasion it snatches a carrot stump from the boy's hands and leaves a smear of saliva there.

At the moment of the second haunting, the clanging sound that became a horse now becomes a hearse, in an interestingly poetic turn. It is a turn that Choy himself does not remember. Rather the association is made for him by his Fifth Aunty:

> Fifth Aunty touched my shoulder with her cane and giggled. Death never scared her. She had seen too much death in Old Chinatown. I told her that, if I won the big lottery, I would see her ride into the sunset in the grandest, and slowest, horse-drawn hearse.
>
> "Remember that day you little boy and saw your very first one, Sonny?" she said. Aunty always went back to the old days.
>
> "No, I don't," I said. "I remember big milk wagons."
>
> "Yes, yes, you remember," she insisted. "We stand on Hastings Street, I hold your hand, and your aunty finally tell you that black thing no fancy milk wagon." Fifth Aunty broke into toothless laughter. "Oh, you looked so surprised that people died, just like your goldfish."
>
> "What did I say?"
>
> "You cry out '*Mah-ma won't die!*'"[61]

The feminine becomes a sign of death, specifically the death of the mother, who herself belongs to the deathly realm in the traditional metaphysical order of things. The milk wagon becomes a death wagon that will eventually take the mother away. The feminine that is fertile becomes both the feminine that obliterates and the feminine that is obliterated.

Choy illuminates for us at the outset a kind of motile liminal space. The mother is both alive—in the story given by the strange woman Hazel, and dead, in Choy's pragmatic recollection of her death and funeral. And so the Choy of the narrative also becomes a figure of Bhabha's interstitial time/space—both a "natural" son of Chinatown and a strange adoptee, the son of a mysterious opera singer, made legitimate through false papers to a mother who herself has become a legitimate citizen on false papers. His mother, Lilly Choy, is officially known as Nellie Hop Wah, who in fact was a married woman who died abroad and whose papers were later sold. The doubleness of life and death becomes also a doubleness of national and familial belonging. Choy and his mother exist inside the nation-state and inside the family on false papers with names that are not their own. Choy does not even know what his birth name, if he had one, might have been. Outside the clearly false sanctioning of citizenship, Choy and his mother are shadows without names or existence. Now his mother turns out not to be his mother, and at least in the suspended moment of the text's opening, turns out to be not dead but alive—a returnee from what Bhabha charmingly calls the "*au dela*."[62] A living woman carries a dead woman's name, finally dies, and then is substituted for another living woman in a bizarre series of oscillations between life and death, being and non-existence.

No wonder, then, that this memoir is haunted. Their lives are doubled images of the home in the world, as Bhabha explains in his articulation of the unhomely beyond:

> The recesses of the domestic space become sites for history's most intricate invasions. In that displacement, the borders between home and world become confused; and uncannily, the private and the public become part of each other, forcing upon us a vision that is as divided as it is disorienting.[63]

I want to ask now whether this unhomely effect comes from the writing of Choy's life or from the experience of life itself. As Joan Scott has described for us, a major tension of the identity politics moment is the tension between experience and writing, often figured as a class tension between those with the education and ability to write and those without. The problem is unresolvable because there is no such thing as unmediated experience.[64] The appearance of haunting in Choy's text can be apprehended only insofar as the text is literary. We need the mysterious clanging noise, the fireflies, the poetic resonance between "horse" and "hearse" in order to arrive at the unhomely effects I have described above. We need them also to recognize the crises of life and death, citizenship and being. These are the things that Evelyn Lau in *Runaway* does not provide. In gesturing towards the void, Choy is able to bring it momentarily to life, to create in that uncanny home, that cave of the bedroom he shared with his mother, a momentary haunting that draws us into history and the churnings of our national politics. As Bhabha says, quoting Morrison's *Beloved*:

> When historical visibility has faded, when the present tense of testimony loses its power to arrest, then the displacements of memory and the indirections of art offer us the image of our psychic survival. To live in the unhomely world, to find its ambivalencies and ambiguities enacted in the house of fiction, or its sundering and splitting performed in the work of art, is also to affirm a profound desire for social solidarity: "I am looking for the join [...] I want to join [...] I want to join."[65]

I seem, at this point, to be arguing in favour of metaphoricity, as more liberatory and more productive than texts that presume to artlessly represent experience, if only because the latter cannot, in the end, produce experience for the reader. As George Yudice argues in the translator's introduction to Nestor Garcia Canclini's *Consumers and Citizens*:

> Literary theory and cultural studies are rife with these assimilations of social problems to philosophical and aesthetic categories: Heidegger's homelessness versus homeless people; Kristeva's abjects vis-à-vis social "deviants"; Freud's uncanny vis-à-vis women's sexuality; and so on.[66]

One could, of course, leave the act of writing altogether, in order to engage other strategies of self- and community presencing, as indeed many activist-writers and activist-artists did in the nineties and continue to do in the current moment. Some writers have also consciously theorized their writing as an active and contingent practice. Roy Miki's notion of "asiancy" describes precisely that engagement for racialized cultural workers striving for social justice in writing, organizing, and art practice.

It certainly does seem that Choy is more conscious of his writing practice as a metaphorical act of representation than Lau is. He consciously makes space for the rupture, even in the way he names himself. He is "Wayson Choy" on the cover of the book, but "Choy Way Sun" as the protagonist of the autobiographical narrative. This slippage parallels two others: the recognition that he is someone other than who he was born and that his mother is also not who her papers say she is. These slippages seem to intentionally rupture the epigraph of the text: "At three, at eighty— the same."[67] This is also a conscious and productive disturbance of the autobiographic pact. In a sense, it is a call to the recognition of the genealogy of names, something Lejeune himself addresses in *Signes de Vie*, his follow-up to *Le Pacte Autobiographique* thirty years later, in which he writes:

> On risque toujours de croire que, parce que des éléments se transmettent, ils restent les mêmes, alors qu'ils se déforment en prenant une autre fonction. Là où l'on voit une continuité, il y a eu mutation. C'est difficile à penser pour nous, parce que tout le travail de construction de notre identité va dans l'autre sens, nous cherchons à enraciner notre présent dans des continuités en partie illusoires.[68]

While Choy playfully recognizes the genealogical mutations of his own name, however, the deeper question of the representation of Asian bodies and spaces remains ambivalent in relation to the stereotypes of Oriental mystery and inscrutability. I don't want to overload Choy or Lau with the burden of representation. On the other hand, stereotyped representations, deployed in the apparent service of truth-telling, reconfirm racist understanding in a newly powerful way. I want to ask whether more is possible, whether there are deeper ways of activating language in order to escape the stereotype of Chinese secretiveness and inscrutability.

Much of the anti-racist liberatory work of the late 80s and early 90s was predicated on a desire by racialized subjects for entry into Canadian cultural life. The introduction of the Canadian Multiculturalism Act in 1988 and the rise of cultural activity in racially marginalized communities in Canada coincided to the great benefit of artists, writers, and their audiences. The moment was fraught, for reasons Monika Kin Gagnon and Richard Fung have documented in *13 Conversations*. What cultural organizers, artists, writers, and critics might not have recognized as we did in that liberatory work was the extent to which we believed in the democratic possibilities of national belonging, in spite of our sometimes quite cutting critique. Or perhaps the critique itself was testament to that faith. While the texts I discuss here are not overtly about entry into a national imagination, I argue that they were published in that context and should be read as such.

The 1991 emergence of the anthology *Many-Mouthed Birds: Contemporary Writing by Chinese Canadians* did much to shape the expectations of what "Chinese Canadian writing" ought to do, positing it both within the national container "Canadian Literature" and outside it at the same time. I register autoethnography not so much in relation to nuances of conventional Western ethnography as with the pressure on Chinese Canadian writers to explain themselves to the white mainstream, and the assumptions which that pressure and its categories produce. To the extent that we "tell the secrets of Chinatown" (to whom?) the work is "autoethnographic" in the self-explaining mode that is so often taken on by racially marginalized subjects in white settler nations, in response to their exclusion from the national culture life. In the Introduction to *Many-Mouthed Birds*, Bennett Lee takes note of SKY Lee's thoughts on *Disappearing Moon Café*:

> Her novel *Disappearing Moon Café* is one break in what Kae, the narrator, terms "the great wall of silence and invisibility we have built around us." She goes on: "I have a misgiving that telling our history is forbidden. I have violated a secret code." The secret code was that reviving the troubled past would serve no useful purpose and should be forgotten or, at the very least, kept within the family. These writers [the contributors to the anthology] have indeed violated the code. By unearthing the past, breathing life into the characters who inhabited those troubled times, giving them a voice and investing them with human frailties and passions, they open up a world with its own colour, texture, weight and dreams.[69]

In *Paper Shadows*, Wayson Choy matter-of-factly addresses the telling of secrets: "The voice on the hotel phone chattered on, spilling out details and relationships, talking of Pender *Gai*, Pender Street, and noting how my novel talked of the 'secrets of Chinatown.'"[70]

The notion of Chinatown as a place of secrets may well have some basis in reality. This doesn't stop it from reinforcing the trope of Chinese inscrutability. Further, it places the second-generation narrators who disclose the "secrets" in the dubious position of traitor (to their first-generation parents), interpreter, and assimilated-but-marked Canadian subject. The "secrets of Chinatown" are traded for national belonging. Of course, the idea of Chinatown secrets is a problematic formulation. The "secrets of Chinatown" may be no deeper or stranger than the secrets of any other neighbourhood—the problem lies in the coincidence of Chinatown secrets with already existing, racist expectations about Chineseness. And so, if to tell those secrets constitutes a kind of autoethnography, it does so on the shaky ground of pandering to exoticist expectation. The problem is first and foremost a problem of reception. The author is not to be blamed. Some racialized writers, however, do consider it their responsibility to take that predictable reception into consideration.

In such a case, the question for the conscientious racialized writer becomes first of all whether national belonging is desirable, and secondly, if it is, how to go about obtaining it without confirming the Orientalist expectations of the mainstream. I think that, for a long time, many racialized Canadian cultural workers did perceive national belonging as something to be desired and striven for, even if the path was always fraught, contradictory, and problematic. We believed in the possibility of democratic equality within the bounds of the Canadian nation.

Today, as I write this essay, the stage of the nation has been radically altered from its early-90s condition by free trade agreements and the rise of militarism, fundamentalism, and war. It is important to understand what the texts did at the moment of their emergence, and what they might do (that is, how they might circulate differently) in the present.

As these texts find their place within the canon of CanLit, it is important to ask whether or not they retain their liberatory possibility. For there is a danger at present that could not have been perceived in the heady moment of their conception. The danger is that, sanctioned through the legitimizing power of the authentic voice, these texts become a new kind of ethnography rife with stereotypes—some old, some new—made all the more salient precisely because it is the native who speaks. Not enough authority has suddenly become too much, though in neither case does the "native speaker" benefit. It is the text, not the body or the history from which it emerges, that is privileged. But it is privileged only in the sense that it is put into the service of the same capitalist white supremacist hegemony under which we still live.

There seems to be a law of belatedness at work here, in the sense that autobiographical texts are a necessary step in the liberation of marginalized peoples, but no sooner do they come into being than their function, or, at least, one of their functions, becomes a very conservative one indeed. There is a parallel here between the writing of autobiography and what Hardt and Negri have to say about the functions of nationalism: that it is liberatory only insofar as it is oppositional—that the nation-state is the poisoned gift of national liberation movements.[71]

Once it has been produced, autobiography can work as a sort of retrospective folding of the marginalized subject into a kind of national cultural belonging. It seems to vindicate the past, but it actually produces a spectral present in the service of a future that requires the redeployment of marginalized bodies in different terms, but often for the same purposes. I am concerned that at the present moment the stories of past wrongs against Asian Canadians get redeployed as a sign of Canada's benevolence, a sign of liberal/multicultural arrival.

What is particularly interesting about Asian Canadian autobiographical texts is the use of historical photographs on the covers, as a way of producing nostalgia for a moment that could never, even at its best, have been particularly romantic. Certainly this is the case with the cover of Wayson Choy's "haunting memoir," which features a sepia-toned photograph of the young "Way Sun" standing in a small yard, and what seems to be age-stained paper covered in Chinese calligraphy. Denise Chong's *The Concubine's Children* is all the more loaded because its cover image is an old photograph of the beautiful concubine, her grandmother May-Ying. The stereotype of the exotic, sexually deviant Asian woman is reproduced and heightened by its archival status.

As Roy Miki deconstructs the cover of the anthology *Many-Mouthed Birds* to illustrate how Chick Rice's playful, ironic photograph of Tommy Wong's face is redeployed through marketing strategy to (re)produce an image of the Asian as "secretive and mysterious,"[72] so one might argue that book cover art using archival photos, whatever their "original" significance, produces a similar effect. But there is also added dimension of a strange kind of nostalgia, as I have said, such that these bodies are belatedly incorporated into the mythos of the nation. The exotic other is retrospectively encrypted into a history that did not want these bodies on the first pass.

Through the logic of the future anterior which Marjorie Garber has described in her discussion of Shakespeare's history plays,[73] we are given an uncanny vision of the present as the future of a past that never was, in spite of all the trappings of authenticity. What are the psychic effects of this incorporation for subjects represented by this history?

The French psychoanalysts Abraham and Torok propose a theory of "inclusion," in which the subject undergoes a traumatic experience she or he cannot admit to memory because it is too overwhelming. Through the mechanism of inclusion, the subject incorporates the experience into his psyche whole, in the form of a crypt. It is painful, it is undigested, it is inarticulable:

> Between the idyllic moment and its subsequent forgetting (we have called the latter "preservative repression"), there was the metapsychological traumatism of a loss or, more precisely, the "loss" that resulted from a traumatism. This segment of ever so painfully lived Reality—untellable and therefore inaccessible to the gradual, assimilative work of mourning—causes a genuinely covert shift in the entire psyche. The shift itself is covert, since both the fact that the idyll was real and that it was lost must be disguised and denied. This leads to the establishment of a sealed-off psychic place, a crypt in the ego. Created by a self-governing mechanism we call *inclusion*, the crypt is comparable to the formation of a cocoon around the chrysalis. Inclusion or crypt is a form of anti-introjection, a mechanism whereby the assimilation of both the illegitimate idyll and its loss is precluded.[74]

What I want to propose here is that through the writing of autobiography, traumatic memory can be momentarily disinterred from its crypt within the psyche of the marginalized subject. I argue, however, that while it might sometimes heal the marginalized subject, it runs an equal danger of reinterment in the collective psyche of the nation. It might be swallowed whole, and left undigested. The only evidence of its existence left in that case is the cover of the book, which maintains the status quo—what Abraham and Torok would call "the original topography"—as the romantic, exotic, Orientalized sign of something roiling beneath the surface.

To be thus "included" into the social-psychic space of the nation may be partially liberatory, but as long as this effect occurs, it cannot be fully so. Vigilance is required against the seeming comfort of its seamless surface, that has in fact incorporated so many racial traumas. Multicultural incorporation does not necessarily expiate the trauma. Insofar as Canada presents itself as a market, an exporter, and a favorable site of overseas Asian investment, it is important that its cultural workers continue to attend to both the articulable and the inarticulable that roil beneath.

NOTES

1 Sigmund Freud, "The Uncanny," in *The Standard Edition of the Complete Psycho-logical Works of Sigmund Freud*, vol. 18, ed., trans. James Strachey (London: Vintage, 2001), 224.

2 Himani Bannerji, *Thinking Through: Essays on Feminism, Marxism and Anti-Racism* (Toronto: The Women's Press, 1995), 55.

3 Ibid., 64.

4 Karl Marx, *The Eighteenth Brumaire of Louise Bonaparte* (New York: International Publishers, 1963), 15. That the ideal of affirmative action in hiring practices rose and became prominent at this time is no coincidence. In some progressive circles the notion of "optics" also became salient. Workplaces and organizations were challenged to find hiring and recruiting strategies to literally up the count of brown bodies in their makeup, as concrete praxis to begin undoing the unjust historically entrenched privileging of white bodies through the ideology of colonialism. These strategies challenged the notion of meritocracy, not as an ideal per se, but as one that could be put into practice without privileging certain already privileged histories, thought systems, and bodies—the white, the European, the male. Liberation politics claimed a gap, and a hypocrisy, between the theory of meritocracy and its practice. They also pointed to the particularity and historical specificity of the white body in ways that those used to thinking of their literatures and experiences as "universal" often found quite difficult to stomach. Within these politics, strategies like affirmative action were always recognized as contingent, as arising out of historical circumstance rather than the Western philosophical notion of first principles, which posits the ideal before the body. Lest I appear to be claiming a pure outside to "Western philosophical notions," however, let me remark that these are fully Marxist strategies, emerging from Marx's observation that politically aware people can build their own histories, but not under conditions of their own choosing (*Eighteenth Brumaire*, 15).

5 Bannerji, *Thinking Through*, 65.

6 Ibid., 82.

7 Ibid.

8 Ibid., 84.

9 Roy Miki, "Asiancy: Making Space for Asian Canadian Writing" in *Broken Entries: Race, Subjectivity and Writing* (Toronto: Mercury Press, 1998), 107. It is important to note here that body politics are oppositional only within the flow of Western philosophical and literary discourse. As the title of Miki's book suggests, for the Japanese Canadian subject, one both does and does not enter racialized subjectivity within a linear flow. Her emergent subjectivity is thus a "broken entry." Insofar as she is other, it is perpetually present. It cannot have a past. Insofar as she is assimilated, she belongs to Western discourse, and is thus a (continuous) product of it.

10 Ibid., 109.

11 Ibid., 110.

12 Ibid., 113.

13 Smith and Watson, *Women, Autobiography, Theory* (Madison: U of Wisconsin P, 1998), 5.

14 Phillippe Lejeune, *Le Pacte Autobiographique* (Paris: Editions du Seuil, 1975), 33.

15 Ibid., 26.

16 Ibid., 26.

17 Miki, "Asiancy," 113.

18 Ibid., 114.
19 Ibid., 116.
20 James Clifford and George E. Marcus, *Writing Culture: The Poetics and Politics of Ethnography* (Berkeley: U of California P, 1996), 4.
21 Ibid., 5.
22 Ibid., 9.
23 Ibid., 10.
24 Ibid., 10.
25 D. Soyini Madison, *Critical Ethnography: Methods, Ethics, Performance* (Thousand Oaks, CA: Sage Publications, 2005), 5.
26 Ibid, 6.
27 Clifford and Marcus, *Writing Culture*, 13.
28 Ibid., 14.
29 Ibid., 14.
30 Miki, "Asiancy," 112.
31 Marc Eli Blanchard, "The Critique of Autobiography," in *Comparative Literature* 34, no. 2 (1982): 101.
32 Ibid., 99.
33 Evelyn Lau, *Runaway: Diary of a Street Kid* (Toronto: Harper and Collins, 1989), 1.
34 Ibid., 1.
35 I am not arguing here that her claims are false, only that they do not tell us anything about the "true identity" of the author.
36 Lau, *Runaway*, 4.
37 Blanchard, "The Critique of Autobiography," 105.
38 Ibid., 106.
39 Lau, *Runaway*, 250–51.
40 Julia Kristeva, *Powers of Horror: An Essay on Abjection*, trans. Leon S. Roudiez (New York: Columbia UP, 1982), 58.
41 Lau, *Runaway*, 251–52.
42 Kaja Silverman, *The Threshold of the Visible World* (New York: Routledge, 1996), esp. Chapter 1.
43 Kristeva, *Powers of Horror*, 12.
44 Julie Rak, "Doukhobor Autobiography As Witness Narrative," in *Biography* 24, no. 1 (2001): 232.
45 Rita Wong, "Market Forces and Powerful Desires: Reading Evelyn Lau's Cultural Labour," *Essays in Canadian Writing* 73 (2001): 122.
46 Robert Stepto, *From Behind the Veil: A Study of Afro-American Narrative* (Urbana: U of Illinois P, 1979): 6.
47 Ibid., 8.
48 Ibid., 15.
49 Rak, "Doukhobor," 232.
50 Judith Butler, "Subjection, Resistance, Resignification: Between Freud and Foucault," in *The Identity in Question*, ed. John Rajchman (New York and London: Routledge, 1995), 236.
51 Lien Chao, *Beyond Silence: Chinese Canadian Literature in English* (Toronto: TSAR, 1997), 159.
52 Lau, *Runaway*, 156.
53 Janice Haaken, "The Recovery of Memory, Fantasy, and Desire in Women's Trauma Stories: Feminist Approaches to Sexual Abuse and Psychotherapy," in *Women,*

Autobiography, Theory: A Reader, ed. Sidonie Smith and Julia Watson (Madison: U of Wisconsin P, 1998), 359.

54 Ibid., 357.

55 Freud, "The Uncanny," 224.

56 Homi Bhabha, *The Location of Culture* (London: Routledge, 1994), 5.

57 Wayson Choy, *Paper Shadows: A Chinatown Childhood* (Toronto: Viking, 1999), 7.

58 Ibid., 6.

59 Ibid., 6–7.

60 I mean this in an associative, poetic sense. Milk is a fluid associated with motherly love and nurturance. One might read the horse's mouth, psychoanalytically, as a kind of feminine opening. Its associative attachment to milk in Choy's system of images makes it doubly feminine. Of course, there is room here if one wants to play with words, for other kinds of gendered associations—the milkman as a man with strong attachments to the mother, the horse as a figure of virility, the horse's mouth as a source of truth, etc., but this is beyond the scope of my argument.

61 Choy, *Paper Shadows*, 11.

62 Bhabha, *The Location of Culture*, 1.

63 Ibid., 9.

64 Writing of a moment in Samuel Delaney's *The Motion of Light in Water*, in which he witnesses gay male sexuality at a bathhouse, as an epiphany of sorts, Scott says:

> For Delaney, witnessing the scene at the bathhouse (an "undulating mass of naked male bodies" seen under a dim blue light) was an event. It marked what in one kind of reading we would call a coming to consciousness of himself, a recognition of his authentic identity, one he had always shared, would always share with others like himself. [This is the kind of reading that Scott eschews.] Another reading, closer to Delaney's preoccupation with memory and self in this autobiography, sees this event not as the discovery of truth (conceived as the reflection of a prediscursive reality), but as the substitution of one interpretation for another. Delaney presents this substitution as a conversion experience, a clarifying moment after which he sees differently. But there is a difference between subjective perceptual clarity and transparent vision; one does not necessarily follow from the other even if the subjective state is metaphorically presented as a visual experience. Moreover (and this is Swann's point), "the properties of the medium through which the visible appears—here, the dim blue light, whose distorting, refracting qualities produce a wavering of the visible," make any claim to unmediated transparency impossible. Instead, the wavering light permits a vision beyond the visible, a vision that contains the fantastic projections ("millions of gay men" for whom "history had, actively and already, created ... whole galleries of institutions") that are the basis for political identification. "In this version of the story," Swann notes, "political consciousness and power originate, not in a presumably unmediated experience of presumably real gay identities, but out of an apprehension of the moving, differencing properties of the representational medium—the motion of light on water. (66–67)

65 Bhabha, *The Location of Culture*, 18.

66 George Yudice, introduction to *Consumers and Citizens*, by Nestor Garcia Canclini (Minneapolis: U of Minnesota P, 2001), xiv.

67 It is interesting that he uses the Western convention of naming (personal name followed by family name) when declaring his authorship (Wayson Choy) but the

Chinese convention (surname followed by generation name followed by personal name—Choy Way Sun) when he is the object of his own text. In another project, it would bear interrogating how voice and silence are enacted through these uses of the name.

68 Philippe Lejeune, *Signes de Vie: Le Pacte Autobiographique 2* (Paris: Editions de Seuil, 2005), 117–18.
69 Bennett Lee and Jim Wong-Chu, *Many-Mouthed Birds: Contemporary Writing by Chinese Canadians* (Vancouver: Douglas and McIntyre, 1991), 4.
70 Choy, *Paper Shadows*, 5. Italics in original.
71 Michael Hardt and Antonio Negri, *Empire* (Cambridge, MA: Harvard UP, 2000), 134.
72 Miki, "Asiancy," 120.
73 Marjorie Garber, "'What's Past is Prologue': Temporality and Prophecy in Shakespeare's History Plays," in *Renaissance Genres: Essays on Theory, History and Interpretation*, ed. Barbara Lewalski (Cambridge: Cambridge UP, 1986), 311.
74 Nicolas Abraham and Maria Torok, *The Shell and the Kernel: Renewals of Psychoanalysis*, ed., trans. Nicholas T. Rand (Chicago: U of Chicago P, 1994), 141.

[chapter five]

The Politics of Gender and Genre in Asian Canadian Women's Speculative Fiction
Hiromi Goto and Larissa Lai[1]

Pilar Cuder-Domínguez

In his 1995 essay "An End to Innocence: The Ethnography of Ethnography," Van Maanen described recent developments in the discipline, and particularly the way in which ethnographers have lately turned against those forms of ethnographic writing that have for a long time contributed to naturalizing its alleged objectivity. For Van Maanen, self- or auto-ethnography is one of several alternatives to ethnographic realism, one in which, by textualizing the culture of the writer's own group, the distinction between the researcher and the researched is obliterated.[2] As a self-reflexive mode of representation, autoethnography can become useful in the interrogation of binary conceptions of self/others and in exploring multiple affiliations of the subject. As Reed-Danahay points out, the term itself has a double sense, "referring either to the ethnography of one's own group or to autobiographical writing that has ethnographic interest."[3] In the context of the growing dialogue across the disciplines, Françoise Lionnet has described autoethnography as "a kind of 'figural anthropology' of the self,"[4] and has further related the autoethnographic impulse to literary autobiography, insofar as the women writers that she critiques deployed this literary genre in order to "articulate a vision of the future founded on individual and collective solidarities, respectful of cultural specificities, and opposed to all rigid, essentializing approaches to questions of race, class, or gender."[5]

Yet, autobiography is not the only literary genre that interrogates the construction of the subject in its overlapping identities, nor is it to be found always in isolation, for, as Lionnet herself points out in her analysis of Zora Neale Hurston's *Dust Tracks on a Road*, the autobiographical voice can ally itself to other narrative forms. Such is the case of fantastic or non-realistic forms like science fiction and utopia, two literary genres that, as Tom Moylan reminds us, "appear to concern themselves realistically with the future [although they] are most concerned with the current moment of history, but they represent that moment in an estranged manner."[6] Since its inception, science fiction has been peculiarly useful as a vehicle for women writers' critique of patriarchy and for unpacking the contradictions of their own position within it. Jane Donaworth describes how "they have returned again and again to the complexities of the questions that Shelley raised [in *Frankenstein*]: making a science that does not exclude women, creating an identity for women as alien, and finding a voice in a male world."[7]

This chapter addresses the politics of the representation and/or performance of gendered Asianness in two speculative novels written by Asian Canadian women at the onset of the twenty-first century: Hiromi Goto's *The Kappa Child* (2001) and Larissa Lai's *Salt Fish Girl* (2002). For the term "performance" I am drawing mainly from recent studies on ethnicity, and so I am referring to the generational repetition of role models. Joshua Fishman has described ethnicity as made up of being, doing, and knowing: *being* because, in his view, ethnicity "has always been experienced as a kinship phenomenon, a continuity within the self and within those who share an intergenerational link to common ancestors"; *doing* because this common paternal lineage moves people to behave as their ancestors did, a specific way that is transmitted from a generation to the next and that is in itself "more meaningful than the goal-directed behaviour theoretically involved through civility, rationality, or other such mundane approaches. The 'doings' of ethnicity preserve, confirm, and augment collective identities and the natural order." Finally, *knowing* because ethnicity offers universal truths, explanations to origins and destinies.[8]

For "speculative fiction" I take as my meaning the deployment of fantastic elements of diverse kinds that disrupt and challenge in some measure the realism of a narrative and thus interrogate and critique the very concept and limits of "reality." In his study on the development of science fiction, Patrick Parrinder convincingly argues that since the 1960s, the future has been "increasingly regarded as a metaphor for the present,"[9] and as a result SF has turned into a form closely related to utopian writing, suggesting hopeful possibilities rather than predicting future developments. Parrinder concludes that "the metaphorical theory of the genre redefines SF as 'speculative fiction' or 'speculative fantasy.'"[10] Therefore, "speculative fiction" is currently a more inclusive term than either "science fiction" or "fantasy," and thus is particularly appropriate for the hybrid blend of generic features that these Asian Canadian authors deploy. Larissa Lai has drawn a post-apocalyptic world featuring policed company compounds and dangerous unregulated zones, and Hiromi Goto's contemporary scene is tinged with the fantastic by means of a trickster figure from Japanese myth. In their novels, the writers foreground Asian women's sexuality as a means to highlight questions ranging from human reproduction, bioethics, and genetic engineering on the broader social level to sexual orientation on the more personal one (but ultimately inextricably social as well). Gender, race, and genre are intimately connected in these novels.

Donna Haraway first suggested the link between women of colour and "cyborgs," in that they could be interesting examples for new identities in high-tech societies, and she turned to the pages of science fiction for their imagined constructions, in the belief that creators of fiction offered new epistemologies that could illuminate our path.[11] Lai in particular seems to be influenced by Haraway's thought, specifically in the wealth of science fiction intertexts that surface throughout her novel, as well as in the way she has pushed forward the Frankenstein myth through the creation of a complex, innovative, Frankenstein creature in the clone Evie.[12] In Goto's and Lai's novels, the deployment of fantasy (whether couched in the form of myth or of dystopian fiction) appears to serve the purpose of helping readers envision performances of racial identity alternative to those traditionally enforced. "Race" in them means not just skin colour, but the conventional hierarchies of race and even sexual orientation ensuing from it, since, as Sandra Harding reminds us, "the social structures of race relationships are interlocked with gender and class systems."[13]

Thus, this essay starts by looking into the representation of the Asian females at the centre of the novels, and attempts to untangle the issues of sameness and difference that they embody. The questions I pursue here are related to the status of the woman of colour as the alien in speculative fiction, which feminist critics such as Jenny Wolmark and Jane Donaworth have examined. Wolmark considers that women writers "use the science fiction metaphor of the alien to explore the way in which the deeply divisive dichotomies of race and gender are embedded in the repressive structures and relations of dominance and subordination."[14] Donaworth has identified "minority women as aliens among us" as one of four categories of the woman as alien in science fiction.[15] All these questions are in turn also intimately related to autoethnography, since the (auto)ethnographic drive emerges in the confessional tone of the sometimes bizarre stories of the women characters in the Canadian novels under discussion. The characters can be seen as involved in an effort to define their individual and communal identity and to establish their solidarities and allegiances. Secondly, the paper addresses the relationship between the representation of Asianness as discussed in the first section and the politics of the speculative fiction that both authors have chosen as the vehicle for their concerns. Finally, it contextualizes their writing within Asian North American writing, in order to determine whether they have managed indeed to move "beyond autoethnography."

Sameness and Difference: Asian Subjectivity, Gender, and Sexual Orientation

Central to both novels are their Asian women characters, who engage in a search for their "imagined community."[16] They each set out to examine themselves in relation to their ethnic community, particularly as it is embodied by their own families. The biological is thus the starting point for the ethnographic exploration of the self, but not necessarily its ultimate destination.

The unnamed narrator of *The Kappa Child* is a second-generation Japanese Canadian woman whose abusive father sets out to grow Japanese rice in the dry soil of the Albertan prairies. She must tease out her identity in the midst of conflicting family allegiances (father/mother, siblings) and with the dubious help of available but unsuitable role models of pioneering life in the prairies. The mother (Emiko) and the four sisters (Slither, the unnamed narrator, PG, and Mice) evolve in different ways under the weight of the father's verbal and physical violence. A man whose main traits are his unpredictability and his stubbornness, he hits them all frequently and at random, and his most common term for them is "bakatare" (idiot). Throughout the girls' childhood, Emiko accepts the role of the submissive wife and mother, seeking invisibility as the safest position, and expressing her suffering only by means of repeated sighs. The oldest sister, Slither, grooms herself into the perfect image of vulnerable Asian femininity. Small and beautiful, Slither's thoughts are constantly on her looks. To the narrator, Slither is weak and spineless—as the name she has created for her suggests—as well as only too willing to conform. The passive behaviour of the two younger sisters also fails to satisfy her. PG retreats behind a screen of words, her childhood refrains, such as "Happy endings, sad endings"[17] and "scary things are not scary if you are not scared of them."[18] The youngest one, Mice, is always frightened and often silent, like a little mouse. The narrator resents her "collect long-distance calls, her breathing and breathing on the phone for two hours straight, just so she doesn't have to breathe alone."[19]

The repetition of patterns that she finds out of joint is not conducive to a productive sense of ethnicity. In the midst of such a dysfunctional family, the narrator has to look for positive role models elsewhere. Throughout her childhood, she had found them in the pages of her favourite book, *Little House on the Prairie*, and in her favourite character, Laura Ingalls, with whom she strongly empathizes, even though many of the items in the book make little sense for the girls:

> "The Ingalls family were from the east so they went west. We're from British Columbia, so we were in the west, but we moved east to get to the same place, funny, huh?" I beamed. [...]
>
> "I don't get it," Slither said. "Why does that Laura girl want to see a papoose so bad? I bet there were a lot of flies in that wagon. It's kinda sad that the dog got swept away in the river. Do you think salt pork is like bacon?"
>
> I scowled. "It's about being pioneers. See, we're like that right now, get it? It's not about salt pork!"
>
> "Did Laura's pa hit the ma?" PG muttered.
>
> "He never hit her! Ever! He played the violin!" I exclaimed. Though something gnawed inside. I hadn't noticed before, but now that I read it out loud, Ma seemed so much weaker than I'd imagined. "*Oh, Charles,*" she said. "*Whatever you think, Charles.*"[20]

Yet, Laura Ingalls, with her obsession to see "a papoose," is sadly wanting as a role model for an Asian child, and the protagonist finds the Ingalls' fictional world more and more restrictive, as she instinctively realizes that it is based on policing the borders of race and gender. An alternative role model for the narrator's survival on the prairies is the one provided by her closer neighbours, the Nakamura family. Janice Nakamura is a Canadian Nisei who lives with her son Gerald, the result of a short-lived marriage with a First Nations husband. Both as a family and individually, the Nakamuras fail to meet the standards of both white and non-white society. First of all, they do not represent the ideal of happy family life embodied by the fictional Ingalls. They are not the standard nuclear family and their lifestyle is too eccentric. Secondly, Janice Nakamura's behaviour is too manly, outspoken, and self-sufficient to fit into the Japanese construction of femininity. She does not speak Japanese, nor does she strictly follow the rules of politeness, but her ways are efficient and she shows the new family where to get water while the narrator's father is vainly digging a well in the dry soil. The children must thus learn not to pass judgment solely on grounds of appearance: Janice's rice balls may look too big to be the

perfect Japanese *onigiri*, but they do taste delicious. Thirdly, Gerald Nakamura's mixed-racedness places him beyond the pale. As a person combining two racial identities, but especially as a native person, he is, to the
narrator, "incomprehensible,"[21] but that in a way brings him close to her,
as one who feels stranded among such diverse identities. The Nakamuras
are truly "aliens" insofar as their performance of a racialized identity is
not based on essentialized repetition, or on biological bonding, but in a more
creative and inclusive subjectivity. Like her *onigiris*, Janice has found her
own version of ethnicity, although it will take a long time for the narrator
to fully understand this.[22]

Goto brings all these elements to bear on the narrator's identity conflict through a supernatural figure drawn from Japanese myth, the Kappa,
a green creature of water and water places. Indeed, the narrator reaches
a crisis in the novel when she feels she is pregnant after having an odd
encounter with an extraordinary Kappa-like female character during a
lunar eclipse. Her increased awareness of her body—which she has always
thought of as ugly—as well as her doubtful pregnancy are the stylistic features that convey the psychological voyage of the character.

The Kappa is the embodiment of the narrator's tensions regarding her
sexuality. Although sexually attracted to two female friends, Genevieve
and Midori, she has repressed her feelings and maintained a strict celibacy
and emotional aloofness that is taking its toll on her. When her two friends
become lovers, Goto's narrator feels excluded to the point of utter loneliness. The encounter with the Kappa leads her to confront her fears and inad-
equacies. This coincides with her mother's unexpectedly walking out on her
husband and departing on her own voyage of self-discovery with a new partner, Janice Nakamura. It becomes a source of wonder for the narrator, who
never dared expect that such liberation could take place. A final confrontation with her father allows the narrator to move away from her childhood
and to accept herself and her siblings as full-fledged adults who may still
have a chance for happiness. Fretting over her mother's whereabouts, the
narrator visits her elder sister, Slither, and in entering her home she is
forced to come to terms with her sisters' adult lives rather than the picture
of them she has held since their traumatic childhoods: "'By the way,' my
sister inclines her head so like Okasan my heart gives a little jump, 'I would
prefer that you called me Satomi. Slither was funny when we were children, but we're adults now.'"[23]

Therefore, in *The Kappa Child* Hiromi Goto explores the dialectics of
sameness and difference by means of blood-related characters. The four siblings are simultaneously seen as extremely similar due to racial background
and upbringing and yet markedly dissimilar in their personalities and

lifestyles. Further complicating the matter is the issue of same-sex love, also resolved when the narrator embarks on a relationship with a Korean Canadian character, Bernie. The novel's final scene displays the two lesbian couples, Genevieve-Midori and the narrator-Bernie, enjoying a night out under the stars and being symbolically blessed by the Kappa when the rain starts to fall:

> The wind feels good, the stars glitter. And somewhere, planets align.
>
> Then, a raindrop falls. Full and round, as big as a Muscat grape, I look up but there's not a cloud. Where has it come from? A perfect orb drops on my lips, seeps to my tongue. Sweet. Then more droplets fall, plump, warm, soft as kisses, they rain down on us. We turn to each other, eyes wide with wonder.[24]

Nature and nurture are finally in harmony. The human-made links between the four friends and lovers are at least as strong, if not more so, than those between the four biological sisters. A sisterhood of the heart seems to displace a sisterhood of the body by the novel's end. Hiromi Goto's exploration of these issues weaves together the real and the fantastic, as we will discuss below.

Larissa Lai's *Salt Fish Girl* (2002) also involves the interaction of a figure from ancient Asian mythology, Nu Wa, and humans. Nu Wa is a shape-shifter and the creator of human beings, but her loneliness pushed her to adopt a human form. Like the Kappa in Goto's novel, such interaction is mainly erotic. However, Lai also develops a parallel plot set in the second half of the twenty-first century, in a post-apocalyptic future where governmental authority has weakened and the big corporations have increased their wealth and power so much that the middle classes are drawn to the comfort and safety of their compounds. In the middle of this fast disintegrating world Lai places an unusual heroine, Miranda Ching, whose strong body odour, described as cat piss and pepper, sets her apart from all other human beings, first in the corporate compound where she lives most of her childhood, and later on outside, in the so-called Unregulated Zone. Her smell recalls that of durians, and Miranda's mother actually ate a piece of that fruit on the day of her conception. Miranda's scent, and by extension, durians, become the sign of her difference, of her Asianness, marking her off from the people around her. Thus, for example, it is mentioned that she is the only Asian child in her school class.[25]

Like the unnamed narrator of Goto's novel, Miranda must sort out the puzzle of her identity by facing up to the model of the previous generation, represented by her mother's successful career in show business. But Miranda's isolation is such that she completely lacks appropriate role models. Her only sibling is over thirty years older, and thus more a parent than a brother. Her parents were in their sixties when they surprisingly conceived her, and this is the reason why they belong to a place and time long gone, one which she can hardly understand. Again like Goto's narrator, Miranda is unable to accept herself, a failure that evolves into self-hatred. She lives in guilt and shame, believing that she is to blame for everything that has befallen her family, including her mother's accidental death:

> For years after my mother's death, I could not bear the presence of mirrors in any room. When I chanced on one by accident, I shuddered at the sight of my own reflection and wished with all my heart that I could erase it. [...] I wasn't suicidal. I just couldn't stand the sight of myself.[26]

Much of Miranda's plight, however, stems directly from her "condition," a condition that, as the story goes along, seems to be affecting more and more people, to the extent that it becomes a real epidemic, which some believe has been intentionally crafted in a lab or is the unintentional result of genetic tampering with the food supply. Here Lai is making deep connections between the personal and the political, between Miranda's individual body and the way capitalist economies market and exploit human bodies. As Lee contends, Lai's novel thematizes the strong hold capitalism has on the body: "Late capitalism wants bodies that are controlled by the global market, and in the case of noncompliant bodies, it will not hesitate to suppress and reshape them into conformity."[27] This sort of connection is missing from Goto's text, where, though the narrator determinedly steps outside the sphere of consumerism and competitiveness that is part and parcel with contemporary life, she does not go out of her way to fight against it, or to proselytize, either. On the contrary, in Lai's fiction it is an unavoidable fact that only the naive or misinformed may ignore.

Things start to change for Miranda when she gets to know and falls in love with a woman who she later learns is a clone. Evie is indebted to many characters in previous works of feminist science fiction, such as those by Mary Shelley (the Frankenstein creature), Angela Carter (Eve/Evelyn in *The Passion of New Eve*), and Margaret Atwood (the subversive Moira in *The Handmaid's Tale*). Evie (originally known as Sonia 113) is part fish, a fact that explains her strong salty body odour. Through her Miranda comes in contact with a community of women, the Sonias, seven other female clones that live and raise children together in a decaying house. Here Miranda experiences at last the recognition of similarity and the troubling beginnings of a community that may not be considered "natural" but is still a community. She at first feels some revulsion at the sight of the likeness of the women, but later she is jealous of their intimacy:

> My eyes turned back to Evie and Sonia 14. I watched them for a long time. I did not feel half so creeped out as I did envious. To have access to oneself as an old woman. Was it like that for them? Did Sonia 14, having lived them, share Evie's foibles? Had she come to an understanding of them? Did she see Evie's life as an extension of her own, as a second shot at those things that had failed the first time?[28]

Miranda recognizes a kind of sisterhood that is a far cry from everything she has known before. But what makes this a real community goes beyond the biological bond and involves the ties brought about by the same kind of suffering and exploitation. In turn, these experiences are inextricably related to race. In Lai's imagined world, Caucasians exploit non-Caucasians. The Sonias have escaped the exhausting work demanded of them by the shoe factories, and they share a subversive purpose, to bring to light and publicize the dehumanizing practices of the capitalist multinationals. Like Goto, Lai imagines a group of "sisters" whose biological bond is superseded in all or in part by socio-cultural ties. What keeps the Sonias together is a common purpose, not a common parent.

Such a community could be entirely disruptive of conventional society, whether in its economic workings (capitalist exploitation) or in its heterosexual normativity. Since the Sonias have found out the secret of fertility without male insemination,[29] their community could entail the birth of a new world order, as Dr. Rudy Flowers very much fears: "'You don't know,' said the doctor, 'what monstrosities might have come of those births. [...] The fertility those durians provided was neither natural nor controllable. It was too dangerous.'"[30] As such, Flowers orders its destruction. When they discover that most of the Sonias have been murdered, Miranda and Evie go into hiding. Lai brings to an end and daringly resolves many of the contradictions of this ambitious tale[31] poetically, with a nativity scene featuring a female trinity: Miranda gives birth with the assistance of her partner, Evie, to a baby girl she has conceived by eating one of those genetically altered durians. Lee has read Miranda's pregnancy as "the creation of a body that asserts ownership over itself through an act of self-production."[32] This new world order, starting out as it does despite all the combined pressures of conventional society, is hailed as a true utopian beginning. The dystopian nature of the tale thus becomes finally suspended in utopian timelessness:

> I thought, we are the new children of the earth, of the earth's revenge. Once we stepped out of mud, now we step out of moist earth, out of DNA new and old, an imprint of what has gone before, but also a variation. By our difference we mark how ancient the alphabet of our bodies. By our strangeness we write our bodies into the future.[33]

Both *The Kappa Child* and *Salt Fish Girl* conclude their ethnographic examination of the self by making use of closing scenes with a strongly utopian
bent. They strive to cancel out the conflicts between self and society examined in the narrative by determinedly asserting the subject's reappropriation of her own body and her proud reclamation of difference.

Genre Politics: the Contours of Speculative Fiction

The representation of the Asian female characters in these novels must be
read ethnographically against the diverse background of the society constructed in each speculative fiction. Hiromi Goto has chosen an Asian myth
to challenge the one-sidedness of the realist script, while Larissa Lai combines Asian mythology with the high-tech quality of science fiction proper.

The Kappa Child has been widely read as science fiction.[34] Goto's novel
won the 2001 James Tiptree Jr. Award "for works that expand and explore
gender roles in SF and fantasy."[35] The main fantastic element is the presence of the Kappa, a mythical water creature that, according to Iwamoto,
became popular in Japanese writing of the late 1920s. It is described as a
small, green figure with webbed fingers and a bowl-shaped head that contains the water it draws its powers from. Further, an entry from *Kenkyusha's
New Japanese–English Dictionary* helpfully annexed to the novel describes
the Kappa's fondness for cucumbers and its interest in sumo wrestling, two
items that will play relevant roles in Goto's fiction.

As a trickster, the Kappa serves a variety of functions in Goto's novel.
First, because it is a water creature, it sets off the displacedness and isolation of the Japanese characters in the dry landscape of the Canadian prairies.
It is a mark of their race and ethnicity, and one of a range of symbols of
the East–West encounter in the novel. Its timeless voice interacts with the
contemporary plot of the narrator and her family. Second, its connection
with water also awakens psychoanalytical associations with human sexuality, and thus the Kappa appears in Goto's novel as a sexually attractive
female stranger, met on the night of the last total lunar eclipse of the twentieth century in Calgary's Chinatown:

> The Stranger was leaning against the wall of the hallway. Wearing a silk red
> wedding dress, snug on her slender body, and slightly worn on the curve of
> a middle-aged belly. A black beret covered an oddly shaped head, strands of
> thin hair hanging long and limp. A heavy leather jacket. In the strange glow
> of the streetlight, the Stranger's complexion looked almost olive.[36]

The Stranger suggests they watch the eclipse, and they end up sumo
wrestling naked on the grounds of the international airport.[37] As the nar-

rator wakes up alone the next morning, she feels an unusual craving for Japanese cucumbers that signals the onset of an even more unusual pregnancy. Although she undergoes a series of tests to determine whether or not the foreign presence in her belly is indeed a baby, obviously no scientific procedure and no human doctor can verify an immaculate conception like the one she claims to have experienced. As the narrative unfolds, it becomes more and more evident that the narrator's is a psychological pregnancy, and that she is bound to give birth only to a renewed self, by overcoming her childhood traumas and accepting her own body and sexual orientation.

As mentioned above, *Salt Fish Girl* also features a mythical creature, Nu Wa, whose voice shares narrative space with a futuristic character, Miranda. Readers learn towards the end of the novel that Nu Wa and Miranda happen to be the same creature in successive reincarnations.[38] All in all, three time periods and two geographical settings are described in Lai's novel: the bank of the Yellow River during a pre-Shang dynasty, where Nu Wa has her original habitat; the late 1800s in South China, where Nu Wa first takes human form as a farmer's daughter; and the second half of the twenty-first century in the North American region of Serendipity and the Unregulated Zone, where Nu Wa is reborn as Miranda. The original Nu Wa is a supernatural water creature like the Kappa, and thus evokes similar sexual echoes:

> Here comes the sound of a river, water rushing in to fill the gap. Here comes the river. Hussssssssh. Shhhhhh. Finger pressed vertically against lips, didn't I tell you? Of course I have lips, a woman's lips, a woman's mouth already muttering secrets under my breath. Look, I have a woman's eyes, woman's rope of smooth black hair extending past my waist. A woman's torso. Your gaze glides over breasts and belly. The softest skin, warm and quivering. And below? Forget modesty. Here comes the tail, a thick cord of muscle undulating, silver slippery in the early morning light. Lean closer and you see the scales, translucent, glinting pinks and greens and oily cobalt blues.[39]

Besides, and again like Goto's Kappa, Nu Wa is connected to a fruit as well, the durian, which, as discussed above, becomes in the novel the perceptible sign of her/Miranda's Asianness, their "essential" difference.

However, and unlike Goto's *The Kappa Child*, *Salt Fish Girl* features a strong sense of history. One must read a kind of historical development in what is, after all, the multi-faceted story of Nu Wa, who decides to mingle with humans out of jealousy for the happiness they experience in sexual bonding. Lai has claimed this is part of an overall project:

> My strategy in recent years has been to make a project of constructing a con-
> sciously artificial history for myself and others like me—a history with women
> identified [as] women of Chinese descent living in the West at its centre.
> [...] It must be artificial because our history is so disparate, and also because
> it has been so historically rare for women to have control over the means of
> recording and dissemination.[40]

It is tempting to read the novel as a bildungsroman, a plot that res-
olutely takes us towards a more enlightened individual who has learnt
from her mistakes, as is the case with Goto's novel. But Lai's, though historically rooted, displays a cyclical development as Nu Wa lives one life
after another, not learning a lot from the incidents in either. Nu Wa's first
life is full of blunders. She proves unable to control her fate, and she is con-
strained by all kinds of obstacles both due to her femaleness and her love
for a woman. Her unwillingness to marry and her choice of spinsterhood
had pained her family, and her mother in particular, and her love affair
with a woman had been outside all social mores. Again and again Nu Wa
fails, unable to meet social expectations for women. Above all, she is isolated, one of a kind.

Nu Wa's second life as Miranda is likewise full of mistakes. Lai con-
trives a similar triangular relationship in both time periods: Nu Wa, the
Salt Fish Girl, and Edwina in the nineteenth-century storyline versus
Miranda, Evie, and Ian Chestnut in the futuristic period. Where both stories greatly differ is in the portrayal of the beloved, whether it is the Salt
Fish Girl or Evie. While the Salt Fish Girl passively worked herself to
blindness and old age in a factory and refused to forgive Nu Wa for her
desertion, Miranda finds in Evie the kind of mentor and teacher that Nu
Wa lacked. Evie is a leader and a rebel who opens Miranda's eyes to the
world around her, and who tries to teach her to act against injustice and
to think through the consequences of her deeds, even while Miranda
repeatedly goes back to conformity and stasis. Miranda herself is aware
of how Evie has influenced her, even if she feels unable to live up to
Evie's expectations: "I grew suddenly aware that I was watching and lis-
tening in a way I had not known how to before," she realizes during an
incident on the bus.[41]

Such a mentor figure is necessary to alert Miranda as well as the readers to the dystopian features of the world she inhabits. It is through her that
Miranda learns that Dr. Rudy Flowers has been engineering clones with the
help of non-human DNA. She describes how Flowers has been selling the
clones for factory work with huge benefits, for these workers are not citizens and therefore have no rights:

"I do know that Nextcorp bought out the Diverse Genome Project around the same time I was born."

"Diverse Genome Project?"

"It focused on the peoples of the so-called Third World, Aboriginal peoples, and peoples in danger of extinction."

"And so all the Workers in the factories [...]"

"Brown eyes and black hair, every single one."

"Stuff like that is not supposed to happen any more."

"Stuff like that never stopped."[42]

Lai thus forcefully points towards the racialization of poverty and the power differential of the First and the Third Worlds that make people of some races expendable, a political purpose for which speculative fiction is a peculiarly suitable vehicle. However, information is not enough. Miranda must learn to her cost how engulfing this system can be, and how difficult it is to resist it. It is only after she has sold her mother's songs for money and a job, and later on, when the experience of being with the powerful has gone to her head so that she betrays even the woman she loves, that she is ready to understand which side she must be on and can take the necessary steps towards her liberation. Once more, she lets herself be guided by Evie, and they leave human society behind in order to embark on a new life together. It is noteworthy that, since the life of women in the West in the twenty-first century offers a wider range of choices, Lai's ending to this storyline is much more hopeful, insofar as Miranda manages to hold on to Evie and they have a child together. Moreover, Miranda and Evie are endowed with the kind of agency that Nu Wa and the Salt Fish Girl had earlier failed to display.

Beyond (Auto)ethnography?

As we have seen, both Hiromi Goto and Larissa Lai have managed to use the speculative form creatively in their fictions, bringing together such diverse features as myth, history, SF proper, dystopia, and pioneer writing. The ensuing hybrid form allows them to interrogate the representation of Asian women's subjectivity, challenging standards of both gender and genre. In their novels, Goto and Lai articulate a multiplicity of subject positions by using a hybrid narrative form that, while sharing some of the objectives of autobiography, resists being labelled as such. Autobiography has been the genre most commonly associated with Asian North American women's writing so far, with the ensuing effects suggested by Asian American critic King-Kok Cheung:

The die-hard tendency to value Asian American works primarily as autobiography or ethnography has perhaps prevented these works from being taken seriously as literature. In tandem with the reading public's preference for autobiographical works is readers' tendency to take selected Asian American texts as representative of an entire ethnic group, a tendency that is reinforced by the current implementation of multiculturalism in the American classroom.[43]

In choosing a generic form outside the realm of autobiography, Lai and Goto are making an effort to free themselves of the burden of representation that weighs on women writers of "visible minorities."[44] Speculative fiction deflects the tendency to read the texts as ethnography by distancing the experiences narrated from the world view of both the author and the reader. In so doing, the writers are effectively escaping from the kind of "ethnic pigeonholing" that other Asian North American authors are riddled with, as Helena Grice has remarked, while still calling into question the politics of racialization.[45]

It should be noted, however, that the authors' use of an alternative, hybrid genre does not indicate their rejection of their cultural and racial heritage or the aims of the autoethnographic project as described at the beginning of this essay. After all, there is not just one form of autoethnography, as Reed-Danahay explicates.[46] First, as described above, both authors successfully braid Asian myths and history in their writing. Second, both novels are firmly rooted in the biological by looking into the performance of ethnicity in a genealogical frame. Rather, what they are resisting are essentialist notions of Asianness, and they do so by developing female characters that are immersed in a constant negotiation of their racialized identities with the dominant culture. Both Goto and Lai move away from an Orientalist portrayal, rendering instead a wealth of subject positions in their Asian characters. As Marilyn Iwama rightly points out concerning Goto:

> As a writer without familial roots in prewar Canadian society, Goto engages with a national discourse that no longer speaks in terms of "the yellow peril." She is, therefore, "free" to engage with a more sophisticated racialization than Kogawa or Takashima or Kitagawa (via Miki) did in the 1970s and 1980s.[47]

Iwama's remarks could apply for Lai as well, since this writer has discussed at some length her views about the politics of writing, or what she describes as "the paradox of claiming a racialized space as a space from which to work":

To claim a racialized space is empowering in that it demands acknowledgement of a history of racism to which the mainstream does not want to admit. It demands acknowledgement of the continued perpetuation of that racism often, though not always, in new forms in the present. On the other hand, to claim that space also confirms and validates that eurocentric racist stance by placing ourselves in opposition to it, enforcing a binarism which itself is a Western social construct.[48]

The aim is not just to disclose the dynamics of race from a biological approach, but to look into constructed bonds. Thus, *The Kappa Child* and *Salt Fish Girl* depict communities of women with a biological basis (siblings, clones) together with erotic (homosexual) relations. The intergenerational and the intragenerational approach blend in the two novels, therefore providing a complex view of the relations of the self and the community that opens up new and wider forms of (auto)ethnography.

NOTES

1 I wish to thank the Department of Foreign Affairs and International Trade for the Canadian Studies Institutional Research Program 2004 award to the research project on "Transnational Poetics: Racialized Women Writers of the 1990s" that started me on this line of research. I am also grateful to the organizers and participants in the conference "Beyond Autoethnography: Writing Race and Ethnicity in Canada" held at Wilfrid Laurier University in 2005 for providing a first, and very stimulating, forum for an earlier draft of this paper.

2 John Van Maanen, "The End of Innocence: The Ethnography of Ethnography," in *Representation in Ethnography*, ed. John Van Maanen (London: Sage, 1995), 1–35. He also lists confessional ethnography, dramatic ethnography, and critical ethnographies as other alternative discourses in the discipline.

3 Deborah E. Reed-Danahay, ed., *Auto/Ethnography: Rewriting the Self and the Social* (Oxford: Berg, 1997), 2.

4 Françoise Lionnet, *Autobiographical Voices: Race, Gender, Self-Portraiture* (Ithaca, NY: Cornell UP, 1989), 99.

5 Lionnet, *Autobiographical Voices*, xii.

6 Tom Moylan, *Demand the Impossible: Science Fiction and the Utopian Imagination* (New York and London: Methuen, 1986), 35.

7 Jane Donaworth, *Frankenstein's Daughters: Women Writing Science Fiction* (Syracuse, NY: Syracuse UP, 1997), xviii. Shelley's legacy has also been the subject of Debra Benita Shaw's *Women, Science, and Fiction: The* Frankenstein *Inheritance* (London: Palgrave, 2000).

8 Joshua Fishman, "Ethnicity as Being, Doing, and Knowing," in *Ethnicity*, ed. John Hutchinson and Anthony D. Smith (Oxford: Oxford UP, 1996), 63–66.

9 Patrick Parrinder, "Science Fiction: Metaphor, Myth or Prophecy?," in *Science Fiction: Critical Frontiers*, ed. Karen Sayer and John Moore (London: Macmillan, 2000), 23–34, 27–28.

10 Ibid.

11 See Donna Haraway, "A Cyborg Manifesto: Science, Technology, and Socialist-Feminism in the Late Twentieth Century," in *Simians, Cyborgs and Women: The Reinvention of Nature* (New York; Routledge, 1991), 149–181; particularly 173ff. for this topic.

12 On this subject, see Robyn Morris, "'What Does It Mean to Be Human?' Racing Monsters, Clones and Replicants," *Foundation: The International Review of Science Fiction* 33 (2004): 81–96.

13 Sandra Harding, "'... Race?': Toward the Science Question in Global Feminisms," in *Whose Science? Whose Knowledge? Thinking from Women's Lives* (Ithaca, NY: Cornell UP, 1991), 215.

14 Jenny Wolmark, *Aliens and Others: Science Fiction, Feminism and Postmodernism* (Hemel Hempstead, UK: Harvester Wheatsheaf, 1994), 27.

15 Donaworth, *Frankenstein's Daughters*, 43.

16 By "imagined community" I am referring to Benedict Anderson's concept of the nation as the community their members can imagine themselves as being part of. See Benedict Anderson, *Imagined Communities: Reflections on the Origin and Spread of Nationalism* (London: Verso, 1991).

17 Hiromi Goto, *The Kappa Child* (Calgary: Red Deer Press, 2001), 29.

18 Ibid., 128.

19 Ibid., 108.

20 Ibid., 43.

21 Ibid., 188–89.

22 The idea of the alien is characteristic of Goto's writing. It appears in manifold guises in her work, for example, in her approach to monstrosity in her collection of short stories *Hopeful Monsters* (2004).

23 Goto, *The Kappa Child,* 268.

24 Ibid., 274–75.

25 Larissa Lai, *Salt Fish Girl* (Toronto: Thomas Allen, 2002), 23.

26 Ibid., 90–1.

27 Tara Lee, "Mutant Bodies in Larissa Lai's *Salt Fish Girl*: Challenging the Alliance between Science and Capital," *West Coast Line* 44 (2004): 94.

28 Lai, *Salt Fish Girl*, 228.

29 Incidentally, parthenogenesis has been a feature of feminist science fiction since its inception. See, for example, Mary E. Bradley Lane's *Mizora: A World of Women* (1881) and Charlotte Perkins Gilman's *Herland* (1915).

30 Lai, *Salt Fish Girl*, 256.

31 For some of these contradictions, see Guy Beauregard, "A Glimpse of Something" (Review of *Salt Fish Girl*), *Canadian Literature* 181 (2004): 149–50.

32 Lee, "Mutant Bodies in Larissa Lai's *Salt Fish Girl*," 108.

33 Lai, *Salt Fish Girl*, 259.

34 Yoshio Iwamoto has pointed out its "ample science fiction elements" in "*The Kappa Child*," *World Literature Today* 77, no. 1 (2003): 102.

35 "Tiptree Award to Hiromi Goto," *Science Fiction Chronicle* 24, no. 7 (2002): 4.

36 Goto, *The Kappa Child*, 88.

37 The location suggests the notion of space travel and therefore highlights the science fiction elements of the tale. It is noteworthy, too, that the narrator's mother later claims to have been an alien abductee for many years.

38 This happens in the chapter entitled "A Seed," (205–9), which describes Nu Wa's leaving the ocean to coil herself around the seed of a durian that Miranda's mother will later eat.

39 Lai, *Salt Fish Girl*, 1–2.
40 Larissa Lai, "Political Animals and the Body of History," *Canadian Literature* 163 (1999): 145–54.
41 Lai, *Salt Fish Girl*, 165.
42 Ibid., 160.
43 King-Kok Cheung, "Re-viewing Asian American Literary Studies," in *An Interethnic Companion to Asian American Literature*, ed. King-Kok Cheung (Cambridge: Cambridge UP, 1997), 19.
44 See Eleanor Ty, *The Politics of the Visible in Asian North American Narratives* (Toronto: U of Toronto P, 2004), for a wide-ranging analysis of the manifold issues concerning the (in)visibility of the Asian North American subject.
45 Helena Grice, *Negotiating Identities: An Introduction to Asian American Women's Writing* (Manchester: Manchester UP, 2002), 83. See the whole of chapter 3, "Genre and Identity," pp. 76–102, for a comprehensive overview of the main issues involving genre in Asian North American writing.
46 Reed-Danahay, *Auto/Ethnography*, 2–9.
47 Marilyn Iwama, "Fantasy's Trickster," *Canadian Literature* 180 (2004): 139.
48 Lai, "Political Animals and the Body of History," 149.

chapter six

"Auto-hyphen-ethno-hyphen-graphy"
Fred Wah's Creative-Critical Writing

Joanne Saul

I n his creative and critical writing alike, poet and critic Fred Wah manages to be both writer and reader in a way that collapses the distance between these two activities and encourages new reading practices. Wah uses the term "poetics"

> not in the theoretical sense of the study of or theory about literature, but in its practical and applied sense, as the tools designed or located by writers and artists to initiate movement and change. That is, "poetics as a sort of *applied poetic*, in the sense that engineering is a form of applied mathematics."[1]

Wah insists on a practical and applied poetics that has the potential to subvert academic authority and to "make things happen."[2] One way Wah's writing "makes things happen" is by what he calls "clanging a noisy hyphen" or animating or "actualizing" the space *between*. For Wah this space includes the space between Chinese and Canadian, between reading and writing, between poetry and narrative, between father and son, between past and present, between public and private, and, as we will see, between photograph and text. Because of its intense focus on the in-between and the problematization of settled assumptions in terms of subjectivity, ethnicity, and genre, Wah's writing engages with many of the issues raised by the term "autoethnography." In fact, by animating all three parts of this complex compound word—"auto," "ethno," and "graphy"—and refusing to let them settle, Wah situates his writing not "beyond autoethnography," but rather he deepens and complicates the project of autoethnography by situating his own writing practice firmly in the middle of it.

There are different ways of thinking about "autoethnography," both as a term and as a practice. The term raises important questions about who is speaking, for whom, and why. It also points to the intersections between autobiography and ethnography and highlights the relationships among self, culture, and writing. Mary Louise Pratt explores the concept in her book *Imperial Eyes*, a study that she describes as her "attempt to suggest a dialectic and historicized approach to travel writing."[3] In her introduction she sets out the three main terms that she manufactures and engages with throughout her study. They are "contact zone," a term that Wah himself makes use of in a number of his works, including his "biotext," *Diamond Grill*; "Anticonquest"; and "autoethnography" or "autoethnographic expression." According to Pratt, "autoethnography" refers to "instances in which colonized subjects undertake to represent themselves in ways that *engage with* the colonizer's own terms. If ethnographic texts are a means by which Europeans represent to themselves their (usually subjugated) others, autoethnographic texts are those the others construct in response to or in dialogue with those metropolitan representations."[4] For Pratt, "autoethnography" is an oppositional term; it is a response to and an interrogation of the authority invested in metropolitan representations, or representations from the so-called "centre."

Importantly, in her work Pratt emphasizes that, in spite of their responsive nature, autoethnographic texts are not "authentic" or autochthonous forms of self-representation; rather they "involve partial collaboration with and appropriation of the idioms of the conqueror," particularly the idioms of travel and exploration writing, that are "merged or infiltrated to varying degrees with indigenous modes."[5] Thus, according to Pratt, "autoethnographic texts are typically heterogeneous on the reception end as well, usually addressed both to metropolitan readers and to literate sectors of the speaker's own social group, and bound to be received very differently by each."[6] In other words, they are necessarily a hybrid form of representation. Joel Martineau has pointed out that one of the troubling aspects of Pratt's definition is that it emphasizes only the "moment of entry into the colonizer's world of textual production"[7] and tends to ignore the long history of production prior to colonization. As a result Pratt's formulation "posits the colonized in a reactive mode, oversimplifying their scope for agency and creativity."[8] In an even more comprehensive critique of Pratt's "exclusively anti-colonialist autoethnography," James Buzard suggests that "the practice of something discernible as autoethnography is derived solely from the identity of the author in the dichotomy between colonizer and colonized."[9] Even more troubling, in Martineau's view, is that in spite of the

interconnectedness or hybrid nature of these expressions, Pratt's definition still maintains the binaristic idea of the "East/tradition" and
"West/modernity." Such binaristic thinking does not adequately capture
the complexity or the multiplicity of subject positions that a writer like
Wah insists upon exploring in his writing.

Nonetheless, Pratt's term does begin to examine the power relations at
work in traditional examples of ethnographic representation and foregrounds the textual nature of these representations. In fact, Pratt also suggests that these autoethnographical expressions are most likely to occur in
the contact zone. A "contact perspective," says Pratt, "emphasizes how
subjects are constituted in and by their relations to each other. It treats
the relations among colonizers and colonized, or travelers and travelees,
not in terms of separateness or apartheid, but in terms of co-presence,
interaction, interlocking understandings and practices, often within radically asymmetrical relations of power."[10] In *The Location of Culture* Homi
Bhabha refers to this ambivalent space of these cultural productions as the
"third Space of enunciation." Bhabha argues that the cultural production
that arises from this ambivalent or in-between space makes any claim to
cultural purity untenable. Bhabha suggests that this space is a reminder that
"in the productivity of power, the boundaries of authority—its reality
effects—are always besieged by 'the other scene' of fixations and phan-
toms."[11] Such theorizations of the contact zone have reverberations with
the kind of in-betweenness that Wah also explores in his writing.

Françoise Lionnet's description of autoethnography picks up on this
sense of co-presence and interaction, rejecting any notion of authentic self-
representation.[12] Focusing specifically on the writing of Zora Neale Hurston,
Lionnet suggests that the book "*Dust Tracks* does not gesture toward a
coherent tradition of introspective self-examination with soul-baring displays of emotion; despite its rich cultural content, the work does not author-
ize unproblematic recourse to culturally grounded interpretations."[13] Later
she argues that "the resulting text/performance thus transcends pedes-
trian notions of referentiality, for the staging of the event is part of the
process of 'passing on,' of elaborating cultural forms which are not static
and inviolable but dynamically involved in the creation of culture itself."[14]
In Lionnet's reading of autoethnography, the "self," and particularly the
"racial self," is seen as a fluid, changing, and performative concept. Lionnet calls autoethnography a form of métissage or cultural creolization that
"opens up a space of resistance between the individual (auto-) and the
collective (-ethno-) where the writing (-graphy) of singularity cannot be
foreclosed."[15] For Lionnet, métissage involves the negotiation of multiple

relations of gender, race, language, class, and nationality. It implies a productive space that avoids the binary of self/other and allows for new articulations of self.

In a more recent collection of essays on autoethnography, Deborah Reed-Danahay suggests that several key concerns emerge through the study of the practice: "questions of identity and selfhood, of voice and authenticity, and of cultural displacement and exile."[16] In his creative-critical work, Wah engages similar issues: he interrogates the sanctity of the unified subject by proposing that the subject is much more than the sum of identities; he gives life and breadth to the "contact zone" so that singular notions of culture (and community) are challenged, and his creative-critical practice explores new ways of writing and provokes new ways of reading that are both productive and animating. His blurring of the lines between the creative and the critical is one way he animates his writing practice. For example, in his introduction to his collection of essays for NeWest Press's "Writer as Critic" series, *Faking It*, Wah writes:

> I think of the essay in the sense of something one tries out, or on. That's why the language and methods of poetry have always seemed right to me; they push at the boundaries of thinking; they play in the noise and excess of language; they upset and they surprise. To write critically I've always written poetry.[17]

Wah's thoughts on his creative-critical writing echo those of his friend Charles Bernstein in several volumes of "essays," collected variously in *My Way*, *A Poetics*, and *Content's Dream*. For example, describing the contents of *My Way*, Bernstein writes:

> The book is arranged so as to put at play formal and thematic relations that cut across the selections. There are essays in poetic lines and prose that incorporates poetics motifs, there are interviews that mime speech and speeches that veer into song. The idea is to put a wide, yet decisive, range of styles into conversation with one another. The point is not to break down generic distinctions as much as to bring genres and styles into rhetorical play with one another.[18]

He refers to his creative-critical writing as "Not unstructured essays but differently structured: not structurally challenged, structurally challenging."[19] Similarly, Wah is uncomfortable with the very idea of a collection of essays, hence the title that he chooses for his collection, *Faking It*. According to Wah, faking it "is a gesture in composition that has consequences for a poetics of equivocation, of betweenness, of hybridity."[20]

More collage than collection, *Faking It* collects two decades of his writing on poetics, including his series of previously published "Poetics" essays

("A Poetics of Ethnicity," "Half-Bred Poetics," "Racing the Lyric Poetic," "Poetics of the Potent," "A Molecular Poetics"), an interview with Ashok Mathur (previously published online and in Mathur's *Filling Station*), and a short "biofiction" arranged in conjunction with a series of black and white photographs. "Strang(l)ed Poetics," offers an inventory of contemporary Canadian poetics, that includes descriptions of proprioceptive verse, the contestatory long poem, and something Wah calls "Trans=geo-ethno=poetics." Interspersed throughout the more conventional essays in *Faking It* are a series of what Wah refers to as "Strangles," short pieces that serve to disrupt generic classification by accosting the boundaries of criticism and autobiography, poetry and prose.

Three of the pieces in *Faking It* reflect Wah's interest in Chinese avantgarde poetry. These "essays" allow Wah to probe a different cultural context in order to further trouble the role of nation in the making of a non-thematic, non-representational poetics. Grouping together a more conventional essay, an interview, and a series of journal entries that document his experiences in China, he foregrounds the diverse entry points that inform his investigation. The "journal journey" describes food and drink as well as conversations and ruminations about poetry, power, and cultural identity. Interspersed with the journal entries are poems (usually separating the entries) that cover material similar to that found in the prose, but serve to distill Wah's experiences and thoughts, seemingly as he is having them. The poems flow less easily than the prose because there are fewer connecting words as the words follow one another like a list. The content of the poems thus appears less distilled, more immediate:

> cloisonné fish
> in the restaurant
> shell fish
> for lunch
> dao fu
> rice w/ cold dish
> of cucumber salad
> slightly picked
> words silent
> beyond the window
> bike stand
> pay for it[21]

The positioning of the poems on the page demands that the reader take notice of the process of writing at work. Several of the essays are dedicated to colleagues and fellow writers. These pieces seem to open onto a.

conversation in midstream. For example, Wah grounds a posthumous and intimate "dialogue" with his friend, the poet bp nichol, in a discussion of nichol's "last notebook." "Dear Hank" is an essay-letter to Hank Lazer; "Loose Change" engages the poetic concerns of Louis Cabri in a discussion of the materiality of language. All three pieces read like conversations already in process, and although they may not openly invite the reader into the critical conversation, they do clearly convey a key principle that characterizes the text as a whole: a deep commitment to a processural poetics. And it is this focus on how the text is put together and on the actual look of the words on the page that helps to animate the "graphy" or the writing component of "autoethnography." Wah is highly self-conscious about the act of writing difference.

In fact, throughout the collection Wah demonstrates how pushing the limits of inherited literary forms has, for him, always been an explicitly political act. In his series of "Poetics" essays, Wah argues that race disrupts genre so that politics and poetics are closely entwined. In his essay "A Poetics of Ethnicity," Wah explores the necessity for a poetics of difference and argues how a tactics of refusal and reterritorialization can "enable a particular residue (genetic, cultural, biographical) to become kinetic and valorized."[22] In "Speak My Language: Racing the Lyric Poetic," he says, "I'm interested in how the colouring of the negotiations, with whatever thread of the inherited lyric, has consequence for a socially informed poetic (not a politics of identity but a praxis in language)."[23] This link between language and politics is similarly expressed by Sherry Simon, who argues that "literary language is not a given, but always an expression of affiliation or transgression."[24] Roy Miki also reinforces the transgressive potential of language when he suggests that "displacement calls for a language to enunciate the radical non-teleological shiftings that perform the present tense or the tense present 'we' are in."[25] Similarly, Myrna Kostash suggests that embracing a poetics of estrangement is an important strategy for ethnic minority writers who wish to foreground their difference from a perceived mainstream: "We may not wish to belong to the club. We may wish to live with tension and distress. We may wish to remind ourselves, over and over, that we live on the wrong side of the tracks, on the edge of town."[26] In other words, a seamless blending in or wanting to belong to some kind of hegemonic writing practice is not the goal of writers such as Wah. He self-consciously writes his difference into his texts by embracing what he calls a non-aligned poetics of ethnicity: "this principle of synchronous foreignicity, of embracing antithesis, polarity, confusion, and opposition as the day-to-day household harmony, is a necessary implement in art that looks for new organizing principles, new narratives."[27]

Although many of the essays in *Faking It* have been previously published, in typical Wah fashion, he has rethought and recast individual essays to reflect his own developing sense of an oppositional poetics. For example, earlier assumptions about estrangement in poetry are qualified by a developing awareness of gender and race. As a result, the collection as a whole documents the "collision" of two extremely important movements in Canadian poetry: the *Tish* poetics of the late 1960s and the growing corpus of racialized and feminist poetics that also began to emerge in Canada in the 1970s.[28] Situated at the centre of these movements, Wah's writing shows how they could in fact complement one another in their questioning of the mainstream.[29] Wah says, "I've grown accustomed to various poetics (improvisational, ethno, the long poem, prose poem, and so forth) as a means to contest the social branding and stranding I felt hailed and held by."[30] As Jeff Derksen explains, Wah's poetry is a challenge to mainstream writing, both poetically and politically:

> The disunity of alienethnic poetics resists normative narrative strategies. This distrust of literary structures parallels a distrust of larger social structures as these structures have rendered writers of colour invisible through assimilation. In this way, narrative is also read as a social structure.[31]

Derksen explores how critical attention to Wah's avant-garde poetics has meant that his work has never been read as reflecting his working-class Chinese-Canadian background. The splitting of form and content has, in the past, set up a binary that separated his racial identity from his poetry. Ignoring this component of Wah's work ignores his ongoing commitment to a poetics of autoethnography. In contrast, Derksen suggests that Wah's racialized identity has always been so deeply embedded within his poetics that the two cannot be separated. In other words, Wah maintains an interest in deepening the project of autoethnography.

This is certainly the case when we look at other examples of Wah's creative-critical writings, including his recent "ramble," "Is a Door a Word?" a piece collected in the special issue of *Mosaic* on "The Photograph." While ostensibly an essay on the "photo-text" (both his own and others,' particularly Roy Kiyooka's "Pacific Windows") as a genre (or anti-genre), this piece is, at the same time, an example of Wah's strategy of writing as reading, and it demonstrates his ability to open up the space of writing as a space of creative potential. Like *Faking It* and *Diamond Grill*, "Is a Door a Word?" is a collage, and difficult to define generically. His term "ramble" (like "strangle," "biotext," and "biofiction") demonstrates his unease with genre in general and the form of the essay in particular. He incorporates both his own and other people's photographs, cover photography from books, excerpts from family albums, poetry, and prose. He mixes fragments of *utanikki* (Japanese travel diary); autobiography; and "biotext," fragments— from various chapbooks (including his latest, *Isadora Blew*), from *Faking It*, from *Diamond Grill*, from *Pictographs from the Interior of B.C.*, from *Tree*, from a collaboration with Mexican photographer Eric Jervaise in the Yucatan and in Banff.

These diverse fragments help to emphasize the importance of collaboration, or working with others. The piece is filled with intertexts. But most important is the way he acknowledges the influence of others on his work, including Daphne Marlatt, Roy Kiyooka, Marian Penner-Bancroft, Robert Kroetsch, and Eric Jervaise. This is also a recurring thread in Wah's work; from his early days as a *Tish* poet, to the collaborations with fellow long poets, to more recent collaborations with a generation of younger poets and students, he locates himself within a group of writers that feed his writing practice. He says, "I like the measure of words reading one's contemporaries reveals."[32] In the process, he destabilizes the notion of the "writer/critic," not only by questioning the very form of the essay, but also by inserting himself into other people's texts (for example, he quite literally photographs himself into Roy Kiyooka's photographs) and he undermines the distance and the objectivity traditionally associated with the critical stance as he becomes both reader and writer, reading others and even writing himself into others' writings. As Andy Weaver argues, Wah's "emphasis on response blurs one of the fundamental boundaries of subjectivity, that of personal, singular authorship; by foregrounding the dialogic relationship between his poems and the texts of other writers, Wah implicitly argues against the self/Other binary."[33] This breaking down of the binary between self and other further demonstrates Wah's preoccupation with evoking the complexities of giving voice to autoethnography.

Throughout the "essay," Wah reflects on the relationship between photo and text, between image and word, drawing attention once again to the interface or the "contact zone" between them. In other words, "Is a Door a Word?" is in effect a "ramble" on hyphenation or in-betweenness and its creative or animating potential. Because the "essay" highlights so many of Wah's concerns, both poetic and political, it is an example of what Wah has elsewhere called a "RE" Poetics, a rewriting and recontextualization of one's own writing.[34] As he himself admits in the opening, "this is a poetry photography reading (in two senses) that I hope inflects some of the lexicon of hybridity, a topic that is crucial to me as a mixed-blood person and as a writer. I've been writing about, in, and around it for years so please forgive me if I sound a little repetitive."[35] His inclusion of fragments of his own previously published writing (including *Tree*, *Pictograms from the Interior of B.C.*, *Faking It*, *Diamond Grill*, and *When I Was Eight*) serves to emphasize the "processural" and cumulative nature of his writing and gives the sense that he is always adding to, amending, reflecting on what he's already written. Poems from his earlier collections show up again and again throughout his oeuvre, revised and rewritten so that similar content is filtered and reworked from different angles within different contexts. For example, the same passage from the poem "from MOUNTAIN" appears in *Lardeau* (1965), *Mountain* (1967), *Among* (1972), and *Loki Is Buried at Smoky Creek* (1980). Similar rewriting occurs in *Breathin' My Name with a Sigh* (1981), *Waiting for Saskatchewan* (1985), and *Diamond Grill*. In "Is a Door a Word?" fragments of past works are included without introduction or commentary; it is their relational quality—how they play off other fragments of text—and their ability to illustrate important concepts that make them such a crucial part of the ongoing "ramble." For example, Wah draws connections between Kiyooka's work on the photoglyph in his "Notes toward a Book of Photoglyphs" and his own use of the pictogram in *Pictograms from the Interior of B.C.* Both, according to Wah, cut "across the contact zone of form to intervent."[36]

Perhaps most importantly, however, throughout the essay, Wah makes a number of signature moves that help to illustrate how his poetics, with its exploration (and challenge to) established notions of the unified self, culture, and writing, engages with a critical term like "autoethnography." For one thing, the sanctity of the self or the "auto" is interrogated, not only by his insistence on dialogue and collaboration, as we have seen, but also in his exploration of subjectivity as a complex construction. Reed-Danahay suggests that the questioning of a coherent, individual self is one of the integral components of contemporary autoethnography.[37] Although Wah's distrust of the lyric subject goes back to his early *Tish*-inspired poetry, it becomes even more pronounced as he begins to negotiate his mixed-race identity in his writing. A third-generation Canadian of a mixed-blood background, in his writing Wah makes tangible a long (albeit fractured and disrupted) Chinese-Canadian history in the prairies and the interior of British Columbia. His father, who was raised in China, was of Chinese-Scots-Irish descent. His mother, who was born in Sweden, was raised in Swift Current, Saskatchewan. "When you're not pure," says Wah in his poetic diary, "Grasp the Sparrow's Tale," "you just make it up."[38] In part because of his mixed-race background, he is acutely aware that identity is always in process, always shifting. Wah thus resists being categorized as "other" in any stable way. This resistance comes from eluding other people's categories and challenging the motives behind their construction. For example, throughout his most recent chapbook, *Isadora Blew*, Wah refers to himself as "Mr. In-Between." In "Is a Door a Word?" Wah explores the creative energy of in-betweenness by referring to himself as "me too" or "me two."[39] The "twoness" resists the closure of "either-or-ness." He chooses to negotiate the both/and as opposed to the either/or. He goes on to describe this condition: "a ME-ness, however, that wants to be there, in between, furnishing that place with its own 'astonishments.' ME. TOO. and ME. TWO. Always need 2 to make anything move—and that between ness is more than its polarities, always in and on, the move."[40]

Wah's reference to "Me too" in this context is also his response to his re-situating himself within a photo-text by his friend Roy Kiyooka. Wah describes how, in a series of photos taken by Kiyooka projected on a wall of a gallery, Wah walks between the projector and the wall and discovers himself as part of the passing scene. Using his digital camera he photographs himself into the street-scene captured by Kiyooka. The result is the shadowy figure of Wah both "of" and, at the same time, "not of" Kiyooka's original piece. Wah's reconfiguring of Kiyooka's photograph raises a number of interesting points about the relationship of the artist to his work and about the function of time and memory in photography as well as breaking down the self/other binary in his autoethnographic practice. Sheryl Conkleton has argued that in many of Kiyooka's photo-texts, he makes himself present so that the "eye/I" of the camera is involved in the scene. According to Reed-Danahay, autoethnography is "a useful term with which to question the binary conventions of a self/society split, as well as the boundary between the objective and the subjective"[41] Referring to a number of Kiyooka's photo-texts, Conkleton suggests, "What he expressed in his multiple image series, sequences, and grids was himself as the individual who both saw and then rewrote what he saw."[42] Kiyooka's work thus collapses the distance between the artist and his subject. By inserting his own image into Kiyooka's photograph, Wah continues this effect. He makes explicit the more implicit "eye/I" present in Kiyooka's work and enacts Kiyooka's own "business of art," which is, "to live in the complete actual present, the complete actual present, and to express the complete actual present."[43] By inserting himself into Kiyooka's photographs, Wah also demonstrates how the photograph can take on new and different meanings over time and how the perceiver of the photograph changes the meaning of the photograph as he experiences it. Here again Wah as autoethnographer interrogates the separation between reader and writer as he rereads and therefore rewrites the original photographic moment.

Another way that Wah manages to capture the sense of the construct-edness of his mixed-race identity and evoke the complexities of autoethnog-raphy is through the self-conscious negotiation of his past or autobiography. As in *Faking It* (and *Diamond Grill*), fragments of autobiography or "bio-text" are woven into the essay. These fragments of life story are non-lin-ear, in motion. Different parts of his past surface and resurface so that it feels to the reader as though the "self" in this "ramble" is one that is becom-ing. He is figuring things out as he goes along. He filters the past through photos and through stories, through collaborations and through memory. He includes parts of his photographic biofiction "When I Was Eight" (a piece that was "originally" a chapbook and was later included in *Faking It*); photos from the family album are lined up alongside text that sometimes corresponds in some way to the images, but often doesn't. For example, the caption, "When I was eight we had a black 1940 Ford two-door coupe with whitewalls and a radio," is lined up beside an image of a 1940 Ford coupe. However, the next caption,

> About a month after my eighth birthday somebody tried to beat up Ernie in the middle of the road on Third avenue but I punched the big kid in the chin then he grabbed me and we landed on the hard snow of the road and rolled around until Ernie shouted watch out here comes the bus up the hill

is aligned with an obviously posed photograph of Wah with his brother Ernie and their mother, all smiling. The photo admits nothing of the drama of the caption.[44]

This playful manipulation of the "photo-text" is another way that Wah experiments with the telling of stories or the constructiveness of narrative. As John Berger has suggested,

> [i]n the relationship between a photograph and words, the photograph begs for an interpretation, and the words usually supply it. The photograph, irrefutable as evidence but weak in meaning, is given a meaning by the words. And the words, which by themselves remain at the level of generalization, are given specific authenticity by the irrefutability of the photograph. Together the two then become very powerful; an open question appears to be fully answered.[45]

However, in Wah's work, the effect of the gap between text and image is somewhat disconcerting, undercutting the literalness of reference, so that the text does not reconstruct the image, rather it creates something new. And such gaps make the reader/viewer work harder, as she reflects on what this gap between image and text might mean. Wah's play with the fam-ily album also raises further questions about the nature of the photograph and the workings of memory, about how the visual contributes to the verbalization of experience, and how pictures play a role in storytelling but cannot tell the whole story. In the process of negotiating the complex relationship between photo and text, the reader turns into a kind of co-creator or collaborator in the work and Wah again carries out the challenge to the self-other binary that is implicit in the practice of autoethnograpy.[46] As Reed-Danahay argues, "the notion of autoethnography foregrounds the multiple nature of selfhood and opens up new ways of writing about social life."[47]

At the same time that any stable version of self or "auto" is being undercut in Wah's ramble, any stable sense of "ethnos" is also difficult to pin down, because the focus on hybridity or on the in-between complicates notions of purity or sameness, centre or margin, self and other. In other words, the second part of the term "auto-ethno-graphy" is negotiated throughout the ramble. As we have seen, Wah refers explicitly to Pratt's work on transculturation in *Diamond Grill*. In "Half-Bred Poetics" Wah refers to Bhabha's work on hybridity and ends with a quotation from Pratt's *Imperial Eyes* that describes the contact zone and a contact perspective. Closely related to theories of hybridity, theories of diaspora also inform Wah's writing. In this respect he is in dialogue with theorists such as Stuart Hall who interrogate where diasporic subjects speak from and the various factors that complicate a unified speaking position. However, as Cynthia Sugars argues, Wah's writing also serves to interrogate theories of diaspora that accept the "constitutive split between the 'centrifugal homeland' and a 'yearning for a sense of belonging to the current place of abode.'"[48] Wah is able to "subvert the identity/hybridity dialectic," suggests Sugars, "by giving voice to an experience of diaspora that is not limited by singular identity constructions, even as his focus remains of the historical contingencies and continuities of diasporic experience."[49] Again Wah breaks down binaries by focusing on the multiplicity of identifications implicit in his practice of autoethnography.

Wah's theorizing of his racial and ethnic identifications has also led him to engage in debates about the nation in contemporary Canadian literature and criticism. He rejects what he sees as "a nationalistic aesthetic that continually attempts to expropriate difference into its own consuming narrative"[50] and engages instead in debates around the constructedness of the Canadian nation and the role of the nation-state in the subject's identification. Cultural nationalism is not considered enabling by Wah. For Wah the idea of Canada is a dangerous one. He claims for himself its margins:

I don't want to be inducted into someone else's story, or project. Particularly one that would reduce and usurp my family's residue of ghost values to a status quo. Sorry, but I'm just not interested in this collective enterprise erected from the sacrosanct great railway imagination dedicated to harvesting a dominant white cultural landscape.[51]

According to Reed-Danahay, his stance is a particularly autoethnographic one: "The most cogent aspect to the study of autoethnography is that of cultural displacement or situation of exile characteristic of the themes expressed by autoethnographers. This phenomenon of displacement.... [b]reaks down dualisms of identity and insider-outsider status."[52] In "A Poetics of Ethnicity," Wah suggests that "the tactical imagination of a 'national unity' is, for some writers, a 'disunity.'"[53] Instead he locates the hyphen—the in-between—as the site of contestation about fixed identities. This space, argues Wah, "could be the answer in this country": "If you're pure anything you can't be Canadian. We'll save that name for all the mixed bloods in this country and when the cities have Heritage Days and ethnic festivals there'll be a group I can identify with, the Canadians."[54] Wah's focus on the local, a focus that in fact goes back to his *Tish*-inspired poetry, helps to challenge all-consuming narratives of nation. In *Faking It* he writes, "That's it, the local. What is meant in the west by the term regional. The immediate 'here,' the palpable, tangible 'here,' imprinted with whatever trailing cellular memory, histology, history, story."[55] In his ramble Wah includes the description of his father's café with its "long green vinyl aisle between booths of chrome, Naugahyde, and formica"[56] as well as images and a poem from his collection *Tree*, a collection grounded in the particulars of southeast British Columbia. By incorporating descriptions of Kiyooka's photo-texts into "Is a Door a Word?" he also evokes a rootedness in the neighbourhood around Hastings Street in Vancouver.

Central to Wah's questioning of identity—ethnic, raced, and national—are the act of writing and the use of language, the third part of the term "auto-ethno-graphy." He is highly self-conscious about his use of language as a means of destabilization. His earlier collections of poetry, including *Lardeau, Mountain, Among*, and *Tree*, show the influence of Black Mountain poets such as Olson, Creeley, and Duncan. Wah not only attended the 1963 Vancouver Poetry Conference, at which he was introduced to the poetry of Olson, he later went on to study with Olson at the State University of New York. Although most often associated with projective verse theory and its practitioners, Wah's poetry is also influenced by the Language poetry that emerged in the mid 1970s. This poetry endorsed Victor Shlovsky's notion of *ostranenie* or "making strange," by which the instrumental function of language is diminished and the objective character of words foregrounded. In his essay "Strang(l)ed Poetics" Wah cites Shlovsky's "oft-quoted" statement about the function of a work of art:

> And art exists that one may recover the sensation of life; it exists to make one feel things, to make the stone stony. The purpose of art is to impart the sensation of things as they are perceived and not as they are known. The technique of art is to make objects "unfamiliar," to make forms difficult, to increase the difficulty and length of perception because the process of perception is an aesthetic end in itself and must be prolonged. Art is a way of experiencing the artfulness of an object; the object is not important.[57]

Most important, in terms of its influence on Wah's work, is the relationship that Language poetry attempts to set up with the reader: "one based less on the recuperation of a generically or stylistically encoded work and more on the reader's participation in a relatively open text."[58] In other words, Language poets confound readers' expectations of a text by focusing attention on the language itself rather than on language as a vehicle for meaning. Bernstein describes it thus: "I want to materialize the word, create a work in which the words remain audible, rather than unsounded and invisible."[59] For Wah, as Bowering suggests, "Language is not a vehicle on which to ride into the mossy backwoods"; instead "home is where the story is."[60] Throughout Wah's poetry, language is not used to describe a reality "out there." Language and reality are closely entwined.

Similarly, language is a site of play in "Is a Door a Word?" Throughout the ramble there is an intense focus on words and sounds of words; repetition of words ("is a door wood / is a door a board / is a door barred / is a door abhorred / is a door locked / is a door shocked / is a door cut / is a door shut / is a door a jar / is a door a lid"), puns, wordplay, compound words, and the breaking down of words into their disparate sounds (and other words—"the Spanglish in anguish/the Sass in disaster"). Columns of words in poems further interrogate syntax so that, as in so much of Wah's writing, there is a creative space of tension here between story and language. This focus on the particulars of language takes attention away from the idea of a finished product in writing so that Wah's ramble is itself tentative, unfinished, in the process of becoming. He quotes Kiyooka, who articulates this same sense of process in his writing: "the narrative I am questing, indeed, veering towards."[61]

As in *Diamond Grill*, the door plays a central role in Wah's ramble. For example, there are echoes of the door in his father's café in *Diamond Grill*: "those kitchen doors can be kicked with such a slap they're heard all the way to the soda fountain."[62] He also includes dozens of photos of doors blown off by hurricane Isadora in Mexico. These blown off doors leave a gap or a space of in-betweenness. In Wah's work, the doorway represents the liminal space of possibility where language may actually create. Cynthia Sugars refers to the function of this "generative space" in *Diamond Grill*: "for the narrator, the swinging doors of the Diamond Grill function not just as a border between 'Occident and Orient,' but as the hyphenated divider and connector between multiple identity markers."[63]

By exploring the relationship of photo and text in a "photo-hyphen-text" (and photoglyph and pictogram), Wah reiterates the importance of the hyphen as a space of immense potential and a tool to reinvigorate the practice of autoethnography. For Wah it is a space of creativity that defies either/or-ness, one that "is more than its polarities, always in and on the move." As Susan Rudy writes, "he pushes for conjunctions and community, for being and beings who are similarly interested in the spaces between, in hybridity, in being among."[64] Referring to the photo-text, Wah says, "Actually it's neither. Picture or Word. But the space between them. A poetics, then, of the hyphen between image and text, the 'actually' not a 'finally' but a between, a hybridity."[65] This focus on the hyphen draws attention to the relationships among the various parts of the term "autoethnography": self and culture and writing. Wah's creative-critical practice engages all three of these terms while querying them. Rather than somehow writing "beyond autoethnography," through his poetics he encourages the reader to question the term, hyphenate it, and then make the hyphen heard: "auto-hyphen-ethno-hyphen-graphy."

NOTES

1   Fred Wah, "A Poetics of Ethnicity," in *Faking It: Poetics and Hybridity* (Edmonton: NeWest Press, 2000), 51.
2   Fred Wah, personal interview with author, May 11, 2000, Toronto.
3   Mary-Louise Pratt, *Imperial Eyes: Travel Writing and Transculturation* (New York: Routledge, 1992), 6.
4   Ibid., 7.
5   Ibid.
6   Ibid.
7   Joel Martineau, "Autoethnography and Material Culture: The Case of Bill Reid," *Biography* 24, no. 1 (Winter 2001): 243.
8   Ibid.
9   James Buzard, "On Auto-Ethnographic Authority," *Yale Journal of Criticism* 16, no. 1 (2003): 61–91.
10 Pratt, *Imperial Eyes*, 7.
11 Bhabha, quoted in Monika Kin Gagnon, *Other Conundrums: Race, Culture, and Canadian Art* (Vancouver: Arsenal Pulp Press, 2000), 43.

12 As has been cited by Kamboureli and others, autoethnography is "the defining of one's subjective ethnicity as mediated through language, history, and ethnographical analysis; in short, [...] a kind of 'figural anthropology' of the self," according to Françoise Lionnet, *Autobiographical Voices: Race, Gender, Self-Portraiture* (Ithaca, NY: Cornell UP, 1989), 99.

13 Ibid., 101.

14 Ibid., 102.

15 Ibid., 108.

16 Deborah Reed-Danahay, *Auto/Ethnography: Rewriting the Self and the Social* (Oxford: Berg, 1997), 3.

17 Wah, introduction to *Faking It*, 1.

18 Charles Bernstein, *My Way: Speeches and Poems* (Chicago: U of Chicago P, 1999), xi.

19 Ibid., 11.

20 Fred Wah and Frank Davey, "Meandering Interview," *Open Letter* 12, no. 3 (Summer 2004): 102.

21 Wah, "China Journal," in *Faking It*, 172–73.

22 Wah, "A Poetics of Ethnicity," in *Faking It*, 51.

23 Wah, "Speak My Language," in *Faking It*, 110.

24 Sherry Simon, "The Language of Difference: Minority Writers in Quebec," in *A/Part*, ed. J.M. Bumsted (Vancouver, *Canadian Literature*, 1987), 121.

25 Roy Miki, "Can I see Your ID?" in *Broken Entries: Race, Subjectivity, Writing* (Toronto: Mercury Press, 1998), 215.

26 Myrna Kostash, "Pens of Many Colours," *Canadian Forum* (June 1990): 19.

27 Fred Wah, "A Poetics of Ethnicity," in *Twenty Years of Multiculturalism: Successes and Failures*, ed. Stella Hryniuk (Winnipeg: St. John's College Press, 1992), 104.

28 The *Tish* poets were a group of writers at the University of British Columbia who founded a newsletter in 1961. They were heavily influenced by the proprioceptive verse of American poets Robert Duncan and Robert Creeley. The *Tish* group marked the beginning of a distinct West Coast writing community.

29 Timothy Yu's work on the intersections of Language poetry and the feminist and multicultural poetics that emerged in the 1960s in the United States is helpful here. In his essay, "Form and Identity in Language Poetry and Asian American Poetry," *Contemporary Literature* 41, no. 3 (Fall 2000): 422–61, he suggests that "the impulses of Language poetry and of minority writing might not be mutually exclusive, but rather complementary," 423–24.

30 Wah and Davey, "Meandering Interview," 120.

31 Jeff Derksen, "Making Race Opaque," *West Coast Line* 29, no. 3 (Winter 1995–96): 74.

32 Fred Wah, "Is a Door a Word?" *Mosaic* 37, no. 4 (2004): 62.

33 Andy Weaver, "Synchronous Foreignicity: Fred Wah's Poetry and the Recuperation of Experimental Texts," *Studies in Canadian Literature* 30, no. 1 (2005): 318–19.

34 Fred Wah, "Poetics of the Potent," in *Faking It*, 203.

35 Wah, "Is a Door a Word?" 39.

36 Ibid., 49.

37 Reed-Danahay, *Auto/Ethnography*, 2.

38 Fred Wah, *Waiting for Saskatchewan* (Winnipeg: Turnstone, 1985), 43.

39 Wah, "Is a Door a Word?" 43.

40 Ibid., 45.

41 Reed-Danahay, *Auto/Ethnography*, 2.

42 Sheryl Conkelton, "Roy Kiyooka '…the sad and glad tidings of the floating world …,'" in *All Amazed for Roy Kiyooka* (Vancouver: Arsenal Pulp Press, 2002), 114.

43 Chris Varley, "Intersections: Interview between Chris Varley and Roy Kiyooka," in *Roy K. Kiyooka: 25 Years* (Vancouver: Vancouver Art Gallery, 1975).

44 Wah, "Is a Door a Word?" 53.

45 John Berger, *Another Way of Telling* (New York: Pantheon Books, 1982), 92.

46 For a further discussion of the relationship between word and image in the photo-text, see W.J.T. Mitchell's *Picture Theory*, Clive Scott's *The Spoken Image: Photography and Language*, and Alex Hughes and Andrea Noble's collection, *Phototextualities*.

47 Reed-Danahay, *Auto/Ethnography*, 3.

48 Cynthia Sugars, "'The Negative Capability of Camouflage': Fleeing Diaspora in Fred Wah's *Diamond Grill*," *Studies in Canadian Literature* 26, no. 1 (2001): 28.

49 Sugars, "'The Negative Capability of Camouflage,'" 29.

50 Fred Wah, "Half-Bred Poetics," in *Faking It*, 75.

51 Fred Wah, *Diamond Grill* (Edmonton: NeWest Press, 1996), 125.

52 Reed-Danahay, *Auto/Ethnography*, 4.

53 Wah, "A Poetics of Ethnicity," in *Faking It*, 66.

54 Wah, *Diamond Grill*, 54.

55 Fred Wah, "Strangle Two," in *Faking It*, 48.

56 Wah, "Is a Door a Word?" 40.

57 Fred Wah, "Strang(l)ed Poetics," in *Faking It*, 24.

58 *The New Princeton Encyclopedia of Poetry and Poetics*, s.v. "Language poetry."

59 Bernstein, *My Way*, 68.

60 George Bowering, introduction to *Loki is Buried at Smoky Creek: Selected Poems*, by Fred Wah, ed. George Bowering (Vancouver: Talonbooks, 1980), 11.

61 Wah, "Is a Door a Word?" 48.

62 Ibid., 40.

63 Sugars, "'The Negative Capability of Camouflage,'" 43.

64 Susan Rudy, "Fred Wah—*Among*," in *Writing in Our Time*, ed. Pauline Butling and Susan Rudy (Waterloo, ON: Wilfrid Laurier UP, 2005), 111.

65 Wah, "Is a Door a Word?" 40.

[part three]

Artistic/Textual/Bodily Politics

chapter seven

Troubling the Mosaic

Larissa Lai's *When Fox Is a Thousand*, Shani Mootoo's
Cereus Blooms at Night, and Representations
of Social Differences

Christine Kim

S hani Mootoo's *Cereus Blooms at Night* (1996) and Larissa Lai's *When Fox Is a Thousand* (1995) both play with readerly expectations of ethnic literature, "moving beyond the politics of identity, beyond what Françoise Lionnet has termed 'autoethnography,' or ethnographic autobiography," and yet these texts have been received critically and commercially in very different ways.[1] Like many other recent texts by ethnic writers, these two novels complicate the connections between individual and cultural identities and ask us to reconsider what is at stake politically in critical engagements with representations of ethnicity. As much as I hope to suggest readings that examine representations of gender and ethnicity in Mootoo's best-known work and Lai's first novel, I also want to provide *readings of their readings,* as a way to "get at" the work these novels perform in the field of Canadian literature. That is, I want to place text and context in dialectical relation to each other to show how, to borrow Pierre Bourdieu's vocabulary, cultural production in Canada is not autonomous from the field of power, but is instead shaped by local and global economic interests as well as the powerful sway of literary taste-makers and dominant academic discourses.[2] I want to focus on the contradiction between feminist small-press production and the postcolonial, in the case of *Cereus Blooms at Night,* or multicultural, in the case of *When Fox Is a Thousand,* politics of consumption to trouble the position of ethnic Canadian fiction within the larger literary field and reflect upon the dominant critical practices that shape how ethnicity is both written and read within Canadian contexts.[3] Reinserting questions of gender back into discussions of these novels reminds us that these are literary texts that trouble multiple kinds of social identities by using a variety of strategies. In an attempt to move away from ethnographic readings of ethnic literature, I want to first consider some of the different factors that encourage reducing ethnic literature to anthropological fieldwork and think about what happens when texts such as Lai's refuse to make such readings possible. My discussion will begin by examining *Cereus Blooms at Night* as a novel that is typically packaged as postcolonial, a move that foregrounds exclusion as it includes it within national culture. The positive response by the mainstream to Mootoo's novel as a postcolonial text implies that part of its symbolic currency stems from its appeal to institutionalized discourses. The ease with which *Cereus Blooms at Night* was embraced by literary institutions suggests an effort to normalize and contain difference within specific frames. After examining aspects of the postcolonial reading of Mootoo's novel that has rendered it so popular within academia, I will argue that Lai's text has not achieved the same levels of critical and commercial success, in part because it critiques dominant representations of Asian Canadians within the nation and troubles discourses of Canadian multiculturalism. The difference between Mootoo's and Lai's texts speaks directly to issues of circulation and institutional success that shape the reading of ethnic literature and its position within broader discourses of the nation, and it encourages us to find new strategies for reading this body of writing.

Prior to writing *Out on Main Street*, Mootoo's first collection of short stories published in 1993 (she released *Cereus Blooms at Night* three years later, and then *The Predicament of Or*, a collection of poetry, in 2001), Mootoo was an established visual artist and experimental video producer. Press Gang, a small feminist publisher based in Vancouver, solicited written texts from Mootoo after seeing her visual art, because the press was interested in the way that her visual work explored intersections between cultural, gendered, and sexual identities.[4] The subsequent release of *Out on Main Street* and *Cereus Blooms at Night* by Press Gang not only helped Mootoo enter the literary field, but also positioned her within a literary network of politicized women writers with strong connections to activism.[5] The publication of Lai's novel, *When Fox Is a Thousand*, also by Press Gang a year earlier, situates her within this same political milieu. Framing Mootoo and Lai as Press Gang writers draws attention to the feminist and lesbian dimensions of their work and encourages reading their texts alongside other Press Gang authors such as SKY Lee, Lee Maracle, and Betsy Warland. Considering Mootoo's and Lai's works in relation to the publications of these other women writers helps illustrate the ways in which the term "feminism" is repositioned within various discourses over time, what the field of women's writing looks like at specific intervals, and the relevance of gender to contemporary debates about the representation of social identities.

In many critical studies of *When Cereus Blooms at Night*, the novel is transformed from a lesbian feminist novel to a queer postcolonial text, a process that draws attention to the institutional frameworks that shape the production, travel, and reception of texts that write cultural difference.[6] As a novel originally published by Press Gang, *Cereus Blooms at Night* emerged out of feminist social and economic networks. Yet the crucial role this small feminist press played in editing, promoting, and distributing the novel is often overlooked in discussions that celebrate *Cereus Blooms at Night* for its relevance to discourses of postcolonial hybridity and mobility. The current position of postcolonial fiction at the centre of the national field needs to be interrogated for its own politics and for the ways that it has displaced the feminist revolutionary politics of an earlier generation within the Canadian literary field.[7] In advocating that we take a closer look at the recent critical shift in Canadian literature away from feminist criticism and towards postcolonial, and more recently, globalization studies, I do not mean to suggest that we abandon the investigation of race and culture in contemporary Canadian writing. Instead, I believe that we need to consider what is at stake in privileging questions of race over those of gender, sexuality, and class. The negotiation of specific kinds of social difference is an especially pressing issue given the expectations that are typically placed on racialized texts, ones that highlight the often fraught intersection of cultural and aesthetic modes of representation. It is precisely this tendency to read autoethnographic elements into texts by ethnic writers that David Palumbo-Liu takes up when he chastises academics that read ethnic literary texts as if they were "authentic, unmediated representations of ethnicity."[8] It is useful here to think of the art-culture system James Clifford maps out when he describes the tendency of Western critics to categorize non-Western objects as "cultural artifacts" and Western ones as "aesthetic works of art," since ethnic texts are framed less often as artistic works and more frequently as examples of cultural difference.[9] I propose instead that Mootoo's and Lai's novels should be read as artistic works that are useful for interrogating representations of cultural and gendered difference.

Cereus Blooms at Night articulates a vision of being able to manipulate social systems such as gender but not being able to be free of them. In the novel, individuals perform gendered identities in unconventional ways that contradict the social norms of their community. Although their performances speak to the proliferation of possibilities within gendered systems, they remain consciously located within these parameters. *Cereus Blooms at Night*, set in the fictional Caribbean island of Lantanacamara, depicts the crossing of various borders—social, sexual, temporal, and national—as it explores conflicted local histories. The narrative focuses on Mala Ramchandin, an elderly woman who is placed in the care of the Paradise Alms House after her familial home burns down. The narrative perspective belongs to Tyler, the male nurse who now tends to her. In *Cereus Blooms at Night*, gender is represented as an unstable signifier and is used to critique biological truths and the naturalization of narratives that uphold them. This is perhaps most evident in the relationship that develops between Mala and Tyler, one that is based on a "shared sense of queerness."[10] The reader is introduced to Tyler's sense of queerness early on in the novel. Despite his nursing qualifications, Tyler is assigned housekeeping duties at the nursing home, an indication of the homophobia of his superiors. Although Tyler is able to survive within this subtle hostility, "quietly proud and [...] not enter[ing] into a façade of denial," it is only after Mala arrives at the home that he begins to explore his professional and personal sense of worth.[11] Only in front of Mala is Tyler first able to don a nurse's uniform and move beyond the feeling of being "[n]ot a man and not ever able to be a woman, suspended nameless in the limbo state between existence and nonexistence."[12] Tyler's exploration of the ambiguities of gender is framed as an act of confidence that is made possible within the confines of Mala's room. Later in the novel, inspired by the possibility of romance, Tyler ventures out in public wearing the nurse's uniform and drenched in "enough scent to make a Puritan cross his legs and swoon."[13] Gender, it is made clear by Tyler's display, is a malleable social system capable of generating multiple possibilities that extend beyond the division into male and female. Otoh, Tyler's love interest, also participates in this act of resignifying gendered markers. Born biologically female but having discarded that identity early on in life, Otoh also exemplifies what Heather Smyth calls an "emphasis on 'in-between' identities, change, and process [that] indicates the mutability of sexuality in the novel."[14] Desire, in this text, transgresses dominant practices of organizing bodies into gendered systems, but is firmly located within individual bodies.

Although Tyler is represented as queer in more visible terms than Mala, the novel considers theirs a "shared sense of queerness."[15] Mala's remaking of gender, however, is not the result of her own desires. Her sense of sexual difference lies, paradoxically, in her participation in the bourgeois model of ideal sexual relations: marriage. After her mother, Sarah, and her lover, Lavinia, are forced to leave Mala and her younger sister, Asha, behind as they flee to the Shivering Wetlands, Mala and Asha are repeatedly molested by their father, Chandin. The novel pairs these sets of relations, the coupling of Sarah and Lavinia and that of Mala and Chandin, to illustrate the danger of unregulated desire. Sarah and Lavinia's romance is an example of how the novel "presents sexuality as a fluid form of identity and parallels sexual indeterminacy or outlaw sexuality with other forms of border-crossing identities."[16] Sarah and Lavinia's crossing of borders to escape from Lantanacamara—a space of obligations to parents and families—carries a number of risks, including the vengeance of Chandin and the loss of Sarah's two daughters. The transgression of social and sexual norms by their mother and Lavinia translates into taxing penalties for Mala and Asha. As a result of his wife's actions, Chandin deteriorates into a state of constant inebriation and, one night, mistakes a daughter for his wife. Instead of regretting the mistake, Chandin continues to molest his children, thereby attempting to recreate the family unit. This sexual violence is compounded by the further symbolic violence Mala is made to endure by also fulfilling the domestic duties of her mother. Despite Mala's eventual confrontation with her father, an act that leads to his death, and despite her mother's flight from her oppressive marriage, both women remain caught within the logic and constraints of normative gendered systems. These negotiations of gender suggest that although this system is open to transformation, its limits cannot be erased.

At the same time, a reading of *Cereus Blooms at Night* and its mainstream success needs to consider not just whether the novel espouses a vision consistent with contemporary feminist politics, but also how that vision is articulated by the novel. For this reason, it is important to remember that while the publication of Mootoo's novel by Press Gang situates it within a conversation about gender, the text also circulates throughout various institutions and is consequently positioned within other kinds of debates that draw out its different aspects. Discussions of the novel frequently invoke its relevance to conversations about postcoloniality. For instance, Smyth's reading of *Cereus Blooms at Night* as an "imagined place [...] inhabited by a coalition of queer subjects who find healing and a space for the performance of their liminal identities" also reminds us that the novel's "fragile sense of 'paradise' is complicated by the sexual, spiritual, and physical violence of colonialism and other forms of oppression."[17] Similarly, Cora Ann Howells points out, "Mootoo's agenda is neither exclusively feminist nor entirely 'queer.' It includes gender troubles of the male sex too, [...] Mootoo's protagonists whose life histories are inscribed within

Caribbean colonial history problems of gender identity and sexual transgression are inevitably bound up with the discourses of colonialism."[18] Although the novel's explorations of gender and sexuality may have been a critical component in Press Gang's decision to invest in it, much of its appeal for literary and cultural institutions is tied to its depictions of a postcolonial space. The confluence of these multiple interests makes it possible for the text to travel through disparate spaces—local, national, and imperial—with relative ease.

Smyth's and Howells' references to colonial discourse demonstrate how *Cereus Blooms at Night*'s relevance to postcolonial debates within universities has helped forge a place for it within the cultural field. As Randal Johnson points out in his introduction to Bourdieu's *The Field of Cultural Production*, the symbolic value associated with cultural products "is sustained by a vast social apparatus encompassing museums, galleries, libraries, the educational system, literary and art histories, centres for the performing arts and so forth."[19] Academic and literary institutions have demonstrated their interest in *Cereus Blooms at Night* and Mootoo's collection of short stories, *Out on Main Street*, by publishing scholarly articles on these texts and by nominating Mootoo's novel for literary awards:

> *Cereus Blooms at Night* [...] is already fast becoming a classic of post-colonial literature. It was short-listed for the Giller Prize and the Chapters First Novel Award, long-listed for the Booker Prize, and is now taught not only at Canadian universities and colleges, but in the United States and Britain as well. It is on bookstore shelves in 14 countries.[20]

The linking of literary prizes and university syllabi in McMaster's description of Mootoo's novel and its popularity confirms Bourdieu's theory that the field of restricted literary production—that is, "legitimate" literature—is "a field that is its own market, allied with an educational system which legitimizes it."[21]

The awarding of prizes to certain positions and not others is random to some degree, but not completely inexplicable. The ability of those vying for honours to position themselves within the interests of granting institutions and those affiliated with the institutions is an obvious advantage for the success of their books. In the case of *Cereus Blooms at Night*, it is relevant that this text not only engages with issues of gender and sexuality but also invokes questions of postcoloniality, since "[p]ostcolonialism, like feminism, has at last become a foundational category of critical analysis within the academy, and for many this is a cause for celebration."[22] The postcolonial currency of the novel is also relevant when considering *Cereus Blooms at Night*'s position on the Booker Prize's long list. According to Luke

Strongman, "The Booker Prize is a crucial award in English letters because it is perceived as one which, from a (former) imperial centre, confers literary recognition on novels that reflect and portray the state of culture after empire."[23] Thus the text's consideration of the aftermath of empire, articulated through the lingering effects that the past continues to have on the present, both within the specific parameters of the family and the larger workings of the Lantanacamara community as a whole, has the advantage of making it a logical candidate for publishers to nominate for the Booker Prize. As a work that expresses difficulty in envisioning a future freed of colonial domination, *Cereus Blooms at Night*, like "[a]ll of the Booker Prize-winning novels ha[s] an implied relationship with empire, whether this be writing in the form of counter-discourse, subscription to imperial rhetoric, nostalgia for empire, or of an articulation of identity in the fluid internationalisms which emerge after empire."[24]

Reading Mootoo's novel through the lens of postcolonial discourse is a double-edged sword. Positioning *Cereus Blooms at Night* as postcolonial raises the visibility and marketability of the text but ultimately locates it within the cultural politics of the academy rather than the lesbian feminist politics of activism out of which it emerged. Reading the novel in this way runs the risk of minimizing the weight of its political interventions. Market and critical success, then, can potentially diffuse a sense of urgency. As Stephen Slemon has argued, "Postcolonial intellectual work—as has happened within other "theoretical" schools that have seen their star rise in the academy—no longer needs a politics, a commitment, a feeling of rage against contemporary economic and cultural imperialism, a risk of engulfment in the thick human matter of history. Instead, postcolonialism becomes no more and no less than practicable critical method."[25] Politics becomes relegated to the past, something that was critical in the incursion of postcolonialism into the academy but is no longer relevant to its daily operations.

Another danger inherent in the academy's celebration of Mootoo's novel as a postcolonial text is that, in attempting to discuss the postcolonial subject, academics may erase her agency by speaking for her. Slemon suggests that this risk is always present because of the way that academic conversations about postcolonialism are regulated:

> In law, the accused does not, or will not, or by common wisdom should not, represent him- or herself: a similar assumption carries forward into the arcane theatre of postcolonial theory, where the language of address is astoundingly difficult at just about every level—clearly, not a language of mutual and coherent understanding between the "subaltern" and the scholar,

but a technical language for the professional advocacy of subaltern issues and concerns, addressed to powerful social bodies and mediated by important protocols of professional competence and rhetorical skill.[26]

Similarly, the interlocutory process regulates the representation of the postcolonial subject within the text as well as about it. For instance, early on in the novel, the reader learns that Mala has been accused of murdering her father who had been physically and sexually abusing her for years. Before the law, Mala is a silent, if not absent, figure on behalf of whom others advocate. When her case is brought before the courts, it is framed as a conversation between Judge Walter Bissey, the prosecution, and the police constable. Instead of providing insight into Mala's state of mind following Judge Bissey's dismissal of the murder charges, the text describes the town's disappointment when they are denied the salacious thrill of having "a woman criminal" and the constable's feeling of frustration "swarming under his skin."[27] The irony of Judge Bissey's position is that he was instrumental in the social ostracism that Mala and her sister, Asha, experienced as children. Walter Bissey, fully aware of their mother Sarah's absence, regulated the social norms among children and decided that, since Sarah had left her family to be with her lesbian lover, the girls could not be permitted to play in a space meant "only for good, decent people."[28] The residents of Lantanacamara perceive Sarah and her lover Lavinia's lesbian relationship as morally transgressive, and, consequently, they brand Mala and Asha as dissolute. The romantic relationship between Sarah and Lavinia is the ultimate transgression because it contradicts the authority of church and father. Chandin's violations of his daughters' bodies offend the community but are more comprehensible through a collective articulation of excuses and rationalization. Walter Bissey and his friends pass judgements on Mala and Asha that uphold the social laws of their community but are unjust. Later, as an adult, Bissey tries to atone for his past behaviour by exonerating Mala of criminal charges, an act that recognizes that "[s]he is the victim and not the perpetrator of a legacy of violence, which is both domestic and historical."[29] Yet Bissey's act of contrition provides only a partial solution to this violent situation given Mala's silence within the courtroom. By not being able to engage in her own defence, Mala is once again silenced and denied justice.

The community tends to view Chandin as a victim because he was once a respected and religious figure "[a]nd, they [...] reason, what man would not suffer a rage akin to insanity if his own wife, with a devilish mind of her own, left her husband and children."[30] Communal sympathy for Chandin is directly linked to the structures of colonialism that shape the town.

Throughout the novel, this imaginary Caribbean island is constantly positioned in relation to the Shivering Northern Wetlands, a site that Smyth
reads as "a stand-in for England," and occasionally in relation to Canada,
the country that provides cold refuge for Asha when she escapes from her
father's abusive home.[31] Even before Chandin becomes the object of town
gossip as a spurned husband, he is a well-known figure in Lantanacamara
because of his relationship with the Thoroughlys. Reverend Thoroughly
and his wife, originally from the Shivering Northern Wetlands, adopt
Chandin as a foster child with the intention of sending him to the seminary.
As the "first Indian child in Lantanacamara to get a title," Chandin is a
prominent figure within his community.[32] While the benevolence of the
Thoroughlys is viewed as good fortune for Chandin's parents—it freed
them from the financial burden of sending him away to be educated—and
a wonderful opportunity for Chandin, it places him in the position of the
colonized subject much like that described by Frantz Fanon in *White Skin,
Black Masks*:

> Every colonized people—in other words, every people in whose soul an infe-
> riority complex has been created by the death and burial of its local cultural
> originality—finds itself face to face with the language of the civilizing nation;
> that is, with the culture of the mother country. The colonized is elevated
> above his jungle status in proportion to his adoption of the mother country's
> cultural standards.[33]

Chandin is subjected to the doubled discourse of colonization: on the one
hand, he is encouraged to think of himself as a brother to the Thoroughly's
daughter, Lavinia (who eventually becomes Sarah's lover). On the other
hand, it is made clear that Chandin is not family. The Thoroughlys leave
Chandin behind when they visit the Shivering Northern Wetlands. Most
difficult for Chandin, however, is the Reverend's use of a rhetoric of inclusion, a belonging to the family, to explain why Chandin must suppress his
romantic interest in Lavinia. The falseness of this rhetoric is revealed when,
upon returning from their family holiday, Reverend Thoroughly announces
to Chandin Lavinia's intention to marry her white cousin, Fenton, a union
that is acceptable because Fenton is adopted and therefore "not a true relation."[34] Reverend Thoroughly's specious logic suggests that Chandin is
what Bhabha calls a colonial mimic, one who fulfills the colonial "desire
for a reformed, recognizable Other, as a subject of a difference that is
almost the same, but not quite."[35]

The ease with which Mootoo's novel lends itself to discussions of postcolonial representation in a cultural moment preoccupied with issues of ethnic relations, global politics, and national identity is surely part of its appeal.

The text's use of garden imagery, for instance, invokes multiple contradictory associations. In addition to Mariam Pirbhai, who looks at the garden as an inverted postcolonial space in her chapter, Sarah Casteel has read the garden as a site in which botanical and colonial histories overlap, in part through its "important connections to hybridity, both metaphorically as a figure for the hybridization of cultures, and historically in that nineteenth-century theories of racial hybridity drew on the science of botany."[36] For Casteel, hybridity is used in Mootoo's novel for its "emphasis on mutability and transformation, in particular on the instability of identity and its connection to place."[37] This engagement with one of postcolonial theory's central themes also occurs in *Out on Main Street*, Mootoo's earlier collection of short stories. For instance, in "A Garden of Her Own," the narrator, Vijai, mourns the emptiness of her newlywed life in North America and her distance from home. To compensate for the loneliness of her Sundays, a day that she used to enjoy with her family, Vijai begins to cultivate a garden on her balcony, an act that lets her forge a connection with her new cultural space. Similarly, botanical images are also used in "Lemon Scent," the second short story of the collection. This time, as the references to "the bird-of-paradise" bushes make clear, the garden is a utopist space for the characters, Kamini and Anita.[38] It is only in the forest that they are able to engage in their affair without fear of being discovered by Anita's husband. Like the "mudra tree" under which Lavinia and Sarah "whisper and giggle" in *Cereus Blooms at Night*, the samaan tree under which Kamini and Anita make love in this story signifies the dual erotics of secrecy and discovery.[39] In these various examples, hybridity (both botanical and cultural) represents a means of escaping the divisive binary of colonizer and colonized as the garden becomes a social-sexual space of germination.

The fecundity of gardens is further explored in the novel when the annual blooming of the cereus plant occurs in a garden overrun with life after Mala kills her abusive father. The momentous event is described as heralding

> [t]he arrival of thousands of moths, already drunk from the smell alone, [that] held Mala spellbound. The sound of a thousand pairs of flapping wings drowned out the screaming crickets and created a draft. Mala rubbed her arms for warmth. Crazed bats swooped by, crisscrossing each other's flight en route to suckle the blossoms. They disturbed the swarms of frantic moths. They brushed their hairy bodies against the blossoms to sample the syrupy, perfumed juices. Then, thirst and curiosity satisfied, they darted off. By two o'clock in the morning, every moth was thirstily lapping sweet nectar, brushing and yellowing its body against the large stamens that waved from the flowers.[40]

The cross-pollinating effects of this plant rooted in Mala's garden are seen in the intersecting routes of moths, bats, and flowers, and by descriptions of strolling lovers and townspeople in satisfied slumber that frame this narrative moment. At the same time, however, reading texts solely through common postcolonial tropes and the popular theoretical lens of hybridity poses its own set of limitations. While individual identities are fluid and open to change in an ideally imagined space of postcolonial hybridity, they remain regulated by intersecting and persistent gendered and classed social systems, such as marriage, that remain difficult to overturn and open up to the potential liberations of hybridity theory.

It is perhaps also relevant that *Out on Main Street*, Mootoo's first published collection of short stories, contains stories that grapple "with the question of what it feels like for a nonwhite woman to live in contemporary multicultural Canada."[41] Unlike *Out on Main Street*, *Cereus Blooms at Night* displaces its sense of dissatisfaction with social regulations onto distant sites. Donald Goellnicht, in his assessment of Asian Canadian literature, suggests that the tendency for a number of South Asian Canadian writers such as Mistry, Selvadurai, and Mootoo to "focu[s] in their fiction on the past in a distant place that still haunts them, another place, not here, rather than writing novels about racism and discrimination *in Canada* may also help to explain why it has been easier for their works to get published by mainstream publishing houses."[42] While Goellnicht makes it clear that he does not intend to criticize this pattern, his reading can be used to consider the widespread popularity of *Cereus Blooms at Night* in comparison to Mootoo's earlier, albeit less stylistically mature, *Out on Main Street* and to Lai's *When Fox Is a Thousand*.

I want to turn now to Lai's first novel, *When Fox Is a Thousand*, and read it against *Cereus Blooms at Night*, as both are texts published by Press Gang in the 1990s that are attuned to questions of gender, race, and sexuality. Lai's novel depicts a community of Chinese-Canadian lesbians living in Vancouver, and despite the fact that it explores issues of representation, culture, and sexuality similar to those in *Cereus Blooms at Night*, it has not received the same kinds of symbolic or economic rewards. This may be attributable to the troublesome position *When Fox Is a Thousand* takes up within dominant ideas of the nation,[43] as the novel demonstrates the limits of official multiculturalism as well as Canadian literature's canon to accommodate textual representations of differences (particularly sexual difference) in the here and now.

Privileging postcolonial aesthetics within the Canadian literary field also has material implications for authors and their publishers. Mootoo's novel highlights the gap between material and ideological circulation. *Cereus Blooms at Night*'s appeal to an already institutionalized discourse of postcoloniality encourages its circulation within various cultural institutions, but ironically creates material problems that make it difficult for these small presses to collect economic and symbolic rewards. The restraints of capital on the literary field are demonstrated by the sequence of events that occurred after *Cereus Blooms at Night* was nominated for literary awards. While small publishers welcome the symbolic capital generated by prizes, they are less pleased by the economic burden of these nominations. Former members of Press Gang Publishers have commented that "[t]he interesting thing about the Giller Prize is that when your book gets nominated, they want you to ante up something like fifteen hundred to two thousand dollars to pay your share of the publicity."[44] While this cost may be minimal for larger publishers, it is a major obstacle for small presses with tight budgets. In addition to the cost of publicity, nominations for literary prizes also require a second printing, a serious expense for a small press. Given these publication demands and promotion costs, Press Gang allowed *Cereus Blooms at Night* to be picked up by McClelland and Stewart. The financial obstacles Press Gang encountered following *Cereus Blooms at Night*'s Giller nomination are a clear demonstration that such awards are geared towards larger publishers and put smaller ones at a serious disadvantage, an observation that other small publishers have also made. The economic challenges faced by small presses draw attention to ways in which material constraints shape the circulation of literature and reading practices. Moreover, the proliferation of difference within liberal capitalism is evident in the fact that minoritarian discourses are enjoying extreme popularity but little is being done to ensure the continued production of these discourses by small and micropublishers. The contradiction between the rhetoric and the economic circumstances surrounding these discourses is linked to the way such textual representations of difference are consumed by the general public and literary institutions.

While small publishers are willing to take risks and produce texts that might not appeal to a wide market, they are often unable to reap the economic and cultural rewards when these texts become successful. In the case of *Cereus Blooms at Night*, subsequent printings bear the imprint of McClelland and Stewart and erase the crucial role played by Press Gang in bringing the book into print in the first place. Given the economic limitations of a small press, it is difficult to envision a situation in which both Press Gang and *Cereus Blooms at Night* might benefit from the nomination. In many ways, this relationship between the small and mainstream presses is similar to the one between postcolonial writers and literary crit-ics, "whereby the colonies produced the raw material (the literary text) and the metropolitan societies added the value (critical judgement, eval-uation, and commentary) and, of course, took most of the profit."[45] Instead of providing a situation in which disadvantaged players are able to reap the economic and symbolic rewards of their risk-taking, nominations for major literary prizes cement these inequalities. While the recognition of Mootoo's novel benefits the author and text, it underlines the difficulties of revising the relations of power within the literary field. As Gareth Griffiths notes in his discussion of postcolonial studies, "merely accreting literatures and lit-erary texts onto a unified model of English studies, even one which accepts a plurality of differences, does not ensure a genuine equality of cultures and of diverse reading and speaking positions."[46] The ongoing problem of unequal distribution of resources makes it increasingly difficult for small publishers to contribute to the literary field given their struggles to remain afloat.

Assessing the relationship between Mootoo's and Lai's works is a com-plicated matter, not only because they consider similar issues and use sim-ilar strategies of shifting temporalities, but also because the two authors openly acknowledge each other's professional and personal influence. Their mutually supportive relationship, as indicated by the writers themselves in the acknowledgements section of their first novels, illustrates the signifi-cance of the social networks that shape the literary field. At the same time, while there are multiple overlaps between these works, they differ in terms of how Mootoo's and Lai's texts have succeeded in the mainstream and how they have been received by various literary institutions. For instance, while *When Fox Is a Thousand* was, like *Cereus Blooms at Night*, shortlisted for the Chapters/Books in Canada First Novel Award and has recently been taken up by critics interested in Asian Canadian writing, overall it has not received the same kind of critical acclaim as the latter. The discrepancy in the levels of symbolic and economic capital each of these novels has been able to generate is indicative of the subtle difference in their positions within literary and cultural institutions. Whereas *Cereus Blooms at Night* mobilizes discourses of postcoloniality to frame its discussion of gendered, sexual, and cultural identity, *When Fox Is a Thousand* critically invokes those of multiculturalism to position its discussion within the parameters of the Canadian nation and investigate notions of citizenship. Mootoo's novel travels throughout global networks and has the advantage of having received legitimation from sites outside Canada, an edge that strengthens its symbolic position within the nation given Canada's fraught history of

British colonialism and American domination. This recognition, most obviously in terms of *Cereus Blooms at Night*'s nominations for literary prizes like the Booker, "facilitat[e] negotiation of the very rates and barriers of such exchange, negotiations which define the true stakes of the game."[47] In contrast, *When Fox Is a Thousand* positions itself primarily within the parameters of the Canadian nation and is therefore less likely to receive critical attention from institutions outside of Canada. For instance, although Artemis, the novel's main character, travels to Hong Kong, her return to Vancouver makes it clear that Canada is the centre of Lai's novel and the object of the text's scrutiny.

The comparative neglect of Lai's novel cannot simply be attributed to its national focus. It is also necessary to note that the text takes up a troublesome position within the nation, one that demonstrates the limits of representation and of both multicultural discourses and literary canons. It is often argued that significant discrepancies exist between the discourses and practices of nationalism. The former "assume[s] that the people [a]re one and shar[e] similar interests, but this [i]s mostly a way of uniting diversity. In practice many groups [a]re ignored, ha[ve] other interests, or continu[e] to be repressed."[48] The gap between these aspects of nationalism is evident in Canada, a former settler colony that continues to grapple with colonial practices within its borders. Arun Mukherjee argues that by continuing to frame its sense of national identity as bicultural, Canada promotes "social and cultural hierarchies" that disadvantage native and visible minority populations.[49] For such writers, their work is often "slotted as immigrant writing" and not perceived as belonging to Canada in the same way as that of white writers.[50] Mukherjee quotes a passage from an article by David Staines, who argues that most "transplanted writers," with the exception of rare instances like Michael Ondaatje, are not able "to sense instinctively and naturally the meaning of here."[51] The solution, for Mukherjee, to this exclusionary and double-voiced discourse of nationalism, is to construct "a new nationalism, one whose grounding premise will be Canada's heterogeneity."[52] In many senses, *When Fox Is a Thousand* participates in precisely this kind of project. By presenting Artemis as part of a community of Asian Canadian women, many of whom have artistic, social, familial, and educational ties to Canada, the novel suggests that the "meaning" of here cannot be "sensed instinctively" but instead must be forged through social networks.

While Artemis and her friends may have been raised in Canada, the text suggests that they are not read by others as what Mukherjee would call "officially Canadian."[53] The text critiques the limits of multicultural discourses that promote difference but are not able to recognize nuances within difference. Thus, as David Bennett notes, "state-managed multi-culturalisms reify and exoticise alterity; addressing ethnic and racial difference as a question of 'identity' rather than of history and politics."[54] The differences among Chinese-Canadians are drawn out in *When Fox Is a Thousand* through the relationship between Artemis and her friend Diane. Fox, a mythological character about to celebrate her thousandth birthday, is the narrative presence who weaves Artemis's story together with her own and that of a ninth-century Chinese poetess. When she introduces the reader to Artemis, she takes care to explain the history of Artemis's name; as a Chinese-Canadian name, it "marks a generation of immigrant children whose parents loved the idea of the Enlightenment and thought they would find it blooming in the full heat of its rational fragrance right here in North America."[55] That her name bridges generations and geographical spaces is emphasized first by her adoptive parents' decision to let Artemis keep both her first and last name, Wong, as "her only keepsake," and, second, by Artemis's own decision to not change her name as an adolescent, something that she later considers "an aesthetic, like fortune cookies, or spaghetti noodles in hot dog soup."[56] While Artemis brings together a number of cultural markers throughout the novel, she is not its sole representative of Chinese-Canadianness. This is underlined when Artemis and Diane meet and Artemis' initial reaction is to think that they "have the same name. [...] Just different versions."[57] The text continues to pull apart easy equations between signifier and signified when it compares Diane's and Artemis's appearances. Artemis points out that while they have "the same kind of hair [...] [a]nd the same kind of eyes," other physical attributes are completely different.[58] Her use of sameness and difference destabilizes dominant discourses of representation and produces an almost nonsensical effect, one that Diane can only read as "funny."[59] But while Diane and Artemis are able to perceive the differences between themselves, others are less successful. The french-fry vendor, despite the multiple differences in appearance between the two women that have just been pointed out to the reader, justifies his mistaking the two women for sisters by claiming that "[s]he looks just like you."[60] As Robyn Morris observes in her reading of *When Fox Is a Thousand*, "There is an implied power in the equating of sameness with otherness and Lai is vitriolic in her critique of an assumption of power that allows whiteness the majesty of, to paraphrase Barthes, looking without seeing."[61] Lai's critique of the ways in which ethnic identity is read within Canada is also relevant for thinking through how writing by ethnic authors tends to be interpreted. Clearly, neither individuals nor their texts can simply be read as representations of their cultural groups.

The novel's interrogation of multicultural logic poses implications for literary history. *When Fox Is a Thousand* suggests that the inclusiveness of this national rhetoric is "a fantasy that deflects the colonial history of white supremacist power," an insight that is relevant given the cultural work that literary canons perform.[62] As Donna Bennett notes in her contribution to *Canadian Canons*, "The notion that a canon is *shaped* also arises out of the relation of canon to national identity, which has been a crucial feature of canons throughout the nineteenth- and twentieth-century eras of nation building."[63] The representative function of literary canons within the parameters of national identity is intriguing given the "'additive' model of representation, which treats minorities as 'add-ons' to the pressure-group spectrum."[64] It is clear, then, that both literary canons and the rhetoric of multiculturalism represent particular ideological fantasies rather than social realities. The partial acceptance of Lai's text suggests that while it, like many texts that have been received as examples of ethnic writing, appeals to literary institutions to the extent that it is assimilable within the category of "immigrant writing," it also disagrees with the tastes of dominant institutions, because it emphasizes the dissonance between the work of representation that literary traditions and their larger national histories set out to do but fail to accomplish. Lorraine Weir notes in her contribution to Robert Lecker's collection of essays on the question of literary canons in Canada that "[w]hat has been canonized is, as always, what can be absorbed with least resistance or noise in the institution."[65] This tendency is illustrated by the success of Mootoo's novel, which fits easily into existing discourses of postcolonialism, unlike Lai's text, which troubles accepted notions of multiculturalism and Canadian nationalism.

The ambivalent recognition of *When Fox Is a Thousand* suggests that while parts of this text can easily be read through the dominant discourses of the nation and the literary institution, other parts resist being read in those terms. By drawing on traditional Chinese lore, Lai's novel demands that the reader become familiar with non-Western cultural texts. Yet the problem with writing a textually and culturally complex text is that, as Lai has observed in an interview, "if you critique what is unfamiliar, people don't recognize it as a critique."[66] Lai's novel also tends to locate its Chinese cultural stories within Canada, and thus this text cannot be as easily exoticized as *When Cereus Blooms at Night*. By depicting the Chinese community in Canada as diverse and Chinese culture as multi-layered, *When Fox Is a Thousand* refuses the familiar representations of alterity that circulate in the West and moves beyond the purview of autoethnography. Lai's insight is upheld by comments made by the judges of the Chapters/Books in Canada First Novel Award.[67] David Helwig critiques *When Fox Is a Thousand* by stating that "[t]he three narrative voices don't seem altogether complementary, and the interweaving of the three never succeeds in providing moments of dramatic enlightenment. They all sound much the same. The characters in the book's present-day narrative are not strongly defined or differentiated, and are not of a lot of interest."[68] While Helwig chastises Lai's novel for not flowing together properly and not drawing sharp enough distinctions, his real dissatisfaction with the novel would appear to be that it does not conform to his reading practices. Lai's investigation of Asian-Canadian communities eschews familiar celebratory discourses of multiculturalism and chooses instead to explore closely the complicated workings of diasporic lesbian communities. Helwig reads Lai's characters as "not strongly defined or differentiated" because a number of them are Chinese lesbians, a combination that ignores the distinct personal histories and interests of each of these female characters.[69]

It is also useful to consider the relative degrees of institutional acceptance that postcolonial theory and literature and Asian Canadian literature have received. Unlike the field of postcolonial studies, which, while still relatively young, has generated a considerable amount of critical debate, Asian Canadian literature, like many other bodies of ethnic writing, has yet to accumulate a comparable body. As Eleanor Ty and Donald Goellnicht have usefully pointed out, "[i]n scholarly works, the texts of Asian Canadians have been studied by Canadianists and postcolonialists rather than Asian Canadian critics."[70] The relative paucity of critical discourse on Asian Canadian literature is perhaps not surprising since the critical popularity of ethnic writing in Canada in general only dates back to the 1980s.[71] Although Asian Canadian writers such as the Eaton sisters have been producing texts for years, it is only quite recently that Asian Canadian texts "have emerged as disciplinary objects of knowledge in Canadian literary culture" and read under the category of race.[72] To be more precise, while Asian Canadian writing had been included in anthologies and journals since the 1970s, academic institutions only began to pay attention to it, and other forms of ethnic writing, in the 1990s.[73] The importance of having a language with which to speak about Asian Canadian texts cannot be underestimated when it comes to generating recognition of the texts' value. Roy Miki suggests that since "the advent of institutionalization works to establish 'the domain of the sayable,' then it also functions as a process through which an entity such as Asian Canadian takes on social and critical appearance and thereby

accrues value as a discursive category, in other words, as a sphere of public knowledge."[74] The institutionalization of Asian Canadian writing such
as Lai's must therefore be read as a necessary act of inclusion, but one that
must also be met with suspicion because such practices are "attempt[s] to
discipline and contain various Asian ethnic groups and their cultural production."[75] While Asian Canadian literature deserves to be read critically,
discussions must avoid lapsing into general celebrations of hybridity and
mobility and neglecting the institutional frameworks that shape the production, travel, and reception of these texts.

I want to conclude this discussion by drawing attention to the division
between production and consumption that *Cereus Blooms at Night* and
When Fox Is a Thousand make visible within the larger Canadian literary
field. In Rey Chow's essay, "Against the Lures of Diaspora: Minority Discourse, Chinese Women, and Intellectual Hegemony," she reminds us of "the
necessity to read and write against the lures of diaspora."[76] Chow warns
that "[a]ny attempt to deal with women or the oppressed classes in the Third
World that does not at the same time come to terms with the historical
conditions of its own articulation is bound to repeat the exploitativeness
that used to and still characterizes most exchanges between West and
East."[77] Her cautionary comment is relevant, not just for thinking through
the construction of Chinese women in Asian studies, but also for the production of a variety of minoritarian discourses in North American cultural
institutions. According to Chow, overlooking the socio-economic conditions of minority struggles runs the risk of reducing them to "signifiers
whose major function is that of discursive exchange for the intellectuals'
self-profit."[78] The proliferation of minoritarian discourses—those that speak,
for example, to women's, feminist, queer, lesbian, ethnic, diasporic, postcolonial, and aboriginal issues—suggests that these struggles within North
America also face the possibility of being transformed into theoretical signifiers divorced from their historical conditions.

In the Canadian context, the dire economic circumstances of small publishing houses devoted to the production of alternate voices contrasts
sharply with the proliferation of minoritarian discourses. Many recent successful books, such as Ann-Marie MacDonald's *Fall on Your Knees* and Rohinton Mistry's Oprah-picked novel, *A Fine Balance*, focus on marginal
identities—sexual, racial, ethnic, and classed—and participate in important
conversations about representation, identity, and diaspora. Increasingly,
the Canadian publishing industry is buoyed by big books, and less room is
being left for texts such as Lai's. Narratives of marginalization have in
many instances proved compatible with this economic model, but some

identities remain beyond the pale. This problem is discussed by Fred Wah, who notes that the "culturally marginalized writer [...] [tends to] engineer approaches to language and form that enable a particular residue (genetic, cultural, biographical) to become kinetic and valorized."[79] What is interesting to Wah is the difference between writers such as Joy Kogawa and Mistry, who explore the condition of marginality "within a colonized and inherited formal awareness," and authors like Roy Kiyooka and Marlene Nourbese Philip, who employ "more formal innovative possibilities."[80] That the former category of writers is more familiar to most Canadian readers than the latter suggests that it may be useful to consider the formal as well as the thematic expectations of ethnic literature as a way to move beyond the impulse to read ethnographically. How these narratives are told is relevant to conversations that attempt to unpack the link between ethnic identity and literary production, especially when considering how the pressure to produce "the next big thing" plays into the hands of large publishing houses rather than small press collectives. Jennifer Andrews and John Clement Ball note that "[f]irst-time authors are coveted by small and large presses alike, who all hope their next release will generate the attention and revenues of Anne Michael's *Fugitive Pieces* or Ann-Marie MacDonald's *Fall on Your Knees*."[81] These high critical and commercial expectations suggest that the book industry is willing to invest in a few authors, a strategy that obviously does not bode well for those writers whose works do not appeal to the dominant taste of literary institutions. *Fall on Your Knees*, like many other novels, speaks to the condition of marginalized peoples, yet it bears the imprint of a major publisher. The transformation of texts about marginalization into economic and symbolic capital for dominant literary institutions is a process that asks us to reconsider the recent emergence of postcolonial Canadian texts within the socio-economic systems that produce them and the ways in which these texts have recently become prominent, in part through media promotion and literary awards. The legitimation of narratives of marginalization by major Canadian publishers suggests that even though discourses of difference are widespread in the literary field, they nonetheless continue to exist in what Miki calls "a normative system of power hierarchies."[82]

While including postcolonial writing within literary institutions has translated into certain kinds of rewards for certain authors, it remains problematic. Instead of reconfiguring the regulations that govern the cultural field, "minority" writers have largely been parcelled into "specialized niche markets within the 'global.'"[83] The larger struggle in the reading practices articulated in relation to texts like Mootoo's and Lai's, then, is not just to create a space within the cultural field, but to try to revise the colonial logic that structures it. Miki suggests that while the "cultural desta-bilizations [...] are radically altering the conditions of visibility and invis-ibility[,] [...] [h]ow these changes will reconfigure the lexicon of current cultural politics—and thus the mutations of racialization—waits to be seen."[84] Similarly, small feminist presses like Press Gang have struggled to produce texts that introduce new ways of thinking about contemporary culture and representations of gender and race. That the consequences of this kind of cultural production are becoming visible and being taken up by conferences such as "Beyond Autoethnography" is significant, as such projects remind us of the importance of the economic to conversations of culture, gender and ethnicity to politics, and publishing to aesthetics, as all influence the Canadian cultural field and shape how we engage with eth-nic literature.

NOTES

1   Eleanor Ty and Christl Verduyn, "Beyond Autoethnography: Writing Race and Ethnicity in Canada," call for papers (2005), http://info.wlu.ca/%7Ewwweng/ety/Ethnicity-conference.

2   Pierre Bourdieu, *The Field of Cultural Production*, ed. Randal Johnson (New York: Columbia UP, 1993).

3   Discourses of postcoloniality and multiculturalism critique different objects. Post-colonial literature and theory discuss structures of colonialism and imperial rela-tions. According to David Scott's *Refashioning Futures* (Princeton, NJ: Princeton UP, 1999), 12,

> [a]s a political-theoretical project, then, postcoloniality has been concerned principally with the decolonization of representation; the decolonization of the West's theory of the non-West. Postcoloniality altered the question about colonialism and provided a new set of conceptual tools with which not merely to revive colonialism as a going problematic, but to reframe it in terms of the relation between colonial power and colonial knowledge. It thereby enabled a systematic reinterrogation of contemporary practices in terms of the extent to which (or the sense in which) they reproduced forms of knowledge that emerged as part of the apparatus of colonial power.

In contrast, discussions of multiculturalism focus on the relations between cultural groups and the nation. Himani Bannerji, for one, has criticized the model of Cana-dian multiculturalism, arguing that it allows

> [a]n element of whiteness [to] quietly ente[r] into cultural definitions, mark-ing the difference between a core cultural group and other groups who are represented as cultural fragments. The larger function of this multicultural-ism not only takes care of legitimation of the Canadian state, but helps in managing an emerging crisis in legitimation produced by a complex political conjuncture evolving through the years after the second world war. (Introduc-tion to *The Dark Side of the Nation*, by Himani Bannerji [Toronto: Canadian Scholars' Press, 2000], 10)

4 Press Gang approached Mootoo through an intermediary figure, Persimmon Black-bridge:

> As an established painter and experimental video producer in the 1980s and early '90s, Mootoo kept a diary to help her articulate the source of her inspiration. She showed these private musings to a fellow artist, Persimmon Blackbridge, who, unbeknownst to Mootoo, passed them on to Press Gang. It was a case of love at first sight. "[Press Gang] called and said they'd heard I was writing and was there anything I could show them," says Mootoo. "I said, "Well, I'm writing, but it's really private stuff." They wouldn't take no for an answer, however, calling about once a month to see if she'd changed her mind. After they sent her a contract (just, they said, so she could see what a contract looked like) and agreed to give her an advance (which they'd never done for anyone else) she finally relented. She soon produced a well-received collection of short stories in 1992 called *Out on the Street* [sic]. (Geoff McMaster, "Mootoo Explores New Ground," *University of Alberta Express News*, January 11, 2002, http://www.expressnews.ualberta.ca/expressnews/articles/printer.cfm?p_ID=1707)

5 Press Gang initially began as a printing operation with male and female members in the 1970s. Eventually, following negotiations for property and access to equipment, the male workers left the press (Lynn Giraud and Sheila Gilhooly, "A Herstory of a Women's Press: Press Gang Printers," *Feminist Bookstore News* 16, no. 2 [August 1993]: 49). With the departure of these members, in 1974 the press became an all-women's organization with explicit feminist and Marxist commitments. Shortly after this change, Press Gang forayed into the field of publishing, a move partly motivated by a desire to give "women at the Press [...] a more active voice in what they were printing—they wanted to publish work they developed" and also "partly out of [a] need to establish a distribution network so that women had more control over getting printed material to readers" (Press Gang, "History of the Press" [unpublished overview of Press Gang's history, private papers of Nancy Pollak and Sarah Davidson], n.p.). Early creative and critical publications such as *Women Look at Psychiatry*, ed. Dorothy E. Smith and Sara J. David (Vancouver: Press Gang, 1975), and Anne Cameron's *Daughters of Copper Woman* (Vancouver: Press Gang, 1981) convey a sense of energy as they explore women's social realities. By publishing writing about women, texts that sometimes led to debates over issues of artistic integrity, social freedoms, and economic realities, this feminist press clearly intended to invoke cultural and political change.

6 For instance, Cora Ann Howells categorizes *Cereus Blooms at Night* as "a postcolonial text that confronts the binary structures inherent in colonialism and in sexual politics" (*Contemporary Canadian Women's Fiction* [New York: Palgrave Macmillan, 2002], 148). The discussion of gendered and sexual issues can only begin for Howells once it has been established that the novel is, in fact, postcolonial. Similarly, Judith Misrahi-Barak situates her reading of Mootoo in the broader context of "post-colonial literatures and particularly in the Caribbean" ("Beginners' Luck among Caribbean-Canadian Writers: Nalo Hopkinson, André Alexis and Shani Mootoo," *Commonwealth Essays and Studies* 22, no. 1 [1999]: 89). In particular, Misrahi-Barak draws out the connections between Mootoo's work and those of André Alexis and Nalo Hopkinson to consider generational shifts. Sarah Casteel also opens her analysis of Mootoo's novel with the claim that "postcolonial studies should benefit from the renewed attention to space"

("New World Pastoral: The Caribbean Garden and Emplacement in Gisèle Pineau and Shani Mootoo," *Interventions* 5, no. 1 [2003]: 12).

7   Recent book publications that examine postcolonial writing in Canada include *Voices of Change: Immigrant Writers Speak* out, ed. Jurgen Hesse (Vancouver: Pulp Press, 1990); Arun Mukherjee's *Oppositional Aesthetics* (Toronto: TSAR, 1994); *Writing Ethnicity*, ed. Winfried Siemerling (Toronto: ECW Press, 1996); *Intersexions*, ed. Barbara Godard and Coomi S. Vevaina (New Delhi: Creative Books, 1996); *Floating the Borders: New Contexts in Canadian Criticism*, ed. Nurjehan Aziz (Toronto: TSAR, 1999); and Smaro Kamboureli's *Scandalous Bodies* (Don Mills, ON: Oxford UP, 2000). As well, *Essays on Canadian Writing* produced a special issue called "Testing the Limits: Postcolonial Theories and Canadian Literatures" in 1995 (56).

8   David Palumbo-Liu, introduction to *The Ethnic Canon: Histories, Institutions and Interventions*, ed. David Palumbo-Liu (Minneapolis and London: U of Minnesota P, 1995), 12.

9   James Clifford, "On Collecting Art and Culture," in *Out There: Marginalization and Contemporary Cultures*, ed. Russell Ferguson et al. (Cambridge, MA, and New York: New Museum of Contemporary Art and Massachusetts Institute of Technology, 1990), 146.

10 Shani Mootoo, *Cereus Blooms at Night* (Vancouver: Press Gang, 1996), 52.

11 Ibid., 16.

12 Ibid., 83.

13 Ibid., 268.

14 Heather Smyth, "Sexual Citizenship and Caribbean-Canadian Fiction: Dionne Brand's *In Another Place, Not Here* and Shani Mootoo's *Cereus Blooms at Night*," *ARIEL* 30, no. 2 (1999): 148.

15 Mootoo, *Cereus*, 52.

16 Smyth, "Sexual Citizenship," 147.

17 Ibid., 156.

18 Howells, *Contemporary*, 152.

19 Johnson, *The Field of Cultural Production*, 15.

20 McMaster, "Mootoo Explores New Ground," n.p.

21 Bourdieu, *The Field*, 129–30.

22 Stephen Slemon, "Afterword: The English Side of the Lawn," *Essays on Canadian Writing* 56 (1995): 275.

23 Luke Strongman, *The Booker Prize and the Legacy of Empire* (Amsterdam and New York: Rodopi, 2002), ix.

24 Ibid., x.

25 Slemon, "Afterword," 282.

26 Ibid., 278.

27 Mootoo, *Cereus*, 8.

28 Ibid., 93.

29 Howells, *Contemporary*, 154.

30 Mootoo, *Cereus*, 211.

31 Smyth, "Sexual Citizenship," 151.

32 Mootoo, *Cereus*, 31.

33 Frantz Fanon, *Black Skin, White Masks*, trans. Charles Lam Markmann (New York: Grove Weidenfeld, 1967), 18.

34 Mootoo, *Cereus*, 48.

35 Homi Bhabha, *The Location of Culture* (New York and London: Routledge, 1994), 86.

36 Casteel, "New York Pastoral," 14.

37 Ibid., 26.

38 Shani Mootoo, *Out on Main Street, and Other Stories* (Vancouver: Press Gang, 1993), 31.

39 Mootoo, *Cereus*, 61.

40 Ibid., 148.

41 Howells, *Contemporary*, 144.

42 Donald Goellnicht, "A Long Labour: The Protracted Birth of Asian Canadian Literature," *Essays on Canadian Writing* 72 (2000): 15.

43 The need to construct a strong sense of national identity has long dominated conversations about Canadian literature and culture. As Tamara Palmer Seiler notes in her description of discussions of Canadian nationalism, "That literature might indeed express national culture was assumed fairly widely in English-speaking Canada from at least the time of the Confederation to the 1970s" ("Multi-Vocality and National Literature," in *Literary Pluralities*, ed. Christl Verduyn [Peterborough: Broadview Press and *Journal of Canadian Studies*, 1998], 48). More recently, in the 1960s, a period of "assertive nationalism in English-speaking Canada, literature (including literary criticism) was widely regarded as a site where the remnants of the old colonial relationship with Britain and the new colonial relationship with the United States could be resisted" (Palmer Seiler, 49). And of more recent developments, Palmer Seiler notes, "the official definition of Canadian culture that emerged in the policy announced by Pierre Trudeau in October of 1971 was "Multiculturalism within a bi-lingual framework," a phrase that arguably highlighted Canadian culture as the site of a complex process/struggle over the nature of Canadian identity and nationhood" (55).

44 Sarah Davidson and Nancy Pollak, interview by author, December 2, 2002, Vancouver, BC.

45 Gareth Griffiths, "The Post-colonial Project: Critical Approaches and Problems," in *New National and Post-colonial Literatures*, ed. Bruce King (Oxford: Clarendon Press, 1996), 166–67.

46 Ibid., 175.

47 James F. English, "Winning the Culture Game: Prizes, Awards, and the Rules of Art," *New Literary History* 33, no. 1 (2002): 126.

48 Bruce King, "New Centres of Consciousness: New, Post-colonial, and International English Literature," in *New National and Post-colonial Literatures*, ed. Bruce King (Oxford: Clarendon Press, 1996), 7.

49 Arun Mukherjee, "Canadian Nationalism, Canadian Literature, and Racial Minority Women," *Essays on Canadian Writing* 56 (1995): 82.

50 Ibid., 85.

51 Ibid., 85.

52 Ibid., 92.

53 Ibid., 89.

54 David Bennett, introduction to *Multicultural States: Rethinking Difference and Identity*, ed. David Bennett (London and New York: Routledge, 1998), 4.

55 Larissa Lai, *When Fox Is a Thousand* (Vancouver: Press Gang, 1995), 10.

56 Ibid., 10, 11.

57 Ibid., 24.

58 Ibid., 63.

59 Ibid., 63.

60 Ibid., 65.

61   Robyn, Morris, "Making Eyes: Colouring the Look in Larissa Lai's *When Fox Is a Thousand* and Ridley Scott's *Blade Runner*," *Australian Canadian Studies* 20, no. 1 (2002): 81–82.

62   Roy Miki, "Can I See Your ID?: Writing in the 'Race' Codes That Bind," *West Coast Line* 31, no. 3 (Winter 1997–98): 90.

63   Donna Bennett, "Conflicted Vision: A Consideration of Canon and Genre in English-Canadian Literature," in *Canadian Canons*, ed. Robert Lecker (Toronto: U of Toronto P, 1991), 134.

64   David Bennett, introduction to *Multicultural States*, 5.

65   Lorraine Weir, "Normalizing the Subject: Linda Hutcheon and the English-Canadian Postmodern," in *Canadian Canons*, ed. Robert Lecker (Toronto: U of Toronto P, 1991), 194.

66   Larissa Lai, "Interview with Larissa Lai," by Ashok Mathur, July 1998, http://www.eciad.ca/%7Eamathur/larissa/larissa.html.

67   I do not mean to overstate the influence of Helwig's opinion, but instead want to treat his comments as symptomatic of a certain kind of critical approach to Asian Canadian literature in order to consider its particular set of expectations. At the same time, however, as one anonymous reviewer for this volume pointed out, it is still necessary to remember that Lai's novel was reprinted in 2004 by Arsenal Pulp Press and is still widely taught. Both indicate the level of success that this novel has achieved and raise questions about readerships, university patronage, and pedagogical complicity. According to Arsenal Pulp publisher Brian Lam, the majority of sales for the reprint of *When Fox Is a Thousand* come from course adoptions. The original Press Gang edition, he believes, likely received more trade sales (Brian Lam, "*When Fox Is a Thousand* Query," August 1, 2007, personal email [August 2, 2007]). The increased circulation of the reprint of Lai's novel within post-secondary contexts coincides with the rising acceptance of Asian Canadian literature within academic institutions.

68   David Helwig, Charles Lillard, and Gayla Reid, "The Chapters/Books in Canada First Novel Award," *Books in Canada* 25, no. 4 (May 1996): 3.

69   Ibid.

70   Eleanor Ty and Donald C. Goellnicht, introduction to *Asian North American Identities*, ed. Eleanor Ty and Donald C. Goellnicht (Bloomington and Indianapolis: Indiana UP), 6.

71   For an extended discussion of the development of ethnic writing in Canada as an object of study, see Christl Verduyn, ed., *Literary Pluralities* (Peterborough, ON: Broadview Press and *Journal of Canadian Studies*, 1998), especially "Introduction": 9–18.

72   Daniel Coleman and Donald Goellnicht, "Introduction: 'Race' into the Twenty-First Century," *Essays on Canadian Writing* 75 (2002): 2.

73   Goellnicht, "A Long Labour," 1.

74   Roy Miki, "Can Asian Adian? Reading the Scenes of 'Asian Canadian,'" *West Coast Line* 33/34, no. 3 (Winter 2001): 57.

75   Goellnicht, "A Long Labour," 3.

76   Rey Chow, "Against the Lures of Diaspora: Minority Discourse, Chinese Women, and Intellectual Hegemony," in *Gender and Sexuality in Twentieth-Century Chinese Literature and Society*, ed. Tonglin Lu (Albany: State U of New York P, 1993), 42.

77   Ibid., 42.

78   Ibid., 42.

79 Fred Wah, "A Poetics of Ethnicity," in *Twenty Years of Multiculturalism: Successes and Failures*, ed. Stella Hryniuk (Winnipeg: St. John's College Press, 1992), 99.
80 Ibid., 99.
81 Jennifer Andrews and John Clement Ball, "Introduction: Beyond the Margins," *Studies in Canadian Literature* 25, no. 1 (2000): 3.
82 Miki, "Can I See," 93.
83 Emily Apter, "On Translation in a Global Market," *Public Culture* 13, no. 1 (2001): 2.
84 Miki, "Can I See," 92–93.

chapter eight

Ken Lum, Paul Wong, and the Aesthetics of Pluralism

Ming Tiampo

With regard particularly to the rituals involving fire, incense and walking the mountain, I remark to Paul Wong that the danger of exotification veers perilously close. In the context of performance art, with its Eurocentric basis, the threat is very real. Who is this for? Both within a Eurocentric practice and outside of it, we have a need to incorporate Asian practices at the same time as altering them to suit the situation, at the same time as protecting them. To bring our own family practices to our new home, within white mainstream institutions, reclaims that space. But in a context in which we and our practices have been exoticized, appropriated, mystified and misrepresented, we still have to worry about how that work may be read.   —Larissa Lai[1]

L arissa Lai presciently evokes the conundrum of autoethnography in this analysis of Paul Wong's *Chinaman's Peak: Walking the Mountain*, which he created for *As Public as Race* at the Walter Phillips Gallery of the Banff Centre for the Arts in 1992.[2] *As Public as Race* was a three-part exhibition series that reflected upon the possibilities of official multiculturalism after the ratification of the Multiculturalism Act in 1988, buoyed by the optimism of having difference newly entrenched in the nation's statutes. Each of the artists—Margo Kane, James Luna, and Paul Wong—were invited by curator Sylvie Gilbert to create work reflecting on race, identity, and stereotype, "commenting in different ways on a society largely blind not only to racist attitudes, but non-white cultural practices in general ... creat[ing] powerful precedents that enable distinctive practices to emerge and flourish."[3] Kane's work, *Memories Springing/Waters Singing*, Luna's *Indian Legends*, and Wong's *Chinaman's Peak: Walking the Mountain* all worked to subvert cultural stereotypes, reclaiming their own cultural voices and the right to represent themselves.

Wong's work, *Chinaman's Peak: Walking the Mountain*, was an installation, video, and performance piece that developed out of a longer feature-length video called *Ordinary Shadows, Chinese Shade* (1988) that the artist produced after returning from an extended voyage in China. The culmination of a period of discovery and reunification of family, language, and culture that began only in 1982, *Ordinary Shadows, Chinese Shade* and *Chinaman's Peak: Walking the Mountain* were exercises in recovery. In his own words, they were an attempt to "recover the lost histories and tend the gravestones left untended for decades."[4] In the performance *Chinaman's Peak*, Wong swept gravesites, lit candles, and paid respect to the spirits of Chinese pioneers, allowing the incense smoke to fill the spaces left empty by mainstream discourse. Wong filled the gap with a palimpsest of memory that layered the commemoration of his father, Chinese railway workers, and the forgotten history of Chinaman's Peak, a mountain so named in 1980 in honour of a Chinese cook who climbed the peak in 1896, whose name, Ha Ling, was not restored until 1997. Wong also filled these silent margins with the memory of friends and lovers who had committed suicide, Paul Speed and Kenneth Fletcher.

Reclaiming stories of the past and rebuilding histories that were assimilated, obscured, and marginalized through (auto)biographical and autoethnographic narratives was an important first step in cultural race politics that mirrored the consciousness raising of first-wave feminism. The priority was then, as Wong declared in the catalogue for the 1991 exhibition *Yellow Peril: Reconsidered*, to be "first seen and heard."[5] However, as Lai points out, when the fragrant streams of incense smoke found their way into "white mainstream institutions,"[6] these voices risked being received as radically other, as exoticism staged for the consumption of audiences in search of the new. Indeed, when other voices first entered into a white discursive field, they were in danger of being perceived as exotic, as excitingly strange. Although first-wave cultural race politics may have eschewed the centre for this very reason, creating safe spaces on the margins where those narratives would not be misunderstood or co-opted, I would argue that the task before us now is more radical: to challenge the very existence of "white mainstream institutions." Not only must racialized identities be re-theorized, but so must what Lai referred to as the "white mainstream." In other words, rather than making circumscribed interventions, insertions, and recoveries, it is essential to disassociate the terms "white" and "mainstream," refiguring the entire texture of discourse and dislocating the authority of the hegemonic voice rather than making measured interventions and insertions.

This chapter examines recent work by Ken Lum and Paul Wong, arguing that both artists self-consciously abandon autoethnographic narratives in order to define a problematic and aesthetics of pluralism. I argue that both artists represent a new recognition that the consequences of pluralism are relevant to all Canadians, as well as the significance of using mainstream discursive structures to generate critical debate around the articulation of a national identity that is heterogeneous. Demonstrating that debates about multiculturalism in the '80s and '90s were concerned about who should define the margins—the centre (the government) or the margins themselves—this paper argues that the terms of those debates were leaving the hierarchy of centre and margins intact. Rather, using the recent work of Ken Lum and Paul Wong to illuminate what an alternative might look like, I suggest that the terms of engagement should be shifted to consider how we define the centre itself, what Slavoj Žižek called the "privileged empty point of universality from which one is able to appreciate (and depreciate) properly other particular cultures."[7]

My analysis of Ken Lum's work includes his Portrait text works (*Portrait Attributes* and *Portrait Repeated Texts)* and *There is no place like home* (2000) series, while my examination of Paul Wong will consider his multimedia *Hungry Ghosts* (2003) and *The Class of 2000: A Refugee Prisoner's Lament* (2000).[8] I consider how both Chinese-Canadian artists actively resist the temptation to focus only on Chinese-Canadian issues without ignoring them, and think instead about what their critical perspectives bring to a consideration of their larger imagined community—the nation. By reflecting on issues of race and ethnicity as categories that touch *all* Canadians, Lum and Wong fragment the fiction of a unified, essential identity for any of us in this diverse and fractured nation. Indeed, I would go so far as to argue that their work functions on an international level, articulating a model of pluralism that is relevant beyond the boundaries of Canada.[9]

The philosophical model of pluralism that Lum and Wong make visible in their work is best articulated by Richard Day, who critiques official multiculturalism as it has been theorized and practised until now as a recognition of minority rights that continues to perpetuate the existence of a majority and a minority, a self and an other.[10] He traces the origins of their theoretical models to the early colonial history of Canadian diversity, arguing that official multiculturalism is a technology of governance that derives from British colonial techniques of managing difference within an expansive empire. Built on these foundations, official multiculturalism and its defenders fortify the construction of a "silent, Invisible Self group that chooses to give, or not to give, gifts of recognition and self-government to noisy, Visible Others."[11] In addition to perpetuating a social hierarchy that will never lead to a nation of equals, Day explains that the consequences of this construct are dire for both the Invisible Self group (that he identifies with English Canada) and the Visible Others. Using psychoanalytic theory, he demonstrates that this inequality leads to an over-investment in the visibility of the others (exotification through recognition) and an inability to define the self due to its symbolic invisibility (lack of recognition), generating both a fetishization of "symbolic ethnicity" and English Canada's soul-searching obsession with "What It Means to Be Canadian."[12] Multiculturalism as a mode of managing otherness thus constructs arbitrary boundaries between self and other that caricature the other and empty the self of everything but relational content (not British, not American, not French …). As Day writes, "[…] if Canadian multiculturalism is to be seen as a technology of governance, then this technology must also be seen as perversely constraining/seducing individual bodies into becoming, that is orbiting about, *nothing at all*."[13]

Day's critique should, however, be distinguished from conservative criticisms of official multiculturalism that emerged during the mid-1990s, accusing it of undermining Canadian national unity and ultimately putting immigrants at a disadvantage. Most vocal were Neil Bissoondath, who wrote of official multiculturalism's "undeniable ghettoization," and Richard Gwyn, who commented that "official multiculturalism encourages apartheid, or to be a bit less harsh, ghettoism."[14] Unlike these critics, Day does not see the terms of pluralism framed as a choice between assimilation into mainstream culture and maintaining separate cultural spheres. Rather, he writes that there is no such thing as a unified, pure notion of mainstream culture in Canada, and argues for a de-territorialization of identity that replaces the categories of self and other with an open discursive field that is in "dynamic and fluid chaos," allowing the "free emergence" of multiple identities.[15] The Canada that Day envisions is thus one where the fiction of sameness within the "canonical Self's" imagined community surrounded by the particularities of the others is supplanted by an acknowledgement that everyone is different, and that the centre, far from being "nothing at all," is teeming with life.

Figuring multiple, overlapping and conflicting narratives in their work, both Lum and Wong employ an aesthetics of heterogeneity to articulate their visions of Canada. They work as storytellers, reinventing the myths of the nation, thus transforming the imagined community itself. They refuse to commodify and whitewash difference, grappling with the difficult seams of pluralism. Resisting the easy sell of revelling in the beauty of diversity, they address issues such as racism, discrimination, refugee status, disease, culture clash, war, and historical injustices. At the same time, they refuse the notion that stories about visible minorities must always be engaged with questions of difference, and indulge in accounts of love, boredom, and everyday life.

In addition to investigating a broad spectrum of human concerns, both artists reflect on the medium of their expression and define the possibility of an aesthetics of pluralism. Rather than reaching for modernist universals, both artists stress the importance of the particular in the constitution of community. Lum, for example, comments that he is interested in the micro-moments of life, "[...] which are seemingly banal and seemingly insignificant but actually can mean a lot because they're so undefinable, so indescribable. They're not like major movements; its not the revolution itself, but the moments of conflict."[16] The visual techniques that they employ emphasize that particularity. Eschewing the timelessness and universal claims of painting, both artists use media (photography and video) associated with the proliferation of images in popular culture, manipulating those images to convey a sense of the microcosm, the tiny pieces that make up our world.

They seek nothing less than to reconfigure the narratives that constitute our imagined community—the term that Benedict Anderson used to describe the psychological feeling of nationhood.[17] For both artists, pluralism is a mainstream issue. Unlike *As Public as Race*, which created a separate space to explore otherness, Lum and Wong open a discursive field in which diversity is constitutive of every Canadian's identity. So committed are they to bringing their provocations into the larger public sphere that they both situate their work on the border between art and non-art, using mass media to reach an audience beyond the gallery-going elite, while maintaining a critical voice that challenges viewers to think for themselves. Using billboards, newspapers, and public airwaves to disseminate their work to a general public, they reach beyond Bissoondath's "ghettos" into mainstream discourse, ultimately reframing "minority questions" as issues of national importance.

Ken Lum

In the late 1980s and early 1990s, the Vancouver artist Ken Lum created a series of large scale *Portrait Text* works that juxtaposed photographs of "characters" in the style of the Vancouver Photoconceptualists with text panels crafted in the visual language of old-style sign painting—a trade that Lum learned from his neighbour in East Vancouver. The *Portrait Text* works can be divided into three groups, the *Portrait Logos*, *Portrait Attributes*, and *Portrait Repeated Texts*, each of which considers a different kind of relationship between text and image. As a group, the *Portrait Text* works weave together many strands of experience, creating a narrative of life in Canada, life perhaps on the east side of Vancouver, that directly engages with issues of pluralism, immigration, and home, as well as examining poverty, love, and teenaged fantasy, among other themes. Lum expands his narrative territory beyond the confines of mandatory ethnicity, yet he also refutes the notion of a utopian post-ethnicity. At times, his works reveal his deep engagement with the discourses of art history, addressing questions of aesthetics, medium, and representation, revealing these "universal" issues as specific to a given context. Operating on multiple levels, Lum's work represents a diverse world without creating a discourse of otherness by weaving together self and other into a fractured, heterogeneous, yet common fabric of experience.

In the *Portrait Repeated Texts* work *Don't be silly, you're not ugly* (1993; see Figure 8.1) for example, Lum analyzes the experience of marginality by using beauty as a cipher for anxieties of belonging. In this piece, a young Asian woman wearing a figure-concealing black dress stands against a chain-link fence in what resembles a schoolyard. She stares at the ground, her badly permed hair tucked behind her ears to reveal a tearful expression on her face. Her friend, an earnest-looking brunette, looks at her intently, worried. This scene is juxtaposed with a purple text panel that reads:

> Don't be silly
> you're not ugly
> You're not ugly
> You're not ugly at all
> You're being silly
> You're just being silly
> You're not
> You're not ugly at all

The words on this sign are arranged idiosyncratically, flirting with references to Symbolist and Dada poetry. In the seventh line of the text, the friend's words of comfort metamorphose into a statement of the real problem: "You're not." You do not exist. The viewer is left to wonder why the crying woman feels that her identity is negated, that she does not belong,

Don't be silly
you're not ugly
You're not ugly
You're not ugly at all
You're being silly
You're just being silly
You're not
You're not ugly at all

Figure 8.1 Ken Lum, *Don't Be Silly, You're Not Ugly*, 1993. Chromogenic print with lacquer and enamel on aluminum. Collection of the Vancouver Art Gallery, gift of Marion and Jack Adelaar, VAG 99.51.2. Photo: Tim Bonham, Vancouver Art Gallery.

that she is in some way objectionable, ugly. Lum allows us to come to our own conclusions about the cause of her inability to belong, be it race, gender, class, or some combination of all three, making us pause and consider the experience of the outsider as a larger conceptual problem.

In this work, as in all the *Portrait Repeated Texts*, Lum uses the text panel on the side of the photograph to *repeat* the character's speech. The works originated from the artist's experience watching a television program in Germany that had been badly dubbed, creating a long time lag between the movement of mouths and the utterance of sound. As Lum comments, "There was a sense of drama and anxiety, which I found really interesting."[18] It is not surprising, then, that these text panels read less as speech bubbles than they do as subtitles or closed-captioning, with the work of representation made as clear as if the text were enclosed by quotation marks. This heightened sense of drama underscores the fact that we are not viewing a moment of someone's life, but a constructed moment of banality, writ large. This strategy of manifest fictionality at once resists the ethnographic gaze that seeks to categorize and know the other, and also claims a position for these narratives in a wider discursive field by unambiguously taking these stories, however particularized, beyond the individual.

In *We Are Sacred Blade* (1990; see Figure 8.2), *Melly Shum Hates Her Job* (1989; Figure 8.3), and *Mounties & Indians* (1989; Figure 8.4), Lum pointedly moves beyond questions of ethnicity and class to other human concerns such as fantasy, ennui, and tourism. In embracing the luxury of being able to be banal, Lum assumes the privilege of speech that is not rationed and does not always have to be political.

Lum humorously plays with teenaged garage-band fantasies in *We Are Sacred Blade*. A group of four white teenaged boys with heavy-metal tresses, dressed in jeans, tight leather pants and snakeskin boots, rock to the sound of their own ecstasy. Despite their dress and showmanship, however, we are convinced by the daytime lighting, shiny linoleum floors, and fake wood panelling of the tiny room that they occupy that they are not in fact performing before a large fan base, but in the rec room of one of their parents' homes. This contradiction between reality and fantasy is further amplified by the composition of the photograph, which emphasizes their delusions of grandeur. The drummer is raised higher than the rest of the band, creating an ironic reference to the technique of pyramidal composition used to aggrandize figures in painting from the Renaissance to Courbet (especially history painting, a subject of great interest for Lum).[19] The monumental size of Lum's photographs (in this case, 121.3 cm × 279.4 cm) also refers to the status of history painting, equating the importance of these micro-narratives with the allegorical themes of history painting. To the left is a violet text panel that reads "We Are Sacred Blade," the text of "Sacred Blade" rendered in a tricoloured gothic font one might see on heavy-metal merchandising or publicity. Weaving together references to history painting—the pinnacle of the Salon hierarchy—with quotations from popular culture, Lum reflects on the boundaries of art and the relationship between painting, photography, and mass media. Because of their histrionic banality and pop-irony, however, these works resist becoming monumentalized. Rather, they begin to question the universality of claims made in the history of art, asking how universal narratives are constituted, whose interests they represent, and what values they convey.

Despite their banality, these works are deeply political. In *Melly Shum Hates Her Job*, Lum treats Shum's ethnicity as a matter of pointed disinterest, concentrating on the almost comical contrast of Shum's gentle, almost subversive smile and passive pose with the words "Melly Shum HATES Her Job," with the word "hates" triple emphasized with colour, form, and outline. The flashy, ironic pop-icon font adds a layer of theatricality, of fiction, to the statement that makes the viewer wonder why this aspect of Melly Shum's life has been represented and inserted into the

Figure 8.2 Ken Lum, *We Are Sacred Blade*, 1990, edition of 2. Aluminum, enamel, c-print, mounted on sintra, 47 3/4 × 110 × 2 1/2 inches. ARG# LK1990–004.1 © Ken Lum. Courtesy Andrea Rosen Gallery, New York.

Figure 8.3 *Melly Shum Hates Her Job*, 1989. Colour print; pressed paper vinyl film letters on Plexiglas, 124.5 × 230.3 cm. Collection of the Winnipeg Art Gallery, gift of Denise Oleksijczuk, accession # G-89–1502. Photo: Ernest Mayer, The Winnipeg Art Gallery.

Figure 8.4 *Mounties & Indians*, 1989. Colour print; pressed paper vinyl film letters on Plexiglas, 204.0 × 124.5 cm. Collection of the Winnipeg Art Gallery, acquired with funds from The Winnipeg Art Gallery Foundation Inc., accession # G-89–1502. Photo: Ernest Mayer, The Winnipeg Art Gallery.

public sphere. Ethnicity is wittily de-essentialized in *Mounties & Indians* as well. The tongue-in-cheek phrase "Mounties and Indians," rendered in the font of vintage storefront signage, dominates the bottom half of the work and sets the viewer up for a kitschy restaging of stereotypes from Hollywood Westerns. Instead, in the photograph, a group of urban Indians pose with Mounties in dress uniforms. Two Mounties of almost identical height

Figure 8.5 Ken Lum, *There Is No Place like Home*, Kunsthalle Vienna, 2000/01. © museum in progress, www.mip.at. Photo: Roman Berka.

pose stiffly, formally, flanking a native family who smile into the camera. At ease with the photographer and posing with the casual gestures of self-representation rather than representation of type, the Indians look like tourists, and the Mounties like the tourist attraction.

By addressing the figure of the native and critiquing historicized stereotypes and perceptions, Lum breaks down the opposition of immigrant and native—those who were here before, and those who came after. In so doing, Lum seems to ask why the opposition? Before and after who? Breaking down the opposition and critically engaging with the politics of race, racialization, and representation for First Nations groups, Lum frames his project as a problematic—not just for Chinese Canadians, not just for immigrants, not just for First Nations peoples—but for all Canadians.

The *Portrait Text* works create a kaleidoscope of meaning that draws strength from the multiplicity of stories that are told. It is, however, only when the works are viewed together that a heterogeneous vision begins to emerge. Both Lum's billboard-sized work, *There Is No Place like Home* (2000; see Figure 8.5) and Paul Wong's *The Refugee Class of 2000* articulate ideas nascent in Lum's *Portrait Text* series, presenting multiple voices within the framework of a single time-space unit, giving rise to an aesthetics of pluralism.

In *There Is No Place like Home* Lum weaves multiple narratives together in one space, refuting the possibility of a unified voice completely, giving form to Day's space of free emergence. This work was an enormous public installation that consisted of twelve visual blocks—six photographs and six text cells on the subject of "home."[20] At first glance, each text cell seems to be associated with the image above or below it: the four visible minorities in the centre expressing ambivalence and anger about the idea of home, the white man telling an imaginary audience, "Go back to where you come from! Why don't you go home?" and a white woman who does not seem to think this applies to her, "Wow, I really like it here. I don't think I ever want to go home!" As with the *Portrait Repeated Text* works, however, the dialogue does not seem to stream unencumbered from Lum's characters. Rather, each text, isolated in its own separate pictorial cell, appears slightly dislocated, underscoring the act of representation. That sense of dislocation is further underscored by the multiplicity of text panels and photo portraits, which does not provide a stated logic for reading the work. The geometry of the work allows for multiple readings, forcing the viewer to become aware of their own assumptions about race, class, and gender when interpreting it. Why, for example, do we assume that the Muslim woman did not say "Wow, I really like it here. I don't think I ever want to go home!" and that the European tourist was not thinking, "I'm never made to feel at home here. I don't feel at home here"?

The twelve panels combine to form a cacophony of reflection on the question of home. The simultaneity of the narratives, complicated by the purposeful ambiguity of text-image relations, creates an impression of chaos, of discursive mastery denied. What emerges is an aesthetics of rupture, of collage, of multiple voices and narratives, a visual space in which no one narrative takes precedence over the others. In this work, Lum examines the question of home from multiple perspectives, using each fictional character as a facet on his prism of analysis. There is no autoethnography here. Not only does Lum examine the question of what home means for other minority groups—for Muslims, the poor, and African Canadians—but he turns his gaze back on what Lai called the "white mainstream," incorporating those narratives into his imagined community. He thus breaks down the categories of self and other in the discourse of the nation to include a multiplicity of voices—voices that contradict; voices that are dissatisfied, cantankerous, and angry; but voices that in the end, are heard.

Despite the far-from-utopian message of this billboard, it was in fact an act of faith and an optimistic vision of pluralism in which airtime is shared even when minorities step beyond the boundaries of cultural festivals into the real political struggles of envisioning society, revising history, and demanding restitution. This is not the multiculturalism of colourful festivals and good Chinese food. This is the pluralism of free emergence as envisioned by Day, where differences are not occluded by ideology and where conflicts are played out in the public sphere. It is this vision of pluralism that was radically inserted into the landscape of Vienna in 2000.

In the year that Jörg Haider, the anti-immigrant leader of the Freedom Party, was elected to office, this billboard was exhibited on the side of the Kunsthalle Vienna. The project began when Lum was invited to create a work for 3,000 poster sites scattered around Vienna by the Museum in Progress, a Viennese non-profit organization that seeks to realize in practice André Malraux's *Museum without Walls*.[21] Planning exhibitions in non-traditional spaces such as subway stations, the Vienna Opera House, and the street using television, newspapers, magazines, billboards, and posters, the group seeks to bring art into the lives of ordinary people. Faced with the rise of the extreme right in Austria and other parts of Europe, Lum felt that he had to respond with a work that would force people to think critically about the political stances that were being taken in that country. What he created was a series of six posters that eventually provided the model for *There is no place like home*, juxtaposing portraits of his characters with brightly coloured text blocks. Installed all over the city, they would have created a consistent visual presence and would have been read as a single poster campaign designed to open dialogue about the question of home. Tellingly, two civic officials with allegiances to the far right coalition party rejected Lum's proposal—the first time any proposal had not just been rubber-stamped to proceed. Given the strength of the opposition, it appeared that Lum's work had touched a nerve. The Museum in Progress persevered.[22] The Kunsthalle Vienna donated the side of their building, and production costs were sponsored by the Canadian Embassy in Austria, the Viennese Fund for Integration, and the Austrian League of Human Rights. Lum waived his fee, re-formatted the work to cover the side of the Kunsthalle (10 m × 54 m), and published three double-page spreads of the work in the Austrian newspaper *Der Standard*.[23]

Using the language and format of commercial advertising, Lum's work does not immediately announce itself as art. Borrowing a concept from performance theory, we can say that the work is "non-matrixed," meaning that it exists outside of the matrix or frame of art.[24] Viewers approaching the work are not alerted to the status of the work, and they perceive it at first as advertising. Viewers thus seek to scan its message, evaluate whether or not that message is useful, then move on to the next image-text module in their environment. Their viewing cycle is, however, disrupted by Lum's work, since it does not provide a clear message that can be consumed.

What is this billboard trying to sell? What is it trying to say? Is it critiquing the Freedom Party's stance on immigration? Or is it anti-immigration, as a careless reviewer of the *Ottawa Citizen* intimated?[25] Discomfited unless they stop to interpret the work for themselves, city dwellers, who are accustomed to receiving hundreds of visual cues daily, are forced to stop and critically engage with the ideas before them. This moment of recognition, of critical reflection borne out of surprise and discovery, creates a heightened engagement with the art object that Lum cherishes. He comments, "I like to play with a kind of deferred recognition of my art as art. Ultimately, it is the status of art that is recognized, but it is a deferred status."[26]

For Lum, the mental effort of recognizing the billboard as art and struggling with its meaning in an unexpected context is critical to the experience of his work. Lum seeks not just to address attitudes about immigration in this work, but to educate people to take a more critical stance towards messages they receive in the media. It is a radical project that seeks to refigure the ways in which people relate to information in the public sphere. He writes,

> A second consideration has to do with how to insert an artistic statement in the cacophony that fills up the experience of contemporary civic space. If indeed as Foucault claim[s], domination insinuates itself into all systems of production and communication, and in language, then I felt my project had to at least try to open up public space by providing an askance view to the domination. By this I mean the work had to resolve the contradiction of acknowledging public familiarity with the structures, codes, and messages of publicly sited discursive conveyances, as well as provide for an articulation different from corporate culture. In other words, my idea had to register as art, familiar [though] it may be to the form of non-art. I wanted a way of using billboards to express disillusionment with [the] public media's manipulative nature.[27]

Mounted on the side of the Kunsthalle in the context of a cosmopolitan city whose population prides itself on its cultural literacy, where Museum in Progress had been working for a decade organizing artistic interventions in everyday spaces, Lum's work was acclaimed by the art press in Vienna. Reviews of the work provided translations of the texts into German, and also pushed the critical dialogue that Lum sought into the public sphere. In particular, a review entitled "Was heißt hier heimat" (What is home called here?) insightfully positioned the work between Vienna and Vancouver, using Lum's culturally diverse home as a model of innovation and pluralism to quell Austrian anxieties about immigration.[28] Its international relevance was not lost on Lum, who toured the work to Innsbruck,

Venice, Ljubljana, Lofoten, Berlin, Duisburg, Rotterdam, Brussels, and Warsaw. The work was not, however, translated from English until it was shown in Canada, as Lum sought to mitigate its specificity to each context, stressing that this is a "problem that transcends borders."[29]

In 2002, a bilingual version of the work was installed at the Canadian Museum of Contemporary Photography in Ottawa.[30] The work was installed in both French and English in order to maintain its neutrality in a Canadian context. Directly facing Parliament, the site where *There is no place like home* was installed on the museum wall was most visible from the country's centres of power. Claiming centre stage, this work re-articulated the nation on a monumental scale. It resisted the temptation of grand heroic gestures that monumentality provokes, however. Representing the tiny fragments of experience that make up our collective and heterogeneous idea of home, *There is no place like home* contributed to the slow and subtle process of remaking the centre.

Paul Wong

As with Lum, the video/installation/performance artist Paul Wong's diversity of interests has created a landscape of work that, through its variety, defies categorization as autoethnography. His work explores questions of poverty, suicide, sexuality, and AIDS, as well as identity and ethnicity, providing a trenchant analysis of social issues that are rendered invisible in the mainstream media. Mixing real-life footage with commentary and fiction, Wong's work takes a no-holds-barred approach to social commentary that does not provide abstractions. His gritty use of real-life footage in his work—the investigation of a murder that he discovered in his neighbourhood in *Murder Research* (1977), or his raw interviews of people recounting their sexual experiences in the multi-channel installation *Confused: Sexual Views* (1984)—opens our eyes to marginalized realities, veering perilously close to Diane Arbus-style voyeurism. Wong makes it difficult for the viewer to visually consume his work, however, since reality is frequently disrupted by irreality. As Monika Kin Gagnon argues, this jarring effect of reality being cast as possible fiction disrupts the viewer's passive viewing practices: "through their refusal of fixed formal genres, [the works] not only disrupt the production of established meanings found in mainstream stereotypes, but they also undermine the security of didactic counter images."[31] As reality is misinterpreted as fiction, and fiction as reality, identities, stereotypes, cultural norms, and expectations are revealed in Wong's work as fragile constructs.

As Larissa Lai implied in the epigraph of this paper, the discursive ambiguity of Wong's work leaves it particularly open to misinterpretation. So open, in fact, that when the artist was commissioned to create a work for the Vancouver Art Gallery in its new space in 1984, the work was rejected two days before the opening by the then director of the gallery, Luke Rombout. His reasoning, and the defence given when Wong sued the Vancouver Art Gallery for breach of contract? *Confused: Sexual Views* is "not art."[32] Because his video practice was so personal—a quality that was intensified by his physical presence in almost all of the early works—each piece taken on its own had the potential of being received as autoethnography, what art critic Sarah Milroy called "reality-TV before it had a name."[33]

Responding perhaps in part to the risks of self-exotification, Wong's recent production has moved away from the first-person narrative. The 2003 work *Hungry Ghosts*, which Wong created for a collaboration between the Neutral Ground gallery in Regina and the Nuova Icona gallery in Venice at the 50th Venice Biennale, seems to carefully resist being read as autoethnography.[34] Curator Elspeth Sage commented,

> Wong is currently in a time of reflection, looking for a new contextualization
> of his work. He has been previously categorized in exhibitions through sexual identity, social issues, race politics, cultural representation, and performance practices. This will be the first time that he will be featured with a focus
> on death, a subject that is found in many of his works. The topics will cover
> suicide, murder, ancestral worship, death rituals, sex, and death through
> AIDS.[35]

It is telling that Sage wrote of the artist rather than the work when she referred to the issues with which he had been identified, as if the artist and the work were one, speech and identity inseparable. "He has been previously categorized in exhibitions through sexual identity, social issues, race politics, cultural representation, and performance practices."[36] *Hungry Ghosts* literally reframed this earlier work, taking charge of its reception by recombining footage from *Murder Research* (1977), *in ten sity* (1978, a performance about Ken Fletcher's suicide), and *Chinaman's Peak: Walking the Mountain* (1992). The video pieces were collaged and installed in a multi-channel format in Venice on a *vaporetto* boat, and in Regina at the Neutral Ground Gallery in two large-format projections and three television screens, accompanied by ten still digital collages. Wong's strategy in Venice in particular was highly effective. While earlier pieces had been misinterpreted as "not art" and thus as a kind of documentary, reporting from the trenches of one or another group, here Wong deftly resists the viewer's desire to identify him with the work. The videos address poverty in East Vancouver, drug use, murder, AIDS, suicide, ritual, cultural longing, and most importantly, loss, using the Chinese figure of hungry ghosts—the ignored and forgotten dead—as a metaphor for the marginalized in society. Here, Chinese mythology no longer risked being the object of the ethnographic gaze, as it did in *Chinaman's Peak: Walking the Mountain*. Rather, Wong used it as a subjective lens through which to refract his larger meditation on death and marginality. Deluging the viewer with multiple and overlapping images from different aspects of his oeuvre, Wong's heterogeneous artistic vision emerged clearly. Trapped on the boat, the viewer had no choice but to view it all.

Video collage has been an especially effective technique for Wong in creating an aesthetics of heterogeneity. In 2000, the artist used this technique to give form to his vision of pluralism in the work *The Refugee Class of 2000: A Refugee Prisoner's Lament*. This work was one of three nationally broadcast public service messages that the artist created for the campaign *Unite Against Racism: See People for Who They Really Are*, sponsored by the Canadian Race Relations Foundation. Wong was one of five artists commissioned by the CRRF to create public service announcements for the campaign, which started in 1999.[37]

Wong took two events from 1999 as an inspiration for this series of videos—the arrival of four boats on the coast of B.C. transporting 599 Chinese migrants without legal documentation, and the inauguration of Adrienne Clarkson as Governor General of Canada. Struck by the outspoken opinions that flooded the press after the arrival of the "boat people," Wong sought to humanize the figure of the refugee, reminding viewers that refugees were people too: mothers, brothers, sisters, and friends.[38] Rather than investigating the personal stories of this particular group of refugees, however, Wong sought to use the notion of the refugee as a conceptual category to investigate the limits of Canadian identity. Instead of asking whether this group of refugees should be allowed to stay in Canada (97 percent of respondents polled by the Victoria newspaper *Times Colonist* said no, send them back home) Wong considered the question of what it means to be Canadian.[39] In Wong's video, a diverse group of people proudly proclaim, "I am a refugee." Framed as a public service announcement and not art, the viewer's immediate response is surprise at the prevalence of refugees in the general population. Taken in the context of Wong's artistic practice, however, the viewer begins to wonder where fact leaves off and fiction begins. With each speaker leaving open the possibility that they too, are a refugee, self and other are broken down as discrete categories in this act of solidarity. The video ends with the most surprising refugee: Adrienne

Clarkson, who arrived in Canada as a refugee from Hong Kong in 1942, and was admitted into Canada despite the 1923 Chinese Immigration Act banning Chinese immigrants except for certain categories from entering the country.[40] A photograph of her face is superimposed with a quote taken from her inaugural speech as Governor General, "try to forgive what is past."

Like Lum's *Home*, which freed itself from the discursive space of the Museum, Wong's *Refugee Class of 2000* makes a direct political intervention into the spaces of real life and interaction.[41] The video is a collage of sound, text, image, and video that pulls the viewer in, inviting us to try and make sense of it. On one level, it is extremely structured—the words that flash across the screen are alphabetized—Aboriginal, AIDS, Arabic, Asylum, Auschwitz—the singsong music repeats over and over, and the young adults speaking into the camera answer the same questions and leave, only to return again. They begin by saying "My name is" then move on to "I am a ..." followed by "I was born in" and "I am in the graduating class of 2000" then "I want to be ...," all of this interspersed with the repeated statement "I am a refugee." This sense of repetition and structure gives the viewer a false sense of order, however, as the radical heterogeneity of the overlapping forms and meanings resist easy consumption, or even comprehension. As the speakers introduce themselves, moments of historical injustice flash by with no logical order: the Chinese Exclusion Act, the Japanese internment, Hindus being asked to swear on the Bible, hunger strikes, police brutality. Quotations from recent refugees scroll along the bottom of the screen, showing that we have not yet transcended historical racisms. "You save us, to be locked up in your prisons. Is this your idea of justice? I do not understand." At other moments, racial slurs appear on the screen. Sound, text, and image combine to form a confusing pastiche, disassociating speech from speaker, text from image, so that one can no longer confidently associate what is being said with who is saying it, confounding the ethnographic gaze. One is left with the impression that all of these racial injustices and racial slurs are an insult to every one of the speakers in the video, no matter what their race. It is not so much that this video envisions a world post-race, but that it imagines one in which racism is an affront to all of us, a world so diverse that mainstream Canadian identity itself becomes a palimpsest of cultures. It is a utopian vision of a world post-hegemony.

Despite Wong's rhetorical flair and his articulation of an aesthetics of pluralism characterized by fragments, overlap, and multiples, there are moments of clarity within this chaos. Having, like Lum, critiqued the validity of a hegemonic voice, Wong uses his constructed spaces of clarity to give us glimpses of what a post-hegemonic world would look like. An East Asian woman appears on the screen: "Are you from Hong Kong?" A South Asian woman replies, "No, I'm not that fluent, we speak English at home." A European Canadian woman responds, "Well, I took Japanese at school..." This exchange takes the ethnographer's expectations and stands them on their head. Not only does Wong address the trope of the second generation who is "not so fluent," he examines the impact of immigration on white Canada, on the girl who took Japanese in high school and is likely more fluent than her Japanese-Canadian friends.

Both Wong and Lum resist the hegemonic voice by undermining its authority and by drowning it out with a cacophony of what they see as Canada's new reality. Refusing to distill that reality into a unified narrative or single subject position, they resist reterritorializing the narrative into something knowable and consumable. They create representations of Canada's freely emerging identities that question the necessity and validity of defining national identity as a unified confluence of language, culture, and race with the state. Rather, both artists, like Richard Day, know that this is not a model that has ever worked in Canada, and they have faith in the fractured, complex, overlapping, and multiple national cultures that are emerging from this negotiation.

The East Asian woman in the red sweater from Wong's Class of 2000 reappears, nods with understanding, and says, "I think when you are in Canada it changes you." I would add further that it is mutual: when you are in Canada, you change it.

NOTES

1 Larissa Lai, "The Site of Memory," in *Paul Wong: Chinaman's Peak: Walking the Mountain*, ed. Sylvie Gilbert (Banff: Walter Phillips Gallery, 1993), 12.

2 *As Public as Race* grew directly out of *Race and the Body Politic*, a summer residency at the Banff Centre for the Arts organized by Chris Creighton-Kelly in 1992.

3 *Singing*, Sylvie Gilbert, exhibition curator; Mary Anne Moser, editor and designer (Banff: Walter Phillips Gallery, 1993), 23. This essay is repeated in each of the catalogues in the *As Public as Race* series.

4 Paul Wong, "Walking the Mountain: Performance Description," in *Feng Shui*, ed. Elspeth Sage (Vancouver: On Edge, 1994), 31.

5 Paul Wong, "Yellow Peril: Reconsidered," in *Yellow Peril: Reconsidered* (Vancouver: On Edge, 1990), 7.

6 Lai, "The Site of Memory," 12.

7 Slavoj Žižek, "Multiculturalism; or, The Cultural Logic of Late Capitalism," *New Left Review* 225 (September–October 1997): 44.

8 All of the works by Lum that I discuss in this paper can be consulted in Kitty Scott and Martha Hanna, eds., *Ken Lum: Works with Photography* (Ottawa: Canadian Museum of Contemporary Photography, 2002). Documentation of Paul Wong's

Hungry Ghosts video installations can be viewed online at the *Hungry Ghosts* project website, http://www.hungryghosts.net/hungryghosts.htm. All three versions of Wong's *The Class of 2000* can be viewed online at www.ccca.ca, the Centre for Contemporary Canadian Art, a database of Canadian artists and their work. See http://www.ccca.ca/artists/artist_info.html?languagePref=en&link_id=744&artist =Paul+Wong.

9   The relevance of Lum's model of multiculturalism to the Austrian context was explored in a review of Lum's *There is no place like home* in the Austrian newspaper *Falter*. Vitus H. Weh, "Was heißt hier heimat" (What is home called here), *Falter*, January 2, 2001.

10   Richard J.F. Day, *Multiculturalism and the History of Canadian Diversity* (Toronto: U of Toronto P, 2000).

11   Ibid., 216.

12   Herbert Gans, "Symbolic Ethnicity: The Future of Ethnic Groups and Cultures in America," *Ethnic and Racial Studies* 2 (January 1979): 1–20; Day, *Multiculturalism and the History of Canadian Diversity*, 205.

13   Day, *Multiculturalism and the History of Canadian Diversity*, 208.

14   Neil Bissoondath, *Selling Illusions: The Cult of Multiculturalism in Canada* (Toronto: Penguin, 1994), 111; Richard Gwyn, *Nationalism Without Walls: The Unbearable Lightness of Being Canadian* (Toronto: McClelland and Stewart, 1995), 274.

15   Day, *Multiculturalism and the History of Canadian Diversity*, 225. On the free emergence theory, see Day, "The Rise of the Mosaic Metaphor," in *Multiculturalism and the History of Canadian Diversity* (Toronto: U of Toronto P, 2000), 146–53.

16   Ken Lum interviewed by Munrow Galloway, "Ken Lum—It's Not the Revolution Itself …," *Artpress* no. 209 (January 1996): 50; quoted in Kitty Scott, "Ken Lum: Works with Photography," in *Ken Lum: Works with Photography*, ed. Kitty Scott and Martha Hanna (Ottawa: Canadian Museum of Contemporary Photography, 2002), 24.

17   Benedict Anderson, *Imagined Communities: Reflections on the Origin and Spread of Nationalism* (London: Verso, 1983).

18   Ken Lum, "Portraits," in *Notion of Conflict: A Selection of Contemporary Canadian Art*, ed. Dorine Mignot (Amsterdam: Stedelijk Museum, 1995), 27.

19   In the article "On Board the Raft of the Medusa," as well as in a number of lectures presented at the Universities Arts Association of Canada and Yale University among others, Lum argued that this pyramidal composition was used subversively in Théodore Géricault's *Raft of the Medusa* (1819) to critique the social hierarchy in France that enslaved Africans as less-than-human. Ken Lum, "On Board the Raft of the Medusa," *Nka: Journal of Contemporary African Art* 10 (Spring/Summer 1999): 14–17.

20   According to the Austrian newspaper *Neue Zeit*, Lum's billboard, which measured 54 m × 10 m, was the fifth time the Museum in Progress had sponsored the creation of the "größte Bild der Welt" (largest picture in the world). Review of *There is no place like home*, by Ken Lum (Museum in Progress, Vienna), "Das größte Bild der Welt, *Neue Zeit*, December 5, 2000.

21   André Malraux, *Le Musée Imaginaire de la sculpture mondiale* (Paris: Gallimard, 1952).

22   The Museum in Progress's support of Lum's work was one aspect of the Viennese cultural community's larger critical response to the rise of the far right that involved concerts, exhibitions, and public projects such as Lum's.

23 This large-scale work was produced using CALSI (Computer Aided Large Scale imagery), which was printed on PVC netting. The images were published in *Der Standard* (two portraits and two text blocks at a time) on the following dates: December 2, 2000; December 16, 2000; January 27/28, 2001.

24 This term was coined by performance theoretician Michael Kirby in 1965 to describe "happenings." Michael Kirby, "The New Theatre," *Tulane Drama Review* 10, no. 2 (1965): 23–43.

25 Jennifer Campbell, "Mural Stirs Debate about Community," *Ottawa Citizen*, September 18, 2002.

26 Ken Lum, email message to author, August 4, 2005.

27 Ken Lum, "Art as Counter-Narrative in Public Space," Museum in Progress website, http://www.mip.at/en/dokumente/1674-content.html (accessed August 8, 2005).

28 Vitus H. Weh, "Was heißt hier heimat" (What is home called here), *Falter*, January 2, 2001.

29 Ken Lum, email message to author, August 4, 2005.

30 This work was produced on a smaller scale than in Vienna, and in different materials. The work in Ottawa was 4.39 m × 20.42 m, produced in acrylic lacquer on vinyl.

31 Monika Kin Gagnon, "Go Ahead, Push My Discursive Limits: The Ambivalence of Paul Wong's Video Works," in *Paul Wong: On Becoming A Man*, ed. Jean Gagnon (Ottawa: National Gallery of Canada, 1995), 25.

32 Miguel Moya and Dave Smith, "Exhibit not art, court told," *Globe and Mail*, February 25, 1984. While Rombout used the argument that the work was "not art" as a defence in court, it is likely that the director feared the reactions of his donors and board to this potentially controversial work. This issue has been discussed extensively in the art press and was a major controversy in its time. See Varda Burstyn, "The Wrong Sex," *Canadian Forum*, no. 741 (August/September 1984): 29–33; Sara Diamond, "Daring Documents: The Practical Aesthetics of Early Vancouver Video," in *Vancouver Anthology: The Institutional Politics of Art*, ed. Stan Douglas (Vancouver: Talonbooks, 1991), 47–83; and Elspeth Sage, "Ethics and Art," *Parallelogramme* 12, no. 4 (April/May 1987): 26–29.

33 Sarah Milroy, "Vindication of an Art Pioneer," *Globe and Mail*, October 22, 2002.

34 Paul Wong, *Hungry Ghosts*, video installation, 2003. Documentation of the video installation can be viewed online at the Hungry Ghosts project website, http://www.hungryghosts.net/hungryghosts.htm.

35 Elspeth Sage, "Curatorial Statement for *Paul Wong: Hungry Ghosts*," Neutral Ground, artist-run centre and gallery, Regina, SK, http://www.neutralground.sk.ca/?page=eventdetail&pageid=1&year=2003&id=200451204212504.

36 Ibid.

37 The other artists were Rion Gonsalves, Michael Jarvis, Dana Inkster, and Cynthia Lickers. I thank Anne Marrian, Program Director of the CRRF, for this information and for her kind co-operation.

38 For more on the media reception of the "boat people," see Joshua Greenberg, "Opinion Discourse and Canadian Newspapers: The Case of the Chinese Boat People," *Canadian Journal of Communication* 25 (2000): 517–37; Paul Wong, in *Commentary from the Producers of Unite Against Racism: See People for Who They Really Are* (Toronto: Canadian Race Relations Foundation, 2005), unedited video recording, Phase II of *Unite Against Racism: See People for Who They Really Are* public awareness campaign. With permission of the Canadian Race Relations Foundation.

39 *Victoria Times Colonist*, July 30, 1999. Quoted in Greenberg, 518.

40 Also known as the Chinese Exclusion Act, the Chinese Immigration Act of 1923 banned all Chinese immigrants except for merchants, diplomats, foreign students, and people under "special circumstances." The act was repealed on May 14, 1947, but Chinese immigration did not begin until 1967, when Canadian immigration policy was liberalized.

41 The video can be viewed online at www.ccca.ca, the Centre for Contemporary Canadian Art, a database of Canadian artists and their work. See http://www.ccca .ca/artists/media_detail.html?languagePref=en&mkey=47728&link_id=744.

[chapter nine]

Potent Textuality
Laiwan's Cyborg Poetics

Tara Lee

Scott McFarlane writes that "the textuality of the political, social, and cultural fabric is more and more in evidence. The nation is written. The nation is graphic. As writing it is doubly marked by identity and otherness."[1] Ten years after McFarlane wrote these words, the graphic nature of the nation has become increasingly more apparent as globalization has altered the ability of the state to maintain naturalized and impenetrable borders. Throughout its past, the Canadian state has constructed a national texture that has masked the heterogeneous and discordant elements within its borders. However, the accelerated movement of people, capital, and goods across Canadian boundaries has destabilized the ability of the nation to claim impermeability. Instead, the more permeable lens of the present has revealed spaces for new voices that claim location in the interconnections and ambiguities of destabilized national space. As Diana Brydon argues, "it's time for a new set of questions"[2] as twenty-first century Canadians move beyond seeing the nation as a static, coherent entity to conceiving of it as a contact zone of identities that are "negotiated, interactive, and open to change."[3] Brydon makes statements that are particularly relevant to poet/writer/artist/filmmaker Laiwan, who responds to shifts in capital, technology, and cultural flows with texts that engage in both form and content with reworked national space. Laiwan negotiates new complex power configurations with equally complex creative representations that defy straightforward textual models. This new, located textuality transforms constructed boundaries into sites for disruption, contestation, and generative change.

The agency within creative textual work is important at a time when "scattered hegemonies"[4] are reconfiguring the once naturalized borders of the nation-state. Writers are adapting to these hegemonies with border-crossing subjectivities and texts that are able to grapple with shifting identity contexts. At first glance, Laiwan appears to be the ultimate border-crossing "nomadic subject" who, as Irene Gedalof describes, puts "all of the emphasis on the going, on the transgressing of boundaries."[5] Laiwan does indeed move and create across shifting cultural, national, and textual spaces. She is an artist of Chinese ancestry who was born in Harare, Zimbabwe, in what was then Rhodesia, and then later moved to Canada in 1977 to escape the civil war in that country. This border-crossing subjectivity is matched by texts that combine different creative media and that cross discursive boundaries. Laiwan travels across the borders of now explicitly permeable national space; nonetheless, she returns back to place in order to claim a newly located identity of mixed and generative change. Her poetics claims an identity apart from the nomad's tendency to "side step, or at least downplay, the question of place in the construction of self."[6] For, as Gedalof writes, "to downplay the question of place makes it particularly difficult to engage seriously with the kinds of differences that race, nation, and ethnicity can make for women."[7] Instead, Laiwan offers a "potent"[8] poetics that engages with and claims productive location within altered national space.

Previously, the discursive and material consolidation of Canadian borders has resulted in both writing and criticism that have operated within a naturalized national framework. In order to claim national membership, Asian Canadian writers have often felt compelled to suppress, deny, and cover over the "foreign" aspects of their identity. They have had to limit their acts of textual creation, frequently writing according to, and not openly against, the confines of the national domestic space. Joy Kogawa states that "after the war Japanese Canadians similarly tried to distance themselves from their ethnicity."[9] Asian Canadians found themselves writing within a claustrophobic space that limited their ability to acknowledge the "outside" creative influences that had inflected and continued to inflect Canadian society. This situation produced texts like Kogawa's *Obasan* that depicted Asian Canadian subjectivity that defined itself primarily through its national connections. These texts contained ambivalent representations of Asian Canadian subjectivity that were the creations of writers who grappled with how to write for the domestic while covering over their racialized difference. In *Diamond Grill*, Fred Wah speaks of this dilemma when he writes of "the racism within me that makes and consumes that neutral (white) version of myself, that allows me the sad privilege of being, in this white white world, not the target but the gun."[10] Just as Wah inhabits a body that can visually "pass," many Asian Canadian writers wrote texts that "passed" by camouflaging their foreign connections. They found themselves reifying artificial boundaries in order to fit into national space.

Meanwhile, the efforts of the state to build a coherent "nation" have been replicated in Asian Canadian writers who have felt the artificial impetus to see identity as a "space" that they must claim from larger national territory. Asian Canadian literature has found itself struggling to claim full membership within the larger body of Canadian literature that dominates the national literary landscape. CanLit's status as *the* national literary body has fuelled such an impetus to belong. This desire persists as Asian Canadian writing continues to exist in an implicit hyphenated position that disconnects it from and yet connects it to the nation and its literature. This position leaves Asian Canadian literature in a state of unfulfilled desire as it strives to belong to something in which it seems forever marked. Miki questions, "What's a racialized text like you doing in a place like this?"[11] as a reminder that racialization marks and contains as "different" those who fall within its constructed borders. The naturalization of the borders of the nation has given rise to a belief that "Asian Canadian" must overcome the failure to achieve a similar identity space. Many critical texts invoke words such as "belonging,"[12] "establish,"[13] and "emergence"[14] that imply that there is a definable national space that "Asian Canadian" must "belong to" and "emerge in" in order to claim its own place of agency.

However, this desire to belong to a naturalized nation has altered as Asian Canadian critics and writers respond to recent shifts in capital, technology, and cultural flows with texts that engage in both form and content with reworked national space. Miki in his article "Altered States: Global Currents, The Spectral Nation, and the Production of 'Asian Canadian'" stresses the present opportunity for a reconceiving of the nation:

> The fragmentation of formerly (more or less) coherent public spheres can provide the motivation for practices of critique, countermoves and alliances. These practices have the capacity to enable a rethinking of "nation" as a complex of heterogeneous global/local formations, constituted not solely as enclaves of identification but more generatively as the instance of negotiations across and within temporalities and boundaries. The time of the nation needs to be reconceived as non-synchronous.[15]

Miki argues that the nation is composed of "heterogeneous global/local formations." Under this reconception, "Asian Canadian" emerges as a production of multiple forces and discourses that defies not only spatial and temporal enclosures but also fixed definitional boundaries. Laiwan is one such creative artist who presages this future for Asian Canadian writing in her exploration of permeable identities that produce through their interconnections.[16] She negotiates new power configurations with equally complex literary representations that defy straightforward textual models. Her works speak from spaces where denaturalized borders rework themselves and take on new creative forms. Up until now, Laiwan has existed on the margins of Asian Canadian literature because her heterogeneous cultural background and the mixed nature of her work have resisted categorization. Laiwan and her work take on new critical importance in a present context of fluctuating economic, technological, and cultural flows.

Most importantly, her work negotiates a space of shifting borders by recreating a relationship to place that is different from both the essentialized claims of the past and the celebratory travelling and becoming of the nomadic subject. Gedalof writes that "we need to think about how our genealogies of 'staying put' are entangled with those of dispersion." She continues, "if we understand the nomadic model to be less about 'the going,' and more about defining a different kind of relationship with the space women inhabit, then this might take us some way towards a strategy of simultaneously problematizing and reconstructing a space/place of identity from which a different kind of subject might speak and act."[17] In other words, there now exists the possibility for a new kind of subject, one who speaks, acts, and claims location within fluctuating and intersectional spaces.

Laiwan constructs such a subject through a cyborg poetics, a powerful textual medium that claims creative agency and place within destabilized identity conditions. Laiwan produces works that address the complexities of twenty-first-century impositions on the body while still engaging with the specific contexts in which the racialized writer produces. Her cyborg poetics extends the concept of "the cyborg," defined by feminist theorist Donna Haraway as "a cybernetic organism, a hybrid of machine and organism, a creature of social reality as well as a creature of fiction,"[18] by using the cyborg as a creative medium for negotiating the multiple material and discursive forces that shape individual subjectivity. Haraway argues that the interpellated body within "the belly of the monster" occupies "a cyborg subject position"[19] that locates itself amidst chaos and ambiguity. According to Gedalof, "Haraway works with a more complicated model that redefines situatedness within impure spaces and offers the possibility of a self that survives and acts by coming to terms with, and working the possibilities available in those spaces."[20] A cyborg poetics claims a similarly productive material presence within what is broken and fragmentary: "here is an image of being *not yet* in this world / a floating, bouncing, jumping shape closer to cyborg than human."[21] This cyborg poetics is a way of reading and creating textuality that has three distinguishing characteristics. First of all, it unfixes borders by revealing the connections that the surface hides; secondly, it claims an embodied location within this fragmentation; and finally, it creates new textuality through impurity and contestation. It is this paradox of claiming location in a space of dislocation that gives cyborg poetics its creative force. Laiwan exemplifies a cyborg poetics because she takes the poetic voice through the many competing connections that compose "body." Haraway describes her own desire to produce similar effects of cyborgian connection: "my diminutive theory's optical features are set to produce not effects of distance, but effects of connection, of embodiment, and of responsibility for an imagined elsewhere that we may yet learn to see and build here."[22] Like Haraway, Laiwan imagines a reconfigured body that owns its connections and responsibility to a recontextualized local space. Her cyborg poetics is an active form of creative production because it locates textual materiality and subjectivity within the contestations of global and technoscientific context.

More importantly, Laiwan proposes a cyborg poetics that conceives of a body that inhabits a world beyond the binary separations between inside/outside, self/other, local/global, and human/technology. Her poetics is closely aligned with Doreen Massey's proposal that "if social space is conceived of as constructed out of the vast, intricate complexity of social processes and social interactions at all scales from the local to the global, then 'a place' is best thought of as a particular part of, a particular moment in, the global network of those social relations and understandings."[23] Similarly, Gedalof writes that a cyborg model "redefines the self by breaking out of the confined and fixed place of origin or 'home' to travel across the apparent certainties and stabilities of community identities. Yet it also holds on to a sense of locatedness in the impure space of power relations."[24] Laiwan recognizes that the "place" of the text must, like the places and bodies she represents, function as a nodal point in a network of "impure" social processes, interactions, and power relations. While the text grapples with the desire to return the body to an isolated state, it brings together many discourses, bodies, and images as an argument for seeing the body as an assemblage of disparate parts. This textual and physical body negotiates its relationship to the "outside" in such a way that it expands to include its many connections. It embraces "processes"[25] that transform the body from a signifier of *"unconditional love"*[26] into a negotiated space: *"never forget / how telling this is: this rashness of blood circulating some kind of insistence / circumnavigating unconditionally a desire to listen to this that so reveals."*[27] Ultimately then, Laiwan's cyborg poetics emerges as a new medium for claiming location and creativity within an altered and explicitly interconnected local space.

A Voice from the Womb: "Notes towards a body II"

Laiwan's body of work includes the poem "notes towards a body II" and the video *Remotely in Touch*, as well as numerous other poems and exhibitions that she has created over the years.[28] "Notes towards a body II" is the sequel piece to the poem, "notes towards a body," that sees the poet break out of Canadian context and insert herself into the local space of Mozambique. There, she discovers the body as a text that is under threat of erasure from those who want remembrance to occur according to their terms. The text interrogates the simultaneous forgetting and remembering of a society that wants to erase traces of its violence and make remembering a contained nostalgic process. Nonetheless, the poet refuses to accept this erasure and instead represents Mozambique as a multi-layered space that maintains remembering as a negotiated and continually evolving act. This earlier poem performs an unpacking of the residual master narratives that stain the body; its sequel piece, "notes towards a body II," moves from Mozambique to a more minute local space, the human body, as it probes similar issues of alienation, memory, and bodily agency. Four technoscientific images launch four sections that each look at the position of the body amidst technologies that penetrate and capture its inner workings: an ultrasound of a fetus in the womb, organs targeted in exploratory surgery, x-rayed hands from the Human Genome Project, and the author's own blood cells under a microscope. The desire for wholeness in the face of such fragmented images collides with and complicates the competing need to form a relationship for the body to these technoscientific representations. In this case, nostalgia centres on the maternal body that stays fluid as the text launches into inside/outside explorations. These explorations reveal the multiple and often invasive representations that the scientific gaze produces and the dislocation that the body experiences as a result of this penetration of its private recesses. Current bodily disintegration finds new poetic possibility as fragmentation and ambivalence weave together into a cyborg textual creation. In the end, the superficial images gain body through a text that engages with them and claims them as its own.

The piece takes as its starting point the nostalgia for an untouched body that offers salvation from current fragmentation. This nostalgia permeates the works as they rethink the body as an agency-producing local space within a context of global dispersal. The conception of the body as a reworked local space resonates with Gedalof, who also stresses that "we need to both account for our locatedness within these specific community identities, while also thinking about alternative ways to imagine both women's embodied locations and the communities which they help to constitute."[29] The poem reimagines "women's embodied locations" by exploring the desire for wholeness in the face of fragmentation. The lines that speak of "*a still life in portrait / longing for body*"[30] acknowledge the wish for materiality in the digital portraits that now define subjectivity. The lack of material presence within these portraits creates a yearning for a new conception of the body that will combat its current despatialized state. This yearning explores its shape and limits in order to transform into an interrogated presence within the textual space.

The text creates this interrogated presence by first of all questioning the nostalgia for a pre-fragmented identity space that is protected from the passage of time and the naming process. It returns to an anterior womb space that is seemingly free of contemporary societal interventions. This womb space offers a retreat through memory to an essentialized past that rids the body of the complexities of late twentieth- and early twenty-first-century life. Here is an imagined past in which "*i am remembering the time i was not yet born / when there was no such thing as time / and no such thing as remembering.*"[31] These lines express a wish to return to a temporal no man's land that is devoid of all memories. In this no man's land, the body exists beyond its past and present in a space of artificially coherent memories. These fabricated memories pose as the "real" in a limbo time "*of being not yet in this world*"[32] when subjectivity is still unformed. The poet interrogates imagined memories that deny current context and mourn a time "*of the not yet born / of the still being born / of the still being and the still born.*"[33] While Arjun Appadurai speaks of the dangers of "'imagined nostalgia,' nostalgia for things that never were,"[34] the foregrounding of this mourning in this work prevents it from naturalizing the essentialized space that it constructs.

It is tempting to erase the markings of the nation, capital, and science, and of the categorizations of gender, sex, sexuality, "race," class, economics, and religion. Anne Balsamo speaks of the "desire to return to the 'neutrality' of the body, to be rid of the culturally marked body"[35] that is extremely powerful given the current hyper-marked surface of the body. The first section of the poem constructs an unmarked surface that casts the body into a time before various categories have marked it with their identity traces. The lines, *"when there was no such thing as time / and no such thing as remembering,"*[36] speak of a moment when relationships between times, places, and people are still unstable and undetermined. This space of indeterminacy frees the poet of the interpellation process and, more importantly, the responsibilities attached to these identity affiliations. She can then drift in this "limbo"[37] space without feeling the impetus to engage with the numerous forces that circulate around her. This dislocation of the body severs her ties to the material and discursive connections that create context. However, as tempting as neutrality is, there is a note of uncertainty as she questions the vulnerability of being *"remembered solely by a frozen image / of a frozen time."*[38]

This engagement with markings works to end the vulnerability of the poet to those who mark her with their representational claims. The first image of the fetus complicates nostalgia by questioning the sanctity of the womb-space. The ultrasound image of an offspring captured in the womb highlights the maternal body as an ambivalent site of security, containment, and permeability. The initial security of the womb fades as it transforms into a critical borderspace that witnesses both the blurring and maintenance of borders. The maternal body, more specifically the womb, emerges as a vehicle for the search for a stable space, apart from the disorder of the outside, where the body felt protected from outside regulation. The mother is the haunting *"her"* and *"she"*[39] who offers the promise of the stability that is missing in a context of fluctuating representational impositions. The desire for comfort in the face of present "inhumanity"[40] impels the text to search out this lost maternal space. Grounding herself in a sense of context becomes difficult without the "unconditional love" and "compassion"[41] that she usually associates with the mother. Instead, this lack becomes the focus as she laments her inability to situate herself and yearns for the security of the maternal body:

> i can no longer feel her. i ignore her as she always available yields.
> mother, forgotten by a surge of inhumanity:
> the one person who could know so well unconditional love
> who could be my body of compassion[42]

The mother comes to represent a body that can overcome the spatial confusion of the ultrasound image and return the fetus to perfect physical union. Only air and silence are left as the poet reaches for the mother to soothe the fragmented pieces that now compose her body. Instead, the search for materiality leads to a grappling with the many fragments that have filled the void that the departure of the mother has created.

Self-consciously, the poet charts the desire to massage fragments into a renewed maternal presence. This inability to locate bodily presence leads to a focus on the maternal body that once housed the fetus before birth. Memories of the mother invoke a sense of nostalgic connection that combats the placelessness that characterizes the dislocated images that introduce each section of the text. The line, "I remember mother feeding me,"[43] refers to a time when a single connection defined the body: the dependency on the maternal body. As E. Ann Kaplan writes, "the mother is the one through whom we come to be subjects in this formation, in our similarity and difference from her: she is therefore deeply lodged in the unconscious. This subjectivity is, moreover, prior to other subject-identities (such as class, race, or nationality)."[44] Remembering maternal materiality is a pathway to confronting a sense of body that is *"eliminated in the process"*[45] of representation. The memories associated with the mother not only invoke a time of wholeness, but are also a pathway for reconstructing "a body."[46] The remembrances that "i am remembering mother's hands,"[47] and that once "my mother was my body,"[48] struggle to recover a sense of physicality. Suddenly, there exists a stable sense of physicality that the poem can access through nostalgic recall.

However, that this recall is limited to parts of the body of the mother and is inflected with nostalgia underlines the need to keep this body fluid. A stable maternal body eludes the text as it continues to negotiate the many strands that compose subjectivity. Instead, there exists a denaturalized space, *"a push and pull effect,"*[49] that necessitates a response that moves beyond nostalgic recall. Nostalgia fades away as the invasiveness of technological and scientific innovations pervades the text. The four images that introduce each section are examples of the ability of technoscience to penetrate the body for its representational purposes. Rosalind Petchesky uses the term the *"panoptics of the womb"*[50] to describe the technologization of the maternal body that has transformed its interior space into a site open for scientific observation. She stresses the need to "image the pregnant woman, not as an abstraction, but within her total framework of relationships, economic and health needs and desires"[51] as a response to the loss of agency that women undergo through visualization technologies. Before the *"i, waiting to be born become[s] remembered solely by a frozen image,"*[52] the poetic voice must negotiate its relationship to scientific panoptics.

The fight against a panoptics that pierces past physical barriers and examines private recesses for scientific purposes becomes paramount. The apparent transparency of these images makes it harder to locate the silences and absences that elude a technoscientific gaze that probes and records the body through its visualization technologies. This scientific mindset has the ability to go in and capture the particles of the body that it encounters: *"I am going in, looking in / to see what i am made of."*[53] The images of the "bowel and intestine area from exploratory surgery" and the blood cells of the author "captured through an electronic microscope"[54] evidence this probing scientific mindset. For example, Barbara Duden speaks of the repercussions of ultrasound technology, arguing that "the pregnant body—formerly the metaphor for the hidden, the secret, and the invisible—is turned into a space for public inspection. Pregnancy—formerly perceived as an aptic somatic experience of being with child—is redefined into the disembodied realization of an optical imputation."[55] This optical going in shifts the body from a private interior space to a site for public exploration of *"this knotted gut / this gutted heart."*[56] *"This disheartened surgery of feeling"*[57] dominates the poem as she explores the repercussions of a scientific gaze that can capture the inner workings of the body with surgical precision.

Consequently, the four images that depict different parts of the body question the scientific ability to make interior spaces into exterior display. The fetus, the hand, the bowel and intestine, and the blood cells in the images are now located exterior to the body through technologies that can capture details that escape the human eye. By drawing attention to the relationship of the body to these visualization technologies, the text challenges the static and disconnected quality of these representations. The poetic voice speaks from a space whose borders are now permeable and where the previously binary distinctions of private/public and self/other are now blurred. The ultrasound, x-ray, and microscope images destabilize readings of the body premised on a fixed separation between inside and outside. Internal workings seize visible public spaces, "this image: this is my blood / outside of me because i had forgotten,"[58] where they create a sense of disconnection and displacement. The blood cells in the image are the property of a technoscientific gaze that examines them for its own purposes. While these representations circulate seemingly beyond reach, they collide within the space of the textual encounter: "this is my body, this is my blood / *no, i am wrong, this is a portrait of me."*[59] The body now inhabits a space in between public and private, "a cramped, unfamiliar freezing space / which could be purgatory, limbo, nowhere / *everywhere,"*[60] one which creates an unstable textual form. Questioning, *"how can i come to know unconditional love,"*[61] the poet examines images in which the barrier between the gaze and its representational object has disappeared.

Moreover, the stark nature of the black and white images in the text highlights the representational power of the scientific gaze that can produce detailed two-dimensional images of interior physical spaces. The "x-ray of hand from the Human Genome Project on the Internet"[62] treats the body as a virtual informational resource that can be catalogued and archived away. The text counters the representational violence that the scientific gaze performs by disrupting and complicating the images that introduce each of the four sections of the poem. This rereading destabilizes the normalization of the scientific appropriation of the body. In their discussion of new technologies and Asian American subjectivities, Rachel Lee and Sau-ling Wong similarly challenge the over-circulation of bodily images when they argue that "when thinking about the Asian and the Asian American in relation to technology, Internet or otherwise, not so much absence but overrepresentation"[63] characterizes this connection. "Notes towards a body II," focuses on this overrepresentation that masks the scientific ability to detach these images from their referents. The question "do we regret contributing to this most dulling of deeds / of removing life from being itself?"[64] critiques a gaze that creates flat, virtual representations that stand in for the "real." *Compassion and memory and body / are shocked into silence*"[65] due to a gaze that penetrates interior spaces and then re-presents them as static, "silent" images. This metamorphosis of the body from material subject to image facilitates a spectating process that freezes the body in virtual space as it is "*named by image then frozen in space.*"[66] These images circulate independently from the poet and her words, leaving her remote and reaching for connections. Reinstated, these connections shatter the smooth façade of technoscientific images and insert materiality back into these virtual representations.

Consequently, the poem uses the materiality of its words and the reconstructed maternal presence in order to fight against a context in which, as Anne Balsamo writes, the "body is redefined as a machine interface."[67] The mother functions as a contested and embodied subject within the poem to disrupt the two-dimensionality of technoscientific images. The maternal presence destabilizes even as it comes into being through the continual questioning, "*how can i come to know unconditional love,*"[68] and the question marks[69] that trail after the memories of the mother. In the lines, "i once believed love originated from my mother's body / i once believed my body came from my mother's love,"[70] the repetition of the "once" emphasizes that the connection between the mother and bodily stability is tenuous and subject to contestation. Instead, the text resists circulating the mother as a given. The constant undercutting of the mother makes the desire for body a negotiated experience that stays fluid and resists reducing itself to an essentialized escape. Stating, "i am remembering unconditional love / in a body tremble or body sweat, I remember / gut feeling,"[71] the poet begins the process of using the nostalgia for the mother as a tool to spur on movement and maintain identity negotiation. In short, the maternal body remains amorphous to keep identity exploration in motion.

Materiality becomes possible in this amorphous and continually moving body because it exceeds the gaze of both the poet and technoscience. By positioning the mother as a borderspace, the text situates "home" *within* the interactions and negotiations of technoscientific connections. Elspeth Probyn speaks of the "moment of being—like the moment when the trapeze artist has let go of one ring but hasn't yet grasped the other. This is an image of momentum and chance that captures for me what belonging is all about."[72] The text similarly captures Laiwan stretching to connect with the mother without providing the final moment of contact. The presence of the mother within fragmentation and absence questions the images that the technoscientific gaze presents:

> i am remembering mother's hands
> *no this is not hers she is not here*
> *not a part of this*[73]

Because the x-rayed hand is a constructed representation, the adoption of a fixed position in relation to the four images is difficult. The maternal body transforms into a productive space that assumes form through the ambiguities of the textual encounter. "*I can no longer feel her*"[74] signals regret that spurs the poetic voice to generate its own materiality through a search for the maternal body amidst its technoscientific connections. And it is precisely because this body is wavering and uncertain that desire can mobilize and textual exploration can continue to produce change.

As a result, the text not only reclaims the maternal space, but meaning and form also work together to create a new cyborgian textual body. The alienation of two-dimensional images dissipates as the poet claims agency in the performance of her fragmented subject position. The words on the page reveal and engage with the fractures in meaning construction in order to find voice in the process of negotiation. Propelled by the longing for body, the poetic voice moves further into its fragmentation and into the individual pieces that strive to make the text whole. As Donna Haraway claims, "knowledge-making technologies, including crafting subject positions and ways of inhabiting such positions, must be made relentlessly visible and open to critical intervention."[75] In this case, the cyborgian poetic practices of the text remain visible through a questioning tone that resists simple answers. For example, the Genome Project x-rayed hand incites the questions "could this be my hand? could this be of my hand?"[76] which deconstruct the "truth" claims of the image as well as confront the complicity of the poet in its production. This ambivalent wordplay continues with the haphazard stanza breaks, the occasional indentation, and the switching back and forth between italicized and non-italicized text that create a work whose body resists packaging. Haltingly, the lines stop and start and frequently dissolve into silence as they struggle to locate meaning. In the line, "*this* my mother was my body,"[77] the disruptive pause between "*this*" and "my mother" is where the heart of the text can be found. Overall, creative production becomes a negotiated act that demands attentiveness to the process of making meaning.

Representation in the poem is a cyborg poetic performance that propels the creative voice towards further identity exploration. By mapping and positioning the body in relation to its many flows, this performance re-establishes connections that technoscience has severed. Textual embodiment exists within flux at the moments at which boundaries collapse and meaning emerges out of contestation. The final image of the blood cells under a microscope confronts the relationship of the body to the texture of the images and words that appear on the page. Their cyborg poetics moves towards awareness as it pieces text and meaning together:

> i look at her and remembering comes flooding back to body
> blood rushes to circulate some kind of lightness
> and day to day motion becomes derailed for this most invisible of flurries."[78]

These lines exemplify a poetics that claims contingency as the force behind meaning construction. The text stays fluid as one line leads on to another and a lack of punctuation keeps the words in constant connection. Moreover, the significant number of verbs in these lines conveys a sense of change without the accompanying need for closure. The body is in the midst of "remembering" a past that is "flooding" back as its materiality "rushes," "circulates," and is in constant "motion." The "derailment" at the end is yet another example of a text that disrupts the easy flow of words in order to consider what lies unspoken and "invisible." This exploration process prevents the closing off from possibility and leaves subjectivity in a space of productive ambivalence. Within this ambivalent movement, textuality becomes both dynamic and interactive.

As a result, by claiming materiality within the fragmentation and negotiation of the creative process, the text challenges the reproduction of technoscientific images. The reconfigured maternal body is a creative force that adds depth to the flatness of technoscientific representations and reworks them into an embodied cyborg text. This text is cyborgian because, like Haraway's cyborg, "it redefines the self by breaking out of the confined and fixed place of origin or 'home' to travel across the apparent certainties and stabilities of community identities. Yet it also holds onto a sense of locatedness in the impure space of complex power relations."[79] In other words, the text travels to dismantle the boundaries that contain it, but at the same time, it also claims a generative location at the point at which these global, technoscientific boundaries are in disarray. For example, the lines "*still / i am breathing deep / so* as *to never neglect / what her body is telling me what my body is telling me / without words, without gesture*"[80] demonstrate that speech is possible even in seeming silence. A cyborg poetics constructs new channels for agency within a context of capital and technoscientific intervention. The poet answers the question "*from where is the cause of my upheaval / this knotted gut / this gutted heart / this disheartened surgery of feeling?*"[81] with the following lines:

> i am remembering the stillness of this moment
> which reminds me of when i once had to be reminded of mortality, of body,
> of blood
> of when i was reminded to be still[82]

The references to "blood" and "the stillness of the moment" attest to a body that is now willing to claim the materiality that emerges in the moment. Whereas the images in the poem decontextualize the body and cover over materiality, the text navigates its multiple and ever-fluctuating physical connections. The recognition that "this image: this is my blood / outside of me because i had forgotten"[83] reassumes ownership over once disconnected fragments and, more importantly, over a renewed, cyborgian sense of materiality. The intermingling of images, text, and the poetic voice itself produces a textual body that rediscovers and reclaims materiality.

Remotely in Touch: A Cyborgian Video Work

Remotely in Touch is a thirteen-minute video that brings together music, text, imagery, narration, and video clips in a cyborg poetic performance. The piece organizes itself around the five elements of earth, fire, water, air, and love as it explores the body imagery that circulates in digital and visual technologies. Longing for body propels the work through spliced images that are individually isolated but that collectively disrupt a stable conception of text. This longing for body extends the concerns of "notes towards a body II" in its explicit engagement with bodily fragments that cross the borders between the natural and the technological. Visual, audio, and written textual fragments circulate within the video to depict the body as a layered, constantly moving local site. The film includes images of Mars, a fetus in the womb, x-rayed hands, blood cells, volcanic smoke, worms burrowing in the earth, and individual bodies performing martial arts in the search for agency within the disorienting state of the body. The text uses its many representational fragments in order to present a complex and ambivalent reading of the body. It explores questions of representation and perception in a technoscientific society as it develops a new, agency-producing cyborg form. Taken as a whole, these various images and media refract the body through a new representational lens and intersect with one another to create a cyborg creative body. The piece is thus a simultaneous opening up and creating of a textual body through the blurring of representational borders.

The piece opens with the words, "are you / remotely / in touch,"[84] to introduce the paradoxical question that appears repeatedly throughout the piece. The images of volcanic smoke, a fetus in the womb, and blood vessels speak of the yearning for touch in a context in which the body feels remote from itself and the many forces that circulate around it. The video work begins with the longing for wholeness but finds the body quickly enmeshed in a multitude of natural and technological forces. The desire for connection amidst the alienating effects of technoscientific intervention is a palpable presence in the images and sounds of the video as it focuses on five elements that connote the basic and the "natural." Most especially, love is one of the five elements, emphasizing the need for the connection and interaction that the body lacks amidst the disorienting flows of technoscience. As Irene Gedalof asserts, it is time for the body to take a stand against dislocation, for "what should be important then, even within the terms of a Deleuzian project, is *not* 'the going,' but a different kind of relationship with the space one inhabits, that resists the striations of binary logic."[85] The impetus to redefine a relationship to place becomes more crucial as the body becomes increasingly detached from the spaces in which it circulates. The film introduces five elements that ground and give substance to the body, then juxtaposes them against technoscientific images that expose how far the body has strayed from its initial base matter. The images of fire, earth, water, air, and love combine with the many other elements of human and technological intervention that now make up body.

The narrator's words, "we know too much to be left with so little,"[86] stress that the current alienation of the body makes it difficult for it to claim its multiple fragments as its own. The feelings of disconnection and the struggle to locate a sense of place parallel the placelessness of science and technology. Space exploration emerges in the video as paradigmatic of a larger technoscientific strategy to alienate the body and displace it from a grounded "home." Black-and-white images of Mars flash in the video to highlight current bodily alienation as the narrator reinforces with the words, "we search the world to find resources, maintaining a vestige of identity from what we are not. A spot in the sky without a trace of humanity."[87] The images of Mars chart the search for resources in alien sites that take the body further away from a sense of "humanity" and "identity." Instead, the seeming normativity of space exploration imagery reveals the extent to which the body has become part of technoscientific projects. The narrator of the video draws attention to a world in which the alien soil of Mars has replaced the security and wholeness of the earth. She says that "in Chinese we say, the earth bears and carries in receptive abandon. Yet this is not earth. Dusty and rocky Mars where soil cannot be earth and does not bear fruit."[88] Whether in images of Mars or of the womb, the narrators in the video lack the ability to recognize and claim materiality. Once again, the longing for body fuels the creative process that seeks to recover materiality through the creation of textuality.

However, despite present alienation, the work finds location within these technoscientific flows as it achieves productive agency. The video commences with five elements, but as its thirteen minutes unfold, more layers contribute to its textual fabric. The combining of underwater volcanic imagery with satellite imagery, images of Mars, and images of x-rayed hands exposes the impurity and contradiction of current bodily context. Donna Haraway argues that "if technoscience by our moment in history is unmistakably 'nature' for us—and not just nature but nature-culture—then understanding technoscience is a way of understanding how natures and cultures have become one world."[89] This one world emerges in the text through "natural" elements that intersect with technoscience to call into question the untouched state of the body. The black-and-white images of Mars bring attention to human complicity in the creation of an alienated bodily condition:

USE
BETRAY
DIVERT
ABANDON[90]

These four verbs function as a call for individuals to hold themselves accountable for the misuse of the resources of the earth. They call attention to the way images have contributed to our conception and exploitation of the world. The spliced images, sounds, and text from a variety of sources confront the impure origins of science, technology, and capital, discovering that the alien is more intimately acquainted with the body than it first appeared to be.

The spliced images, sound, and text force an awareness of the body as a technologically invested entity that demands a cyborg poetic response. *Remotely in Touch* performs bodily impurity by placing different media in coexistence without drawing them together into a single representation. N. Katherine Hayles writes, "Bruno Latour has argued that we have never been modern; the seriated history of cybernetics—emerging from networks at once materially real, socially regulated, and discursively constructed—suggests, for similar reasons, that we have always been posthuman."[91] Hayles makes comments that apply to a film performance that exposes the body as a networked node. In other words, the posthuman, like a cyborg poetics, sees wholeness as a construction that masks the position of the body within a network of technological and discursive connections. The exposure of fragmentation maps out a web of connections that challenges a singular reading of the body. The network of images jars, disconcerts, and connects to produce many different representations of the body. These creative movements are in dialogue with one another to prevent their voices from merging into stable meaning. For example, as images of smoke and fire appear on the video screen, a narrator declares that "fast movement will make me not breathe again, will catch my breath, inhabiting spirit gets lost with speed."[92] The images of the fire and the narrator's words intersect to present a body that moves in and out of discourses and media in its search for meaning. The overlay of so many stimuli ensures that the text is located in the zone where limits dissolve and come into question. The variation contained within this blurred space produces meaning that is in fluctuation as it interacts and engages with its diverse connections.

This state of becoming is an argument for the body as an intersectional point. Hayles proposes, "when the human is seen as part of a distributed system, the full expression of human capability can be seen precisely to *depend* on the splice rather than being imperilled by it."[93] The images, sounds, and words form productive connections that work to locate the body amidst all these flows. The words in the film "things of the world are fleeting and transitory. There will be nothing left but this breath"[94] describe a video project that incorporates images, sound, and written text to arrive at further ambivalence. The fleeting connections between the various images create textuality that is in tension with itself as meaning slips past

the borders that it erects. The desire for connection in the face of disconnection keeps the representational process in dialogue. The video is "a
body bursting in form of heat and light and energy"[95] because of the many
layers inserted into its textual body. Akin to the cyborg poetic performance in "notes towards a body II," the film privileges movement even as it
searches for "humanity"[96] in many different images and sounds. The productivity within movement derives from keeping negotiation in play and
not permitting the body to become static.

However, despite the exploratory nature of the text, the video images
are linked in their allegiance to the physical and textual body. The video
fragments combat their alienation by relocating themselves in their connections to the other components that circulate within the piece. No matter where the text travels or what speeds of exploration it reaches, it returns
to the body and its materiality. The video clips are "too fast" and are "unable
to be secured or caged"[97] because they are concerned with intensifying
and energizing bodily connections. Donna Haraway argues that "what I
mean to emphasize is the *situatedness* of situated. In other words it is a way
to get at the multiple modes of embedding that are about both place and
space in the manner in which geographers draw that distinction."[98] The text
strives to find a new form of situatedness that challenges images that
decontextualize. It eventually develops a sense of locatedness that pauses
to situate the body within context before it shifts to its next representation.
This materiality grounds itself in textuality that accepts fragmentation and
then proceeds to work with it. The images—of the rocky ground, of the
worms burrowing, of the cells and organs of the body, of the moving and
producing human body—present bodily presence in slightly variant ways
but together form an argument for a material presence. Despite their singularity, they each stress the need to keep the body at the forefront of the
representational gaze.

These fragments appear in a strategic constellation that reclaims the bodies contained in these images. This materiality of ambiguity asserts presence in the pause between the destabilization and restabilization of borders,
arguing that materiality still exists even in the images when the body seems
most compromised. The reading of the body as ambiguous and compromised resonates with Hayles, who comments that "located within the dialectic of pattern/randomness and grounded in embodied actuality rather than
disembodied information, the posthuman offers resources for rethinking
the articulation of humans with intelligent machines."[99] The manipulation
of the dialectic of pattern/randomness serves as a creative engine for
reclaiming a body within technological flows:

presence
pattern
absence
randomness[100]

The words that appear on the video screen stress that the interplay between seeming oppositions produces textuality. The paradoxical relationship between presence and absence, pattern and randomness, ensures that bodily texture is a contestation. Each word and image construct a materiality that takes what is fixed and present and looks deeper to uncover and engage with their silences and inconsistencies.

In particular, the footage of the writer who is in the process of putting words to paper is a reminder that the creative body is also a part of the network of meaning that it creates. This body is then made an explicit presence in the video not only to draw attention to the constructed nature of the representational project but also to recognize that meaning making is a dynamic and interactive process. Its image keeps the text and the representation gaze in conversation. The juxtaposition of these various media with the body of the writer shows that, as Hayles writes, "it is not a question of leaving the body behind but rather of extending embodied awareness in highly specific, local, and material ways that would be impossible without electronic prosthesis."[101] The writer finds location through her awareness of her position in relation to the web of images she maps out. Moreover, the writer in motion shows that embodiment emerges out of fluctuation. As the camera pans over a rocky piece of ground, a voice declares, "we have traveled so far to see. We are at the beginning and the end, rotating and reinforcing."[102] In other words, groundedness occurs as the writer and the other bodies in the text "rotate and reinforce" in their search for material presence. The film finds embodiment as it creates texture through the combining of different images, voices, and representation media.

This creative work witnesses the construction of two bodies, the text and the poet herself, as it explores where the "longing for body" will take it. Irene Gedalof argues that the birth of a body that claims materiality within change and fluidity offers individual subjects opportunities for agency:

> Drawing on the break-points and dissonances in dominant models of identity, we argue with Haraway that birth is always the birth of (an)other, and not the reproduction of the same. A differently imagined body and birth might provide a different basis on which the birth-based identities of communities are imagined, one which places change and fluidity-fluency at its centre.[103]

Remotely in Touch creates two texts through its struggles within silence and ambiguity. The two bodies that emerge from this creative project are both cyborgian in their bringing together of capital and technoscience with a variety of representational media. More significantly, these creative productions differentiate themselves and claim agency as they speak of their individuality. The voice in the video describes this creative process in the following way: "I have searched dark and anti-matter for life. Does not yield heat willingly nor easily. Not as this body with desire. Her presence wills body into light."[104] In the search for "light," the film delves into "dark" and "anti-matter" and eventually locates itself within the efforts to construct textuality. It finds generative agency within the gaps, silences, and disruptions of textuality itself. The production of the text is a fraught passage into meaning; it represents a hard-fought struggle that claims textuality word by word and image by image. The advice, "gently label it / as 'thinking' / then let it go,"[105] encapsulates a creative project that creates a body while still allowing it to exceed the borders of its representations.

The poet therefore responds to the longing for body with a creative voice that engages in a cyborg poetics that speaks to current destabilized identity conditions. After so long on the margins of Canadian literature and its criticism, Laiwan moves to the forefront of the critical lens as her cyborg poetics offers condensed examples of the power of textuality to disrupt, question, and destabilize once-naturalized boundaries. The representational process transforms into a journey that sees Laiwan moving from one creative media to another and from one textual body to the next as she resists the creation of stable bodily representations. The question that opens the video, "are you / remotely / in touch,"[106] describes two works that bring together the remote and the intimate to produce connection. Laiwan comes to know the body in its ambivalence and disarray through the weaving of disconnection and connection. As the words and photographs appear on paper, as the video images move across the screen and the narrators speak out of presence and absence, the poet forms connections to her texts and to her own body. She eventually locates a body that claims a "home" in the ambivalences, fluctuations, and silences of textuality itself.

She said be still and learn how to move me[107]

NOTES

1 Scott McFarlane, "The Haunt of Race: Canada's Multiculturalism Act, the Politics of Incorporation, and Writing Thru Race," *Fuse* 18, no. 3 (1995): 20.

2 Diana Brydon, "It's Time for a New Set of Questions," *Essays on Canadian Writing* 71 (2000): 14.

3 Brydon, "It's Time," 16.

4 Interpal Grewal and Caren Kaplan, "Introduction: Transnational Feminist Practices and Questions of Postmodernity," in *Scattered Hegemonies: Postmodernity and Transnational Feminist Practices*, ed. Interpal Grewal and Caren Kaplan (Minneapolis: U of Minnesota P, 1994), 7.

5 Irene Gedalof, *Against Purity: Rethinking Identity with Indian and Western Feminisms* (New York: Routledge, 1999), 128.

6 Ibid.

7 Ibid.

8 Donna Haraway, "The Promise of Monsters: A Regenerative Politics of Inappropriate/d Others," in *Cultural Studies*, ed. Lawrence Grossberg, Cary Nelson, and Paula A. Treichler (New York: Routledge, 1992), 311.

9 King-Kok Cheung, *Articulate Silences: Hisaye Yamamoto, Maxine Hong Kingston, Joy Kogawa* (Ithaca, NY: Cornell UP, 1993), 6.

10 Fred Wah, *Diamond Grill* (Edmonton: NeWest Press, 1996), 138.

11 Roy Miki, *Broken Entries: Race Subjectivity Writing* (Toronto: Mercury Press, 1998), 160–80.

12 Himani Bannerji, *The Dark Side of the Nation: Essays on Multiculturalism, Nationalism and Gender* (Toronto: Canadian Scholars' Press, 2000), 65.

13 Lien Chao, "Anthologizing the Collective: The Epic Struggles to Establish Chinese Canadian Literature in English," in *Writing Ethnicity: Cross-Cultural Consciousness in Canadian and Quebecois Literature*, ed. Winfried Siemerling (Toronto: ECW Press, 1996).

14 Guy Beauregard, "The Emergence of 'Asian Canadian Literature': Can Lit's Obscene Supplement?" *Essays on Canadian Writing* 67 (1999): 57–75.

15 Roy Miki, "Altered States: Global Currents, the Spectral Nation, and the Production of 'Asian Canadian,'" *Journal of Canadian Studies* 35, no. 3 (2000): 43–72.

16 Other recent texts are representing a national space that renegotiates a new role for itself within local and global interpenetrations that differs from its previous naturalized identity claims. These texts not only express a willingness to travel past national borders; they also bring the fruits of their travels back to a newly permeable national space. The identities that they propose are mixed, fluid, and, most of all, situated in a local space with a globally inflected sense of context. Examples include Dionne Brand, *What We All Long* (Toronto: Knopf Canada, 2005); Hiromi Goto, *Hopeful Monsters* (Vancouver: Arsenal Pulp Press, 2004); Larissa Lai, *Salt Fish Girl* (Toronto: Thomas Allen Publishers, 2000); Ashok Mathur, *The Short Happy Life of Harry Kumar* (Vancouver: Arsenal Pulp Press, 2001); Kerri Sakamoto, *One Hundred Million Hearts* (Toronto: Knopf Canada, 2003); Rita Wong and Larissa Lai, "sybil unrest," *West Coat Line* 38, no. 2 (2004): 39–60.

17 Irene Gedalof, "Identities in Transit: Nomads, Cyborgs and Women," *The European Journal of Women's Studies* 7 (2000): 345.

18 Donna Haraway, "A Cyborg Manifesto: Science, Technology, and Socialist-Feminism in the Late Twentieth Century," in *The Cybercultures Reader*, ed. David Bell and Barbara M. Kennedy (New York: Routledge, 2000), 291.

19 Haraway, "The Promise of Monsters," 300.

20 Gedalof, "Identities in Transit: Nomads, Cyborgs and Women," 347.

21 Laiwan, "notes towards a body II," in *Swallowing Clouds: An Anthology of Chinese-Canadian Poetry*, ed. Andy Quan and Jim Wong-Chu (Vancouver: Arsenal Pulp Press, 1999), 146.

22 Haraway, "The Promise of Monsters," 295.

23 Doreen Massey, "Double Articulation: A Place in the World," in *Displacements: Cultural Identities in Question*, ed. Angelika Bammer (Bloomington: Indiana UP, 1994), 115.

24 Gedalof, "Identities in Transit: Nomads, Cyborgs and Women," 351.

25 Laiwan, "notes towards a body II," 150.

26 Ibid., 149.

27 Ibid., 151.

28 Others works by Laiwan include "notes towards a body," *Capilano Review* 2, no. 24 (1998): 11–13; "Untitled," *West Coast Line* 33/34, no. 3 (2001): 54–55; "Untitled (3)," in *History: Portraits from Vancouver*, ed. Karen Love, 30–33 (Vancouver: Arsenal Pulp Press, 2002); *Machinate: a projection in two movements*, http://www.htmlles.net/2000/webart/laiwbe.html, *Kiss: a film loop for two projectors*, http://artgallery.dal.ca/engaging/LAIWAN.html; *Language of Mesmerization The Mesmerization of Language*, http://www.belkin.ubc.ca/_archived/mesmerization/.

29 Gedalof, "Identities in Transit: Nomads, Cyborgs and Women," 345.

30 Laiwan, "notes towards a body II," 147.

31 Ibid., 146.

32 Ibid., 146.

33 Ibid., 147.

34 Arjun Appadurai, *Modernity at Large: Cultural Dimensions of Globalization* (Minneapolis: U of Minnesota P, 1996), 77.

35 Anne Balsamo, "Forms of Technological Embodiment: Reading the Body in Contemporary Culture," in *Feminist Theory and the Body*, ed. Janet Price and Margrit Shildrick (Edinburgh: Edinburgh UP, 1999), 287.

36 Laiwan, "notes towards a body II," 146.

37 Ibid., 146.

38 Ibid., 147.

39 Ibid., 147.

40 Ibid., 147.

41 Ibid., 147.

42 Ibid., 147.

43 Ibid., 148.

44 E. Ann Kaplan, *Motherhood and Representation: The Mother in Popular Culture and Melodrama* (London: Routledge, 1992), 45.

45 Laiwan, "notes towards a body II," 148.

46 Ibid., 149.

47 Ibid., 148.

48 Ibid., 149.

49 Ibid., 149.

50 Rosalind Pollack Petchesky, "Foetal Images: The Power of Visual Culture in the Politics of Representation," in *The Gendered Cyborg: A Reader*, ed. Gill Kirkup et al. (London: Routledge, 2000), 180.

51 Ibid., 188.

52 Laiwan, "notes towards a body II," 147.
53 Ibid., 149.
54 Ibid.,151.
55 Barbara Duden, "The Fetus on the 'Farther Shore': Toward a History of the Unborn," in *Fetal Subjects, Feminist Positions*, ed. Lynn M. Morgan and Meredith W. Michaels (Philadelphia: U of Pennsylvania P, 1999), 24.
56 Laiwan, "notes towards a body II," 149.
57 Ibid., 149.
58 Ibid., 151.
59 Ibid., 150.
60 Ibid., 146.
61 Ibid., 149.
62 Ibid., 151.
63 Rachel C. Lee and Sau-ling Cythia Wong, introduction to *AsiaAmerica.Net: Ethnicity, Nationalism, and Cyberspace* (Princeton, NJ: Princeton UP, 1999), xvi.
64 Laiwan, "notes towards a body II," 148.
65 Ibid., 148.
66 Ibid., 148.
67 Balsamo, "Forms," 283.
68 Laiwan, "notes towards a body II," 149.
69 Ibid., 148.
70 Ibid., 149.
71 Ibid., 149.
72 Elspeth Probyn, *Outside Belongings* (New York: Routledge, 1996), 42.
73 Laiwan, "notes towards a body II," 148.
74 Ibid., 147.
75 Donna Haraway, *Modest_Witness@Second_Millennium.FemaleMan©_Meets_OncoMouse™* (New York: Routledge, 1997), 36.
76 Laiwan, "notes towards a body II," 148.
77 Ibid., 149.
78 Ibid., 150.
79 Gedalof, "Identities in Transit," 351.
80 Laiwan, "notes towards a body II," 150.
81 Ibid., 149.
82 Ibid., 150.
83 Ibid., 151.
84 Laiwan, *Remotely in Touch*, videotape (Toronto: V-Tape, 1998).
85 Gedalof, "Identities in Transit," 343.
86 Laiwan, *Remotely in Touch*.
87 Ibid.
88 Ibid.
89 Donna Haraway, quoted in Thyrza Nichols Goodeve, *How Like a Leaf: Donna J. Haraway: An Interview with Thyrza Nichols Goodeve* (New York: Routledge, 1998), 156–57.
90 Laiwan, *Remotely in Touch*.
91 N. Katherine Hayles, *How We Became Posthuman: Virtual Bodies in Cybernetics, Literature, and Informatics* (Chicago: U of Chicago P, 1999), 291.
92 Laiwan, *Remotely in Touch*.
93 Hayles, *How We Became Posthuman*, 290.
94 Laiwan, *Remotely in Touch*.

95 Ibid.
96 Ibid.
97 Ibid.
98 Donna Haraway, quoted in Goodeve, *How Like a Leaf*, 71.
99 Hayles, *How We Became Posthuman*, 287.
100 Laiwan, *Remotely in Touch*.
101 Hayles, *How We Became Posthuman*, 291.
102 Laiwan, *Remotely in Touch*.
103 Irene Gedalof, *Against Purity*, 220.
104 Laiwan, *Remotely in Touch*.
105 Ibid.
106 Ibid.
107 Ibid.

[part four]

Global Affiliations

[chapter ten]

"Do not exploit me again and again"

Queering Autoethnography in Suniti Namjoshi's
Goja: An Autobiographical Myth

Eva C. Karpinski

Suniti Namjoshi's work occupies an "elsewhere" territory on a map of contemporary postcolonial transnational literature. She is a border subject who resists reterritorialization into a framework of nationally defined studies of literature. It is possible to call her an expatriate Canadian South Asian author currently living in England, where, in turn, she would probably be labelled an Anglo-Indian or Indo-English writer. A cosmopolitan, former academic, and former member of the prestigious Indian Civil Service, she stands apart from "the realm of dispossessed postcolonials."[1] Compared to other writers of the Indian diaspora, her work does not fit in a tradition of either Bharati Mukherjee's realism or Salman Rushdie's postmodernism. She has shown a penchant for irreverent experimentation in all her work, defying an easy generic classification. Her best-known titles include *Feminist Fables* (1981), *From the Bedside Book of Nightmares* (1984), *The Conversation of the Cow* (1985), *The Blue Donkey Fables* (1988), *The Mothers of Maya Diip* (1989), and *St. Suniti and the Dragon* (1994), all of which have built her reputation as a fabulist, fantasy writer, and mythmaker. Her novel *Building Babel* (1996) is an unprecedented attempt to co-opt readers into collaborative fiction writing using the Internet. Namjoshi's relation to both Indian and Western mainstream audiences is complicated by her lesbian feminist perspective, unique intertextuality, and "the absence of tangible India" in her writing.[2] Written in 2000, *Goja: An Autobiographical Myth* is her life-writing project; funded by an arts grant from the Canada Council, written in England, and published in Australia, even the material circumstances of the book's production reflect other productive instabilities of Namjoshi's positioning.

Goja offers a fascinating case study of how the conventions of autoethnography that are traditionally bound up with representation of culturally mediated racial, ethnic, or other group "difference" can be challenged. Deborah E. Reed-Danahay situates origins of autoethnography at the intersection of three genres: native anthropology, produced by researchers who study their own groups; ethnic autobiography, written by members of ethnic or racial minorities; and autobiographical ethnography, combining cultural analysis with the ethnographer's personal experience.[3] On the whole, these anthropological genres share with literary autoethnography a common focus on autobiographical voices of marginalized people, setting the stage for the ethnographic subject to "write back" to the metropolitan culture. Autoethnographic discourses deployed in literature and anthropology are usually situated within the framework of binary oppositions between centre/periphery, dominant/dominated, native informant/mainstream public, subject/object of the gaze, or speaking "for"/speaking "from." Not only do such discourses often inadvertently re-inscribe the above oppositions and their hierarchical power dynamics, but they are also problematic insofar as they are founded upon certain assumptions of "cultural essentialism," including both its universalist (sameness) and relativist (difference) versions.[4] Feminist criticism of autoethnography examines possible subversions of the genre in women's writing that creates "a space of resistance between the individual (*auto-*) and the collective (*-ethno-*) where the writing (*-graphy*) of singularity cannot be foreclosed."[5] As has been noted in previous chapters, Françoise Lionnet foregrounds "a position of fundamental liminality" as she discusses autoethnography.[6] Similarly, Julia Watson describes this type of writing as boundary-crossing, hybrid texts, products of complex "contact zones," braiding together multiple discourses of the self and the social.[7] In *Goja*, Suniti Namjoshi taps the tradition of self-representation by radical women of colour by recalling Audre Lorde's "biomythography" through her subtitle. Like Lorde, she conceptualizes her narrative as a combination of autobiography, fiction, and myth, encompassing a vast range of formal/aesthetic, political, and ethical concerns.[8]

Grappling with questions of intersubjectivity, reflexivity, historical memory, and ethics, Namjoshi's experimental text is a compelling example of venturing "beyond autoethnography." She experiments with mythopoiesis, projecting herself into the spaces of radical otherness through spectacular displays of discursive heteroglossia, combining Western and Asian traditions, Christian, Hindu, and Greek symbolism. She embraces cultural hybridity as an inescapable outcome of colonial education, conflating Western and

Indian "gods and goddesses" in her fabulation, while also moving beyond the double consciousness of the colonizer-colonized binary to include multidirectional border crossings between social classes and castes, different positionalities of gender and sexuality, diverse ages, and various forms of privilege and oppression. Speaking from a traumatized body, as a survivor of sexual abuse, an ethnic "other," and a lesbian, but also from the body marked by her privileged class position as a member of Indian aristocracy and a Western postcolonial intellectual, she attempts to deconstruct power and oppression as shifting, not fixed categories. Defined by her outsiderness, she gestures towards the ethics of connection and connectedness, implying a rejection of the logic of polarities, a logic that frequently determines complicitous choices for many autoethnographic subjects.

Goja as an autoethnographic text also rewrites lesbian autobiography or lesbian coming-out stories in the postcolonial context, which gives it a potentially radical, transgressive, and transformational character. For Namjoshi, lesbianism is "an important feminist concern because of the intersection of power with sexuality, because of sexual politics, because of the ways in which heterosexual institutions work to maintain the *status quo*."[9] Her writing belongs in the line of queer dissidence that can be identified as "a Wittig-type" utopianism.[10] Monique Wittig in *The Straight Mind* strategically essentializes and politicizes homosexual desire/identity as a third category outside the binary sex/gender system. What she calls "the straight mind" is "a conglomerate of all kinds of disciplines, theories, and current ideas" comprising "a totalizing interpretation of history, social reality, culture, language, and all the subjective phenomena at the same time."[11] The straight mind maintains rigid hierarchies and polarities in order to sustain wider social inequalities, but to embrace queer identification means to place oneself outside of the heterosexual social contract and move toward utopian possibilities of a new social order and new categories. Wittig speaks of the need to rethink "the potentiality and virtuality of humanness," not from the privileged centre (occupied by Western, white, heterosexual, propertied men), but "from an oblique point of view" exemplified by a lesbian.[12] Lesbian identity represents a threat to patriarchy and a vantage point from which to envision a new, off-centre or queer humanism. Echoes of Wittig's thought can be found in Namjoshi's vision as she also gestures toward the possibility of utopian transformation. *Goja* culminates in a teleological allegory of Love and Charity, with its inevitable Christian, Hindu, lesbian, and mythological overtones. Consequently, from the outset, there appears a possibility of construing Namjoshi's autoethnographic project as a quest for a utopian, new humanist ethics.

The autobiographical narrator of *Goja* negotiates her multiple identities and locations following a trajectory of her successive geographical displacements from India, to "cold Canada" and "later" England. *Goja* invokes what Susan Stanford Friedman calls a "geographics of subjectivity," different from the chronology of identity. The geographics of identity "figures identity as a historically embedded site, a positionality, a location, a standpoint, a terrain, an intersection, a network, a crossroads of multiply situated knowledges."[13] It maps out different subject positions of the narrating "I" while at the same time emphasizing the relationality of identity as inseparable from its social and intersubjective context. Making sense of the self requires recognition of the interdependence and interrelatedness of the stories of the self with those of others. Namjoshi's autobiographical "I" avoids situating herself as autonomous, singular, or whole. It is produced through the interplay of tropes, images, and objects of identification. She analyzes complex power dynamics involved in constructing the intersubjective space of memory, the archive of her multiple and former selves situated relationally against the two important figures in her life: her maternal grandmother, Goldie (the Ranisaheb), and her elderly nanny, Goja (the maidservant).

Throughout her spatial mappings, Namjoshi interrogates the idea of non-unitary subjectivity described by Leslie Rebecca Bloom as "an alternative view of the self located historically in language, produced in everyday gendered, racialized, and cultural/social experiences, expressed in writing and speaking, and employed as a political feminist strategy."[14] The non-unitary subjectivity emerges as a product of the geographics of identity, of how constructions of gender, race, class/caste, and sexuality are destabilized and infused with different meanings from the perspective of the subject's shifting positionalities. Namjoshi's diasporic wanderings, together with her experiences in India, have given her an understanding of the relationship between place and self, demonstrating that "a transferral of the body to a new place re-encodes it with a new meaning and within a new dynamic of power relations."[15] She is also aware of the role language plays in the ongoing process of mapping the geographics of subjectivity: "*Where one is* is a word. *Who one is* is a word—Indian, lesbian, poet, Hindu, donkey, monkey, dying animal. [...] And much of one's life is just a matter of exploring words to see which ones fit comfortably, and in which forest of words one might live and breathe" (83).[16] Still, identity is far more than just a discursive problem, and Namjoshi, right at the beginning of her narrative, alerts us to the consequences of living a particular identity when she says of being female in India that "it's possible to die of that" (3).

As a tale of coming out to Goldie and Goja, viewed against the back-drop of Indian sexism and homophobia, Namjoshi's text projects on Goldie and Goja an emotional tangle of her relationship to her native country. Her position in relation to India is complicated: on the one hand, she is secure and even privileged because of her high caste, but on the other hand, there is a certain level of discomfort caused by her lesbianism and her use of English.[17] She voices her charge against Goldie and Goja, that they didn't let her "live honourably and peacefully in [her] own country and in [her] own home" (126), thus forcing her to choose exile in response to the suppression and denial of female sexuality in India. At the same time, she is trying to examine the intersectionality of gender, race, and caste/class politics that have shaped Goldie's and Goja's lives. In this sense, the narrative illustrates a political use of memory, especially Namjoshi's memories of "house and home as the basis for writing histories about the impossibility of dwelling comfortably 'at home.'"[18] The traditional Indian upper-caste Hindu home, with its secluded space for women (the *zenana*), has historically been a contested ideological space in both colonial and postcolonial discourses. Both British imperialists and Indian nationalists used constructions of gender, and especially femininity, to support their political aims. Against the common British accusations of backwardness and effeminacy, male nationalists resorted to discourses of idealized domesticity and rigid heteronormativity to reclaim a "lost" native masculinity.[19] There is also a documented tradition of Indian anti-colonial politics figuring India itself as a home and placing a high value on the Indian woman's domestic virtues.[20] Namjoshi remakes the boundaries of "home" as an oppressive space, reflecting outside changes and "made evil by the fact of servants" (129). The ancestral home "is made to bear witness to the past; and often, its ghostly interiors are made to stand in for the unspeakable violence of what has come before."[21]

Through the allegorized configuration of Goldie and Goja, the Rani and the nanny, Namjoshi is ironically rewriting the Indian nationalist constructions of motherhood, a transgressive move, especially in reclaiming Goja as a mother figure. The lady and the servant represent a polarity between the rich and the poor, a high-caste Hindu woman and a subaltern. Their relationship dramatizes the dependence of indigenous elite women on the labour of other women subordinated by caste and class. Namjoshi is repaying her debt to Goja as one of those servants whose lives "go unrecorded [and who] go unnoticed. They disappear silently" (7). Written out of Indian history, the subalterns—tribals, landless people, agricultural labourers, factory workers, prostitutes, and servants—must be distinguished from the privileged colonial subjects and postcolonial elites.[22] On the other hand, the Ranisaheb's story, despite her privilege in relation to Goja, reveals the double standard of the ideology of womanhood in India. Although she is worshipped as "everybody's mother, everybody's grandmother" (139), Goldie occupies a dependent position in the context of two patriarchies, Indian and British, as well as imperial hierarchies. Both the Rani and the servant are "part of a power structure that they can neither alter nor avoid."[23] This power structure is fractured by different kinds of unequal relations that destabilize the local caste and class hierarchy through racialization, forcing rich and poor Indians alike into another polarity of "brown against white, black against pink" (6). However, caste divisions preclude racial solidarity, in fact pitting one colonized group against the other.

The impact of empire is also felt in the sphere of sexual politics in India, which is largely responsible for Namjoshi's decision to emigrate. According to Leela Gandhi, "empire introduced a virulent strain of homosexual anxiety/homophobia at home and abroad in the colonies," as a result turning the postcolonial nation into a profoundly heteronormative project.[24] Through her dialogue with Goldie and Goja, Namjoshi confronts the repressive culture of compulsory heterosexuality that has made loving another woman illegal in India: "To be a lesbian in those days [...] was so appalling, so terrible, that it was like putting one's head on the block. One risked so much for love that love had to mean everything" (55). She clearly articulates her indictment, claiming that "sexuality in itself is not a moral issue. It's the willingness to use it to hurt other people that is really immoral" (127). In India, she could not live her "romantic dream" (58), but she refused to live a lie. Namjoshi has been closeted for her family and, by her own admission, even after her emigration for a long time she has kept her books out of India, fearing a scandal.[25] Her search for love in *Goja* is doubly coded and refers also to finding her "paradise" through romantic self-fulfillment. She can find her sexual identity in the West, where she won't cause a "scandal" or "tarnish" the family name (75) even though she learns that "the West had its own brand of homophobia and its own kind of sexism, and it had racism as well" (77) and that lesbian love poses a danger to heterosexual society anywhere.

Her coming out to Goldie and Goja is staged as a dialogue or a three-way conversation, with the two grandmothers becoming her "auditors" rather than "audience" (114). They participate actively in the act of narration, often interrupting, contradicting, and cross-examining the narrator. Namjoshi establishes language as dialogic and intersubjective, requiring "a

Speaker and a Listener" (114), while hinting simultaneously at her view of memory "as a collective rather than a recollective faculty."[26] She thus engages in a practice of ghost writing, inviting the dead into her narrative and allowing herself to be inhabited by the ghostly presences of the Ranisa-heb, the servant, and others. Death pierces and enters the text (55) even in the form of her beloved cat (40) or through digressions to extratextual moments such as the passing of Namjoshi's favourite aunt during the writing of the book. But Goldie and Goja can only be constructions of monstrous intersubjectivity, the conjoined "we" speaking "with one voice" (10), combined in the image of a three-headed monster:

> The body is inhabited anyway. The body is infested. The Goja-monster, the Raja-monster, the Goldfish-monster, the Mummy-monster, the Daddy-monster, everyone I've ever known takes root, grubs for sustenance, even the servant who molested me. [...] All these people are jostling one another, entering into me, living with me. I am an ark. All these people I repudiate are part of me. *They are me.* (30–31)

They are "The Needy" to whom she refers through the title of Chapter Three and, in a double sense, they are also the poor whose lives remain unstoried. Their presence challenges the notions of "sacrosanct identity and the integrity of the personality," reminding the reader "that we are all composites, that we are all parts of each other. [...] A mishmash speaking with one voice, and not even realizing that the voice is garbled" (41). Multiplying a series of metaphors of subjectivity as the ark, or the theatre of memory, Namjoshi's narrative vividly dramatizes the non-unitary self of autoethnography. Her dramatis personae are "internal and external" (41), as the writing is visited also by "ghosts" of younger versions of herself "at the age of ten, eleven, twelve, thirteen" (38), further reinforcing the image of self as a multiplicity of selves. The meaning of ghost writing as a form of constructing intersubjective spaces extends to intertextuality. The writing subject and the text are coeval, both haunted and inhabited by intricate traces of others and other writing, by intertexts as ghosts. Namjoshi frankly admits that the picture of Goja can only be sketchy and one-dimensional and her life can only be imagined as filtered through the narrator's own subjectivity. Such self-reflexive moments prevent the author from accusations of romanticizing in her constructions of radical difference, whether lesbian or subaltern. Rather, she insists that the other is not totally available and keeps a respectful distance to the unknown.[27] Her ghost writing is a way of honouring life through words that have the power "to say that every living thing flamed and died; and that it did so matters" (115). In addition, the attraction of death in this ghost narrative can be partly explained by the fact that death too is a great equalizer and that as ghosts, Goja and the Rani can "speak as equals" (19). Namjoshi contemplates the divisions of caste and class and colonial hierarchies as part of her project of denaturalizing inequality. She has made a choice for her writing "to claim centre stage for the dispossessed and to challenge the traditional assumptions."[28] As her questioning of power shows, privilege can be unfixed when viewed in the context of a larger system of interlocking oppressions. This recognition can be used to perpetuate further separations and divisions, but it can also lead to finding commonality and connection. So there is a potential for gender solidarity in patriarchy, and Goja and the Rani can be "sisters"—"unequal in rank, but equal at the bottom" because men rule (17). In a patriarchal society women are always "second-class human beings" while lesbians "third-class." In the West she is "an alien three times over, as a woman, a lesbian, and an Indian (97). *Goja* can be seen as an invitation to break social taboos of caste and age between women and to "acknowledge each other" (103). The feminist subtext of Namjoshi's work consists in the possibility of bonding between women and the need to challenge persistent social prejudices and hierarchies: "It's time we told each other stories about both the West and the East" (87). In that sense, her narrative partakes of the tradition of migrant women writers who "forge a sort of female bonding across time, culture, race, and class [...] they turn to their past—their mothers and grandmothers—to trace their links through a matriarchal lineage [...] they establish links horizontally, too, connecting women of different classes and races to break the barriers separating woman from woman."[29] Namjoshi's voice is projected from the liminal space where the geographics of identity literally translates into "diasporic" and "queer" and where the subject speaks simultaneously to the past and to the future of her virtual readership, while transcending the vertical and horizontal distances in the present. A political potential of this type of feminist autoethnography lies in challenging the unidirectionality of traditional autoethnographic representations that address themselves in either resistant or complicit ways primarily to what they inscribe as a dominant perspective.

Indeed, such questioning of inequality would be incomplete without Namjoshi's examination of her own complicity with power. In post-Independence India, where her grandfather the Raja was a cabinet minister and where she worked in the Indian Administrative Service in her region, she becomes disillusioned with powerful elites and is shocked by the discrepancy between the poor and the rich. She offers admissions of guilt: "I did nothing. The poor were shadows" (63). She tries to do her job in an honest and competent manner, but contends that "to fail to do evil is hardly to do good" (66). She also rejects philanthropy of the rich as a way "to fix up things" (63); it is false charity that is mostly self-serving. Similarly, she later mocks the liberal guilt of the West as insincere (109). The gap between the rich and the poor exists in the West too, but she finds it more appalling in India because of the colonial legacy. The corruption of power seems inescapable: "Under the new system I'm a serf of capitalism. And I hate it. Would I prefer to be a lord? Yes. And therein I'm corrupt" (110). Nevertheless, she gets radicalized by the West, and her position contrasts with the acquiescence of the dispossessed voiced by Goja: "When inhumanity reaches such proportions perhaps those who perpetrate it are not human? Would I be angry with a tiger that was eating me? Just afraid and in pain" (151). Although all people are born into a set-up, into a power structure that defines their place, for Namjoshi, if not for Goja, there is always a choice of "refusing to be who I was supposed to be" (140). Given her expressed "unwillingness to serve" (17), she can voluntarily renounce parts of her relative privilege and model an option of nonconformity.

While deconstructing the erasure and silence of the poor, Namjoshi learns new lessons about power in the West when she experiences social marginalization "as a woman, a lesbian, and a brown-skinned person" (16). Paradoxically, her status in the new world gives her the "freedom of near invisibility" (71), a "privilege" gained at the cost of humiliation, hurt, and the trauma of racism and ethnocentrism. She discovers that polarities are kept in place through ignorance that helps to create separations among people and maintain the status quo. During her year of study in the United States, she is herself drawn into a vicious cycle of power/powerlessness that reproduces stereotyping on both sides. Sarcasm and irony become her weapons against the Americans who, for her, embody the power of stupidity until her perspective is slightly modified by time:

> I understand now that there was nothing that belonged to a particular nationality about what it was that hurt me. This willful, unprocessed, unameliorated ignorance I'm calling stupidity is a function of power. The powerful are stupid. Citizens of Rome are stupid in relation to the rest of the world. Human beings are stupid in relation to the rest of creation, masters are stupid in relation to servants, men in relation to women, adults in relation to children, the rich in relation to the poor [...].(74)

What she calls stupidity is such an attitude that cultivates binary, hierarchical thinking about difference and justifies lack of empathy and knowledge about the other.

Namjoshi deconstructs power also in another sense, as a consensual construct, corroborated through language and performance: "If enough people say something happened, then it did happen" (65). She credits her politicization and activism in the gay and lesbian movements for being able "to understand how language ha[s] power over power itself. Over years, language mediated everything: my struggle with powerlessness and loss of identity, my understanding of who defined whom and how effectively, and my need to work out what really mattered and somehow to say it" (79). *Goja* puts language at the centre of reflection and, in fact, Namjoshi names language as another reason for going abroad: "The English language had colonized my brain, but I had never seen the reality behind the words" (66). Her choice of writing in English is linked both to her inherited condition of postcoloniality and to her adopted politics of dissent. In India the West is not merely a geographical space; rather, "it takes on a psychological existence. This is the colonialism that survives the death of Empires."[30] But she also chooses English because she identifies as an outsider, a lesbian feminist talking back from the fringe, who secedes from either culture, be it British or Indian, finding it repressive and restrictive in one area, but worth hanging on to in other areas. As her sexual self-definition is initially possible only through English, the colonizer's language is here embraced as a tool of defiance and liberation, without losing its associations with foreignness and domination. In this way, Namjoshi further confounds and complicates the already ambivalent politics of language often present in postcolonial autoethnography, with its notions of the native informant's epistemic privilege and double consciousness resulting from the writing subject's familiarity with two unequal languages and cultures.

Namjoshi's subjectivity has historically been constructed by her ascent into English: "I was educated in English, and think in English. Though we spoke Marathi at home, I was never formally taught Marathi" (176). English was an equally strong formative influence on her as the surrounding Indian cultural context, and she admits in an interview that she has been carrying the weight of its powerful cultural tradition.[31] However, she was "supposed to learn English without becoming Anglicized (or Americanized)" and was instructed to "learn what they teach you, but never become one of them" (40). Thinking in English posits a challenge to her as a postcolonial writer. Her native Marathi "wasn't good enough" for her to become a poet (82). As she describes her predicament to an interviewer: "What I had to grapple with was trying to make language say what was alien to that language. How does one talk about the familiar in a language that makes it exotic?"[32] In a striking reversal of the autoethnographic perspective, she tries to explain to Goldie and Goja her dwelling in "an alien language" (47), "exotic" and "foreign" English (96).

Probing the relationship between language, identity, and landscape is another way to discover that "the heritages of postcoloniality do not go away materially even in performance."[33] Namjoshi identifies with Western Maharashtra as her landscape and her people (61), the landscape that could absorb emotion and grief (57). How durable the imprint is that this landscape leaves on her is conveyed by the metaphor of the bones: "in this arid and sunburnt landscape, my bones are your bones, and in the chemical analysis of your ashes and my dust there is no difference!" (10) Even in displacement, the body remains symbolically tied to place. Contrariwise, the estrangement of the self from landscape is what she experiences in exile. Again, she explores this experience through the metaphor of language as an enchanted forest: "Entering the States, and then a year later Canada, was like entering a forest of words" (80). Namjoshi finds comforting affinities between her alienation and "the discomfort of the English-speaking Canadians" (83) that results from Canada's postcolonial sense of incongruity between language and landscape. However, for her a disjunction stems from an imposition of colonial rule on the familiar (and familial) land while the obverse is true in Canada, where the foreignness of the land causes a deterritorialization of language and a sense of being not quite at home. A disjunction between language and landscape, self and place, can be seen in the ironic haunting of "Indian" in "East Indian" (99).

The motif of contamination by colonial violence returns in Namjoshi's treatment of the story of her sexual abuse by a male servant when she was five years old. The three-headed monster of intersubjectivity (the narrator and her two grandmothers) reveals a gaping absence of her mother, personified by the Queen of Spades, who through abandonment offers her black piglet child "to the gods that be, to the fighting, fucking, powerful men—of whom she is afraid" (26). Neither of her two grandmothers could protect her from "a nightmare made up of blood and guts and childhood fear" (25). Namjoshi asks how the telling of abuse is possible, and she invents a dissociative way of telling the story of abuse through an allegory of playing cards. Reminiscent of fairy tales and Lewis Carroll, a splintered narrative foregrounds the sinister irony of pedophiliac associations while trying to invent some restorative strategies for the wounded subject, so she can "inhabit [her] own body" (29). Examining the relationship between sexual abuse and colonialism, one might perhaps gain a different understanding of the ruptures and fragmentations that seem to be characteristic of postcolonial autoethnography. In her study of a rupture of trauma, Jodi Lundgren observes that "[i]n the case of both incest and colonization, the oppressed are objectified, and subject and writing 'emanate from […] a position of damage.'"[34] However, while the splits and fragmentations of Namjoshi's narrative can be interpreted as "one possible permutation" of the trauma of abuse and colonization, at the same time, she embraces a politics of fragmentation from both contestatory and celebratory positions of the postcolonial and postmodern subject.

Namjoshi's postmodern sensibility is visible in an awareness of the power of language to fashion "multiple realities" and multiple meanings, coupled with her understanding of subjectivity as non-unitary. Her recognition that identity is an arbitrary, provisional, and unstable construct stems from the juxtaposition of her experiences in India and the West. In India her job with the civil service was the most coveted post one could aspire to. She "became 'someone'" only to fall into anonymity and marginalization when she was a student in North America (65). Similarly, another consciousness-raising moment is brought to her by the realization that she has been placed inside contradictory constructions of herself as either "mainstream" or "Third World." However, subjectivity exceeds the space of social construction that is usually the focus of autoethnographic representation, and she questions her grasp of the essence and continuity of the self: "But surely I existed before? The knowledge that with or without recognition one continues to live was what sustained me when I was stripped of my identity" (65). In Namjoshi's case, sources of fragmentation of identity can be found not only in her direct experience of displacement or the postmodern deconstruction of the unitary subject, but also in Hindu beliefs and lesbian theorizing. The notion of plural and shifting selves is "in consonance with the Hindu concept of transmigration of souls and it enables her to de-construct not only gender-hierarchy but also hierarchization of living species."[35] As she explains this connection in an interview: "a Hindu grows up thinking that identity is arbitrary […] because you are one thing in this life and another in the next. You may not believe it, but it is a metaphor and that becomes part of your thinking."[36] Namjoshi's tales and fables are populated with mythological and animal "eccentric" creatures. Drawing upon affinities between the human and nonhuman worlds, she foregrounds "hitherto 'exiled' figures, turning them into autonomous subjects and having them tell their tales in their own distinct ways."[37]

Biddy Martin observes that lesbian life writing renders problematic the term "lesbian" itself.[38] Influenced by both poststructuralist and queer theory, lesbian autobiography rejects essentialist identities and embraces identities as shifting and mutable. According to Gita Rajan, Namjoshi employs a "strategy of constructing essentialism"[39] that might also be applied to describe the ethical stance she adopts as an autoethnographer. She short-circuits the binary politics of difference by deploying side-by-side discourses of fragmentation and homogenization. In the context of lesbian identity, Namjoshi's strategy of constructing essentialism might be related to what R. Radhakrishnan says about identity vis-à-vis relations of domination and subordination, namely, that "the dominant position requires acts of self-deconstruction" while the subordinate position entails collective self-construction."[40] The autoethnographic subject of *Goja* fluctuates between these positions. Playful postmodernism of fragmentation is countered by Namjoshi's analysis of the politics of power and her ethical universalism. Otherwise, the experience of non-unitary subjectivity would threaten individual sanity (41). She balances indeterminism and arbitrariness by focusing on commonalities of human experience and on universal values that ought to command everyone's respect. Her version of new humanism is an antidote to a postmodern sense of fragmentation and relativism.

The construction of non-unitary subjectivity and the continuous displacement of polarities are necessary restorative steps towards finding an answer to the problem of misuse of power. Namjoshi admits in an interview that she is concerned in all her works with "considering the moral position of a human being"[41] and with the problem of how to be a good person. She confronts "the dilemmas of living a moral life without either being thoroughly exploited or exploiting other people."[42] In *Goja* she presents an outline of an ethical system that I would call "conjunctural ethics." The term is derived from ethnographic criticism of James Clifford, who defines "conjuncturalism" as a process of moving between cultures necessitated by the breakup of discrete cultures with their essentialist conceptions of identity.[43] In Namjoshi's case, the term "conjunctural ethics" seems preferable to "syncretic ethics" because "conjuncture" connotes "conjunction, union; a combination of circumstances or events usually producing a crisis"—in contrast to "syncretism," which is more like a fusion and implies a harmonious unity.[44] It also seems to be an appropriate term for Namjoshi, classified by Gita Rajan as a representative of Abdul JanMohammed's category of the "specular border intellectual," who utilizes "her interstitial cultural space as a vantage point from which to define, explicitly or implicitly, other utopian possibilities of group formation."[45] By contrast, the "syncretic border intellectual" is more "at home" in the cultures that she inhabits.

Suniti Namjoshi does not shy from saying that we need ethical idealism. She takes a position of high ground, speaking from above the chasm between the rich and the poor in her native India, the gap between the West and the colonies and later the postcolonial world, and the divisions between the West's own haves and have-nots. It is a chasm that opens up whenever and wherever one human being exploits or degrades another. She is speaking from "the appalling knowledge that we are not two different species: [and that] what was being done, we were doing to ourselves" (61). In the face of global poverty and international exploitation, she offers her "conjunctural ethics," contained in what she labels "The Moral Imperative" of respect for life: "Thou shall not exploit other people and feed off their flesh! To be born is not a birthright, but once born, to be allowed to grow and live, and if at all possible, to be happy, surely these things should be inalienable" (61). The text brings up the question of forgiveness in the final part, staging a meeting between the oppressor and the oppressed, the rich and the poor. The narrator demands that the Rani apologize and ask Goja for forgiveness. However, the narrator makes it clear that "to say to Goja, 'Forgive me that I exploited you, day in and day out, year after year'—[is] a travesty" (144). The powerful have no right to ask for forgiveness from the powerless even if they want to apologize. Demanding that the powerless forgive and forget would be tantamount to expecting that they surrender themselves totally to the powerful. Understandably, Goja refuses to collude (152).

According to Namjoshi, we all have internalized polarized thinking although we are pained by polarities. If we search for a way of being in the world that would ease the pain of divisions between the powerful and the powerless, we must find love and charity. They are the Grail of her quest, necessary for the healing of her traumas and the wounds of the world. She believes that love and charity can redeem human beings who are forced to live in a world structured by power and domination, but she is aware that in this world, "being able to love seems absurd sometimes, even foolish, certainly not prudent" (53). However, at least to make an attempt is love's "paradoxical victory." She envisions the possibility of change, meaning that we would have to take the conjunctural ethics literally and live it on every micro and macro level in everyday life. It requires a leap of imagination to break a cycle of abuse, violence, and oppression. A "miracle" would occur if the rich world could overcome its indifference to the poor world and if suffering did not automatically breed hatred. On the horizon of her ethical stance, there is a certain utopianism, derived from both Christian and Hindu traditions and from lesbian utopianism. Paradoxically, for Namjoshi such conjunctural ethics is legitimate in the age of globalization; it accords with her oppression and privilege, with her identity and history as a lesbian, feminist, postcolonial subject at the same time as it bespeaks the luxury of her caste and education.

Interestingly, Namjoshi's ethics of love "as the most noble of human endeavours"[46] can be seen as a bold synthesis of all her diverse influences, Hindu and Christian. In a sense, it is an ironic reworking of traditional Hindu culture with its ideology of high-caste womanhood as fulfilled through love and devotion to her husband, where a Hindu female is defined by "her immense capacity for love and devotion."[47] Namjoshi is also an heir to J. Krishnamurti's philosophy of love, one of the basic tenets of which is the possibility of transformation through love. She was influenced by his teachings while attending Rishi Valley School, and she even quotes one of J. Krishnamurti's axioms: "Where there is fear there cannot be love" (48).[48] Similarly, her relation to the Christian concept of love is referenced through the figure of Jesus as "a likeable god" whose "story acquired meaning to [her]" (52). An important part of her allegory is the idea of bringing love to public life: "as long as Charity is confined to the private sphere, and Power to the public and political one—nothing works!" (136). She develops an argument for substituting the concept of brotherhood of men with "the Motherhood of Men" (34) that eventually might lead to the transformation of human nature. Her reflection on human needs grows from exploring the connections between childhood (including her own personal experience of abandonment and abuse), the continuing existence of social injustice (motivated by power and desire), and the possibility of change. If the originary basic human need is the need of every child to be loved, all that is needed for a truly revolutionary change in social relations to occur is for everyone to respond to this basic need for love. It is ethical idealism to the highest degree, and "perhaps it can't all be done in one sitting, but we could get started" (37).

Namjoshi's vision anticipates the possibility that Richard King describes as "a vision of the twenty-first century as an era which would be globally 'postwestern' rather than Eurocentrically 'postmodern.'"[49] Despite possible accusations of ideological glibness and universalism that may inhere in Namjoshi's quest for love and charity, there are innovative elements in her thinking contained in the effort to historicize and politicize a contemporary moral allegory. Her moral stance is not intended to encourage passivity and quietism. She manages to tease out multiple ironies from the juxtaposition of millennial utopianism and global transnationalism, both of which are couched in the religious rhetoric of salvation. Reading *Goja* it is impossible to forget that Christianity has after all been a tool of colonialism just as the ideology of globalization remains an effective tool of transnational capitalism. Confronted by an impasse of history caused by long-term adherence to polarized thinking, Namjoshi has taken risks trying to revive a kind of conjunctural ethical stance for the twenty-first century when, according to her, human beings are expected "to live with a degree of kindness toward the whole creation under circumstances that [make] it impossible" (52).[50]

Returning to the question of how autoethnography as a genre can accommodate the ethical, Namjoshi's "ghost writing" certainly opens up new possibilities. She foregrounds her accountability to multiple audiences as she undertakes to "explain" the West (mostly Canada) to the East—that is, to her dead grandmothers—rather than addressing herself primarily to her Western readers. Her account is "Janus-faced" (85), that is, looking both ways, shifting and reversing perspectives. Namjoshi occupies the space in between and, according to Gita Rajan, "is never fully an exile, or immigrant, or anthropologist," but rather stresses "the border instead of the territory on either side."[51] The irony of explaining "the Fabulous West to the Mysterious East" (mocking essentialist stereotypes of both) is that the "truths" about the West all turn out to be relative differences, of degree rather than of substance: fewer people sleep on the streets; there's more freedom for women; the gap between the rich and the poor is not so great in the West (89). Conversely, comparing English and Marathi, she asks rhetorically, "Is Marathi less racist, less sexist, less class- and caste-conscious?" (109). Without ignoring the West-East asymmetries, it is the inhumanity of both worlds that is Namjoshi's target.

Goja persistently frustrates traditional ethnographic expectations of cultural complicity by resisting "the ongoing tendency to dichotomize and reify the distinction between 'East' and 'West.'"[52] There is nothing in Namjoshi's narrative that can be neatly packaged as separate "Indian culture" or "Western culture," as both are fractured, intertwined, and changing, revealing "internal plurality, dissension, and contestation over values."[53] Her approach seems to be consistent with Uma Narayan's call to avoid both cultural essentialism and cultural relativism by taking "account of the multiplicity of real differences in values, interests, and worldviews that traverse contemporary national and transnational contexts."[54] But that also means being able to recognize concerns and values common to both worlds. For Namjoshi, "the girders that [bridge] two worlds" are the politics of "sex, power, and language" (86). Likewise, she believes that the quest for Love and Charity should matter in both worlds and that both East and West would benefit from ethics. Her conjunctural ethics is never resolved into the harmony of either "sameness" or "difference," but keeps the tension between the two always present on the horizon of our thinking. Such thinking is possible from Namjoshi's oblique or queer outsider/insider position that allows her to use her marginalization as "the filtering consciousness" from which to re-evaluate the norms of a patriarchal, heterosexist society.[55] Resisting regulation and coercion of the self to conform to heteronormativity, domesticity, Christian norms, whiteness, and other dominant values, she weaves several oppositional discourses and, "in doing so, supplies an idiom for expansive (and utopian) sympathies with hetcrodox/marginalized/subjugated beings, ideas, and knowledges."[56] To borrow the title of Phillipa Kafka's book, Namjoshi is always "on the outside looking in(dian)" and dreaming of a culture that would "allow strangers in."[57]

NOTES

1 Sandra Ponzanesi, *Paradoxes of Post-Colonial Culture: Contemporary Women Writers of the Indian and Afro-Italian Diaspora* (Albany: State U of New York P, 2004), 60.

2 Anannya Dasgupta, "'Do I Remove My Skin?' Interrogating Identity in Suniti Namjoshi's Fables," in *Queering India: Same-Sex Love and Eroticism in Indian Culture and Society*, ed. Ruth Vanita (New York and London: Routledge, 2002), 102.

3 Deborah E. Reed-Danahay, ed., *Auto/Ethnography: Rewriting the Self and the Social* (Oxford, UK: Berg Publishers, 1997), 2.

4 Uma Narayan, "Essence of Culture and a Sense of History: A Feminist Critique of Cultural Essentialism," in *Decentering the Centre: Philosophy for a Multicultural, Postcolonial, and Feminist World*, ed. Uma Narayan and Sandra Harding (Bloomington and Indianapolis: Indiana UP, 2000). She brilliantly demonstrates that "'assumptions of difference' have been deployed for cultural imperialist ends no less expeditiously than 'assumptions of sameness'" (94–95).

5 Françoise Lionnet, *Autobiographical Voices: Race, Gender, Self-Portraiture* (Ithaca, NY: Cornell UP, 1989), 108.

6 Ibid., 99.

7 Julia Watson, "Autoethnography," in *Encyclopedia of Life Writing: Autobiographical and Biographical Forms*, ed. Margareta Jolly (London and Chicago: Fitzroy Dearborn Publishers, 2001), 83.

8 In contrast to Audre Lorde, Namjoshi belongs to a group of privileged cosmopolitan writers who inhabit transnational spaces and for whom "the links between class status and mobility are critical to the kinds of histories they [are] able to write." Antoinette Burton, *Dwelling in the Archive: Women Writing House, Home and History in Late Colonial India* (New York: Oxford UP, 2003), 17.

9 C. Vijayasree, "An Interview with Suniti Namjoshi," in *Suniti Namjoshi: The Artful Transgressor* (Jaipur and New Delhi: Rawat Publications, 2001), 182.

10 Leela Gandhi, "Loving Well: Homosexuality and Utopian Thought in Post/Colonial India," in *Queering India: Same-Sex Love and Eroticism in Indian Culture and Society*, ed. Ruth Vanita (New York and London: Routledge, 2002), 89.

11 Monique Wittig, *The Straight Mind and Other Essays* (Boston: Beacon Press, 1992), 27.

12 Ibid., 46.
13 Susan Stanford Friedman, *Mappings: Feminism and the Cultural Geographies of Encounter* (Princeton, NJ: Princeton UP, 1998), 19.
14 Leslie Rebecca Bloom, *Under the Sign of Hope: Feminist Methodology and Narrative Interpretation* (Albany: State U of New York P, 1998), 6.
15 Ralph J. Crane and Radhika Mohanram, eds., *Shifting Continents/Colliding Cultures: Diaspora Writing on the Indian Subcontinent* (Amsterdam: Rodopi, 2000), xi.
16 All subsequent parenthetical references in this essay are from Suniti Namjoshi, *Goja: An Autobiographical Myth* (Melbourne: Spinifex, 2000).
17 Dasgupta, "Do I Remove My Skin?," 102.
18 Burton, *Dwelling in the Archive*, 5. In her study Burton notes "the enduring discursive influence of house and home on Indian women's autobiographical productions" (19).
19 Cf. Gandhi, "Loving Well," 89. See also Carla Petievich, "Doganas and Zanakhis: The Invention and Subsequent Erasure of Urdu Poetry's 'Lesbian' Voice," in *Queering India: Same-Sex Love and Eroticism in Indian Culture and Society*, ed. Ruth Vanita (New York and London: Routledge, 2002), 57.
20 Cf. Burton, *Dwelling in the Archive*, 9. See also Rebecca Sultana, "'Many Souls, Many Voices': Multiple Transformations of Meena Alexander's Nomadic Characters," in *Discussing Indian Women Writers: Some Feminist Issues*, ed. Alessandro Monti and R.K. Dhawan (New Delhi: Prestige Books, 2004). She discusses Mahatma Gandhi's representations of women that "promoted an ideology wherein female sexuality was legitimately embodied only in marriage, wifehood, motherhood, domesticity" (Sultana, 235).
21 Burton, *Dwelling in the Archive*, 15.
22 Teresa Hubel, *Whose India?: The Independence Struggle in British and Indian Fiction and History* (Durham, NC and London: Duke UP, 1996), 121. She quotes Jenny Sharpe, saying that "the voice of the indigenous elite is too frequently made to represent all of the subject population by critics of the West. The subaltern is effaced by such practices" (Hubel, 119). Hubel also disputes as problematic Gayatri Spivak's claim that "the voice of the colonial subject or indigenous elite is inevitably inauthentic (119).
23 Vijayasree, *Suniti*, 166.
24 Gandhi, "Loving Well," 88.
25 Chelva Kanaganayakam, "An Interview with Suniti Namjoshi," in *Configurations of Exile: South Asian Writers and Their World* (Toronto: TSAR, 1995), 52.
26 Vijayasree, *Suniti*, 170.
27 Namjoshi's respectful stance and her acknowledgement of epistemological and ontological aporias in relation to Goja might be helpful in trying to defend her from the charge of voice appropriation. Nevertheless, the ethical questions involved in writing about the subaltern woman inevitably haunt the text, ironically resonating in the words attributed to Goja: "Do not exploit me ..." Creating Goja, Namjoshi ventures into a contested territory opened up by Gayatri Spivak's question: "Can the subaltern speak?" As Alison Donnell writes, "the insistence on authentic voices with situated knowledge make[s] a false assumption that speaking for is always 'speaking as' or 'talking over,' rather than 'speaking of' or 'speaking alongside.'" Alison Donnell, "When Writing the Other Is Being True to the Self: Jamaica Kincaid's *The Autobiography of My Mother*," in *Women's Lives into Print: The Theory, Practice and Writing of Feminist Auto/Biography*, ed. Pauline Polkey (New York:

St. Martin's Press, 1999), 129. Namjoshi's attempt to speak "of" and "alongside" Goja is coupled with her dehegemonizing of her own position. Similarly, Françoise Lionnet talks about one particular manifestation of cultural relativism that takes the form of a hands-off approach to the study and representation of subaltern subjects, which can further undermine "feminist political solidarity." Françoise Lionnet, *Postcolonial Representations: Women, Literature, Identity* (Ithaca, NY: Cornell UP, 1995), 2.

28 Vijayasree, *Suniti* 177.

29 C. Vijayasree, "Alter-Nativity, Migration, Marginality and Narration: The Case of Indian Women Writers Settled in the West," in *Shifting Continents/Colliding Cultures: Diaspora Writing on the Indian Subcontinent*, ed. Ralph J. Crane and Radhika Mohanram (Amsterdam: Rodopi, 2000), 129.

30 Hubel, *Whose India?* 123.

31 Vijayasree, *Suniti*, 176.

32 Kanaganayakam, "An Interview," 49.

33 Sivamohan Sumathy, "Becoming Woman: Travelling Gender and Identity Politics in Four Women's Texts," in *Discussing Indian Women Writers: Some Feminist Issues*, ed. Alessandro Monti and R.K. Dhawan (New Delhi: Prestige Books, 2004), 290.

34 Jodi Lundgren, "Writing 'in Sparkler Script': Incest and the Construction of Subjectivity in Contemporary Canadian Women's Autobiographical Texts," *Essays on Canadian Writing* 65 (Fall 1998): 237.

35 Vijayasree, *Suniti*, 28.

36 Kanaganayakam, "An Interview," 49.

37 Vijayasree, "Alter-Nativity," 133.

38 Biddy Martin, "Lesbian Identity and Autobiographical Difference(s)," in *Life/Lines: Theorizing Women's Autobiography*, ed. Bella Brodzki and Celeste Schenck (Ithaca, NY: Cornell UP, 1988), 77.

39 Gita Rajan, "(Con)figuring Identity: Cultural Space of the Indo-British Border Intellectual," in *Writing New Identities: Gender, Nation and Immigration in Contemporary Europe*, ed. Gisela Brinker-Gabler and Sidonie Smith (Minneapolis: U of Minnesota P, 1997), 91.

40 After Sally Robinson, *Engendering the Subject: Gender and Self-Representation in Contemporary Women's Fiction* (New York: State U of New York Press, 1991), 3.

41 Coomi S. Vevaina, "An Interview with Suniti Namjoshi," *ARIEL: A Review of International English Literature* 29, no. 1 (January 1998): 195.

42 Ibid., 196.

43 Kamala Visweswaran, *Fictions of Feminist Ethnography* (Minneapolis: U of Minnesota P, 1994), 11. The adjective "conjunctural" appears in feminist discussions of identity. Visweswaran also identifies "the converging practices of 'conjuncturalism' emerging within feminist theory and ethnographic criticism," in particular the "feminist conjuncturalist" approach of Ruth Frankenberg and Lata Mani (Visweswaran, 11–12). For James Clifford, ethnographic conjunctures represent shuttling between cultures.

44 *Webster's Ninth New Collegiate Dictionary* (Springfield: Merriam-Webster, 1998).

45 Rajan, "(Con)figuring Identity," 80.

46 Petievich, "Doganas and Zanakhis," 55. In the light of Petievich's discussion, Namjoshi's celebration of lesbian love can be related to a rich and centuries-old tradition of Indian poetry, both Hindu and Muslim.

47 Hubel, *Whose India?* 140.

48 However, Namjoshi offers a barbed comment suggesting that perhaps he treated love like a commodity. Nevertheless, she credits the school for fostering her need to idealize (51).

49 Richard King, *Indian Philosophy: An Introduction to Hindu and Buddhist Thought* (Edinburgh: Edinburgh UP, 1991), 233.

50 In different contexts, the assessment of a recent turn to ethics in contemporary criticism and theory has been paradoxical. As Tina Chen observes, critics skeptical of the turn toward ethical criticism are often concerned that "an emphasis on ethics as both reading and teaching practice reflects a desire to escape from politics in favour of an over-emphasis on moralism and 'self-righteousness.'" According to Chen, such concerns that an ethics-based approach is evidence of a conservative tendency to depoliticize "the study of race and cultural difference in favour of more general humanistic questions" seem to be misconstrued. Tina Chen, "Towards an Ethics of Knowledge," *MELUS* 30, no. 2 (Summer 2005): 159.

51 Rajan, "(Con)figuring Identity," 95–96.

52 King, *Indian Philosophy*, 236.

53 Narayan, "Essence of Culture and a Sense of History," 96.

54 Ibid., 96.

55 Dasgupta, "Do I Remove My Skin?" 100. One might question at this point if "outsiderism" (or the position of radical difference) is absolutely necessary in order to dream utopia. It seems that such a position is not automatically idealist or progressive. By the same token, utopias are sometimes conservative projects.

56 Gandhi, "Loving Well," 94.

57 Cf. Phillippa Kafka, *On the Outside Looking In(dian): Indian Women Writers at Home and Abroad* (New York: Peter Lang Publishing, 2003). The last phrase is from Gillian Hanscombe and Suniti Namjoshi, "Writing the Rag-Bag of Empire," in *Engendering Realism and Postmodernism: Contemporary Women Writers in Britain*, ed. Beate Neumeier (Amsterdam: Rodopi, 2001), 399.

[chapter eleven]

An Ethnos of Difference, a Praxis of Inclusion
The Ethics of Global Citizenship in Shani Mootoo's
Cereus Blooms at Night

Mariam Pirbhai

Break a vase, and the love that reassembles its fragments is stronger than that love which took its symmetry for granted when it was whole.
—Derek Walcott[1]

You will hear little more of me as I apply myself to the story of Mala Ramchandin, fashioning a single garment out of myriad parts. —Shani Mootoo[2]

Traditionally defined as a "nation,"[3] the "ethnos" connotes group identification, based on the presence of shared traits which serve, in turn, as markers of differentiation from other groups. If autoethnography signals a shift from the "retrieval of a repressed dimension of the *private* self [to] the rewriting of [. . .] ethnic history,"[4] or the relocation of the self within the ethnic community, what are the conceptual and aesthetic limits of autoethnography when the ethnos itself is configured as a group of migrant hybrid subjects, affiliated through difference and allied through "otherness"? Conversely, what are the possibilities for writing or imagining the ethnos "beyond" these limits?

Shani Mootoo's *Cereus Blooms at Night* tentatively poses this and other questions of (self-) representation for those whose subject positions are, by virtue of the multiple sites of identification and "situatedness" associated with diasporic and migrant identities, simultaneously local and global. Moreover, in foregrounding communities as affiliative and filiative bodies which travel across the asymmetrical contact zones of culture as much as they erect the seemingly impenetrable boundaries of exclusion, Mootoo strives to widen the epistemology of the ethnos and, by extension, the relationship between the self and the ethnic community. By redrawing the self and the ethnos within the correlative relationship between the local and global, Mootoo's engagement with the autoethnographic project rejects any overreliance on "a spatially localized people,"[5] that does not acknowledge the already dislocated and globalized positionality of the diasporic subject. This is not to suggest that Mootoo sacrifices historical and cultural specificity for a utopian[6] vision of belonging or a postmodern de-territoriality. Rather, in situating the ethnos as part of the wider human community, Mootoo's text appears to advocate an ethics of global citizenship which considers the interdependent relationship of past and present hegemonies as they are, in turn, simultaneously (re-)constituted within local and global geographies.

The widening of the episteme of belonging and community plays itself out as a productive tension between time frames, narrative modes and perspectives, private and public spheres, the "here" and necessary "elsewheres" of diasporic experience, etc. Set in a fictitious island that is nonetheless fully evocative of the Caribbean, *Cereus Blooms at Night* conflates myth, history, and fantasy, as well as the inexplicable alongside the ordinary. As Vivian May suggests, the novel offers a "mythical version of Trinidad"[7] which echoes other kinds of quasi-fictive locales found across the body of Caribbean women's writing, wherein the "critical utility of a fictional island setting" offers "opportunities to remember identities and histories differently."[8] Within its own multiple, shifting time frames and narrative frames alike, Mootoo's hybrid text also bears the traces of magical realism in its attempt to accommodate the Caribbean's creolized space as a fusion of different cultural groups, as well as of the diasporic subjects whose private selves bespeak a history of dislocation and rupture therein. The novel's "deliberate haziness [...] in time as well as place"[9] further imbues the text with allegorical possibility. In other words, the text becomes meaningful both within and "beyond" the framework of its historical and cultural specificities.

The story of Mala Ramchandin, a victim of incest and protracted sexual abuse, is presented as an amateur biographer's attempt to re-*member* "differently"—that is to say, outside the delimiting framework of ideological and (af)filiative rupture—the history and identity of one such fractured self. Mootoo's wholly self-conscious narrator, Tyler, engages in a metafictional exercise in which authorship is at best a tenuous enactment of narrative control, subject to self-reflexive "lapses, for there are some."[10] Moreover, as soon as Tyler discloses his potential for narrative slippage, so too does the text assume an added writerly dimension of autobiography, for, as he tells us, to have erased the lapses "would have been to do the same to myself." Thus, from our first introduction to Tyler, we are presented with a text that inhabits multiple hybrid discursive spaces. In this case, the interchangeable and intersubjective project of (auto-)biography serves as a generic echo of the dialectical relationship between self and other in which Tyler and his subject Mala are mutually engaged. Indeed, Tyler only begins the process of reconstructing Mala's story in his growing identification with his subject, or, rather, in his increasing recognition of the intertwined fabric of their history/identity.

Cultural Citizenship Across the Colonial and Postcolonial Divide

As I have suggested, one aspect of the novel's unorthodox and subversive teleology is its oscillation between the real and the imaginary. What appears to be an indeterminate fictive island setting in one instance transmogrifies, in the next, into a text that is replete with historical, cultural, and physical markers that are specific to the Caribbean region, and to Mootoo's native Trinidad in particular. On the one hand, historical realism emerges tentatively and symbolically, such as in naming practices which foreground South Asian languages and customs: Mala, Chandin, Ramchandin, and perhaps even "Lantanacamara,"[11] the name of the enigmatic island setting itself. Colonial history also surfaces indirectly in the symbolic naming of local streets and haunts, such as Otoh's family dwelling on "Government Alley," itself a residual echo of the official nomenclature of British imperial administration. Similarly, in her naming the rehabilitation facility for which Tyler works "Paradise Alms House," one finds tongue-and-cheek reversals of reductive tropical island stereotypes,[12] particularly those of the island as an Edenic space, at once the site of spiritual degradation and its inverse, the symbol of pre-lapsarian innocence and purity. Names metonymically reveal the archipelago's post-Columbian history as a palimpsest of multiple discursive sites, which are nonetheless subsumed by the meta-narrative of European colonial history as an unrelenting struggle for power, conquest, supremacy, and dominance.

Colonial history is fully underscored, however, in the concerted degree of realism with which Mootoo portrays the cross-generational saga of Indo-Caribbean peoples who immigrated to the Caribbean under the auspices of the British Raj, as a solution to the labour shortage on colonial plantations in the aftermath of emancipation. The fact that Mootoo is one of a small but steadily growing circle of Indo-Caribbean authors who anchors her characters in the economy and historical trajectory of indentured labour assumes added significance in light of the fact that the Indo-Caribbean population has traditionally left little impression on the imaginative landscape of their Afro-Caribbean counterparts. For example, Barbadian novelist George Lamming confesses that he, like many Afro-Caribbean peoples, "lived in an involuntary, almost unconscious segregation from the world of Indians,"[13] in spite of the fact that the "Indian presence is no less Caribbean in its formation than that of their African comrades."[14]

As Frank Birbalsingh explains, there are several factors that account for the Indo-Caribbean's relative segregation within the dominant Creole cultural community. First, South Asians brought with them altogether alien "languages, customs, religions, dress and culture in an English-speaking, Christian society,"[15] and in a creolized culture bearing African roots. Second, in their exclusive function as a workforce bound to the bidding of the European plantocracy, they were vastly a rural community relegated to the boundaries of the plantation estate. The image of Afro-Caribbean and Indo-Caribbean diaspora cultures as that of two relative solitudes finds its political confirmation in Trinidad and Guyana, home to two of the largest Indo-Caribbean communities. In both postcolonial states, national identity has often capitulated into an oppositional discourse of race, whereby each diasporic community can be seen to retreat within a self-protective space in response to the essentializing gaze of the other.

In her wholly unidealized version of the Indo-Caribbean community, Mootoo not only lifts the veil of mystique surrounding its population but also stretches the imaginative canvas of the Caribbean to include other expressions of difference, of the ethnos. To this end, Mootoo reveals a heterogeneous diasporic body whose responses to history are as varied as they are complex. The racial delineations still prevalent in the emergent postcolonial state, together with the kind of unrealistic claims of each community's relative freedoms within the colonial infrastructure, are quite explicitly foregrounded in the following lament over the social inequities meted out through the colonial education system:

> Since the Africans let go from slavery, all eyes on how the government treating them. It have commissions from this place making sure that the government don't just neglect them. They have schools, they have regular and free medical inspection. Now, you see any schools set up for our children, besides the Reverend's school? When we get sick and we have pains, who looking after us? We looking after our own self, because nobody have time for us. Except the Reverend and his mission from the Shivering Northern Wetlands. All he wants from us is that we convert from his religion.[16]

In the above example, historical specificity can be seen to resurface in the rather loose fictionalization, through the character and missionary zeal of Reverend Thoroughly, of the Canadian Presbyterian Mission established in Trinidad.[17] The education system is revealed to be a catalyst for familial dysfunction and the subsequent patterns of individual and collective *dis*-integration that it sets in motion. This is a direct attack on deracinating and exploitative practices which traditionally denied the "colonized" full citizenship, even at the price of religious conversion. In fact, in the trope of racial (af)filiation, Chandin becomes the ironic "black sheep" of the Reverend's family. Indeed, Chandin is soon disappointed to learn that even as an adopted son, his "definitive place"[18] in the Reverend's family is not as a filial equal but as a paternalistically acknowledged subordinate. Thus what begins as an invitation to fully belong as one of the Reverend's, or God's, children soon dovetails into a "chaos of uprootedness."

It is not surprising that Chandin attempts to escape his acute sense of racial "difference" in the sanctuary of a more readily available ethnic affiliation: "Chandin wanted nothing more than to collapse in the security of a woman, a woman from his background, and Sarah was the most likely possibility."[19] However, Chandin's retreat into the uncontested fold of the ethnos can hardly be viewed as an act of group identification. Rather, it is a performative gesture of differentiation from the imperial other, both in terms of Chandin's literal extrication from the Thoroughly family and in his internalization of their racial stereotypes about "Indians." The process is ironically epitomized in descriptions of Chandin's metamorphosis "back" into the "Indian" labourer in the coda of "mimicry," suggesting the degree to which conversion as a coercive measure forecloses the possibility of ethnic belonging: "he shed Wetlandish fashion and fell into dressing like an overseer,"[20] housing his wife and children in a "two-storey house typical of modest dwellings in the area."[21]

Chandin's attempt at widening the parameters of citizenship is doomed to failure given his recourse to false essentialisms which hold him hostage to self-deracinating constructs of self/other, both within and without the protective boundaries of the ethnos. Although we clearly agonize over Mala and Asha's sexual and physical abuse at the hands of their father, in Chandin's violation of his children we witness not simply a binary of violator/violated, but a far more insidious history of colonial hegemony of which Chandin, himself, is an unfortunate casualty. In fact, the weight of what Amon Saba Saakana refers to as the colonial legacy of "psychic trauma"[22] is projected through Chandin's downward spiralling narrative of alcoholism, economic decay, violence, and moral/sexual deviancy.

Chandin's story as a casualty of the civilizing mission is by now a familiar one. What is interesting in Mootoo's depiction of Chandin's breakdown is her concomitant emphasis on the complex motives behind the diasporic community's willing surrender of its offspring to the assimilative practices of a missionary education. In the composite multi-generational portrait of the Ramchandin family, Mootoo confirms historian Hugh Tinker's contention that indenture was but "a new system of slavery," particularly as it refers to the dehumanizing conditions of the plantation system. As a disenfranchised labour force, the first generation of immigrant labourers, such as the Ramchandin family, were provided little to no social infrastructures, excepting the rare access to a missionary education offered, towards the end of the nineteenth century, by the likes of the Reverend.

In the Ramchandin family patriarch's reminiscences, however, both indenture and castehood are described through the vocabularies of enslavement and servitude: "Old man Ramchandin thought about life in the *barracks* and life in India before his recruitment to Lantanacamara. There was no difference. But by making the long journey across two oceans, he hoped to leave behind, as promised by his recruiter, *his inherited karmic destiny as a servant labourer*, if not for himself, at least for his son who had been born just before they left India."[23] It is important to note the shift in focus in Ramchandin's motivations for migration from the general tribulations of servitude to the specific fate of castehood, such that the new land offers not so much a release from hardship as it does the hope that his male progeny will escape the shackles of caste. In other words, the Ramchandin family's migratory history is prefigured as an attempt to break out of the delimiting parameters of the ethnos; in this particular case, the social and psychic boundaries of castehood.

Accordingly, Chandin and his father's ethno-histories are at various times constituted as sites of resistance and sites of oppression. On the one hand, the Ramchandin men are doubly marginalized in their lower-caste status and as subordinate racial "others." On the other hand, Chandin's role as a violent sexual predator is implicitly sanctioned by the colonial and Hindu patriarchal authority that affords his privileged status as an Indian male and never holds him accountable for his actions; similarly, the father's albeit naive rejection of one form of bondage (castehood) for another (indenturehood) renders inadequate the image of passivity associated with the colonized subject. Here, Mary Louise Pratt's earlier conceptualization of autoethnography as the colonized subject's articulation of resistance to the colonizing gaze and its modes of representation[24] is problematized in a text that draws attention to the ethnos as a paradoxical and highly complex site of intersecting hegemonies. As Chandin's "his-story" resonates beyond the textual limits of imperial ideology, Tyler's narrative similarly demands a wider discursive and epistemological framework, one which may better accommodate the multiple representational and discursive sites from which the diasporic subject speaks, and one in which the binary logic of Pratt's model of autoethnography as an inherently decolonizing reclamation of "representational space"[25] loses considerable ground.

(En)Gendering Citizenship Beyond the Strictures of Patriarchy

As a member of an even smaller circle—that of Indo-Caribbean women writers—Mootoo offers with her text a critical intervention in the canon of an Afro-Caribbean and male-dominated literary tradition.[26] Much like Lakshmi Persaud, Trinidad's first published Indo-Caribbean woman novelist,[27] Mootoo resists the perpetuation of the "myth of the 'eternal feminine' in which women have been marginalized by a particular strategy of 'narrative petrification' [. . . as] passive receptacles of the male writer's unconscious."[28] For just as cultural citizenship is revealed to be a highly fraught and individuated process of identification and *dis*-identification, those practices which deny equal citizenship to members of a given community are equally multi-fold and complex. This is particularly true for women who are circumscribed by the discursive and proscriptive codes of patriarchy and religious orthodoxy.

As Jeremy Poynting suggests in his study of Indo-Caribbean women's writing, the relationship between gender and ethnicity is often "experienced as a contradiction,"[29] not only in terms of the double marginalization of women in a colonial context, but also as it is attributable to other factors of differentiation such as caste, class, and sexuality. As Mootoo illustrates in the absence of her female characters' recourse to colonial or communal law, the rigid boundaries—in legal and physical terms—of the plantation estate quite often rendered invisible the indentured labourers' minority female constituency. Drawing on the concept of "Hindu-Brahmin-hetero-patriarchy" as a multiple interweaving of religious, cultural, and patriarchal discursive practices, Brenda Mehta writes:

> While women's participation in community building is actively solicited, their commensurate recognition in the form of equal citizenship and direct participation in communal policymaking has been largely ignored. Located outside citizenship [...] women are excluded from the process of self-definition

within their community, [and] they are reduced to a certain homogeneity in which they are deprived of their subjective particularities.[30]

As a minority whose subordinate position seemed already edified upon arrival in the new land in the language of cultural chauvinism, gender inequalities were simply compounded for the migrant female labourer. At the same time, Indian female sexuality was often even more "strictly controlled"[31] in the diasporic context than in the originary homeland, as a means of policing the signs of assimilation to the dominant culture. Interestingly, then, while Chandin's father wishes to free his son of a lifetime of servitude, the mother, fearing cultural assimilation, enacts the stirrings of a religiously centred cultural nationalism:

> The few times he went back to the barracks to visit it was evident his mother had not really converted to Christianity. [...] [H]e noticed that the number of statues of Hindu gods and goddesses lining the walls had increased since his move to the Reverend's house. Sometimes sacred camphor and incense used in Hindu prayers coloured the air, and always a faint cloud of pooja smoke permeated his parents' hair and clothes, replacing the odour of coals and spices that used to emanate from his mother's body.[32]

It is worth recalling, once again, Ramchandin's wistful desire to escape the shackles of servitude inherent in castehood and indenture; there is no parallel evocation of hope for Ramchandin's wife, who, all things being (un)equal, should warrant similar claims to freedom.[33]

Transgressing the "Border Zones" of Sexual Citizenship

In Mootoo's text, ethnic affiliation is not only complicated by gender differences but also by sexual coda; in this sense, the ethnos is always constructed as heteronormative, given the multiple and varied instances of what the community might deem to be sexually deviant behaviour, such as Sarah and Lavinia's lesbian affair, Tyler's cross-dressing or Otoh's androgyny. In other words, the "others" against which the community might define itself are more often than not its own marginalized members, albeit along different kinds of affiliative trajectories. As both insiders and outsiders, interlopers and citizens, therefore, the members of the ethnos who do not fully conform to the fixed and fictive version of citizenship, destabilize, from within, the "boundaries" that are ostensibly meant to distinguish them from other groups.

In her article "Sexual Citizenship and Caribbean-Canadian Fiction: Dionne Brand's *In Another Place, Not Here* and Shani Mootoo's *Cereus*

Blooms at Night," Heather Smyth rightly notes that the homophobic and (hetero-)sexist dimensions of Caribbean nationalist discourse delimit lesbian interventions in the creation of a decolonized nation-space. Moreover, for the migrant Caribbean subject, whose movements between the inside (the Caribbean island-nation) and the outside (the migrant's Western locales) are seen as a relinquishment of cultural and political citizenship, the homophobic and heterosexist dimensions of nationhood can result in further denials of belonging:

> [...] diasporic movement, from "another place" to "here" and back, should not prevent full cultural citizenship of Caribbean lesbians in Canada and the Caribbean. [...] Brand's and Mootoo's novels sever the link between homophobic or heterosexist allocation of Caribbean cultural citizenship and the work of decolonization and bring together an anti-racist politics with an affirmation of Caribbean gay men's and lesbians' cultural belonging. Both texts address the issue of cultural citizenship or social enfranchisement through the use of a semi-utopian imagining of this cultural belonging.[34]

Tyler conforms to Smyth's portrait of the doubly excluded diasporic queer subject. As a gay male nurse who has recently returned after pursuing higher education abroad, Tyler at first perceives his homosexuality, his profession, and his status as a returned immigrant as forms of "perversion" or social deviancy. But it is precisely in his transgressive presence in the "Paradise" community that he is shown to be best suited to deciphering the unspeakable "scandal" of Mala Ramchandin's family history. First, Tyler's profession as a nurse functions as a metaphor of healing that permeates the text: he is able not only to identify with Mala's own transgressive status as "some in-between unnamed thing,"[35] but also to lovingly piece together the fragmented shards of her history in his instinctual empathy for her plight as another kind of casualty of exclusive socio-cultural practices. Thus, in his own self-recognition as both outcast and outsider, Tyler embodies that which his community denies: that is, the hybrid and often-fractured nature of its own collective consciousness.

In his cross-dressing, homosexuality, and entry into a traditionally female profession, Tyler transgresses multiple codes of convention and engages in numerous border crossings which better reflect his own multiple positioning as a hybrid subject. In *Vested Interests: Cross-Dressing and Cultural Anxiety*, Marjorie Garber suggests that cross-dressing functions as a "failure of definitional distinction, a borderline that becomes permeable, that permits border crossings from one apparently distinct category to another."[36] In fact, Tyler's narrative, like Tyler's hybrid "nature," mirrors the way he moves across epistemological and geopolitical fields, slipping as he does between past and present and the first and third person as effortlessly as he slips in and out of codes of dress.

This is not to suggest that Tyler is presented in the postmodern semantics of a privileged, free-floating cosmopolitan; rather, Tyler's mobility is distilled as a grounded sensibility that is relationally anchored in the "concrete history of institutions."[37] As a twice-displaced diasporic subject who shifts between multiple cultural and geographic locations, he comes to inhabit a contrapuntal framework that exposes the shifting and relative processes of "othering." Where his status as a visible minority excludes him from full citizenship in a xenophobic Canada, his sexual orientation becomes the site of cultural alienation in a homophobic Caribbean:

> After much reflection I have come to discern that my desire to leave the shores of Lantanacamara had much to do with wanting to study abroad, but far more with wanting to be somewhere where my "perversion," which I tried diligently as I could to shake, might be either invisible or of no consequence to people to whom my foreignness was what would be strange.[38]

Tyler's cross-cultural habitations—in the homeland and host society—enables a coterminous awareness of the signs of difference to which he, in particular, is subject (namely, colour and sexuality), together with the manner in which they are variously deployed in the politicization and stabilization of identity. Moreover, Tyler's position between or across different sites also serves as a filter through which the contact zones of culture are given expression, such that "foreign discourses are refashioned and mixed in with local discourses of citizenship."[39] As a migrant subject, then, Tyler's border crossing derails ethnographic readings of the local as a "contained site with its own autonomous logic,"[40] thereby mobilizing the ethnos beyond the spatial parameters of the local and effectively "globalizing" its fields of discourse.

Interestingly, Tyler's awareness of the performative and relative deployment of identity not only confirms the fictive nature of the ethnos as a stable category of identification, but also corresponds with Jasbir K. Puar's problematization of "queer diasporas" as monolithic entities. As he suggests, "diasporic queers have not only various relationships to different states but indeed different relationships to common states, determined by highly diverse histories of ethnicity, migration, class, generation, gender, and religious identity."[41] In Tyler's relative assessments of selfhood, nationhood, and cultural belonging, we are privy to what Puar rightly suggests to be the complex factors of differentiation that are operative within queer "states" as they are variously experienced across different socio-cultural contexts and economies of being: "what one might conceive of as oppositional and contestatory in one location may well be complicit and oppressive in another."[42]

Transgressive expressions of gender and sexuality thus serve as metaphors for the hybrid nature of the ethnos itself. This is nowhere more pronounced than in the character of Otoh. As a transgendered subject, even Otoh's nickname is a reflection of his "in-betweenness": "Ever since the days of early high school, where he excelled in thinking but not in doing, this trait of weighing 'on the one hand' with 'but on the other' earned him a name change."[43] Otoh's fluid sexual identity, like nature itself, not only brings to bear the straitjacket of fixed and binding proscriptions of sexual behaviour but also signals the way in which sexual identity, itself, "is not exhausted by two possibilities of object-choice. The better we get to know ourselves and our friends, the more we realize [...] how idiosyncratic and various, how unsystematic sexuality is [...]."[44]

Otoh's transgendered identity is not so much outside the bounds of the community's experience as it is purposefully ignored by its members. As Otoh's mother eventually reveals, her son/daughter's hybrid sexuality is not only a "normal" aspect of the community's identity, but also symbolic of the community's tendency to transcend its definitional codes/boundaries, whether in overt or subliminal terms: "Now the fact of the matter is you're not the first or the only one of your kind in this place. You grow up here and you don't realize almost everybody in this place wish they could be somebody or something else. That is the story of life here in Lantacanamara [...]."[45] It is in the desire to maintain the seemingly homogeneous and impenetrable border zones of the ethnos that the community engages in its own performative oblivion to Otoh's gender crossings. Here, the community's response to Otoh underlines what Peter Stallybrass and Allon White refer to as the "psychological dependence upon precisely those Others which are being rigorously opposed and excluded at the social level. It is for this reason that what is *socially* peripheral is so frequently *symbolically* central."[46]

The sexual hybridity of Mootoo's characters disorients rigid binaries while simultaneously exposing its intersecting hegemonies. In their hybrid sexualities, Tyler and Otoh counter an inherently exclusionary heterosexual/patriarchal discourse that fixes the ethnos within the semantics of binary codes of being. In their separate attempts to confront both their own sexual identities and to find a way to "unabashedly declare"[47] themselves, therefore, Tyler and Otoh begin to reconstruct the community's identity in more inclusive terms.

Reimagining the Ethnos of Difference Through Metaphors of Hybridity

In the natural imagery that pervades the text and serves, in the image of the cereus flower, as its central metaphor, Mootoo continually pits the heterogeneity found in nature against the artifice of the ethnos as fixed and homogeneous. Furthermore, the forms of (af)filiation that might otherwise seem to comprise the basis of human relationships, that is, the singular points of identification which hold them in place—be they biological (e.g., parent/child) or social (e.g., citizen/community)—are exposed as fragile constructs prone to internal collapse at the slightest deviation from the "norm." Hence, the mutability and diversity of the natural world becomes a metaphor for a new kind of community, one which emerges on the basis of the ties that purportedly "divide" or "differentiate" rather than those that bind. Moreover, the natural world becomes a figuratively democratic space wherein the ethnos can be reimagined anew.

Tyler's role in Mala's recovery, and, conversely, Mala's role in Tyler's coming to terms with (his) "nature," begins with the character's empathy for the other's sense of marginalization. In fact, for both Tyler and Mala, recovery and survival are synonymous with a mutual recognition of their "shared queerness."[48] For Mala, marginalization is twice reified, through her status as a "fallen woman" at the hands of an abusive father and her status as a "madwoman" at the hands of a dissociative community. Similarly, Tyler's marginalized position in Lantanacamara is felt both as a returned immigrant and as a homosexual. But it is through Mala's affiliation with the laws and dictates of nature that she is able to see in Tyler's "deviance" an inverted "normalcy." For instance, when Mala nudges Tyler to don a dress and a pair of stockings, Tyler recognizes the fact that she sees in his cross-dressing "not something to either congratulate or scorn—it simply was. She was not one to manacle nature, and I sensed that she was permitting mine its freedom."[49]

Interestingly, Mala's egalitarianism is expressed as an instinctual rather than intellectual or political gesture of inclusion, since it is indelibly linked to her philosophy of nature—a philosophy that plays itself out as a practiced and lived experience. This contrasts sharply with Ambrose, Mala's childhood sweetheart, and his own intellectual and scientific pursuits as an entomologist. On the one hand, Ambrose's love for Mala stems from their shared view that there are no hierarchies in nature:

> Unstated but certainly implied is the assumption that humans are by far superior to the rest of all nature, and that's why we are inheritors of the earth.

Arrogant, isn't it? What's more, not all humans are part of this sun. Some of us are considered to be much lesser than others—especially if we are not Wetlandish or European or full-blooded white.[50]

On the other hand, Ambrose cannot make the leap of faith it takes to enact in society what he sees to be the democracies of nature. With his cultivated Queen's English, his loveless but socially sanctioned marriage and his oblivion to his child Otoh's shifting gender, Ambrose is trapped within a debilitating sphere of contradictory discourses, to the extent that he is unable to bridge the distance between word and deed, philosophy and praxis. In this sense Ambrose stands as an antithesis to Otoh's "ability to imagine [and articulate] many sides of a dilemma,"[51] as well as to Mala's radical identification with the natural world as a liberating counter-site to human laws. Mala's garden stands at the metaphorical centre of Mootoo's text: the overgrown and increasingly uncultivated garden is permitted its freedom, so to speak, undergoing a process of regeneration that dismantles the delineation between interior and exterior space, and mirrors Mala's psycho-social development outside the proprietorial eye of the community.

The garden metaphor around which the novel pivots becomes particularly poignant in the context of a tropical island setting. Part jungle, part "paradise," the garden invariably calls to mind the Edenic motif alluded to earlier. The biblical imagery underpinning the tropics as a dual site of pleasure and sin echoes Elizabeth Deloughery's description of an essentializing "island discourse" as the "convergence of imperial, scientific, literary, and anthropological discourses which have constructed an isolated, atemporal space which is entirely divorced from its archipelagic neighbours and which suppresses the complex processes of island migration."[52] Mootoo, herself a visual artist, must perforce be cognizant of the way the island has been and continues to be (through the all-pervasive North American tourist industry) imagined, through visual *mis*-representation, as a sexualized playground and undomesticated wilderness, a place to conquer (at the risk of being conquered by) its savage beauty.

In Mala's garden, therefore, tropical island stereotypes are inverted in several strategic ways. Mala's garden is first and foremost a space where sexuality functions as an extension of natural procreative laws, in their species-laden variation, rather than as a space that sanctions the sexual objectification of its inhabitants. It is here, then, that Mala is able to recover from the ravaging memories of her father's sexual predation. Second, Mala's garden is a space that lives outside the economies of empire and neo-imperial practices alike. Mala is thus a kind of spiritual guardian for the flora and fauna of Lantanacamara, protecting species on the verge of extinction from commercial forms of predation. In this regard, Mala's extrication from her garden-home results in the immediate poaching of "peekoplats," the virtually extinct species of bird said to be living in her mudra tree. The poaching of the birds, in turn, signals the islanders' reversion to speaking of the flora and fauna in the language of commodification and ownership, while also hinting at the "nature" of the already "globalized" economy in which the locals live:

> As the bird catchers passed, he heard them talk. "In a pinch ten birds could live for about two or three days in a cage."
> "You know how much one peekoplat fetching these days?"
> "Divide up, a third each, a mudra that size would make each one of us a rich man. I myself putting in a bid for the lower third of the base."[53]

As a veritable refuge from the violence implicitly embedded in her community's dissociative response to the signs of difference that it feels unable to accommodate, as well as the explicit acts of violence carried out through her father's abuse, Mala's garden, at least in the figurative construct of her albeit fragile protective embrace, also reverses the historic association of the Caribbean landscape with the history of conquest. As Helen Tiffin suggests, "relationships with the land itself, and the practices of agriculture and horticulture were necessarily associated by different Caribbean populations with dispossession, slavery, and servitude, torture, exile and colonisation."[54] Figuratively divested of colonial and other histories of domination—that is, in its symbolic and spiritual clearing of old hegemonies—Mala's garden becomes an inverted positivist space. This is made possible through the regenerative potential of nature as a cyclical process where "'Endings are but beginnings that have taken to standing on their heads.'"[55]

Of course, the garden metaphor finds its greatest resonance as a translocatable symbol of plurality and shared ownership, one which must be nurtured and protected, as an interdependent fraternity, in the image of the nocturnal cereus flower signalled in the title. Significantly, the flower first appears as a gift from Lavinia, the Reverend's daughter, to Mala's mother, Sarah. The gift then changes hands as it is propagated in different gardens, from Sarah/Mala's garden to the community garden at the Paradise Alms House. Here, it is lovingly replanted by Tyler and the gardener Hector. Significantly, the transference of the unruly cereus flower into the facility's otherwise structured grounds becomes a collaborative act between Tyler, the homosexual outsider, and Hector, the heterosexual insider. As a metaphorical process of collective re-*membering*, Hector even recognizes in Tyler a familiar face, that of his long-lost "queer" brother now living in exile. In other words, the cereus ties together the different members of the Lantanacamaran community, across racial, temporal, spatial, and other factors of differentiation. The "tangle of leafage"[56] of the cereus flower becomes the metaphorical corollary, in nature, of interrelation not as a neatly compartmentalized and spatially bound unit but a rhizomatic inter-weaving of its hybrid and heterogeneous parts.

Towards a Poetics and Praxis of Inclusion: The Ethics of Global Citizenship

As I have pointed out, Mootoo's characters are also diasporic beings whose multiple positioning within a complex and dynamic network of individual, communal, national, transnational, and ancestral ties displaces rigid bina-ries or linear trajectories across time and space. However, in the different instances in which the ethnos is prefigured as a paradoxical site of both exclusion and inclusion, Mootoo's text illustrates the way diaspora cultures quite often inhabit the critical juncture between ontological ambivalence and an essentializing politics of identity. Moreover, when the ethnos is exposed as an unstable category of affiliation, the syncretic interstices of its "'[...] border zones'"[57] reveal the dynamic and processual "nature" of identifica-tion. In this sense, the border zone *is* the metaphorical and metamorphic space that is the community's shared "state." However, without a concomi-tant praxis of inclusion, the border zone remains a signifier of division rather than a liberatory site of differentiation, diversity, and difference.

The interrelated tropes of reconstruction, healing, and the regenerative properties of nature function as a necessary salve to the historical wounds of fragmentation, rupture, and self-enclosure (evidenced as much in indi-viduals such as Mala as in the community that ostracizes her). In this sense, Tyler's attempt at "fashioning a single garment out of myriad parts"[58] echoes poet/dramatist Derek Walcott's image of the reassembled "broken vase" as a metaphor for the Caribbean archipelago, itself a paradoxical site of unity-in-fragmentation. The regenerative potential implicit in the act of restora-tion further suggests that to give voice to the Caribbean is akin to re-mapping the islands anew, along with the seemingly disparate diasporic groups who have come to inhabit them. Here, the artist's restitution of the vase is not merely an atavistic attempt at memorialization—that is, an attempt to reproduce the diasporic community as a discrete and somehow uncontaminated whole in the wake of dislocation. Rather, it is a restora-tive act which recognizes in the "ill-fitting" fragments of its "broken shards"

the possibility for a new kind of wholeness, through an agential realign-
ment of self and community based not on ethnic affiliation but on a shared
difference—where difference itself serves as the metaphorical glue that
restores the disparate fragments into a cartographic whole.

Mootoo's novel thus delights in the conviction that in "difference" there
is not opposition but empathy, not instability but coherence, not the mechanical preservation of self but the compassionate triumph of survival. As such,
it motions toward a new poetics and praxis of inclusion, one that situates
the local community within the wider frame of the global community. In
fact, Tyler addresses the global community from the outset of his narrative,
through the form of the implied "you":

> By setting this story down, I, Tyler [...] am placing trust in the power of the
> printed word to reach many people. [...] It is my ardent hope that Asha
> Ramchandin, at one time a resident in the town of Paradise, Lantanaca-
> mara, will chance upon this book, wherever she may be today, and recog-
> nize herself and her family. If you are not Asha Ramchandin—who could,
> for all anyone knows, have changed her name—but know her or someone
> you suspect might be her or even related to her, please present this and ask
> that she read it.[59]

Mala's story becomes a way for Tyler to work through the oppressions and
exclusions of the Lantanacamaran community, thereby reimagining the
ethnos anew, through the likes of his and Mala's "difference." As such,
Mootoo's text echoes Lionnet's reconceptualization of autoethnography
as a space of resistance insofar as the writing "of singularity cannot be
foreclosed."[60]

But more than this, Tyler's implicit appeal to the global, indeterminate
subject suggests that the ethnos is also the human community of which
he, Mala, and her long-lost sister Asha are a part. Indeed, Mootoo writes
beyond the limits of autoethnography by relocating the individual within
the at once codifying and shifting networks of diasporic experience, configured in Tyler's "Paradise" as a simultaneously "bordered" and hybridized
contact zone, or in the cereus flower as an at once elusive and ubiquitous
"gift" of nature. This is neither a utopian nor an idealized clearing of representational space in the interest of de-territorialization; rather, it is an epistemological reconfiguration of centre and margin, self and other, individual
and community, local and global. For the migrant diasporic subject writing both within and across the real and imagined boundaries of the ethnos—an ethnos that is reimagined through difference and otherness—the
democratization of representational space best arises in the reconstitution
of the community within the interdependent economies and intersecting

historical and discursive trajectories of a globalized "ethno-scape." In this sense, Tyler's "ardent hope" is that *we* will be both the actively engaged and "empathetic" reader who, in sifting and sorting through the pages of Mala's story, might recognize *our* history, our-*selves*.

NOTES

1 Derek Walcott, "The Antilles: Fragments of Epic Memory," *Georgia Review* 44, no. 1 (1995): 294–306.

2 Shani Mootoo, *Cereus Blooms at Night* (Vancouver: Press Gang, 1996), 105.

3 The *Oxford English Dictionary* briefly defines *ethnos* as "nation," from which the Greek root "ethno-" is derived. I will use the term ethnos as a noun throughout this paper in the evocation of its broader etymological sense of group identification, rather than its more frequently misused application, insofar as the "ethnic" group is seen strictly on the basis of its differentiation to Western cultural or racial characteristics, itself a vestige of colonial anthropological and ethnological practice.

4 Françoise Lionnet, *Post-Colonial Representations: Women, Literature, Identity* (Ithaca, NY: Cornell UP, 1995), 39.

5 James Buzard, "On Auto-Ethnographic Authority," *Yale Journal of Criticism* 16, no. 1 (2003): 63.

6 Heather Smyth, in her comparative reading of Mootoo's novel with Brand's *In Another Place Not Here*, speaks of each author's "semi-utopian imagining of … belonging" (146) as resistant to homophobic and heterosexist nationalist discourse. While my own use of the term "citizenship" is in dialogue with that of Smyth, I believe that Mootoo's text redefines the notion of citizenship to a far greater degree than is found in Smyth's reading of "citizenship" as an assertion of gay rights.

7 Vivian M. May, "Dislocation and Desire in Shani Mootoo's *Cereus Blooms at Night*," *Studies in the Literary Imagination* 37, no. 2 (Fall 2004): 97.

8 Ibid., 98.

9 Mary Conde, quoted in May, "Dislocation and Desire," 98.

10 Mootoo, *Cereus Blooms at Night*, 3.

11 "Lantanacamara" has the multi-syllabic lilt of South Indian languages, which metonymically ties the novel to the Indo-Trinidadian community that Mootoo describes.

12 Later in the paper, I discuss at greater length the way island stereotypes are deconstructed in the text. For this aspect of my argument, I am indebted to Elizabeth Deloughery's discussion of "island discourse" as another kind of essentializing discursive practice prevalent in the colonial era.

13 George Lamming, "The Indian Presence as a Caribbean Reality," in *Indenture and Exile: The Indo-Caribbean Experience*, ed. Frank Birbalsingh (Toronto: TSAR, 1989), 47.

14 Ibid., 54.

15 Frank Birbalsingh, Introduction, in *Jahaji: An Anthology of Indo-Guyanese Fiction*, ed. Frank Birbalsingh (Toronto: TSAR, 2000), xi.

16 Mootoo, *Cereus*, 28–29.

17 See Verene Shepherd's "Official Policy Towards the Education of Children of Indian Immigrants and Settlers in Jamaica, 1879–1950," in *Sojourners to Settlers: The*

Indian Migrants in the Caribbean and the Americas, ed. Mahin Gosine and Dhanpaul Narine, http://www.saxakali.com/indocarib/sojourner1.htm. See also Arthur Niehoff and Juanita Niehoff, East Indians in the West Indies (Milwaukee, WI: Milwaukee Public Museum, 1960).

18 Mootoo, Cereus, 31.

19 Ibid., 45.

20 Ibid., 49.

21 Ibid., 50.

22 Amon Saba Saakana, The Colonial Legacy in Caribbean Literature (Trenton: Africa World Press, 1987), 26.

23 Mootoo, Cereus, 26. Emphasis added.

24 See Mary Louise Pratt, Imperial Eyes: Travel Writing and Transculturation (New York: Routledge, 1992).

25 Joel Martineau, "Autoethnography and Material Culture: The Case of Bill Reid," Biography 24, no. 1 (2001): 243.

26 Caribbean scholars such as Frank Birbalsingh and Jeremy Poynting contend that Caribbean Literature was primarily dominated by an Afro-Caribbean male perspective, up until the flurry of publications, since approximately the 1960s, by Black Caribbean women writers as well as Indo-Caribbean writers such as V.S. Naipaul (who brought to view the unique cultural perspective of the South Asian diaspora in the Caribbean). This position is reiterated through a chronological overview of Caribbean writing produced over the past century, by Allison Donnell and Sarah Lawson Welsh in The Routledge Reader in Caribbean Literature (London: Routledge, 1996).

27 Lakshmi Persaud has authored four novels to date: Butterfly in the Wind, Sastra, and For the Love of My Name, all three of which are published by Peepal Tree Press, and her most recent novel, Raise the Lanterns High, published by Black Amber Books.

28 Brenda Mehta, "Cultural Hegemony and the Need to Decentre the Brahmanic Stranglehold of Hindu Womanhood in an Indo-Caribbean Context: A Reading of Lakshmi Persaud's Sastra and Butterfly in the Wind," Journal of Commonwealth and Postcolonial Studies 6, no. 1 (1999): 125.

29 Jeremy Poynting, "'You Want to Be a Coolie Woman?': Gender and Ethnicity in Indo-Caribbean Women's Writing," in Caribbean Women Writers: Essays from the First International Conference, ed. Selwyn R. Cudjoe (Wellesley: Calaloux, 1990), 99.

30 Brenda Mehta, "Cultural Hegemony," 134.

31 Shalini Puri, "Race, Rape, and Representation: Indo-Caribbean Women and Cultural Nationalism," Cultural Critique 36 (1997): 121.

32 Mootoo, Cereus, 29–30.

33 See Moses Seenarine's "Indentured Indian Women in Colonial Guyana: Recruitment, Migration, Labor and Caste," in Sojourners to Settlers: The Indian Migrants in the Caribbean and the Americas, ed. Mahin Gosine and Dhanpaul Narine, http://www.saxakali.com/indocarib/sojourner1.htm.

34 Heather Smyth, "Sexual Citizenship and Caribbean-Canadian Fiction: Dionne Brand's In Another Place, Not Here and Shani Mootoo's Cereus Blooms at Night," ARIEL 30, no. 2 (1999): 145–46.

35 Mootoo, Cereus, 71.

36 Marjorie Garber, Vested Interests: Cross-Dressing and Cultural Anxiety (New York: Routledge, 1992), 16.

37 Michael Burawoy, "Grounding Globalization," in *Global Ethnography: Forces, Connections and Imaginations in a Postmodern World* (Berkeley: U of California P, 2000), 339.

38 Mootoo, *Cereus*, 47–48.

39 Michael Burawoy, "Grounding Globalization," 339.

40 Michael Burawoy, "Preface," in *Global Ethnography*, xii.

41 Jasbir Puar, "Transnational Sexualities: South Asian (Trans)nation(alism)s and Queer Diasporas," in *Q&A: Queer in Asian America*, ed. David L. Eng and Alice Y. Hom (Philadelphia, PA: Temple UP, 1998), 409.

42 Ibid., 418.

43 Mootoo, *Cereus*, 110.

44 David M. Halperin, *One Hundred Years of Homosexuality* (New York: Routledge, 1990), 44.

45 Mootoo, *Cereus*, 237.

46 Peter Stallybrass and Allon White, *The Politics and Poetics of Transgression* (Ithaca, NY: Cornell UP, 1986), 5.

47 Mootoo, *Cereus*, 247.

48 Ibid., 48.

49 Ibid., 77.

50 Ibid., 198.

51 Ibid., 110.

52 Elizabeth Deloughery, "'The litany of islands, the rosary of archipelagos': Caribbean and Pacific Archipelagraphy," *ARIEL* 32, no. 1 (2001): 24.

53 Mootoo, *Cereus*, 187.

54 Helen Tiffin, quoted in Vivian May, "Dislocation and Desire," 103.

55 Mootoo, *Cereus*, 170–71.

56 Ibid., 22.

57 Françoise Lionnet, *Post-Colonial Representations*, 8.

58 Mootoo, *Cereus*, 105.

59 Ibid., 3.

60 Françoise Lionnet, *Autobiographical Voices: Race, Gender, Self-Portraiture* (Ithaca, NY: Cornell UP, 1989), 108.

chapter twelve

Ying Chen's "Poetic Rebellion"
Relocating the Dialogue, In Search
of Narrative Renewal

Christine Lorre

In a collection of essays published in 2004 entitled *Quatre mille marches: un rêve chinois*, Ying Chen retraces what she proposes to call a "poetic rebellion"[1] based on two main claims. The first is her refusal to be identified by her Western readers as a minority writer, that is to say, a spokesperson for China and the Chinese or for Quebec's Chinese minority. The second, connected to the first, is her literary interest in the individual rather than the group, the personal rather than the collective quest. These claims shed light on the way her writing has evolved, particularly between her first three novels and the three subsequent ones.[2] *La mémoire de l'eau* (1992), *Les lettres chinoises* (1993), and *L'ingratitude* (1995) are, respectively, the history of a family in China as told by a young woman who emigrates to North America, an exchange of letters between two young Chinese lovers— a man recently emigrated to Montreal and his girlfriend who is preparing to join him—and the story of a young Chinese woman who is contemplating suicide because of her difficult relationship with her mother (ironically, she gets killed by a truck before she has time to take her life). In contrast, *Immobile* (1998), *Le champ dans la mer* (2002) and *Querelle d'un squelette avec son double* (2003), which have the same unnamed woman protagonist and narrator, are conspicuously devoid of specific time and space indications, as well as of ethnic markers, so that unlike the previous novels, they cannot clearly be linked to Chinese society or to the experience of Chinese immigration to North America.

Chen was born in Shanghai in 1961, emigrated in 1989 to Montreal, where she started writing fiction in French, and now lives in Vancouver. The development of her works and her explicit positioning of herself in relation to the question of the writing of race and ethnicity are particularly relevant to the present discussion on Canadian literature's development "beyond autoethnography." If one accepts the premise formulated by Françoise Lionnet in her conclusion to *Autobiographical Voices* that it is "not possible to escape from the voice of tradition," then what form does Chen's move away from her Chinese heritage take?[3] To quote Lionnet again, how to get round the alienation of the self in language "when culture, ethnicity, and historical contradictions inscribe their identifying codes on our bodies"?[4] This is precisely the challenge Chen addresses, for her agenda resembles a decision to make race and ethnicity irrelevant, in response to a literary context in which these two issues are predominant. How does Chen relocate her writing, having decided to move away from autoethnographic fiction? At first, her most recent novels may seem puzzling, dehistoricized, adrift because cut off from any specific social context, bent on rootless contemplation, and boiling down to a floating existential search. But what is performed through them is a search for a different form of writing, which in shifting the narrative framework leads to an unusual type of dialogue between reader and writer. This paper will approach Chen's work in this double perspective, reading the texts both individually and together, against the context in which they were produced, so as to identify the writing strategies at work. It will focus first on her first three novels, then her subsequent three, to examine the question of where she locates herself as a writer, and to show how she evolved towards a more experimental kind of writing, in a move that has taken her away from explicitly autoethnographic fiction. Paradoxically, it is by returning to tradition—Chinese and Western—and elaborating on it, that Chen escapes the "voice of tradition," in the process underlining the universal dimension of the ethnic subject.

Autoethnographic Fiction: Stories of Uprooting and Displacement of the Self

Displacement of the self is the theme that runs through Chen's first three novels. *La mémoire de l'eau* relates stories inherited from the protagonist's grandmother and ends with her arrival in New York. *Les lettres chinoises* deals with the experience of emigrating from China to Canada. In different ways, these first two novels are both clearly part of the tradition of immigrant fiction. Although set in China and devoid of the experience of emigration, *L'ingratitude* also presents a form of displacement, since the protagonist radically removes herself from her mother's authority when she gets killed, an event she relates from the limbo state which follows her death, in a moment of suspension that lasts as long as her narrative. In these three works, Chen relies on various narrative strategies in connection with her own experience of emigration.

La mémoire de l'eau consists of ten units focusing on various characters, with the endearing grandmother standing as the common bond between them, unifying the narrative and framing the book: she is present in the first sentence—"Ma grand-mère Lie-Fei avait cinq ans lorsque le dernier empereur fut chassé de son trône. C'était l'année 1912."—and the last one—"« La petite me ressemble », avait dit grand-mère."[5] The book is dedicated "Pour grand-mère,"[6] which suggests that it draws on stories heard from the author's own grandmother. The last two units focus on the narrator, who on her flight to New York has a dream of the people she left behind in China, from her grandmother to Mao. Although the narrative seems to put the past at a distance, the conclusion shows the narrator missing her grandmother and failing to feel the relief she had expected to experience on arriving in New York. Throughout, the grandmother stands out as a strong, intelligent, resourceful woman who managed to adapt to changing circumstances and skilfully sail through life, sticking to her Taoist moral principle to always keep a middle position. The narrator rejects her grandmother's moderation and acceptance of whatever happens to her, an independence of mind that foreshadows her decision to leave. Chronological sequence provides unity and flow to the narrative as a whole, recreating the history of a family and their close relations against the backdrop of twentieth-century China, from the end of empire in 1912 to, one guesses, the 1980s. The buildup is that of the gradual opening of the country to the outside world, which is paralleled by the progressive liberation of women, leading to the narrator's departure. Considered separately, the stories stand as so many individual ways of negotiating one's personal fate through the vicissitudes of China's recent history.[7] The book thus looks back at the past and the land left behind in a tribute to the narrator's grandmother, while opening space for a new life in the New World, a life that remains to be written, but is placed from the start under the sign of symbolic nostalgia and disappointment with the effects of displacement. Thematically and formally, the book is characteristic of a first book of fiction by an immigrant writer.[8]

The ethnographic dimension of the narrative is omnipresent. Time and space are clearly characterized, in a way that reflects an awareness on the author's part of the needs of a Western audience. The historical framework is set, from beginning, with the end of empire, to end, with the post-Mao period, providing the framework necessary to understand the developments of the narrative—for example, the reappearance of high heels after Mao's death. Chinese phrases and their connotations are explained when their meaning matters: "« Mon père a perdu son chapeau ? » demanda [ma grand-mère]. Et tout le monde rit, car « perdre son chapeau » était une expression qui se disait de quelqu'un quittant volontairement ou non son poste" (20).[9] Chinese customs, such as the choice of the date for a wedding by a seer, are referred to. Similarly, the extended metaphors that run through the narrative are Chinese motifs whose symbolism can easily be deciphered by a Western audience.

The tropes of water, mud, lotus flowers, and roots are central to the narrative.[10] The water of the title is first of all that of the Grand Canal the grandmother sails on when she departs from Beijing for Shanghai with her husband and youngest son, the narrator's father-to-be, leaving behind her two older sons. At first, she hopes that her family's departure from Beijing will bring renewal, and the water of the Grand Canal that takes her to Shanghai, in the short story entitled "L'eau qui chasse,"[11] is supposed to cleanse and purify her life as the daughter of a man who used to be close to the former imperial power, a situation which by 1933 reeked of decadence. But on the boat, the grandmother loses the baby she was then carrying, and from then on water to her is synonymous with darkness, rot, and stench, a recurring image which comes to her mind whenever she is overcome by sadness. In the novel as a whole, water thus represents time flowing and the hardships that life brings: when her granddaughter prepares to leave China, the resigned grandmother expresses her view that "l'odeur de l'eau était partout la même" (115).[12] The granddaughter's subconscious reworks the water image as she leaves China: in the dream she has on the plane to New York, she is sitting by a river that carries the people who mattered to her in China. As she wakes up and looks out the window, she sees a dark irregular line on the ground: "Ce devait être la rivière qui avait nourri mes ancêtres et moi. La rivière qui avait toujours pesé si lourd dans mon cœur comme elle le faisait pour les fleurs de lotus dans les saisons d'automne, et qui me paraissait si fragile maintenant qu'elle était vue d'en haut" (114).[13] As she leaves the land of her past, her life seems lighter, but also more fragile to her.

The lotus flower is a conventional symbol of beauty, recalling the attainment of the purity that transcends desire, and is occasionally used as a metaphor for bound feet, which are "un signe de noblesse, de richesse, de beauté, de pureté, de tout ce qui pourrait apporter le bonheur à une femme."[14] But upon examination of the lotus roots that people in Shanghai eat, the grandmother comes to the conclusion that bound feet resemble the roots rather than the flowers of lotus, the former being soiled with mud inside as well as outside. Maoist rhetoric also uses the metaphor of mud to justify its brainwashing, following an organic logic in which there is a direct connection between feet and head: women whose feet were bound have feudal mud in their heads, while the heads of women who took to wearing modern high heels when they came into fashion are full of bourgeois mud. The narrator's attitude to roots, mud and women's feet and heads unravels this metaphorical bond and its ideological implications:

> J'ai appris à l'école que toute chose a une raison biologique. [...] Si les racines de lotus ont maintenant un bout rond et l'autre pointu, c'est parce qu'elles en ont besoin. On pourrait juger qu'elles sont laides ou qu'elles ne le sont pas. Ça n'a rien à voir avec elles. Elles ne se forment pas elles-mêmes. Ce qui les forme, c'est l'eau, ou plutôt le torrent qui va et qui vient, en enlevant une boue qu'une autre remplacera. (99)[15]

With this fresh set of metaphors, the narrator points at a logical vision of history, rather than an ideological one: the torrent of time brings mud, or ideas, that shape individuals into historical subjects. In the process of examining old metaphors and replacing them with new ones, she establishes a distance between herself and accepted discourse.

La mémoire de l'eau is the book of Chen's symbolic formation. Through the narrator's stories evoking her family background, she takes stock of her origin: the place she comes from, the collective and personal history, the people who nurtured her, the images that fed her imagination. In doing so, she also gives her Western reader an ethnographic account of that background, at the same time pointing at what prompted her to emigrate— the sense of a decaying society she is still fond of nonetheless.

Chen's epistolary novel, *Les lettres chinoises*, is explicitly autoethnographic in many ways: its title clearly states its ethnic content, and the novel openly deals with the question of emigration from China to North America, as Sassa exchanges letters with Yuan, her fiancé, and Da Li, her college friend, who have both gone to Montreal while Sassa stayed behind in Shanghai, planning to join Yuan as soon as possible. In their letters they compare various aspects of the two societies, discussing for example the notion of freedom, and the meaning of exile and of being an outsider, depending where one is. The novel also alludes to the treatment of Asian immigrants in North America and other challenges of immigration. Yet, for all its apparent clarity, the narrative presents an ambiguity. Da Li and Sassa's correspondence is mostly about a Chinese man Da Li meets and falls in love with in Montreal, but it is an impossible love for the man is already engaged to a woman back in China. The main ambiguity of the novel is whether it is Yuan that Da Li writes about in her letters, which every-thing points at, without it ever being clearly confirmed. The reader, like Sassa, thus remains in uncertainty about the actual meaning of Da Li's letters, and double reading is constantly at work.[16] This suspicion must be particularly painful for Sassa, who is reluctant to emigrate and whose only reason for moving to Montreal is to join Yuan. Behind their discussion on the benefits and drawbacks of emigration, what is at play then in the exchange of letters is a game of love and chance among the three protag-onists. This aspect of the novel gives the question of emigration an entirely different dimension, perhaps the most important one to all three protag-onists after all.

It is significant that Chen wrote two versions of *Les lettres chinoises*, which were published in 1993 and 1998.[17] The rewriting of the novel was analyzed in an article by Emile Talbot, who points out that "this virtually unnoticed re-edition represents an important revision of the novel, reduc-ing the number of letters from 69 to 56, suppressing all the letters between Yuan and his father,[18] eliminating material from other letters, and expung-ing all references to characters ... who, while not themselves writers of letters, played roles in the original edition."[19] Talbot convincingly argues that "the erasure of ... information transfers more hermeneutic responsi-bility to the reader while inviting him to focus on more fundamental human pulsions."[20] The revisions brought by Chen to the second version of her novel contribute to the shift in focus of this emigration story, from the dilemmas of emigration to those of love.

Les lettres chinoises shifts focus in other ways too, in particular with the geographical displacement of Yuan and Da Li. In the tradition of Mon-tesquieu's *Lettres persanes*, the epistolary novel relies on the principles of uprooting and displacement as ways to open the mind to new truths. The comparison of two societies, Eastern and Western, with radically different ways and customs, is a theme that occupies a good part of the letter writ-ers' correspondence. The freshness of the Chinese newcomers' view of Montreal and its inhabitants catches some of the most striking wrongs of Western society, such as excessive consumption and obsession with food, people's loneliness, their impatience. Da Li's letters vividly express her amazement, as her inner gaze goes back and forth between Montreal and China. And although Sassa is still in China, she fully participates in the game of comparing, based on indirect knowledge. Her attitude towards Western ways is a mix of dislike and disapproval, and fascination tinted with sarcasm, the latter being spurred by her silent suspicion that the man Da Li has fallen in love with is probably Yuan. Being far away from her lover, she senses that she is losing him, this loss being another major theme of *Les lettres*.

The losses examined in the letters are those linked to exile, and the exchange Chen imagines is comparable to the one Nancy Huston and Leïla Sebbar decide to initiate in *Lettres parisiennes: Autopsie de l'exil*, because "raconter, autopsier l'exil, c'est parler d'enfance et d'amour, de livres, de vie quotidienne, mais aussi de la langue, de la terre, de l'âme […]."[21] In both books, the narrators consider the possibility of choosing between two cultures, and they go through stages of enthusiasm for the new culture and nostalgia for the old. Thus Yuan's mood varies between, on the one hand, being irresistibly drawn to the type of freedom North America allows and, on the other, fearing its magnitude. In the letters Sassa and Da Li exchange, this freedom has a lot to do with Da Li and the Chinese man she is in love with. She eventually decides to leave Montreal because "Nous ne serons jamais vraiment libres. Nous n'arrivons pas à être ensemble sans nous sentir coupables. Je me rends compte de mon immoralité et lui de sa trahison. Ni lui ni moi ne pouvons oublier le passé. Nous avons eu beau quitter notre terre, l'esprit de Maître Con nous a suivis jusqu'ici, écrasant notre simple bonheur et nous compliquant la vie."[22] The paradox is that at the same time, in China, "freedom" is taking on a new meaning, as Sassa reports to Yuan: "Depuis ton départ, on dirait que le mot « liberté » n'est plus aussi péjoratif qu'auparavant. Il n'est plus synonyme d'irresponsabilité, d'immoralité ou même de criminalité. On parle maintenant d'une bonne et d'une mauvaise liberté. Mais comme le terme est encore trop chargé, on a eu la précaution de trouver un terme pour désigner la bonne liberté : « ouverture »" (61).[23] Change is under way for Chinese immigrants to Canada, but also for people back in China like Sassa, who feels like an outsider in her own hometown and ends up reacting negatively to this feeling. Through Sassa, Chen reiterates a principle that is at work in *Lettres persanes*: perspectives are reciprocal, and one is always somebody else's outsider.

One of the central questions of the book is what it means to be "un étranger"—a foreigner, an outsider, a stranger. As the *Lettres persanes* did in a satirical way, Chen's novel makes the point of the reciprocity of perspective about otherness: there is no absolute "other"; wherever you are, there is always an "other." In fact, the self can feel alienated at home, as Sassa's letters demonstrate. By the end of the exchange of letters, she has become bitter and angry at her powerlessness. She previously expressed to Yuan the feeling that, after his departure, she felt like an outsider in her own place, and that, in another country like Canada, she had no fear of being an outsider, but only feared becoming too visible, having lost pride in herself and her country. She admitted to Da Li that she too felt uprooted, as if she was born a foreigner in her own country. She feels that she is the one who constantly has to adjust to others. She eventually envies the feeling of humility that outsiders and foreigners must have, she who feels cheated of her rights:

> La Shanghaïenne que je suis n'arrive pas à réprimer totalement ce sentiment qui me fait croire que ceux qui se promènent dans « notre » rue et travaillent dans « nos » entreprises sans parler shanghaïen sont des étrangers. [...] Un sentiment qui tolère mon constant mécontentement envers le gouvernement, lequel est supposé me rendre heureuse, plus heureuse que les autres si c'est possible, parce que mes arrières-grands-parents sont nés dans cette ville. (137)[24]

This reversal in Sassa, this eruption of anger, reflects her powerlessness in the face of the changes that affect her own country and hometown. She laments these changes throughout the book, but is nonetheless capable of empathy for a French friend of hers who has to pay more for everything because she is so obviously a foreigner. Her loss of bearings leads her to experience extreme and contradictory feelings that range from discomfort in her own city, and empathy for her friend Da Li as a foreigner in Montreal, to anger and bitterness at the presence of outsiders who upset the existing order of things. In contrast, Yuan and Da Li have a much lighter view of what they call exile, the former comparing it to human migrations and to the migration of birds which can leave everything behind without a second thought. The latter views her situation as that of a leaf in the wind, a rootless plant, and wishes to simply be able to follow the flow of things. Sassa cannot stand the unknown or change and prefers fullness to emptiness: "Croyant bêtement que la plénitude incarne le bonheur, je n'aime toujours pas les lunes croissantes ni les récits ouverts" (55).[25] Her eventual bitterness is expressed in her rejection of uncertain love, outsiders, and open stories.

In *Les lettres chinoises*, Chen explores the importance of love in the decision to emigrate. She also holds a mirror up to her Western reader, pointing at how in Shanghai too, xenophobia grows out of insecurity, be it related to love or social status. What happens in the novel is the beginning of a dialogue between East and West through Chinese interlocutors and situations. This is a strategy Chen also uses in her next novel, *L'ingratitude*.

Although *L'ingratitude* is entirely set in China, a mirror effect between China and Canada is achieved, similar to that at work in *Les lettres chinoises*. In the monologue of a young woman who has just died, Chen addresses through an oppressive mother–daughter relationship the issue of rebellion against tradition, an issue familiar to Chinese and Western women alike, and one in which Western feminist thinkers such as Luce Irigaray have played a leading role.[26] In a talk she gave in Montreal in 1980, Irigaray put the difficulties women were facing in a patriarchal society in terms of speech: "leur parole n'est pas entendue."[27] Because their desires are repressed, they, in turn, have become oppressive, especially towards their daughters: as a psychoanalyst, Irigaray contends that "le rapport mère-fille est le *continent noir* du *continent noir*,"[28] and that mothers and daughters should break the silence: "Ne nous laissons pas être les gardiennes du mutisme, d'un mutisme de mort."[29] She concludes by calling for a liberation of women's speech, arguing for a "parole" that would be truly feminine. Chen's fiction of a mother-daughter relationship gone wrong is thus both specific to China and universal,[30] although by locating her protagonist in a limbo that spans the last moments of life and death after cremation, she has already started the process of removal from a well-defined framework that characterizes her subsequent works. The monologue represents an original search for a feminine "parole," not accessible otherwise. Through it, the protagonist accomplishes the talking her grandmother urged her to do at the beginning of the narrative: "Il faut que tu parles. Tu peux maudire ta pauvre mère, si tu le préfères, maudire tout le monde et m'accabler d'injures. Mais parle ! Sur notre tête, décharge ton chagrin. Ainsi, tu auras un voyage facile. Et nous ne serons pas consolés autrement ..."[31]

The Chinese society of *L'ingratitude* is structured upon an oppressive Confucian social order, based on the respect of a male-defined hierarchy and the strict observation of family values, in spite of the official condemnation of Kong-Zi, "le père de notre féodalisme" (13),[32] in Maoist times. The narrator sees through this system, analyzing the reasons that cause her mother to be so destructive with herself: "Si seulement papa avait pu partager un peu avec moi l'énorme responsabilité de rendre heureuse cette femme qui avait tant fait pour moi et pour lui, j'aurais pu mieux respirer et peut-être vivre plus lontemps. [...] C'était bien lui qui m'avait créé, en quelque sorte, une ennemie" (30).[33] The mother's attitude to her daughter's boyfriends is also dictated by her own experience of tradition and arranged marriage. As Irigaray notices about women:

> Le désir d'elle, son désir à elle, voilà ce que doit venir interdire la loi du père – de tous les pères. [...] Toujours, ils interviennent pour censurer, refouler, en tout bon-sens et bonne santé, le désir de la mère. [...] [C]e qui apparaît dans les faits les plus quotidiens comme dans l'ensemble de notre société et de notre culture, c'est que [les femmes] fonctionnent originairement sur un matricide.[34]

This observation finds parallels in the patriarchal Chinese society of Chen's novel, where the father's law takes on literal meaning and translates into arranged marriage and the fact that women's lives could not be envisaged outside male authority, be it the father's, the husband's or the son's. The daughter cannot bear her feeling of being trapped in society, nor her mother's toughness, so she aims to enact a form of matricide through her own planned suicide, which equates a rejection of everything the mother stands for—that is to say, everything the daughter can reasonably hope for—and leads to a form of renewal: "J'étais censée devenir la reproduction la plus exacte possible de ma mère. J'étais sa fille. Il fallait donc détruire cette reproduction à tout prix. Il fallait tuer sa fille. Il n'y avait pas d'autres moyens de la rendre plus sage. Je ne pouvais pas être moi autrement" (111).[35] Although very real, the death of the daughter is primarily a symbolic death, one that is necessary for the mother to recover her role as an emotional mother, as opposed to a reproducer of the system through procreation. Similarly, the daughter recovers her emotions by removing herself from the system of social reproduction.

By the end of the novel, the daughter discovers gratitude: "Je comprends maintenant que notre mère est notre destin. On ne peut se détourner de sa mère sans se détourner de soi-même. [...] [L]es traîtres à leur mère continueront, morts comme vivants, à vagabonder, à se voir exclus du cycle de la vie, à être partout et nulle part. A ne pas être" (150).[36] By then, the daughter's monologue reaches a peaceful tone, and closes on a cry of revelation: "Maman !" (155) In contrast with the letter she never managed to write to her mother before attempting to take her life, she achieves, with her narration, a "parole féminine"[37] that eventually brings her to understand the importance of her relationship with her mother and its impact on her own destiny, therefore to understand herself. Related haltingly, this "parole" is part of a difficult maieutic process which puts an end to the young woman's alienation when a rebirth of the self is accomplished—only too late.

The rebirth achieved by the protagonist of *L'ingratitude*, in a backwards movement from death to (re)birth, is performed through a monologue addressed to her mother. In Chen's eyes, literary writing is a personal quest, the aim of which is to establish this kind of dialogue and break down barriers. She explains her position as a writer and her view of literature in an essay entitled "Entre la fin et la naissance":

> [J]'accepte de temps à autre de jouer un rôle qui ne me convient pas, après avoir parlé dans beaucoup d'endroits de l'immigration, de l'intégration, des chocs culturels, du charme de la langue française, de la nostalgie de la mère

patrie, du régime communiste, de la situation des femmes chinoises, après avoir épuisé tous les sujets de ce genre propres aux écrivains dans ma situation. [...] Sans doute la tâche ne peut-elle que me dépasser, puisque même si certains de mes textes donnent à croire à des sujets vastes, au fond je n'ai jamais parlé que de moi. Je n'ai jamais été les personnages de mes romans, mais mes personnages sont toujours imprégnés de mon âme. À notre époque d'une extrême désindividualisation qu'on voudrait corriger en recourant, à tort et à travers, au patriotisme, si la littérature doit avoir un sens, c'est justement celui de cultiver une vision du monde microscopique, de transformer si possible le dialogue des cultures en des dialogues entre des individus, sinon en monologues.[38]

By rejecting the status of spokesperson on things Chinese, Chen discourages the interpretation of her writing as autoethnographic fiction and rules out her own role as native informant, redirecting the eyes of her readers away from race and ethnicity, towards the writing and the self. By defining a different writing strategy, Chen removes herself and her work from the discussion on identity politics. She carries out this task in her writing itself by virtually leaving out time, space, and ethnic markers in her subsequent novels. In revising traditional narrative strategies, she shifts the reader's bearings, and in relocating her narrative position, she demands of her reader a similar repositioning. By displacing the ongoing dialogue between East and West, she expands its scope beyond its immediate national, racial, and ethnic context. She thus carries further the process of reterritorialization that, according to Deleuze and Guattari, minority literature goes through, making language itself a tool in the search for meaning.[39]

Away from Autoethnographic Fiction: Exiled in Language, in Search of Narrative Renewal

Immobile, Le champ dans la mer, and *Querelle d'un squelette avec son double* depart from the familiar Western narrative form and technique of Chen's first three novels dealing with the experience of emigration from China: in the later novels, ethnographic markers are made irrelevant, but other elements of Chinese culture can be traced in the narrative dynamic and structure. Indeed, while Chen's writing results from multiple influences, both Eastern and Western, it often relies on a dynamic of full and empty that points at the Chinese thought system as influenced by Taoism, and on landscape images borrowed from classical poetry and painting, all these elements being subject to much transformation as they mix with others. Chen's own metaphor for culture and the way it influences and shapes each subject is a Chinese one in which the individual is in harmony with the landscape:[40] she likens culture to the current of a river, flowing and espousing the various shapes of the earth while transforming it, sometimes merging with other currents, sometimes disappearing, the water itself never entirely vanishing, and the subject being like a stone sitting amidst this current,[41] like an erratic boulder shaped and forgotten by time.

The theme of exile, symbolized in the protagonist's inner wanderings, is central to the three novels considered here, echoing the sense of displacement and uprooting of the earlier novels. In an essay entitled "La vie probable," Chen identifies with the writer in exile, whom she characterizes as follows:

> C'est un enfant qui, faute de foyer et condamné à la route, n'a pas appris à marcher, ne grandit jamais. Il écrit pour moquer sa propre maladresse et pour passer son temps inutile. Il revient souvent sur ses mots, se montre contradictoire et anxieux, car il doute de la fiabilité des mots autant qu'il est tenté par le vertige tonifiant que semble promettre une danse avec des langues. Rien à montrer, rien à dire vraiment. Tout est déjà inscrit dès le commencement. [...] J'écris parce que je n'arrive pas à oublier l'épouvantable chute de mon enfant et les incidents de la sorte qui peuplent ma vie jusqu'ici, qui m'incitent à fuir hors de l'illusion de l'identité, parfois, hors de moi, à errer constamment entre le plein et le vide.[42]

The writer in exile is defined primarily by her human condition and existential anxieties; her life is marked by rootlessness, repetition, and aimlessness, a sense of quest, away from "the illusion of identity." Thus, in *Immobile*, *Le champ*, and *Querelle*, exile is put in abstract terms of empty and full, not in terms of national identity. These novels offer three parallel looks at the same woman's life,[43] or lives, since she claims that she has lived several. In these narratives, Chen goes back to less visible, more spiritual forms of Chinese culture, to look for a way out of the aporia of exile figured by the protagonist's aimless inner wanderings, which cause her to be stuck in history and leave her unable to cope with the present.

Before examining each of Chen's later novels individually, it is worth noting that her aesthetic choices present significant parallels with the ones made by Nathalie Sarraute in her time. Sarraute famously talked of the "era of suspicion" towards character in its traditional, nineteenth-century, Balzacian guise: how could a reader still believe in puppet-like characters after modernism had revealed and explored the uncanny of the human psyche? Sarraute decided to "take his possession [the character] back from the reader" and bring him onto the writer's ground, by removing codified characterization and focusing instead on the character's point of view.[44] This is how she came to define her writing technique:

> On ne pouvait plus écrire des romans à personnages. Le personnage de roman avait éclaté, une substance nouvelle le débordait de toutes parts. Le simple nom donné à un personnage sentait la convention. [...] Quand j'ai écrit, en 1932, un premier texte [...], il m'a semblé que j'exprimais une sensation spontanée qui ne pouvait pas entrer dans le cadre du récit ou de la nouvelle. [...] Je m'efforçais de montrer cette sensation en elle-même, pour ainsi dire à l'état pur, telle qu'elle se déploie pendant quelques instants chez un personnage qui n'en est que le porteur, le lieu à peine visible. Toute mon attention se concentrait sur les sensations que produisent certains mouvements à peine conscients, des mouvements qui se développent en nous en l'espace de quelques minutes – parfois de quelques secondes – et qu'ici j'essayais de rendre par des images et par le mouvement de la phrase, comme grossis et vus au ralenti.[45]

Chen's move away from autoethnographic fiction echoes Sarraute's search for alternatives to traditional characters and, later, "littérature engagée." In her aesthetic search, it is likely that Chen found inspiration in Sarraute's ideas,[46] possibly because of their compatibility with the Taoist focus on the inner life. Chen's characters, like Sarraute's, lack traditional characterization and naming, and little happens to them within the scope of the narrative. Further, Chen's mineral image for change and sensations, that of a stone being shaped by the water that runs around it in a river, finds an equivalent in Sarraute's organic metaphor of "tropismes," that is, the process of plants slowly turning towards the light. Finally, both writers, to use terms employed by Linda Hutcheon, write self-reflective fiction that aims for mimesis of process—how characters evolve and tell their stories—rather than mimesis of product, in the realist tradition, which makes for original, experimental writing.[47]

The contrast between the inner life of the protagonists in Chen's later novels and the world around them is stressed by duality, which functions as a recurring motif and a structuring principle in these three narratives. In *Immobile*, the protagonist sees her life as two lives: her present one as the wife of an archeologist, whom she refers to as A., and her past one as an opera singer who married a prince and then had a love affair with a slave, referred to as S.[48] From one life to the other, she has crossed centuries, but in the present, she feels like a puppet whose strings are pulled by the forces of a former life. She alternatively thinks that she is a reincarnation, a ghost, that her condition is nostalgia, or a sickness, that she is undergoing mental breakdown, or is in a state of delirium. All these possibilities are expressed with a degree of doubt, so that no single interpretation of her predicament is definite, but whichever reading one adopts, there is only one conclusion to the narrative: "Je suis l'exemple vivant des méfaits de la mémoire. [...] Je préfère traîner mes jours indignes et vains, dans les ténèbres de la mémoire, loin de [A.], loin de tout espoir de guérison, afin que tout s'achève naturellement. Alors je reste là, immobile et sans défense. Comme un rocher."[49] Her present life seems to be a shadow of her former one, by far the most lively and passionate in the narrative. Unable to cope with the present, she eventually decides to simply let time sweep through her:

> J'ai perçu le grand mensonge que fabrique la machine de l'histoire. L'illusion collective. Les quelques siècles de vicissitudes racontées dans d'innombrables livres égalent le néant que j'ai traversé en un clin d'œil. Personne ne veut l'avouer. C'est pourtant facile à constater. On aime tant la fiction. On ignore le vide. Tout le monde vient du vide et personne ne s'en souvient. (118)[50]

Her discourse runs counter to premises of Western thought when stating that time itself has no finality, that history has no direction, that no progress is possible. What there is is emptiness, which is not synonymous with a lack, a void, as a Western mind would have it. Rather, the narrator's convictions and her decision to remain immobile echo the Chinese belief in the role of emptiness as original strength in the natural order of the world, and the individual search for a balanced position in that world, not doing anything often being the most desirable option. In that system, emptiness does not simply equate nothingness, but is a crucial site for transformation. François Cheng explains in *Vide et plein* that "dans l'optique chinoise, le Vide ... constitue le lieu par excellence où s'opèrent les transformations, où le Plein serait à même d'atteindre la vraie plénitude."[51] Similarly, the harmony of a person's life depends on a dynamics based on empty and full:

> Selon la pensée chinoise, et surtout celle des taoïstes, ce qui garantit d'abord la communion entre l'homme et l'univers, c'est que l'homme est un être non seulement de chair et de sang mais aussi de souffles et d'esprits : en outre, il possède le Vide. [...] Par le Vide, le cœur de l'Homme peut devenir la règle ou le miroir de soi-même et du monde, car possédant le Vide et s'identifiant au Vide originel, l'Homme se trouve à la source des images et des formes. [...] Lorsque le cœur humain devient le miroir de soi-même et du monde, alors seulement commence la véritable possibilité de vivre.[52]

No such true possibility of life is available to the narrator of *Immobile*, for there is no correspondence between her heart and the world around her: she feels totally alienated from it, is lost in modernity and keeps returning to her love story with S. She fails to devise a way of living for herself in her "new," modern life and the novel closes on an image that likens the narrator to rubbish, to remains that time would have forgotten by the side of the road. The novel thus ends in aporia, although by then A.'s wife has realized that A. and S. are similar in many ways, including through the master-slave relations they get involved in, a realization which only confirms her sense that history is repetitive and aimless.

Duality, aimlessness, and disconnectedness also underlie *Le champ dans la mer*. In that novel, A...'s wife is diagnosed as someone whose memory is troubled: she is rid of her obsession for S..., the former lover of a former life, and is about to embark on another monologue, another story, but the lack of consistency from one story to another poses a problem: "Tout souvenir nouveau me fait douter de mes croyances, du sérieux de mes histoires, m'oblige à lâcher toute prétension à la consistance, à la cohérence."[53] Her stance as a storyteller is a shifty, uncomfortable one. In quasi-metafictional comments, she relates her confusion at what she sees as two distinct lives, two worlds separated by nothingness: the childhood of her past and her present life as A...'s wife.

> Je désirais tant acquérir une histoire cohérente, rester fidèlement auprès des êtres, saisissant les choses à ma portée, les retenant à tout prix, quitte à me trahir, à me vendre. J'aurais pu alors à mon tour résumer ma vie, comme si je n'en avais eu qu'une à vivre. Je serais devenue, moi aussi, capable de m'acheminer d'un bout à l'autre, d'un début à une fin, selon une chronologie bien établie, sur une fine ligne suspendue entre des falaises. Une ligne néanmoins toujours trop courte, parce que l'écart entre les falaises est plus grand qu'il n'y paraît. (102)[54]

The felt lack of consistency of her story is linked to a missing sense of direction in life, which is rendered in terms of an imaginary line that, if it were there, would create a pattern and enable her to locate herself in space. But her environment and her life are marked by a repeated sense of loss and rupture through exile, which takes on many shapes.

Forms of exile accumulate in *Le champ*, starting with birth, the first form of uprooting, continuing with the end of childhood, of a first love, or of an era of rural civilization. In her youth, with the end of her story with a boy referred to as V..., the narrator fathoms human feelings: "Il s'agissait d'une première intuition, non seulement de l'inconsistance de l'amour, mais de la fragilité de tous les rapports humains" (54).[55] The end of this first love becomes emblematic of the fragility of one's bonds to others, one's place in space, one's connections to the rest of the world. As the narrative unfolds, other ruptures with what nurtured her contribute to destroy her sense of belonging, of being part of a whole: "Depuis que je me suis fait écraser comme un rat, que les os de mes parents se sont dissous sous les pieds des villageois, que V... laboure le champ à la place de ses parents ou qu'il s'applique à je ne sais quelle autre entreprise, vraisemblablement à la fabrication des briques, je n'ai plus de patrie" (32).[56] The narrator has been in exile since the world of childhood, symbolized by the rural "civilization of corn," has vanished. Her story thus finds a form of dramatization in history, which is another sort of accumulation of loss.

The transformations that occur, generating a feeling of living in exile, are epitomized in the title of the novel, which alludes, in referential terms and in terms of setting, to the image of the cornfields of the past and the seaside the narrator visits in her adult life, in a juxtaposition of two contrasted locations. But the title also corresponds, in Chinese writing, to the combination of the images of sea and field into a metaphor of contiguity which means universal transformation, or the vicissitudes of human life.[57] By choosing minimal elements of characterization for the setting of the novel—a beach, a cornfield—and by using them in a combination similar to that of ideograms, so that their metaphorical meaning matters most, Chen aims to give to her writing a dimension that goes beyond traditional referentiality, sharing with classical Chinese poetry the ideal of a poetry with resonance reaching beyond its simple explicit meaning.[58]

Chen's bald style is part of what François Jullien, after Roland Barthes in 1975, called an "aesthetic of blandness" in classical Chinese art. In *Éloge de la fadeur*, Jullien explains why blandness is the most authentic flavour, the flavour of wisdom: unlike flavours which establish contrasts, blandness links various aspects of reality and makes them communicate with one another; it is a tone that suits the whole and helps apprehend the world and existence beyond the narrowness of individual viewpoint, giving a sense of their true scope.[59] However, how can this aesthetic of blandness, in its detachment, not lead to indifference to the outside world? Jullien explains how, in a counterintuitive way for a Western mind, blandness can express emotion:

> Pour les Chinois, l'émotion ... est d'autant plus profonde en nous que ce à quoi nous réagissons – à l'extérieur de nous – est important – d'un grand enjeu. Aussi, plus elle est profonde, moins elle est individuelle, limitée à notre intérêt personnel (égocentrée) : plus elle nous fait éprouver, au contraire, la richesse du lien qui nous relie au monde et combien nous sommes partie prenante du grand procès des choses. Elle ouvre alors notre subjectivité à la solidarité des existences, à l'interdépendance des réalités, la fait sortir de son point de vue particulier – exclusif et borné. C'est en raison de cette intensité qu'elle est en mesure de nous faire « communiquer » au travers du réel, de nous

élever à une perspective communautaire ... : plus elle est profonde, donc, plus elle est morale.[60]

However, Jullien does acknowledge further that the harmony which results from blandness, if pushed to its utmost limit, can only lead to nothing-ness.[61] In *Le champ*, the condition of A...'s wife leads her to search for a form of harmony with the world around her. Yet her intensely self-centered focus tends to ignore or deny that world, and she fails to reach any form of last-ing harmony. The penultimate image of the novel is one of escape or diver-sion through play: "Ces jeux sur la plage, aussi faux et lucides qu'ils soient, auront la vertu de me faire oublier momentanément mon patri-moine"(107).[62] But the very final image, as in *Immobile*, is one of waiting for the final voyage, sailing the sea on the father's coffin. Through this vision, the filiation to Chinese culture is suggested through the return to the ancestral land, while the protagonist turns her back to life and procre-ation (with the previous image of children playing) and awaits death.

The search for a way out of the aporia of exile runs through Chen's work and is found again in *Querelle d'un squelette avec son double*. It takes place in the form of a dialogue rather than a monologue, between A.'s wife and a woman who claims to be her double, but the narration is ambigu-ous and the two voices may be heard as the two sides of the same person-ality, pertaining to one single person.[63] The narrator's double is trapped in the ground after an earthquake, a dramatic situation which to some extent takes the plot away from the stillness of the two previous novels—but it may all be only a dream. The status and the genre of the narrative are vol-untarily left ambiguous, as the disturbing second voice suggests in a diegetic remark that is also a comment on the narrative: "*Sachez que je suis presque vous, c'est-à-dire une ombre de votre écrasante personne, une représentation, une fragile doublure, un rêve ou une métaphore, on pensera ce qu'on voudra.*"[64] A.'s wife is disturbed by her own conscience, a voice only she can hear, which implores her for help and solidarity in the name of their similarity and reveals the hollow chasm of her own existence to her. The effect achieved by the dialogue form is to disturb the tranquil surface of the nar-rator's life and any smoothness the narrative may have. In this search for a viable way out of her alienation from the outside world, language is used and viewed ever more intensely, the way the Chinese language is viewed—that is to say, to quote Cheng, as "un langage conçu non plus comme un système dénotatif qui « décrit » le monde, mais comme une représentation qui organise les liens et provoque les actes de signification."[65] These links between elements of the world include parallels, gaps, and images.

Querelle spans one day in the life of A.'s wife and is structured on the parallel between two opposed worlds: one is clean, is protected from the outside world, insists on appearances and manners, and has, at its centre, a patisserie from which come irresistible fragrances and where A.'s wife is a regular customer; her day revolves around the dinner party she is to supervise for her husband's friends that night. In sharp contrast, the other world is the post-earthquake environment from which the second voice comes, a land of chaos, darkness, dirt, and desolation. These symmetrical locations are part of two cities separated by a river, the two banks of which mirror each other. In this symbolic characterization of place, the second woman stands as a subterranean alter ego of the first one, a darker side of the same person. Both cling to life in different ways, for different reasons: one feels she has to justify her privileged status; the other one fights against entrapment and chaos. The whole novel is structured on this contrasted mirror effect in which the two voices respond to each other while the huge gap between them acts as a medial space between emptiness and fullness, where transformations take place.[66] It also allows a deeper probe into the soul of the main character, an allegorical self that mirrors East and West in their cultural relation, but also North and South in their economic relation, thus adding another dimension to the relation to the other.

Guilt is shifting and fluctuating in the empty space that separates the two voices. The calls of the second voice are a symbolic dramatization of the need for solidarity between communities, peoples, human beings, which A.'s wife rejects: "Pourquoi encore du patriotisme ? De l'union ? De la parenté ?. [...] Non merci, pas de « nous ». L'invention de ce pronom est une erreur ou une ruse. Il n'y a que « je » et les autres" (49).[67] The quarrel between the two voices takes the form of a Sartrian "huis-clos" in which, to the protagonist, hell is other people, and her bad faith is challenged by her double. The latter denounces her twin's existence as an immense lie and points out to her that the ties that bind them are what should give meaning to her fake existence: "*Notre parenté extraordinairement étroite n'est-elle pas ce qui vous reste de plus cher de cette vie fausse et profondément solitaire, de ce quartier trop concret pour vous et qui, en fin de compte, vous le savez bien, ne sera jamais le vôtre ?*" (76).[68] The former eventually acknowledges her guilt as an inheritance: "Beaucoup d'autres que je n'ai jamais rencontrés ont été moi. J'ai dû prendre à mon propre compte leurs dettes, les atrocités qu'ils ont commises. J'ai dû les en soulager en alourdissant ma conscience, le sac que je porte toujours sur mon dos, depuis le début, depuis je ne sais plus quand, le sac déjà plein à craquer" (123).[69] The symbolic bag of guilt the protagonist feels she has to carry around can work on various levels. In particular, it may encompass the guilt of the difficult heritage of Chinese history, or that of the wealthy "North" in relation to the struggling "South," or that of the privileged writer in relation to the working class. It can thus function within an enclosed space—that of a strongly hierarchized society—or between two spaces, alien to each other but linked.

In the empty space between the two women, the value of the protagonist's storytelling is also closely examined. It is denounced by the woman underground as a diversion from truth: she recurrently dismisses the stories of A.'s wife as repetitive, narcissistic, pointless, selfish, hollow, lifeless, and inadequate to people like herself, "[les] enterrés" (42)—the buried people who symbolize underdogs of all hues. The storytelling is condemned as a fraudulent activity that only serves as a way to invent bearings in the life of the storyteller, making her seem alive when she is but a shadow. The double is ruthless on this point:

> Si vraiment l'existence dans ce temps vous amusait encore, peut-être auriez-vous pu repeupler des terrains dévastés, peut-être seriez-vous tentée de « refaire le monde » comme un enfant donne naissance à des bulles multi-colores en soufflant de l'eau savonneuse. Mais, narcissique, vous vous contentez de libérer votre propre spectre. (20)[70]

Both voices come to agree on the playful nature of making stories, of writing as diversion, that is, a human activity that takes attention away from suffering. But because the narrator has lost sight of that playful dimension, she is a poor performer in her daily life, as her double reminds her: "*Vous jouez mal, ma chère amie, parce que vous avez tendance à oublier que le jeu est un jeu, et que parfois vous refusez d'en sortir. Vous prenez trop au sérieux ce qui se déroule à l'instant même sous vos yeux, dans votre rue et dans votre maison*" (116).[71] Diversion takes on its full Pascalian meaning, making the player miserable; to quote Pascal's aphorism: "La seule chose qui nous console de nos misères est le divertissement. Et cependant c'est la plus grande de nos misères. Car c'est cela qui nous empêche principalement de songer à nous, et qui nous fait perdre insensiblement."[72]

The protagonist herself underlines this paradox about her stories: the closer she gets to truth, the less others understand or believe her stories; so she lies to look real, exposing herself to hollowness in the process: "il faut se méfier d'un rôle fictif qui finit par nous avoir, par s'infiltrer en nous, par nous manger du dedans. [...] Car si on se laisse remplacer par le rôle qu'on joue, si on cède trop d'éléments à un cadavre, au point de se vider soi-même comme lorsqu'on donne trop de sang, si on devient sentimental au fur et à mesure du jeu, c'est qu'on joue mal, très très mal" (133).[73] "Se vider" here is synonymous not with the emergence of a creative space, as in Chinese thought, but with its Western associations of hollowness, or sterile emptiness. By the end of the narrative, the value of full and empty, the meaning of fulfillment and destitution, have been inverted within the fluctuating "empty" space that separates the two voices: the earthquake woman, despite her present entrapment, reiterates that the main narrator's life is one of dryness and decay, while the last moments of her own life are full of lucidity and hope pegged onto a symbolical son embodying the generation to come.

The initial opposition ends up being turned upside down: the main narrator's life seemed the fullest at first, while the chaos following the earthquake had given way to emptiness. Through the dialogue that takes place between the two women, the emptiness between them becomes a site of interaction, confrontation, transformation, and eventually points at the way out of aporia. Paradoxically, although no peaceful harmony is reached by the end of the novel, turmoil—the protagonist's inner agitation, her double's struggle against entrapment—becomes a source of light.

In her three later novels, Chen establishes a different narrative mode. In order to remove herself from autoethnographic fiction, she returns to principles that prevail in the Chinese view of language and aesthetics, and combines them with elements of Western thought (for example, as found in the works of Sarraute, Sartre, Pascal), to proceed with the reterritorialization process of her writing. This shift demands a displacement on the part of her reader as well, whose bearings are altered, but the result is the beginning of a different dialogue between writer and reader, in a way recalling the great dialogue that the Tao has always tried to encourage.[74]

Chen's poetic rebellion against the prevailing forms of writing race and ethnicity in her time is achieved through a strategy that includes going back to her cultural roots in search of new ways of writing. The result is a highly symbolic, abstract style. Can it be said that Chen's writing lies "beyond autoethnography"? No, to the extent that her work relies heavily on Western and Chinese poetic traditions, and yes, since these traditions serve as fertile ground for a new form of writing to emerge, thus offering an original perspective on the discussion of race and ethnicity, based on a constantly dialogic approach. What about the location of her writing and her aporetic sense of being a writer in exile? One should distinguish between two linked dimensions of exile. One is the exile the immigrant experiences, a part of the process of gradually severing the ties with the native country. The other is the universal sense of existential exile that takes on many forms and drives the search for origin. While the former may be temporary, the latter is more deeply rooted and is tied to Chen's view of history as repetitive and devoid of finality and progress, which may be traced both in Chinese thought and Western modernism. It is epitomized in the ironical title of her book of essays and the Chinese image of four thousand steps (in which she once more stages an inversion of who the other is): Chen doesn't espouse the "Chinese dream" of climbing four thousand steps up to a stupendous view at the top of the Yellow Mountain that foreign visitors to China like so much, but identifies instead with Camus's Sisyphus, who is condemned to endlessly push his rock up the mountain, as if there were only an endless process of starting over.

NOTES

1 "Une révolte poétique," *Quatre mille marches: Un rêve chinois* (Montreal: Boréal; Paris: Seuil, 2002), 104.
2 Since this article was written, Chen has had another novel published, *Le mangeur* (Paris: Seuil, 2005), which is parallel to the previous three.
3 Françoise Lionnet, *Autobiographical Voices: Race, Gender, Self-Portraiture* (Ithaca, NY: Cornell UP, 1989), 278.
4 Ibid.
5 ["My grandmother Lie-Fei was five years old when the last emperor was removed from his throne. That was in the year 1912." "'The little one looks like me,' said grandma."] The translations of passages in French are given in endnotes, in brackets. All translations are by the author. Ying Chen, *La mémoire de l'eau* (Montreal: Léméac, 1992; Arles: Actes Sud-Babel, 1996), 11, 115. The first reference to a book by Ying Chen is given in an endnote; subsequent page references are given in parentheses, in the text.
6 ["For grandma."]
7 On Chen's view of history and people's lives, see the Master's in Creative Writing she completed at the Department of French language and literature at McGill University, entitled "Roman et Histoire dans *Les dieux ont soif* suivi de *Les fleurs de lotus*." In her analysis of *Les dieux ont soif*, Anatole France's historical novel, Chen wrote: "les guerres, les traités de paix, les bouleversements politiques ne sont que la partie extérieure et peu importante de l'histoire; par contre, le facteur réellement décisif c'est la vie réelle, immédiate, matérielle, spontanée du peuple lui-même." ["Wars, peace treaties, political upheavals are only the outside and unimportant part of history; on the other hand, the truly decisive factor is the real, immediate, material, spontaneous life of the people itself."] The other, creative part of her thesis, *Les fleurs de lotus*, is the manuscript that was then published as *La mémoire de l'eau*. See Isabelle Girard, "Stylistique et esthétique dans trois fragments de *La mémoire de l'eau* de Ying Chen (hypothèses d'analyse socio-critique)," *Tangence* 68 (Winter 2002): 137, 151.
8 See the previous note, on Chen's training as a writer.
9 ["'Has father lost his hat?' asked my grandmother. And everyone laughed, because 'to lose one's hat' was a phrase used to refer to someone quitting a post, whether of one's own free will or not."]

10 The original title of the manuscript was *Les fleurs de lotus*. The fact that Chen chose a less obviously "Oriental" title for the publication of her work is an early sign of her subsequent self-distancing from ethnic markers.

11 ["Flushing water."]

12 ["The smell of water was the same everywhere."]

13 ["It must have been the river that nourished my ancestors and myself. The river that had always weighed so heavily in my heart as it did for the lotus flowers in the autumn seasons, and which seemed so fragile to me now that I was seeing it from above."]

14 ["A sign of nobleness, of wealth, of beauty, of purity, of everything that may bring happiness to a woman."] Jacques Pimpaneau, *Dans un jardin de Chine* (Arles: Philippe Picquier, 2000), 34, 14.

15 ["I have been taught at school that everything has a biological reason. If lotus roots now have a round end and a pointy one, it is because it is necessary. One could consider that they are ugly or that they are not. It has nothing to do with them. They don't shape themselves. What shapes them is the water, or rather the torrent that comes and goes, taking away one kind of mud that will be replaced by another."]

16 Critics read this ambiguity variously: some consider that to Sassa, Yuan is clearly the man Da Li has fallen in love with (Eileen Sivert, "Ying Chen's *Les lettres chinoises* and Epistolary Identity," in *Doing Gender: Franco-Canadian Women Writers of the 1990s*, eds. Paula Ruth Gilbert and Roseanna Dufault (Madison, NJ: Fairleigh Dickinson UP; London: Associated U Presses, 2001), 217; Emile Talbot, "Rewriting *Les lettres chinoises*: The Poetics of Erasure," *Quebec Studies* 36 (Fall 2003/Winter 2004): 88), others see Yuan and Da Li's relationship as ambiguous (Roseanna Dufault, "Identity and Exile in Shanghai and Montreal: *Les lettres chinoises* by Ying Chen," *Frontières flottantes: Lieu et espace dans les cultures francophones du Canada/Shifting Boundaries: Place and Space in the Francophone Cultures of Canada*, ed. Jaap Lintvelt and François Paré (Amsterdam: Rodopi, 2001), 163), while yet others simply point out the ambiguity in Chen's writing (Irène Oore, "*Les lettres chinoises* de Ying Chen: Le mobile et l'immobile," *Studies in Canadian Literature/Études en littérature canadienne* 29, no. 1 [2004]: 74, 80).

17 The present analysis is based on the second edition of the novel.

18 In fact, all but one: letter 29.

19 Emile Talbot, "Rewriting *Les lettres chinoises*: The Poetics of Erasure," *Quebec Studies* 36 (Fall 2003/Winter 2004): 83.

20 Ibid., 87, 88.

21 ["To tell of exile, to examine it the way you examine a dead body, is to talk about childhood and love, books, daily life, but also about language, territory, the soul."] Although the letters are personal, not fictional ones, they were also written with the awareness that they may ultimately be read by others—and perhaps even published: "Pour la première fois, elles se parlent d'elles, seule à seule, par lettres, sachant bien que cette correspondance ne sera pas secrète et que d'autres la liront." ["For the first time, they talk about themselves, one to one, in letters, knowing well that this correspondence will not be secret and that others will read it too."] Nancy Huston and Leïla Sebbar, *Lettres parisiennes: Autopsie de l'exil* (1986; Paris: J'ai lu, 1999), 6. Chen mentions Huston's notion of "le traduisible" in *Quatre mille marches* (71), a sign that she has read Huston's work. It is likely she would have read *Lettres parisiennes*.

22 ["We will never be truly free. We cannot manage to be together without feeling guilty. I realize that I am immoral and he realizes that he has betrayed. Neither he nor I can forget the past. Even though we have left our land, the spirit of Master Con has followed us here, crushing our simple happiness and making our lives complicated."] Ying Chen, *Les lettres chinoises* (Montreal: Léméac, 1993; Arles: Actes Sud-Babel, 1998), 129.

23 ["Since you left, it has been as if the word 'freedom' were not as pejorative as it used to be. It is no longer synonymous with irresponsibility, immorality or even criminality. People now talk of good and bad freedom. But as the term is still too loaded, people have been cautious enough to come up with a term to refer to good freedom: 'openness.'"]

24 ["The Shangainese that I am cannot completely repress the feeling which makes me think that those who walk on 'our' streets and work in 'our' companies without talking Shanghainese are foreigners. This feeling survives despite my constant discontent towards the government, which is supposed to make me happy, happier than others if possible, because my great-grand-parents were born in this city."]

25 ["Because I stupidly believe that plenitude embodies happiness, I still do not like waxing moons or open stories."]

26 It is worth noting that the novel has often been dealt with by critics along with other novels which have no link to China, the focus being on the mother-daughter relationship as a universal issue rather than on questions having to do with ethnicity per se. See for example Lori Saint-Martin, "Infanticide, Suicide, Matricide, and Mother–Daughter Love: Suzanne Jacob's *L'Obéissance* and Ying Chen's *L'Ingratitude*," *Canadian Literature* 169 (Summer 2001); and Oore, "*Les lettres chinoises* de Ying Chen."

27 ["What they have to say is not heard."] Luce Irigaray, *Le corps-à-corps avec la mère* (Montreal: Pleine lune, 1981), 13.

28 ["The mother–daughter relationship is the dark continent of the dark continent."]

29 ["We must not let ourselves be the guardians of silence, of a deathly silence."] Irigaray, 61, 29.

30 Chen herself argues that mothers like Yan-Zi's "existent ici [au Canada] aussi," ["also exist here in Canada"] stressing the universal dimension of her novel. See Micheline Lachance, "Des vies à l'encre de Chine: Ying Chen écrit à Montréal des romans bouleversants qui se passent à Shanghai," *L'Actualité* 20, no. 18 (Nov. 15, 1995): 90.

31 ["You must talk. You can curse your poor mother, if that is what you prefer, curse everyone and heap abuse on them. But talk! Pour your sorrow upon our heads. Your journey will then become easy. And we will not be consoled otherwise ..."] Ying Chen, *L'ingratitude* (Montreal: Léméac, 1995; Arles: Actes Sud-Babel, 1996), 8.

32 ["the father of our feudalism"]

33 ["If only father could have shared with me part of the huge responsibility of making happy the woman who did so much for me and for him, I could have breathed better and perhaps I could have lived longer. He was the one, in a way, who had made me an enemy."]

34 ["The desire of her, her own desire, that is what the father's law—the law of all fathers—must come to forbid. Always, they intervene to censure, repress, in all common sense and good health, the desire of the mother. What appears in the most daily facts, as in our society and our culture as a whole, is that women originally function on a matricide."] Irigaray, 15.

35   ["I was supposed to become the most accurate reproduction possible of my mother. I was her daughter. So I had to destroy that reproduction at any cost. I had to kill her daughter. There was no other way of making her wiser. I couldn't be myself otherwise."]

36   ["Now I understand that your mother is your destiny. You cannot turn away from your mother without turning away from yourself. Traitors to their mothers will carry on, dead or alive, to wander, to see themselves excluded from the cycle of life, to be everywhere and nowhere. To not be."]

37   ["a feminine way of talking"]

38   ["I agree from time to time to play a part that does not suit me, having talked in many places about immigration, integration, cultural shocks, the charm of the French language, the nostalgia for the motherland, the Communist regime, the situation of Chinese women, having exhausted all the kinds of topics that are typical of writers in my situation. No doubt I can only be overwhelmed by the task, since even though some of my texts may lead the writer to believe that they deal with vast topics, in fact I have never talked about anything else than myself. I have never been the characters of my novels, but my characters are always impregnated with my soul. In our time of extreme dis-individualization, which people would like to check by resorting, wrongly, to patriotism, if literature is to have a meaning, it is precisely to cultivate a microscopic vision of the world, to transform, if possible, the dialogue of cultures into dialogues amongst individuals, if not into monologues."] Chen, *Quatre mille marches*, 43–44.

39   Although Chen resents being identified as a minority writer in the sense of a spokesperson for a minority, her early writing does match Deleuze and Guattari's triple definition of minority literature: it is de-territorialized (Chen writes in a language that is not her mother tongue, in a place that is not predominantly French-speaking), political (her individual stories of life in twentieth-century China, emigration, and a daughter's oppression all have political impacts), and collective (Chen is identified as a writer of Chinese origin). See Gilles Deleuze and Félix Guattari, "Qu'est-ce qu'une littérature mineure?" in *Kafka: Pour une littérature mineure* (Paris: Minuit, 1975), 29–50.

40   On the place of landscape in Chinese culture, see François Cheng on the tradition of landscape painting in tenth-century China: "Exprimant, à travers la représentation de paysages grandioses ou mystiques, le mystère même de l'univers et du désir humain, [les artistes] inaugurent la grande tradition du paysage qui deviendra, on le sait, le courant majeur de la peinture chinoise." ["By expressing, through the representation of grand or mystical landscapes, the very mystery of the universe and of human desire, artists inaugurated the great tradition of the landscape which became, as we know, the main trend of Chinese painting."] *Vide et plein: Le langage pictural chinois* (Paris: Seuil, 1991), 19. See also Pimpaneau, on Chinese garden painting: "il ne s'agit pas de copier des paysages de régions lointaines et inhabitées, mais, au contraire, de rappeler sans cesse cette fusion de l'humain dans la nature ; de permettre à un individu de se retrouver dans une atmosphère où, à la différence de celle des villes, cette harmonie est reconstituée, où les personnes peuvent se sentir pleinement humaines car intégrées dans l'univers." ["The aim is not to copy landscapes from faraway or uninhabited regions but, on the contrary, to recall the fusion of the human and nature, to enable an individual to find himself in an atmosphere where, unlike that of cities, this harmony is reconstituted, where people can feel fully human because they are integrated in the universe."] *Dans un jardin de Chine*, 31.

41 Sylvie Lisiecki-Bouretz, "Actualités: Rencontres littéraires franco-chinoises: Interviews de quatre écrivains chinois: Questions à Ying Chen," August 2, 2005, http://chroniques.bnf.fr/archives/decembre2001/

42 ["It is a child who, for lack of a home, and being condemned to the road, never learnt to walk, and never grows up. He writes to mock his own awkwardness and to pass his pointless time. He often shows himself to be contradictory and anxious, because he doubts the reliability of words as much as he is tempted by the tonifying vertigo that a dance with languages seems to promise. Nothing to show, nothing to tell really. Everything is already written from the start. I write because I cannot forget the horrible fall of my child and similar incidents that have populated my life so far, and which urge me to run away from the illusion of identity, sometimes, out of myself, to err constantly between full and empty."] Chen, *Quatre mille marches*, 79, 81.

43 See Ying Chen, interview with Yvon Le Bras, *Lingua Romana: A Journal of French, Italian and Romanian Culture* 1, no. 1 (Fall 2002), http://linguaromana.byu.edu/yinchen.html, about *Immobile* and *Le champ* (*Querelle* had not been published yet): "Disons qu'ils sont parallèles, car il ne s'agit pas d'une suite. Je n'ai pas cherché à raconter la même histoire dans ces deux romans. Seule la narratrice qui vit dans le monde actuel est semblable." ["Let's say that they are parallel, because it is not a sequence. I didn't try to tell the same story in these two novels. Only the narrator who lives in the contemporary world is the same."] See also Chen, *Quatre mille marches*, 97: "[*Le champ dans la mer*], qui suit *Immobile* et qui précède *Querelle d'un squelette avec son double*, fait partie d'un ensemble romanesque que je suis en train de composer, ayant comme personnage central une femme de nature ambiguë qui raconte ses vicissitudes désencadrées du temps et de l'espace." ["*Le champ dans la mer*, which follows *Immobile* and which precedes *Querelle d'un squelette avec son double*, is part of a sequence of novels that I am composing, and which has as its central character a woman of ambiguous nature, who tells about her vicissitudes that are outside a timeframe or a setting."]

44 Nathalie Sarraute, "L'Ère du soupçon," *Œuvres complètes* (Paris: Gallimard Pléiade, 1996), 1585. See also "Roman et réalité," *Œuvres complètes*, 1645–56.

45 ["One could no longer write novels based on characters. The characters in novels had exploded, they were overflowing with a new substance. The mere name one gave to a character reeked of convention. In 1932, when I wrote a first text, it seemed to me that I was expressing a spontaneous sensation which could not fit into the framework of the novel or the short story. I did my best to show this sensation for itself, in its pure state, so to speak, as it unfolds for a few moments in a character who is only its bearer, its barely visible location. All my attention was focused on the sensations that certain movements that are barely conscious produce, movements that develop in us within a few minutes—sometimes a few seconds—and which I was trying to render here through images and through the movements of the sentence, as if magnified and seen in slow motion."] Sarraute, "Forme et contenu du roman," *Œuvres complètes*, 1667–68.

46 Asked in an email message if she agreed that there was a link between her writing in *Immobile*, *Le champ dans la mer*, and *Querelle*, and the *Nouveau Roman*, especially Nathalie Sarraute's writing, Chen simply responded that she had read a few writers of what is called the *Nouveau Roman*, including Claude Simon and Nathalie Sarraute, and that she appreciated their singular voices (August 14, 2005). However, in previous interviews, she clearly stated Sarraute's influence on her writing. See "Journée internationale des femmes: Sept portraits de femmes,"

La Presse, March 6, 1999, D10 ("Parmi ses guides [les guides de Ying Chen]," l'écrivaine Nathalie Sarraute, "une écrivaine tout à fait moderne, qui m'inspire beaucoup."); ["Among her guides, the writer Nathalie Sarraute, 'a very modern writer, who inspires me a lot.'"]); "Ying Chen, une fiction originale qui témoigne de la diversité des lettres chinoises contemporaines: Un tumulte intérieur," Entretien de Ying Chen avec Alain Nicolas, *L'Humanité*, November 6, 2003, 20 (Chen: "En français, j'ai d'abord lu les classiques du XIXe siècle, surtout Balzac, évidemment. J'aimais Proust, Camus, et surtout Nathalie Sarraute, qui, je pense, a été très importante pour moi."); ["In French, I first read the 19th century classics, especially Balzac, of course. I liked Proust, Camus, and most of all Nathalie Sarraute, whom I think has been very important for me."]); "Ying Chen. D'est en ouest," Revue de *Quatre mille marches* par Caroline Montpetit, *Le Devoir*, May 29, 2004, F1 ("Ying Chen a pourtant quitté la Chine de son plein gré. Née en pleine Révolution culturelle, elle a découvert la littérature française à partir de 1979, à travers les œuvres de Camus, Sartre, Nathalie Sarraute, etc."). ["Ying Chen left China of her own will though. She was born in the middle of the Cultural Revolution, and discovered French literature from 1979 onwards, through the works of Camus, Sartre, Nathalie Sarraute, etc."]). See also the interview of Annie Curien, a sinologist, on the occasion of the 2004 Paris book fair, when China was guest of honour: "Des archipels pour un continent," *L'Humanité*, March 20, 2004, 39 (L'Humanité: "Y a-t-il d'autres littératures étrangères qui attirent les écrivains chinois? Qu'en est-il de la littérature française?" Annie Curien: "Les littératures étrangères sont maintenant bien traduites et bien connues en Chine. Il est donc plus difficile de repérer des pôles massifs. Avant la littérature latino-américaine, il y a eu les grands romans du XIXe siècle les Français, puis les Russes. Par la suite, le Nouveau Roman a effectivement beaucoup frappé les esprits."). ["L'Humanité: "Are there other foreign literatures that Chinese writers are drawn to? What about French literature?"; Annie Curien: "Foreign literatures are now well translated and well known in China. So it is more difficult to spot major poles. Before Latin-American literature, there were the great 19th-century French novels, and the Russians. Later on, the Nouveau Roman did fire people's imaginations."]).

47 See Linda Hutcheon, *Narcissistic Narrative: The Metafictional Paradox* (Waterloo, ON: Wilfrid Laurier UP, 1980), 5. Warm thanks to Claire Omhovère for pointing out this critical text to me.

48 Written S... in *Le champ*, but S. again in *Querelle*. The same goes for A.../A.

49 ["I am the living example of the ravages of memory. I prefer to drag myself through my vain and disgraceful days, in the darkness of memory, far away from A, far from any hope of healing, so that everything will end naturally. And so I stay here, immobile and defenseless. Like a rock."] Ying Chen, *Immobile* (Montreal: Boréal; Arles: Actes Sud, 1998), 146, 147.

50 ["I have caught sight of the great lie that is produced by the machine of history. The collective delusion. The few centuries of vicissitudes told in inumerable books equate the void that I crossed in the wink of an eye. No one wants to admit it. It is so easy to observe though. We like fiction so much. We ignore emptiness. Everyone comes from emptiness and no one remembers it."]

51 ["In Chinese thought, Emptiness constitutes the location par excellence where transformations happen, where Fullness should be able to reach its true plenitude."] Cheng, *Vide et plein*, 45–46.

52 ["In Chinese thought, and especially for Taoists, what first guarantees the communion betwen man and the universe is that man is not only a being of flesh and

blood but also of breath and spirits; further, he possesses Emptiness. With Emptiness, the heart of Man can become the rule or the mirror of oneself and of the world, because, owning Emptiness and identifying with the original Emptiness, Man finds himself at the source of images and shapes. When the human heart becomes the mirror of itself and of the world, only then can there be a true possibility of life."] Cheng, *Vide et plein*, 62–63.

53 ["Any new memory makes me doubt my beliefs, the earnestness of my stories, and forces me to let go of any pretension to consistency, to coherence."] Ying Chen, *Le champ dans la mer* (Montreal: Boréal; Paris: Seuil, 2002), 78.

54 ["I so much wanted to acquire a consistent story, to remain faithfully by other beings, grasping things within my reach, holding on to them at any cost, even if it meant betraying myself, selling myself. I could then have had my turn at summing up my life, as if I had had one to live. I too would have become capable of going from one end to the other, from a beginning to an end, according to a well-established timeline, on a fine line hanging between cliffs. A line that would nonetheless always be too short, because the gap between cliffs is broader than it seems."]

55 ["It was about a first intuition, not only of the unreliability of love, but of the fragility of human relationships."]

56 ["Since I was crushed like a rat, since the bones of my parents dissolved under the feet of the villagers, since V… has been ploughing the field in his parents' place or has been involved in whichever other endeavour, most likely the making of bricks, I no longer have a homeland."]

57 François Cheng, *L'écriture poétique chinoise, suivi d'une anthologie des poèmes des Tang* (1977; rev. ed., Paris: Seuil, 1996), 115–117. Citations are to the 1996 edition.

58 Cheng, *L'écriture*, 90. Chen characterizes her own style as "peu descriptif, dépouillé à l'extrême, avec une intensité intérieure" ["not very descriptive, extremely sparse, with inner intensity"] (*Quatre mille marches*, 99), and likens her writing, starting from *Immobile*, to poetry (Ying Chen, interview with Le Bras). Besides, she has read a lot of Chinese classical poetry, which is characterized as very bald and suggestive (email to the author, August 14, 2005).

59 François Jullien, *Éloge de la fadeur. À partir de la pensée et de l'esthétique de la Chine* (Arles: Philippe Picquier, 1991), 47.

60 ["For the Chinese, emotion is all the deeper in us that what we respond to—outside ourselves—is important, of considerable stake. Thus, the deeper it is, the less individual and limited to our personal interest—egocentric—it is: the more it makes us feel, on the contrary, the richness of the link that ties us to the world and how we play a full part in the great process of things. It then opens our subjectivity to the solidarity of existences, to the interdependence of realities, and makes it come out of its particular viewpoint—exclusive and narrow. Because of this intensity, it is capable of making us 'communicate' through reality, of raising us to a community perspective: the deeper it is, then, the more moral it is."] Jullien, *Éloge de la fadeur*, 95–96.

61 Jullien, *Éloge de la fadeur*, 125.

62 ["These games on the beach, as false and lucid as they are, will have the virtue of making me forget momentarily my patrimony."]

63 To an interviewer asking about the two narrators in *Querelle*, "Qui est la copie, qui est l'originale?" Chen replied: "Le livre pourrait être lu d'une autre façon, ce pourrait être l'histoire d'un seul personnages qui est la femme de A., les deux

voix pourraient provenir d'une même personne. La querelle deviendrait alors un travail sur la conscience, un combat intérieur entre deux voix d'une même personne en contradiction avec soi, montrant deux faces d'un individu divisé." [Q: "Who is the copy, who is the original?"; A: "The book could be read another way, it could be the story of a single character who is A.'s wife, the two voices could come from the same person. The quarrel would then become a study on conscience, an inner struggle between the two voices of one and the same person in contradiction with herself, showing the two sides of a divided individual."] (Éric Paquin, "Madame et son fantôme" (May 29, 2003), *Voir*, Aug. 2, 2005, http://www.voir.ca/publishing/article.aspx?article=26384&section=10).

64 ["Let me tell you that I am almost you, that is to say a shadow of your overwhelming person, a representation, a fragile stand-in, a dream or a metaphor, people may think what they like."] Ying Chen, *Querelle d'un squelette avec son double* (Montreal: Boréal; Paris: Seuil, 2003), 39. The typography of the quotes replicates that used in the novel: quotes in italics correspond to the second voice; quotes not in italics correspond to the first voice, A.'s wife.

65 ["A language conceived not as a denotative system that 'describes' the world, but as a representation which organizes links and creates acts of significance."] Cheng, *L'écriture*, 15.

66 Cheng, *Vide et plein*, 45–50.

67 ["Why more patriotism? Union? Relatives? No thank you, no 'we.' The invention of that pronoun is a mistake or a trick. There is only 'I' and others."]

68 ["Isn't our very tight relation the dearest thing you are left with of that false and profoundly solitary life of yours, of that neighbourhood that is too concrete for you and which, after all, and you know it well, will never be yours?"]

69 ["Many others whom I never met have been me. I had to take responsibility for their debts, and the atrocious crimes they committed. I had to relieve them from all that by making my conscience heavy, that bag I am still carrying upon my back, which I have been carrying since the beginning, since I can't remember when, that bag which is about to burst because it is already so full."]

70 ["If existence at that time still entertained you, perhaps you could have repopulated wasted lands, perhaps you would be tempted to 'make the world over' as a child makes many-coloured bubbles by blowing soapy water. But, narcissistic as you are, you merely liberate your own ghost."]

71 [*"You act poorly, my dear, because you tend to forget that the game is but a game, and you sometimes refuse to step out of it. You take too seriously what is happening right now under your eyes, in your street and in your house."*]

72 ["The only thing that consoles us from our misery is diversion. And yet it is the greatest of our miseries. For it is what keeps us from thinking mainly about ourselves, and it makes us lose insensibly."] Blaise Pascal, "Papiers découpés en attente de classement," fragment 393, *Pensées*, in *Œuvres complètes II* (Paris: Gallimard Pléiade, 2000), 675.

73 ["We should be suspicious of a fictive role that finally defeats us, that sneaks into ourselves, and devours us from the inside. For if you let the role you play take over, if you give away too much to a dead body, to the point of emptying yourself as when you give too much blood, if you become sentimental as the game unfolds, then it means that you are acting badly, very badly."]

74 Cheng, *L'écriture*, 92–93. See also François Cheng, *Le dialogue: Une passion pour la langue française* (Paris: Desclée de Brouwer, 2002), 60: "si j'ai embrassé la langue française et, à travers elle, épousé toute une tradition poétique en Occi-

dent, je n'ai jamais cessé d'être inspiré par ma tradition poétique native qui, loin de m'alourdir, continue à me porter dans le sens de la croissance, telle une vieille nourrice fidèle. Entre le terreau ancien et toutes les nouvelles plantes que j'y ai fait pousser s'est opéré, à n'en pas douter, un fécond va-et-vient."

["Even though I adopted the French language and, through it, espoused a whole poetic tradition in the West, I have never ceased to be inspired by my native poetic tradition which, far from weighing me down, carries on lifting me in the direction of growth, like an old and faithful nurse. Between the old compost and all the new plants I grew out of it, there is no doubt that fruitful comings-and-goings have been taking place."]

[bibliography]

Abraham, Nicolas, and Maria Torok. *The Shell and the Kernel: Renewals of Psycho-analysis*. Ed. and trans. Nicholas T. Rand. Chicago: U of Chicago P, 1994.

Agamben, Giorgio. *Means without End: Notes on Politics*. Trans. Vincenzo Binetti and Cesare Casarino. Minneapolis: U of Minnesota P, 2000.

Anctil, Pierre, ed. *Through the Eyes of the Eagle: The Early Montreal Yiddish Press (1907–1916)*. Trans. David Rome. Montreal: Véhicule Press, 2001.

Anderson, Benedict. *Imagined Communities: Reflections on the Origin and Spread of Nationalism*. London: Verso, 1983.

———. *Imagined Communities: Reflections on the Origin and Spread of Nationalism*. London: Verso, 1991.

Andrews, Jennifer, and John Clement Ball. "Introduction: Beyond the Margins." *Studies in Canadian Literature* 25, no. 1 (2000): 1–11.

Appadurai, Arjun. *Modernity at Large: Cultural Dimensions of Globalization*. Minneapolis: U of Minnesota P, 1996.

Apter, Emily. "On Translation in a Global Market." *Public Culture* 13, no. 1 (2001): 1–12.

Aziz, Nurjehan, ed. *Floating the Borders: New Contexts in Canadian Criticism*. Toronto: TSAR, 1999.

Balakrishnan, T.R., and Feng Hou. "Residential Patterns in Cities." In *Immigrant Canada: Demographic, Economic and Social Challenges*, ed. Shiva S. Halli and Leo Dreidger, 116–47. Toronto: U of Toronto P, 1999.

Baldwin, James. *Giovanni's Room*. New York: Dell, 1988.

Balsamo, Anne. "Forms of Technological Embodiment: Reading the Body in Contemporary Culture." In *Feminist Theory and the Body*, ed. Janet Price and Margrit Shildrick, 215–37. Edinburgh: Edinburgh UP, 1999.

Bannerji, Himani. *The Dark Side of the Nation: Essays on Multiculturalism, Nationalism and Gender*. Toronto: Canadian Scholars' Press, 2000.

———, ed. *Returning the Gaze: Essays on Racism, Feminism and Politics*. Toronto: Sister Vision Press, 1993.

———. *Thinking Through: Essays on Feminism, Marxism and Anti-Racism*. Toronto: The Women's Press, 1995.

Banting, Pamela. *Body, Inc.: A Theory of Translation Poetics*. Winnipeg, MB: Turnstone Press, 1995.

Bass Jenks, Elaine. "Searching for Autoethnographic Credibility: Reflections from a Mom with a Notepad." In *Ethnographically Speaking: Autoethnography, Literature, and Aesthetics*, ed. Arthur P. Bochner and Carolyn Ellis, 170–86. Walnut Creek: AltaMira Press, 2002.

Beauregard, Guy. "Asian Canadian Literature: Diasporic Interventions in the Work of SKY Lee, Joy Kogawa, Hiromi Goto, and Fred Wah." PhD diss., U of Alberta, 2000.

———. "The Emergence of 'Asian Canadian Literature': Can Lit's Obscene Supplement?" http://www.ucalgary.ca/UofC/eduweb/engl392/492/beauregard.html.

———. "A Glimpse of Something." *Canadian Literature* 181 (2004): 149–50.

Beauregard, Guy, and Yiu-Nam Leung, eds. *Asian Canadian Studies*. Special issue of *Essays in Canadian Writing* 85 (2005).

Benita Shaw, Debra. *Women, Science, and Fiction: The* Frankenstein *Inheritance*. London: Palgrave, 2000.

Bennett, David. "Introduction." In *Multicultural States: Rethinking difference and identity*, ed. David Bennett, 1–26. New York: Routledge, 1998.

Bennett, Donna. "Conflicted Vision: A Consideration of Canon and Genre in English-Canadian Literature." In *Canadian Canons*, ed. Robert Lecker, 131–49. Toronto: U of Toronto P, 1991.

Berger, John. *Another Way of Telling*. New York: Pantheon Books, 1982.

Bernstein, Charles. *My Way: Speeches and Poems*. Chicago: U of Chicago P, 1999.

Bernstein, Richard J. *Freud and the Legacy of Moses*. Cambridge: Cambridge UP, 1998.

Bhabha, Homi. *The Location of Culture*. London: Routledge, 1994.

Billingham, Susan. "Migratory Subjects in Shani Mootoo's *Out on Main Street*." In *Identity, Community, Nation: Essays on Canadian Writing*, ed. Danielle Schaub and Christl Verduyn, 74–88. Jerusalem: Hebrew U Magnes P, 2002.

Birbalsingh, Frank. "Introduction." In *Jahaji: An Anthology of Indo-Guyanese Fiction*, ed. Frank Birbalsingh, 7–33. Toronto: TSAR, 2000.

Bissoondath, Neil. *Selling Illusions: The Cult of Multiculturalism*. Toronto: Penguin, 1994.

Blanchard, Marc Eli. "The Critique of Autobiography." *Comparative Literature* 34, no. 2 (1982): 97–115.

Bloom, Leslie Rebecca. *Under the Sign of Hope: Feminist Methodology and Narrative Interpretation*. Albany: State U of New York P, 1998.

Bourdieu, Pierre. *The Field of Cultural Production*. Ed. Randal Johnson. New York: Columbia UP, 1993.

Bouretz, Sylvie Lisiecki . "Actualités: Rencontres littéraires franco-chinoises. Interviews de quatre écrivains chinois."http://chroniques.bnf.fr/archives/decembre2001/

Bowering, George. "Introduction." In *Loki Is Buried at Smoky Creek: Selected Poems*, 9–22. Vancouver: Talonbooks, 1980.

———. "The Poems of Fred Wah." *Concerning Poetry* 12, no. 2 (1979): 3–13.

Brand, Dionne. *What We All Long For*. Toronto: A.A. Knopf Canada, 2005.

Brown, Stephen Gilbert, and Sidney I. Dobrin, eds. *Ethnography Unbound: From Theory Shock to Critical Praxis*. Albany: State U of New York P, 2004.

Brydon, Diana. "It's Time for a New Set of Questions." *Essays on Canadian Writing* 71 (2000): 14–25.

Budde, Robert. "After Postcolonialism: Migrant Lines and the Politics of Form in Fred Wah, M. Nourbese Philip, and Roy Miki." In *Is Canada Postcolonial? Unsettling Canadian Literature*, ed. Laura Moss, 282–94. Waterloo, ON: Wilfrid Laurier UP, 2003.

Burawoy, Michael, Joseph Blum, Sheba George, Zsuszsa Gille, Teresa Gowan, Lynne Haney, Maren Klawiter, Steven H. Lopez, Sean O. Riain, and Millie Thayer. *Global Ethnography: Forces, Connections, and Imaginations in a Postmodern World*. Berkeley: U of California P, 2000.

Burstyn, Varda. "The Wrong Sex." *Canadian Forum* 741 (August/September 1984): 29–33.

Burton, Antoinette. *Dwelling in the Archive: Women Writing House, Home and History in Late Colonial India*. New York: Oxford UP, 2003.

Butler, Judith. "Subjection, Resistance, Resignification: Between Freud and Foucault." In *The Identity in Question*, ed. John Rajchman, 229–250. New York and London: Routledge, 1995.

Buzard, James. "On Auto-Ethnographic Authority." *Yale Journal of Criticism* 16, no. 1 (2003): 61–91.

Cameron, Anne. *Daughters of Copper Woman*. Press Gang: Vancouver, 1981.

Cameron, Elspeth, ed. *Multiculturalism and Immigration in Canada: An Introductory Reader*. Toronto: Canadian Scholars' Press, 2004.

Campbell, Jennifer. "Mural Stirs Debate about Community." *Ottawa Citizen*, September 18, 2002.

Cariou, Warren. *Lake of the Prairies*. Toronto: Random, 2003.

Casteel, Sarah Phillips. "New World Pastoral: The Caribbean Garden and Emplacement in Gisele Pineau and Shani Mootoo." *Interventions* 5, no. 1 (2003): 12–28.

Chao, Lien. "Anthologizing the Collective: The Epic Struggles to Establish Chinese Canadian Literature in English." In *Writing Ethnicity: Cross-Cultural Consciousness in Canadian and Quebecois Literature*, ed. Winfried Siemerling, 145–70. Toronto: ECW Press, 1996.

———. *Beyond Silence: Chinese Canadian Literature in English*. Toronto: TSAR, 1997.

Chao, Lien, and Jim Wong-Chu, eds. *Strike the Wok: An Anthology of Contemporary Canadian Chinese Fiction*. Toronto: TSAR, 2003.

Cheah, Pheng. "Given Culture: Rethinking Cosmopolitical Freedom in Transnationalism." In *Cosmopolitics: Thinking and Feeling Beyond the Nation*, ed. Pheng Cheah and Bruce Robbins, 290–328. Minneapolis: U of Minnesota P, 1998.

Chen, Tina. "Towards an Ethics of Knowledge." *MELUS* 30, no. 2 (Summer 2005): 157–73.

Chen, Ying. *Le champ dans la mer*. Paris: Seuil, 2002.

———. *Immobile*. Arles: Actes Sud, 1998.

———. *L'ingratitude*. Arles: Actes Sud-Babel, 1996.

———. *Les lettres chinoises*. Arles: Actes Sud-Babel, 1998.

———. *Le mangeur*. Paris: Seuil, 2005.

———. *La mémoire de l'eau*. Arles: Actes Sud-Babel, 1996.

———. *Quatre mille marches: Un rêve chinois*. Paris: Seuil, 2004.

———. *Querelle d'un squelette avec son double*. Paris: Seuil, 2003.

Cheng, François. *Le dialogue: Une passion pour la langue française*. Paris: Desclée de Brouwer, 2002.

———. *L'écriture poétique chinoise, suivi d'une anthologie des poèmes des Tang*. Paris: Seuil, 1996.

———. *Vide et plein: Le langage pictural chinois*. Paris: Seuil, 1991.

Cheung, King-Kok. *Articulate Silences: Hisaye Yamamoto, Maxine Hong Kingston, Joy Kogawa*. Ithaca, NY: Cornell UP, 1993.

———. *An Interethnic Companion to Asian American Literature*. Cambridge: Cambridge UP, 1997.

Chong, Denise. *The Concubine's Children: Portrait of a Family Divided*. Toronto: Viking, 1994.

Chong, Kevin. *Baroque-a-Nova*. Toronto: Penguin, 2001.

Chow, Rey. "Against the Lures of Diaspora: Minority Discourse, Chinese Women, and Intellectual Hegemony." In *Gender and Sexuality in Twentieth-Century Chinese Literature and Society*, ed. Tonglin Lu, 23–45. Albany: State U of New York P, 1993.

———. *The Protestant Ethnic and the Spirit of Capitalism*. New York: Columbia UP, 2002.

———. "The Secrets of Ethnic Abjection." In *Race" Panic and the Memory of Migration*, ed. Meaghan Morris and Brett de Bary, 53–77. Hong Kong: Hong Kong UP, 2001.

Choy, Wayson. *Paper Shadows: A Chinatown Childhood*. Toronto: Viking, 1999.

Chuh, Kandice. *Imagine Otherwise: On Asian Americanist Critique*. Durham, NC: Duke UP, 2003.

Clifford, James. "On Collecting Art and Culture." In *Out There: Marginalization and Contemporary Cultures*, ed. Russell Ferguson et al., 141–69. Cambridge, MA: New Museum of Contemporary Art and Massachusetts Institute of Technology, 1990.

———. *Routes: Travel and Translation in the Late Twentieth Century*. Cambridge, MA: Harvard UP, 1997.

Clifford, James, and George E. Marcus, eds. In *Writing Culture: The Poetics and Politics of Ethnography*. Berkeley: U of California P, 1986.

Coleman, Daniel, and Donald Goellnicht. "Introduction: 'Race' into the Twenty-First Century." *Essays on Canadian Writing* 75 (2002): 1–29.

The Concise Oxford Dictionary. 10th ed. Oxford: Oxford UP, 1999.

Conkelton, Sheryl. "Roy Kiyooka '… the sad and glad tidings of the floating world …'" In *All Amazed for Roy Kiyooka*, 101–116. Vancouver: Arsenal Pulp Press, 2002.

Coombe, Rosemary J. "The Properties of Culture and the Possession of Identity: Postcolonial Struggle and the Legal Imagination." *Canadian Journal of Law and Jurisprudence* 6, no. 2 (1994): 249–85.

Craib, Ian. *Psychoanalysis: A Critical Introduction*. Cambridge: Polity, 2001.

Crane, Ralph J., and Radhika Mohanram, eds. *Shifting Continents/Colliding Cultures: Diaspora Writing of the Indian Subcontinent*. Amsterdam: Rodopi, 2000.

Dabydeen, Cyril, ed. *Another Way to Dance: Asian Canadian Poetry*. Stratford, ON: Williams-Wallace, 1990.

———, ed. *A Shapely Fire: Changing the Literary Landscape*. Oakville, ON: Mosaic Press, 1987.

Dasgupta, Anannya. "'Do I Remove My Skin?' Interrogating Identity in Suniti Namjoshi's Fables." In *Queering India: Same-Sex Love and Eroticism in Indian Culture and Society*, ed. Ruth Vanita, 100–10. New York: Routledge, 2002.

Davidson, Donald. *Inquiries into Truth and Interpretation*. Oxford: Oxford UP, 1984.

Day, Richard J.F. *Multiculturalism and the History of Canadian Diversity*. Toronto: U of Toronto P, 2000.

Deer, Glenn. "Asian North America in Transit." *Canadian Literature* 163 (Winter 1999): 5–15.

Deleuze, Gilles, and Félix Guattari. "Qu'est-ce qu'une littérature mineure?" In *Kafka: Pour une littérature mineure*, 29–50. Paris: Minuit, 1975.

Deloughery, Elizabeth. "'The litany of islands, the rosary of archipelagos': Caribbean and Pacific Archipelagraphy." *ARIEL* 32, no. 1 (2001): 21–53.

Derksen, Jeff. "Making Race Opaque: Fred Wah's Poetics of Opposition and Differentiation." *West Coast Line* 29, no. 3 (1995–96): 63–76.

Derrida, Jacques. *Without Alibi*. Ed. and trans. Peggy Kamuf. Stanford, CA: Stanford UP, 2002.

Diamond, Sara. "Daring Documents: The Practical Aesthetics of Early Vancouver Video." In *Vancouver Anthology: The Institutional Politics of Art*, ed. Stan Douglas, 47–83. Vancouver: Talonbooks, 1991.

Diehl-Jones, Charlene. "Fred Wah and the Radical Long Poem." In *Bolder Flights: Essays on the Canadian Long Poem*, ed. Frank Tierney and Angela Robbeson, 139–49. Ottawa: U of Ottawa P, 1998.

Donaworth, Jane. *Frankenstein's Daughters: Women Writing Science Fiction*. Syracuse, NY: Syracuse UP, 1997.

Donnell, Alison. "When Writing the Other Is Being True to the Self: Jamaica Kincaid's *The Autobiography of My Mother*." In *Women's Lives into Print: The Theory, Practice and Writing of Feminist Auto/Biography*, ed. Pauline Polkey, 123–36. New York: St. Martin's Press, 1999.

Donnell, Alison, and Sarah Lawson Welsh, eds. "General Introduction." In *The Routledge Reader in Caribbean Literature*, 1–26. London: Routledge, 1996.

Dorscht, Susan Rudy. "'mother/father things I am also': Fred(,) Wah, Breathin' His Name with a Sigh." In *Inside the Poem: Essays and Poems in Honour of Donald Stephens*, ed. W.H. New, 216–24. Toronto: Oxford UP, 1992.

Duden, Barbara. "The Fetus on the 'Father Shore': Toward a History of the Unborn." In *Fetal Subjects, Feminist Positions*, ed. Lynn M. Morgan and Meredith W. Michaels, 13–25. Philadelphia: U of Pennsylvania P, 1999.

Dufault, Roseanna. "Identity and Exile in Shanghai and Montreal: *Les lettres chinoises* by Ying Chen." In *Frontières flottantes: Lieu et espace dans les cultures francophones du Canada / Shifting Boundaries: Place and Space in the Francophone Cultures of Canada*, ed. Jaap Lintvelt and François Paré, 161–67. Amsterdam: Rodopi, 2001.

Ellis, Carolyn. *The Ethnographic I: A Methodological Novel about Autoethnography*. Walnut Creek, CA: Altamira, 2004.

Ellis, Carolyn, and Arthur P. Bochner. "Autoethnography, Personal Narrative, Reflexivity." In *Handbook of Qualitative Research*, 2nd ed., ed. Norman K. Denzin and Yvonna S. Lincoln, 733–68. London: Sage, 2000.

English, James F. "Winning the Culture Game: Prizes, Awards, and the Rules of Art." *New Literary History* 33, no. 1 (2002): 109–35.

Essays on Canadian Writing 56 (1995). Special issue. "Testing the Limits: Postcolonial Theories and Canadian Literatures."

Fanon, Frantz. *Black Skin, White Masks*. Trans. Charles Lam Markmann. New York: Grove Weidenfeld, 1967.

Fischer, Michael M.J. "Ethnicity and the Post-Modern Arts of Memory." In *Writing Culture: The Poetics and Politics of Ethnography*, 194–33. Berkeley: U of California P, 1986.

Fishman, Joshua. "Ethnicity as Being, Doing, and Knowing." In *Ethnicity*, ed. John Hutchinson and Anthony D. Smith, 63–66. Oxford: Oxford UP, 1996.

Freud, Sigmund. "*The Uncanny*." In *The Standard Edition of the Complete Psychological Works of Sigmund Freud*, Vol. 18, ed. and trans. James Strachey, 217–52. London: Vintage, 2001.

Frideres, James. "Managing Immigrant Social Transformations." In *Immigrant Canada: Demographic, Economic and Social Challenges*, ed. Shiva S. Halli and Leo Dreidger, 70–90. Toronto: U of Toronto P, 1999.

Friedman, Susan Stanford. *Mappings: Feminism and the Cultural Geographies of Encounter*. Princeton, NJ: Princeton UP, 1998.

Gagnon, Monika Kin. "Go Ahead, Push My Discursive Limits: The Ambivalence of Paul Wong's Video Works." In *Paul Wong: On Becoming A Man*, ed. Jean Gagnon, 20–35. Ottawa: National Gallery of Canada, 1995.

———. *Other Conundrums: Race, Culture, and Canadian Art*. Vancouver: Arsenal Pulp Press, 2000.

Gagnon, Monika Kin, and Richard Fung. "(Can) Asian Trajectories." In *13 Conversations about Art and Cultural Race Politics*, 97–125. Montreal: Artextes Editions, 2002.

Galloway, Munro. "Ken Lum—It's Not the Revolution Itself …" *Artpress* 209 (January 1996): 48–53.

Gans, Herbert. "Symbolic Ethnicity: The Future of Ethnic Groups and Cultures in America." *Ethnic and Racial Studies* 2 (January 1979): 1–20.

Garber, Marjorie. "'What's Past Is Prologue': Temporality and Prophecy in Shakespeare's History Plays." In *Renaissance Genres: Essays on Theory, History, and Interpretation*, ed. Barbara Lewalski, 301–31. Cambridge: Cambridge UP, 1986.

———. *Vested Interests: Cross-Dressing and Cultural Anxiety*. New York: Routledge, 1992.

Garber, Marjorie, Beatrice Hanssen, and Rebecca L. Walkowitz. "Introduction." In *The Turn to Ethics*, vii–xii. New York: Routledge, 2000.

Gedalof, Irene. *Against Purity: Rethinking Identity with Indian and Western Feminism*. New York: Routledge, 1999.

———. "Identities in Transit: Nomads, Cyborgs and Women." *European Journal of Women's Studies* 7 (2000): 337–54.

Ghandi, Leela. "Loving Well: Homosexuality and Utopian Thought in Post/Colonial India." In *Queering India: Same-Sex Love and Eroticism in Indian Culture and Society*, ed. Ruth Vanita, 87–99. New York: Routledge, 2002.

———. *Postcolonial Theory: A Critical Introduction*. New York: Columbia UP, 1998.

Gilbert, Sylvie. "As Public as Race." In *Margo Kane: Memories Springing, Waters Singing*. Banff, AB: Walter Phillips Gallery, 1993.

Gilroy, Paul. "The Black Atlantic as a Counterculture of Modernity." In *Theorizing Diaspora: A Reader*, ed. Jana Evans Braziel and Anita Mannur, 49–80. Oxford: Blackwell, 2003.

Girard, Isabelle. "Stylistique et esthétique dans trois fragments de *La mémoire de l'eau* de Ying Chen (hypothèses d'analyse socio-critique)." *Tangence* 68 (Winter 2002): 137–53.

Giraud, Lynn, and Sheila Gilhooly. "A Herstory of a Women's Press: Press Gang Printers." *Feminist Bookstore News* 16, no. 2 (August 1993): 47–53.

Goellnicht, Donald C. "A Long Labour: The Protracted Birth of Asian Canadian Literature." *Essays on Canadian Writing* 72 (Winter 2000): 1–41.

Goodeve, Thyrza Nichols. *How Like a Leaf: Donna J. Haraway: An Interview with Thyrza Nichols Goodeve*. New York: Routledge, 1998.

Goto, Hiromi. *Hopeful Monsters*. Vancouver: Arsenal Pulp Press, 2004.

———. *The Kappa Child*. Calgary, AB: Red Deer Press, 2001.

Greenberg, Joshua. "Opinion Discourse and Canadian Newspapers: The Case of the Chinese Boat People." *Canadian Journal of Communication* 25 (2000): 517–37.

Grewal, Interpal, and Caren Kaplan. "Introduction: Transnational Feminist Practices and Questions of Postmodernity." In *Scattered Hegemonies: Postmodernity and Transnational Feminist Practices*, 1–36. Minneapolis: U of Minneapolis P, 1994.

Grice, Helena. *Negotiating Identities: An Introduction to Asian American Women's Writing*. Manchester: Manchester UP, 2002.

Griffiths, Gareth. "The Post-colonial Project: Critical Approaches and Problems." In *New National and Post-colonial Literatures*, ed. Bruce King, 164–77. Oxford: Clarendon Press, 1996.

Guillory, John. "The Ethical Practice of Modernity: The Example of Reading." In *The Turn to Ethics*, ed. Marjorie Garber, Beatrice Hanssen, and Rebecca L. Walkowitz, 29–46. New York: Routledge, 2000.

Gwyn, Richard. *Nationalism Without Walls: The Unbearable Lightness of Being Canadian*. Toronto: McClelland and Stewart, 1995.

Haaken, Janice. "The Recovery of Memory, Fantasy, and Desire in Women's Trauma Stories: Feminist Approaches to Sexual Abuse and Psychotherapy." In *Women, Autobiography, Theory: A Reader*, ed. Sidonie Smith and Julia Watson, 352–66. Madison: U of Wisconsin P, 1998.

Halperin, David H. *One Hundred Years of Homosexuality*. New York: Routledge, 1990.

Hanscombe, Gillian, and Suniti Namjoshi. "Writing the Rag-Bag of Empire." In *Engendering Realism and Postmodernism: Contemporary Women Writers in Britain*, ed. Beate Neumeier, 391–406. Amsterdam: Rodopi, 2001.

Haraway, Donna. "A Cyborg Manifesto: Science, Technology, and Socialist-Feminism in the Late Twentieth Century." In *Simians, Cyborgs and Women: The Reinvention of Nature*, 149–81. New York: Routledge, 1991.

———. "A Cyborg Manifesto: Science, Technology, and Socialist-Feminism in the Late Twentieth Century." In *The Cybercultures Reader*, ed. David Bell and Barbara M. Kennedy, 291–324. New York: Routledge, 2000.

———. *Modest_Witness@Second_Millennium.FemaleMan©_Meets_OncoMouse™*. New York: Routledge, 1997.

———. "The Promise of Monsters: A Regenerative Politics of Inappropriate/d Others." In *Cultural Studies*, ed. Lawrence Grossberg, Cary Nelson, and Paul A. Treichler, 295–337. New York: Routledge, 1992.

Harding, Sandra. "'... Race?': Toward the Science Question in Global Feminisms." In *Whose Science? Whose Knowledge? Thinking from Women's Lives*, 191–217. Ithaca, NY: Cornell UP, 1991.

Hardt, Michael, and Antonio Negri. *Empire*. Cambridge, MA: Harvard UP, 2000.

Hayles, N. Katherine. *How We Became Posthuman: Virtual Bodies in Cybernetics, Literature and Informatics*. Chicago: U of Chicago P, 1999.

Heath-Stubbs, John. "The Hero as a Saint: St. George." In *The Hero in Tradition and Folklore*, ed. H.R.E. Davidson, 1–15. London: Folklore Society, 1984.

Helwig, David, Charles Lillard, and Gayla Reid. "The Chapters/Books in Canada First Novel Award." *Books in Canada* 25, no. 4 (May 1996): 2–4.

Hesse, Jurgen, ed. *Voices of Change: Immigrant Writers Speak Out*. Vancouver: Pulp Press, 1990.

Hilf, Susanne. "'Hybridize or Disappear': Exploring the Hyphen in Fred Wah's *Diamond Grill*." In *Towards a Transcultural Future: Literature and Society in a 'Post'-Colonial World*, ed. Geoffrey Davis, Peter Marsden, Bénédicte Ledent, and Marc Delrez, 239–47. New York: Rodopi, 2005.

Howells, Cora Ann Howells. *Contemporary Canadian Women's Fiction*. New York: Palgrave MacMillan, 2002.

Hubel, Teresa. *Whose India? The Independence Struggle in British and Indian Fiction and History*. Durham, NC: Duke UP, 1996.

Hughes, Alex, and Andrea Noble. *Phototextualities*. Albuquerque: U of New Mexico P, 2003.

Huston, Nancy, and Leïla Sebbar. *Lettres parisiennes: Autopsie de l'exil*. Paris: J'ai lu, 1999.

Hutcheon, Linda. *Narcissistic Narrative: The Metafictional Paradox*. Waterloo, ON: Wilfrid Laurier UP, 1980.

Hutcheon, Linda, and Marion Richmond, eds. *Other Solitudes: Canadian Multicultural Fictions*. Toronto: Oxford UP, 1990.

Irigaray, Luce. *Le corps-à-corps avec la mère*. Montréal: Pleine lune, 1981.

Ishiguro, Kazuo. *The Remains of the Day*. New York: Knopf, 1989.

Iwama, Marilyn. "Fantasy's Trickster," *Canadian Literature* 180 (2004): 138–39.

Iwamoto, Yoshio. "The Kappa Child." *World Literature Today* 77, no. 1 (2003): 102.

JanMohamed, Abdul R., and David Lloyd, eds. *The Nature and Context of Minority Discourse*. New York: Oxford UP, 1990.

Jullien, François. *Eloge de la fadeur: À partir de la pensée et de l'esthétique de la Chine*. Arles: Philippe Picquier, 1991.

Kafka, Philippa. *On the Outside Looking In(dian): Indian Women Writers at Home and Abroad*. New York: Peter Lang Publishing, 2003.

Kamboureli, Smaro. "Faking It: Fred Wah and the Postcolonial Imaginary." *Études canadiennes/Canadian Studies* 54 (2003): 115–32.

———. "The Limits of the Ethical Turn: Troping Towards the Other, Yann Martel, and Self." *University of Toronto Quarterly* 76, no. 3 (Summer 2007): 937–61.

———, ed. *Making a Difference: Canadian Multicultural Writing*. Toronto: Oxford UP, 1996.

———, ed. *Making a Difference: Canadian Multicultural Writing*. 2nd ed. Don Mills, ON: Oxford UP, 2006.

———. *Scandalous Bodies*. Don Mills, ON: Oxford UP, 2000.

Kamuf, Peggy. "On the Limit." In *Community at Loose Ends*, ed. Miami Theory Collective, 13–18. Minneapolis: U of Minnesota P, 1991.

Kanaganayakam, Chelvanayakam. *Counterrealism and Indo-Anglian Fiction*. Waterloo, ON: Wilfrid Laurier UP, 2002.

———. "An Interview with Suniti Namjoshi." In *Configurations of Exile: South Asian Writers and Their World*, 45–58. Toronto: TSAR, 1995.

Kaplan, Ann E. *Motherhood and Representation: The Mother in Popular Culture and Melodrama*. London: Routledge, 1992.

Kim, Elaine H., and Norma Alarcón, eds. *Writing Self, Writing Nation: Essays on Theresa Hak Kyung Cha's* Dictee. Berkeley, CA: Third Woman Press, 1994.

King, Richard. *Indian Philosophy: An Introduction to Hindu and Buddhist Thought*. Edinburgh: Edinburgh UP, 1991.

Kirby, Michael. "The New Theatre." *Tulane Drama Review* 10, no. 2 (1965): 23–43.

Kirby, Vicki. "'Feminisms, Reading, Postmodernisms': Rethinking Complicity." In *Feminism and the Politics of Difference*, ed. Sneja Gunew and Anna Yeatman, 20–34. Halifax, NS: Fernwood Publishing, 1993.

Kogawa, Joy. *Obasan*. Toronto: Penguin Books, 1983. (1981).

Kostash, Myrna. "Pens of Many Colours." *Canadian Forum* (June 1990): 17–19.

Kristeva, Julia. *Powers of Horror: An Essay on Abjection*. Trans. Leon S. Roudiez. New York: Columbia UP, 1982.

Kutz, Christopher. *Complicity: Ethics and Law for a Collective Age*. Cambridge: Cambridge UP, 2000.

Kymlicka, Will. *Multicultural Citizenship: A Liberal Theory of Minority Rights*. Oxford: Clarendon Press, 1995.

Kyung, Theresa Hak. *Dictee*. New York: Tanam Press, 1982.

Lachance, Micheline. "Des vies à l'encre de Chine: Ying Chen écrit à Montréal des romans bouleversants qui se passent à Shanghai." *L'Actualité* 20, no. 18 (November 15, 1995): 89–90.

Lai, Larissa. "Political Animals and the Body of History." *Canadian Literature* 163 (1999): 145–54.

———. *Salt Fish Girl*. Toronto: Thomas Allen, 2002.

———. "The Site of Memory." In *Chinaman's Peak: Walking the Mountain*, ed. Paul Wong, Sylvie Gilbert, Larissa Lai, 1–19. Banff, AB: Walter Phillips Gallery, 1993.

———. *When Fox Is a Thousand*. Vancouver: Press Gang, 1995.

Lai, Larissa, and Jean Lum. "Neither Guests Nor Strangers." In *Yellow Peril Reconsidered*, ed. Paul Wong, 20–24. Vancouver: On Edge, 2000.

Laiwan. *Kiss: a film loop for two projectors*. http://artgallery.dal.ca/engaging/LAIWAN.html.

———. *Language of Mesmerization The Mesmerization of Language*. http://www.belkin.ubc.ca/_archived/mesmerization/.

———. *Machinate: A Projection in Two Movements*. http://www.htmlles.net/2000/webart/laiwbe.html.

———. "notes towards a body." *Capilano Review* 2, no. 24 (1998): 11–13.

———. "notes towards a body II." In *Swallowing Clouds: An Anthology of Chinese-Canadian Poetry*, ed. Andy Quan and Jim Wong-Chu, 146–47. Vancouver: Arsenal Pulp Press, 1999.

———. "Untitled." *West Coast Line* 33/34, no. 3 (2001): 54–55.

———. "Untitled 3." In *History: Portraits from Vancouver*, ed. Karen Love, 30–33. Vancouver: Arsenal Pulp Press, 2002.

Lamming, George. "The Indian Presence as a Caribbean Reality." In *Indenture and Exile: The Indo-Caribbean Experience*, ed. Frank Birbalsingh, 45–54. Toronto: TSAR, 1989.

Lane, Mary E. Bradley. *Mizora: A World of Women*. New York: G.W. Dillingham, 1890. Reprinted with an introduction by Joan Saberhagen. Lincoln: U of Nebraska P, 1999.

Lau, Evelyn. *Runaway: Diary of a Street Kid*. Toronto: Harper and Collins, 1989.

Le Bras, Yvon. "Interview with Ying Chen." *Lingua Romana* 1, no. 1 (Fall 2002). http://linguaromana.byu.edu/yinchen.html.

Lee, Bennett, and Jim Wong Chu, eds. *Many-Mouthed Birds: Contemporary Writing by Chinese Canadians*. Vancouver: Douglas and McIntyre, 1991.

Lee, Rachel C., and Sau-Ling Cynthia Wong. "Introduction." In *AsiaAmerica.Net: Ethnicity, Nationalism and Cyberspace*, xiii–xxxv. Princeton, NJ: Princeton UP, 1999.

Lee, Tara. "Mutant Bodies in Larissa Lai's *Salt Fish Girl*: Challenging the Alliance between Science and Capital." *West Coast Line* 38, no. 2 (Fall 2004): 94–109.

Leiter, Brian. "The Hermeneutics of Suspicion: Recovering Marx, Nietzsche, and Freud." In *The Future for Philosophy*, ed. Brian Leiter, 74–105. Oxford: Clarendon Press, 2004.

Lejeune, Phillippe. *Le Pacte Autobiographique*. Paris: Editions du Seuil, 1975.

———. *Signes de Vie: Le Pacte Autobiographique 2*. Paris: Editions de Seuil, 2005.

Lingis, Alfonso. *The Community of Those Who Have Nothing in Common*. Bloomington: Indiana UP, 1994.

Lionnet, Françoise. *Autobiographical Voices: Race, Gender, Self-Portraiture*. Ithaca, NY: Cornell UP, 1989.

———. *Post-Colonial Representations: Women, Literature, Identity*. Ithaca, NY: Cornell UP, 1995.

Lorde, Audre. *Zami: A New Spelling of My Name*. Berkeley, CA: Crossing Press, 1983.

Lum, Ken. "Art as Counter-Narrative in Public Space." Museum in Progress website. http://www.mip.at/en/dokumente/1674-content.html.

———. "Das größte Bild der Welt." *Neue Zeit*, December 5, 2000.

———. "On Board the Raft of the Medusa." *Nka: Journal of Contemporary African Art* 10 (Spring/Summer 1999): 14–17.

———. "Portraits." In *Notion of Conflict: A Selection of Contemporary Canadian Art*, ed. Dorine Mignot. Amsterdam: Stedelijk Museum, 1995.

Lundgren, Jodi. "Writing 'in Sparkler Script': Incest and the Construction of Subjectivity in Contemporary Canadian Women's Autobiographical Texts." *Essays on Canadian Writing* 65 (Fall 1998): 233–47.

Mackey, Nathaniel. *Discrepant Engagement: Dissonance, Cross-culturality, and Experimental Writing*. New York: Cambridge UP, 1993.

Madison, D. Soyini. *Critical Ethnography: Methods, Ethics, and Performance*. Thousand Oaks, CA: Sage Publications, 2005.

Malraux, André. *Le musée imaginaire de la sculpture mondiale*. Paris: Gallimard, 1952.

Manalansan, Martin F., IV. "Introduction: The Ethnography of Asian America: Notes towards a Thick Description." In *Cultural Compass: Ethnographic Explorations of Asian America*, 1–16. Philadelphia, PA: Temple UP, 2000.

Martin, Biddy. "Lesbian Identity and Autobiographical Difference(s)." In *Life/Lines: Theorizing Women's Autobiography*, ed. Bella Brodzki and Celeste Schenck, 70–103. Ithaca, NY: Cornell UP, 1988.

Martineau, Joel. "Autoethnography and Material Culture: The Case of Bill Reid." *Biography* 24, no. 1 (Winter 2001): 242–58.

Marx, Karl. *The Eighteenth Brumaire of Louise Bonaparte*. New York: International Publishers: 1963.

Massey, Doreen. "Double Articulation: A Place in the World." In *Displacements: Cultural Identities in Question*, ed. Angelika Bammer, 110–21. Bloomington: Indiana UP, 1994.

Mathur, Ashok. "Interview with Larissa Lai." July 1998. http://www.eciad.ca/%7Eamathur/larissa/larissa.html.

———. *The Short Happy Life of Harry Kumar*. Vancouver: Arsenal Pulp Press, 2001.

May, Vivian M. "Dislocation and Desire in Shani Mootoo's *Cereus Blooms at Night*." *Studies in the Literary Imagination* 37, no. 2 (Fall 2004): 97–122.

McFarlane, Scott. "The Haunt of Race: Canada's Multiculturalism Act, the Politics of Incorporation, and Writing Thru Race." *Fuse* 18, no. 3 (1995): 18–31.

McGifford, Dianne, and Judith Kearns, eds. *Shakti's Words: An Anthology of South Asian Canadian Women's Poetry*. Toronto: TSAR, 1990.

McGraw-Hill Encyclopedia of Science and Technology, 5th ed. "Tide." http://www.answers.com/topic/tide.

McMaster, Geoff. "Mootoo Explores New Ground." *University of Alberta Express News*, January 11, 2002. http://www.expressnews.ualberta.ca/expressnews/articles/printer.cfm?p_ID=1707.

Mehta, Brinda. "Cultural Hegemony and the Need to Decentre the Brahmanic Stranglehold of Hindi Womanhood in an Indo-Caribbean Context: A Reading of Lakshmi Persaud's *Sastra* and *Butterfly in the Wind*." *Journal of Commonwealth and Postcolonial Studies* 6, no.1 (1999): 125–52.

Melissaris, Emmanuel. "Review of *Complicity: Ethics and Law for a Collective Age*, by Christopher Kutz." *Law and Politics Book Review* 14, no. 6 (2004): 420–23.

Miki, Roy. "Altered States: Global Currents, the Spectral Nation, and the Production of 'Asian Canadian.'" *Journal of Canadian Studies* 35, no. 3 (2000): 43–72.

———. "Asiancy: Making Space for Asian Canadian Writing." In *Broken Entries: Race, Subjectivity and Writing*, 101–24. Toronto: Mercury Press, 1998.

———. *Broken Entries: Race, Subjectivity, Writing*. Toronto: Mercury Press, 1998.

———. "Can Asian Adian? Reading the Scenes of 'Asian Canadian.'" *West Coast Line* 34, no. 3 (Winter 2001): 56–77.

———. "Can I See Your ID? Writing in the 'Race' Codes that Bind." *West Coast Line* 31, no. 3 (Winter 1997–98): 85–94.

————. "Can I see Your ID?" In *Broken Entries: Race, Subjectivity, Writing*, 205–15. Toronto: Mercury Press, 1998.

Milroy, Sarah. "Vindication of an Art Pioneer." *Globe and Mail*, October 22, 2002.

Misrahi-Barak, Judith. "Beginners' Luck among Caribbean-Canadian Writers: Nalo Hopkinson, André Alexis and Shani Mootoo." *Commonwealth Essays and Studies* 22, no. 1 (1999): 89–96.

Mitchell, W.J.T. *Picture Theory, Essays on Verbal and Visual Representation*. Chicago: U of Chicago P, 2004.

Montesquieu, Charles Louis de Secondat and baron de la Brède. *Lettres persanes*. 1721. Paris: Livre de poche, 1984.

Montpetit, Carole. "Ying Chen. D'est en ouest." *Le Devoir*, May 29, 2004, F1.

Mootoo, Shani. *Cereus Blooms at Night*. Vancouver: Press Gang, 1996.

————. *He Drown She in the Sea*. Toronto: McClelland and Stewart, 2005.

————. *Out on Main Street, and Other Stories*. Vancouver: Press Gang, 1993.

Morris, Robyn. "Making Eyes: Colouring the Look in Larissa Lai's *When Fox Is a Thousand* and Ridley Scott's *Blade Runner*." *Australian Canadian Studies* 20, no. 1 (2002): 75–98.

————. "'What Does It Mean to Be Human?' Racing Monsters, Clones and Replicants." *Foundation: The International Review of Science Fiction* 33 (2004): 81–96.

Moya, Miguel, and Dave Smith. "Exhibit Not Art, Court Told." *Globe and Mail*, February 25, 1984.

Moylan, Tom. *Demand the Impossible: Science Fiction and the Utopian Imagination*. New York: Methuen, 1986.

Mukherjee, Arun. "Canadian Nationalism, Canadian Literature, and Racial Minority Women." *Essays on Canadian Writing* 56 (1995): 78–95.

————. *Oppositional Aesthetics*. Toronto: TSAR, 1994.

Namjoshi, Suniti. *Gojo: An Autobiographical Myth*. Melbourne: Spinifex, 2000.

Narayan, Uma. "Essence of Culture and a Sense of History: A Feminist Critique of Cultural Essentialism." In *Decentering the Centre: Philosophy for a Multicultural, Postcolonial, and Feminist World*, ed. Uma Narayan and Sandra Harding, 81–100. Bloomington: Indiana UP, 2000.

New, W.H. *A History of Canadian Literature*. 2nd ed. Montreal: McGill-Queen's UP, 2003.

The New Princeton Encyclopedia of Poetry and Poetics. "Language Poetry." Princeton, NJ: Princeton UP, 1993.

Niehoff, Arthur, and Juanita Niehoff. *East Indians in the West Indies*. Milwaukee, WI: Milwaukee Public Museum, 1960.

Ondaatje, Michael. *Anil's Ghost*. Toronto: Vintage Canada, 2000.

————. *Running in the Family*. Toronto: McClelland and Stewart, 1982.

Oore, Irène. "*Les lettres chinoises* de Ying Chen: le mobile et l'immobile." *Studies in Canadian Literature/Études en littérature canadienne* 29, no. 1 (2004): 74–83.

Padolsky, Enoch. "Canadian Ethnic Minority Literature in English." In *Ethnicity and Culture in Canada: The Research Landscape*, ed. J.W. Berry and J.A. Laponce, 361–86. Toronto: U of Toronto P, 1994.

Palmer, Howard. "Social Adjustment." In *Immigration and the Rise of Multiculturalism*, 44–53. Toronto: Copp Clark, 1975.

Palmer-Seiler, Tamara. "Multi-Vocality and National Literature." In *Literary Pluralities*, ed. Christl Verduyn, 47–63. Peterborough, ON: Broadview Press, 1998.

Palumbo-Liu, David. "Introduction." In *The Ethnic Canon: Histories, Institutions and Interventions*, 1–30. Minneapolis: U of Minnesota P, 1995.

Paquin, Éric. "Madame et son fantôme." *Voir*. http://www.voir.ca/publishing/article.aspx?article=26384&section=10.

Parrinder, Patrick. "Science Fiction: Metaphor, Myth or Prophecy?" In *Science Fiction: Critical Frontiers*, ed. Karen Sayer and John Moore, 23–34. London: Macmillan, 2000.

Pascal, Blaise. *Œuvres complètes II*. Paris: Gallimard, Pléiade, 2000.

Patron Saints Index, Catholic Forum Online. "Saint George." http://www.catholicforum.com/saints/saintg05.htm.

Pedersen, Carl. "Sea Change: The Middle Passage and the Transatlantic Imagination." In *The Black Columbiad: Defining Moments in African American Literature and Culture*, ed. Werner Sollors and Maria Diedrich, 42–51. Cambridge, MA: Harvard UP, 1994.

Perkins Gilman, Charlotte. *Herland*. 1915. *Herland and Selected Stories*, ed. Barbara H. Solomon. New York: Signet Classics, 1992.

Perreault, Jeanne, and Sylvia Vance. *Writing the Circle: Native Women of Western Canada*. Edmonton, AB: NeWest, 1990.

Petchesky, Rosalind Pollack. "Foetal Images: The Power of Visual Culture in the Politics of Representation." In *The Gendered Cyborg: A Reader*, ed. Gill Kirkup et al., 171–92. London: Routledge, 2000.

Petievich, Carla. "Doganas and Zanakhis: The Invention and Subsequent Erasure of Urdu Poetry's 'Lesbian' Voice." In *Queering India: Same-Sex Love and Eroticism in Indian Culture and Society*, ed. Ruth Vanita, 47–60. New York: Routledge, 2002.

Petrone, Penny. *Native Literature in Canada: From the Oral Tradition to the Present*. Toronto: Oxford UP, 1990.

Philip, Marlene Nourbese. *She Tries Her Tongue, Her Silence Softly Breaks*. Charlottetown, PE: Ragweed Press, 1989.

Pimpaneau, Jacques. *Dans un jardin de Chine*. Arles: Philippe Picquier, 2000.

Pivato, Joseph. "Representation of Ethnicity as a Problem." In *Literary Pluralities*, ed. Christl Verduyn, 152–62. Peterborough, ON: Broadview Press, 1998.

Ponzanesi, Sandra. *Paradoxes of Post-Colonial Culture: Contemporary Women Writers of the Indian and Afro-Italian Diaspora*. Albany: State U of New York P, 2004.

Poynting, Jeremy. "'You Want to Be a Coolie Woman?': Gender and Ethnicity in Indo-Caribbean Women's Writing." In *Caribbean Women Writers: Essays from the First International Conference*, ed. Selwyn R. Cudjoe, 98–105. Wellesley, MA: Calaloux, 1990.

Pratt, Mary-Louise. *Imperial Eyes: Travel Writing and Transculturation*. New York: Routledge, 1992.

———. "Transculturation and Autoethnography: Peru 1615/1980." In *Colonial Discourse/Postcolonial Theory*, ed. Frances Barker, Peter Holme, and Margaret Iverson, 24–46. Manchester: Manchester UP, 1994.

Probyn, Elspeth. *Outside Belongings*. New York: Routledge, 1996.

Puar, Jasbir K. "Transnational sexualities: South Asian (Trans)nation(alism)s and Queer Diasporas." In *Q&A: Queer in Asian America*, ed. David L. Eng and Alice Y. Hom, 405–23. Philadelphia, PA: Temple UP, 1998.

Puri, Shalini. "Race, Rape, and Representation: Indo-Caribbean Women and Cultural Nationalism." *Cultural Critique* 36 (1997): 119–64.

Rajan, Gita. "(Con)figuring Identity: Cultural Space of the Indo-British Border Intellectual." In *Writing New Identities: Gender, Nation, and Immigration in Contemporary Europe*, ed. Gisela Brinker-Gabler and Sidonie Smith, 78–99. Minneapolis: U of Minnesota P, 1997.

Rak, Julie. "Doukhobor Autobiography as Witness Narrative." *Biography: An Interdisciplinary Quarterly* 24, no. 1 (Winter 2001): 226–41.

Reed-Danahay, Deborah E., ed. *Auto/Ethnography: Rewriting the Self and the Social*. Oxford: Berg, 1997.

Ricoeur, Paul. *Freud and Philosophy: An Essay on Interpretation*. Trans. Denis Savage. New Haven, CT: Yale UP, 1970.

Riley, Patrick. *Character and Conversion in Autobiography: Augustine, Montaigne, Descartes, Rousseau, and Sartre*. Charlottesville: U of Virginia P, 2004.

Robinson, Sally. *Engendering the Subject: Gender and Self-Representation in Contemporary Women's Fiction*. New York: State U of New York P, 1991.

Rudy, Susan. "Fred Wah—*Among*." In *Writing in Our Time*, ed. Pauline Butling and Susan Rudy, 103–14. Waterloo, ON: Wilfrid Laurier UP, 2005.

Rychlak, Joseph F. "Morality in a Mediating Mechanism? A Logical Learning Theorist Looks at Social Constructionism." In *Social Discourse and Moral Judgement*, ed. Daniel N. Robinson, 43–60. San Diego, CA: Academic Press, 1992.

Saakana, Amon Saba. *The Colonial Legacy in Caribbean Literature*. Trenton, NJ: Africa World Press, 1987.

Sage, Elspeth. "Curatorial Statement for *Paul Wong: Hungry Ghosts*." Neutral Ground gallery, Regina, SK. http://www.neutralground.sk.ca/?page=eventdetail &pageid=1&year=2003&id=200451204212504.

———. "Ethics and Art." *Parallelogramme* 12, no. 4 (April/May 1987): 26–29.

Saint-Martin, Lori. "Infanticide, Suicide, Matricide, and Mother–Daughter Love: Suzanne Jacob's *L'Obéissance* and Ying Chen's *L'Ingratitude*." *Canadian Literature* 169 (Summer 2001): 60–83.

Sakamoto, Kerri. *One Hundred Million Hearts*. Toronto: A.A. Knopf Canada, 2003.

Sarraute, Nathalie. "L'ère du soupcon." In *Œuvres complètes*, 71–72. Paris: Gallimard, Pléiade, 1996.

————. "Forme et contenu du roman." In *Œuvres complètes*, 1663–79. Paris: Gallimard, Pléiade, 1996.

————. "Roman et réalité." In *Œuvres complètes*, 1643–56. Paris: Gallimard, Pléiade, 1996.

Sartre, Jean-Paul. *Huis-clos*. Paris: Gallimard, 1947.

Saul, Joanne. "Displacement and Self-Representation: Theorizing Contemporary Canadian Biotexts." *Biography: An Interdisciplinary Quarterly* 24, no. 1 (2001): 259–72.

Scott, Clive. *The Spoken Image: Photography and Language*. London: Reaktion Books, 1999.

Scott, David. *Refashioning Futures*. Princeton, NJ: Princeton UP, 1999.

Scott, Kitty, and Martha Hanna, eds. *Ken Lum: Works with Photography*. Ottawa: Canadian Museum of Contemporary Photography, 2002.

Sedgwick, Eve. "Teaching Experimental Critical Writing." In *The Ends of Performance*, ed. Peggy Phelan and Jill Lane, 104–50. New York: New York UP, 1998.

Seenarine, Moses. "Indentured Indian Women in Colonial Guyana: Recruitment, Migration, Labor and Caste." In *Sojourners to Settlers: The Indian Migrants in the Caribbean and the Americas*, ed. Mahin Gosine and Dhanpaul Narine. http://www.saxakali.com/indocarib/sojourner1.htm.

Seyhan, Azade. *Writing Outside the Nation*. Princeton, NJ: Princeton UP, 2001.

Shepherd, Verene A. "Official Policy Towards the Education of Children of Indian Immigrants and Settlers in Jamaica, 1879–1950." In *Sojourners to Settlers: The Indian Migrants in the Caribbean and the Americas*, ed. Mahin Gosine and Dhanpaul Narine. http://www.saxakali.com/indocarib/sojourner1.htm.

Shikatani, Gerry, and David Aylward, eds. *Paper Doors: An Anthology of Japanese Canadian Poetry*. Toronto: Coach House, 1981.

Siemerling, Winfried. *The New North American Studies: Culture, Writing and the Politics of Re/Cognition*. New York: Routledge, 2005.

————, ed. *Writing Ethnicity*. Toronto: ECW Press, 1996.

————. *Discoveries of the Other: Alterity in the Work of Leonard Cohen, Hubert Aquin, Michael Ondaatje, and Nicole Brossard*. Toronto: U of Toronto P, 1994.

Silverman, Kaja. *The Threshold of the Visible World*. New York and London: Routledge, 1996.

Simon, Sherry. "The Language of Difference: Minority Writers in Quebec." In *A/Part*, ed. J.M. Bumsted, 119–27. Vancouver: Canadian Literature, 1987.

Singer, Linda. "Recalling a Community at Loose Ends." In *Community at Loose Ends*, ed. Miami Theory Collective, 121–34. Minneapolis: U of Minnesota P, 1991.

Sivert, Eileen. "Ying Chen's *Les lettres chinoises* and Epistolary Identity." In *Doing Gender: Franco-Canadian Women Writers of the 1990s*, ed. Paula Ruth Gilbert and Roseanna Dufault, 217–34. Madison, NJ: Fairleigh Dickinson UP, 2001.

Slemon, Stephen. "Afterword: The English Side of the Lawn." *Essays on Canadian Writing* 56 (1995): 274–86.

Smith, Dorothy E., and Sara J. David, eds. *Women Look at Psychiatry*. Vancouver: Press Gang, 1975.

Smith, Sidonie. *A Poetics of Women's Autobiography: Marginality and the Fictions of Self-Representation*. Bloomington: Indiana UP, 1987.

Smith, Sidonie, and Julia Watson. *Women, Autobiography, Theory*. Madison: U of Wisconsin P, 1998.

Smyth, Heather. "Sexual Citizenship and Caribbean-Canadian Fiction: Dionne Brand's *In Another Place, Not Here* and Shani Mootoo's *Cereus Blooms at Night*." *ARIEL* 30, no. 2 (1999): 143–60.

Srikanth, Rajini. *The World Next Door: South Asian American Literature and the Idea of America*. Philadelphia, PA: Temple UP, 2004.

Stallybrass, Peter, and Allon White. "Introduction." In *The Politics and Poetics of Transgression*, 1–26. Ithaca, NY: Cornell UP, 1986.

Statistics Canada. "100 Years of Immigration to Canada: 1901–2001." http://www12.statcan.ca/english/census01/products/analytic/multimedia.cfm.

Stepto, Robert. *From Behind the Veil: A Study of Afro-American Narrative*. Urbana: U of Illinois P, 1979.

Strongman, Luke. *The Booker Prize and the Legacy of Empire*. Amsterdam: Rodopi, 2002.

Sugars, Cynthia. "'The Negative Capability of Camoflage': Fleeing Diaspora in Fred Wah's *Diamond Grill*." *Studies in Canadian Literature* 26, no. 1 (2001): 27–45.

Sultana, Rebecca. "'Many Souls, Many Voices': Multiple Transformations of Meena Alexander's Nomadic Characters." In *Discussing Indian Women Writers: Some Feminist Issues*, ed. Alessandro Monti and R.K. Dhawan, 216–46. New Delhi: Prestige Books, 2004.

Sumathy, Sivamohan. "Becoming Women: Travelling Gender and identity Politics in Four Women's Texts." In *Discussing Indian Women Writers: Some Feminist Issues*, ed. Alessandro Monti and R.K. Dhawan, 247–93. New Delhi: Prestige Books, 2004.

Talbot, Emile. "Rewriting *Les lettres chinoises*: The Poetics of Erasure." *Quebec Studies* 36 (Fall 2003/Winter 2004): 83–91.

Taylor, Charles. "The Politics of Recognition." In *Multiculturalism*, ed. Amy Gutman, 25–73. Princeton, NJ: Princeton UP, 1994.

Thomas, Jim. *Doing Critical Ethnography*. Newbury Park, CA: Sage, 1993.

Tinker, Hugh. *A New System of Slavery: The Export of Indian Labour Overseas, 1830–1920*. Oxford: Oxford UP, 1974.

"Tiptree Award to Hiromi Goto." *Science Fiction Chronicle* 24, no. 7 (2002): 4.

Ty, Eleanor. *The Politics of the Visible in Asian North American Narratives*. Toronto: U of Toronto P, 2004.

Ty, Eleanor, and Donald C. Goellnicht, eds. *Asian North American Identities Beyond the Hyphen*. Bloomington: Indiana UP, 2004.

Ty, Eleanor, and Christl Verduyn. "Beyond Autoethnography: Writing Race and Ethnicity in Canada." Call for papers, 2005. http://info.wlu.ca/%7Ewwweng/ety/Ethnicity-conference.

Van Den Abbeele, Georges. "Introduction." In *Community at Loose Ends*, ed. Miami Theory Collective, ix–xxvi. Minneapolis: U of Minnesota P, 1991.

Van Maanen, John. "The End of Innocence: The Ethnography of Ethnography." In *Representation in Ethnography*, ed. John Van Maanen, 1–35. London: Sage, 1995.

Varley, Chris. "Intersections: Interview between Chris Varley and Roy Kiyooka." *Roy K. Kiyooka: 25 Years*. Vancouver: Vancouver Art Gallery, 1975.

Vassanji, M.G., ed. *A Meeting of Streams: South Asian Canadian Literature*. Toronto: TSAR, 1985.

Verduyn, Christl, ed. *Literary Pluralities*. Peterborough, ON: Broadview Press, 1998.

Vevaina, Coomi S. "An Interview with Suniti Namjoshi." *ARIEL* 29, no. 1 (January 1998): 195–201.

Vijayasree, C. "Alter-Nativity, Migration, Marginality and Narration: The Case of Indian Women Writers Settled in the West." In *Shifting Continents/Colliding Cultures: Diaspora Writing of the Indian Subcontinent*, eds. Ralph J. Crane and Radhika Mohanram, 123–33. Amsterdam: Rodopi, 2000.

———. "An Interview with Suniti Namjoshi." In *Suniti Namjoshi: The Artful Transgressor*, 175–82. Jaipur: Rawat Publications, 2001.

Visweswaran, Kamala. *Fictions of Feminist Ethnography*. Minneapolis: U of Minnesota P, 1994.

Wah, Fred. "China Journal." In *Faking It: Poetics and Hybridity*, 159–84. Edmonton, AB: NeWest Press, 2000.

———. *Diamond Grill*. Edmonton, AB: NeWest, 1996.

———. "Half-Bred Poetics." In *Faking It: Poetics and Hybridity*, 71–96. Edmonton, AB: NeWest Press, 2000.

———. "Is a Door a Word?" *Mosaic* 37, no. 4 (2004): 39–70.

———. "A Poetics of Ethnicity." In *Faking It: Poetics and Hybridity*, 51–66. Edmonton, AB: NeWest Press, 2000.

———. "A Poetics of Ethnicity." In *Twenty Years of Multiculturalism: Successes and Failures*, ed. Stella Hryniuk, 99–110. Winnipeg, MB: St. John's College P, 1992.

———. "Poetics of the Potent." In *Faking It: Poetics and Hybridity*, 194–208. Edmonton, AB: NeWest Press, 2000.

———. "Speak My Language." In *Faking It: Poetics and Hybridity*, 109–126. Edmonton, AB: NeWest Press, 2000.

———. "Strang(l)ed Poetics." In *Faking It: Poetics and Hybridity*, 21–44. Edmonton, AB: NeWest Press, 2000.

———. "Strangle Two." In *Faking It: Poetics and Hybridity*, 45–50. Edmonton, AB: NeWest Press, 2000.

———. *Waiting for Saskatchewan*. Winnipeg, MB: Turnstone, 1985.

Wah, Fred, and Frank Davey. "Meandering Interview." *Open Letter* 12, no. 3 (Summer 2004): 98–122.

Wah, Fred, and Susan Rudy. "Fred Wah on Hybridity and Asianicity in Canada." In *Poets Talk: Conversations with Robert Kroetsch, Daphne Marlatt, Erin Mouré, Dionne Brand, Marie Annharte Baker, Jeff Derksen and Fred Wah*, ed. Paula Butling and Susan Rudy, 143–70. Edmonton: U of Alberta P, 2005.

Walcott, Derek. "The Antilles: Fragments of Epic Memory." *Georgia Review* 44, no. 1 (1995): 294–306.

Watada, Terry. "To Go for Broke: The Spirit of the 70s." *Canadian Literature* 163 (1999): 80–92.

Watson, Julia. "Autoethnography." *Encyclopedia of Life Writing: Autobiographical and Biographical Forms*, ed. Margareta Jolly, 83–86. London and Chicago: Fitzroy Dearborn Publishers, 2001.

Weaver, Andy. "Synchronous Foreignicity: Fred Wah's Poetry and the Recuperation of Experimental Texts." *Studies in Canadian Literature* 30, no. 1 (2005): 309–25.

Webster's Ninth New Collegiate Dictionary. Springfield, MA: Merriam-Webster, 1988.

Weh, Vitus H. "Was heißt hier heimat" (What is home called here). *Falter*, January 2, 2001.

Weir, Lorraine. "Normalizing the Subject: Linda Hutcheon and the English-Canadian Postmodern." In *Canadian Canons*, ed. Robert Lecker, 180–95. Toronto: U of Toronto P, 1991.

Wittgenstein, Ludwig. *Culture and Value*. Ed. G.H. von Wright. Trans. Peter Winch. Chicago: U of Chicago P, 1980.

Wittig, Monique. *The Straight Mind and Other Essays*. Boston: Beacon Press, 1992.

Wolmark, Jenny. *Aliens and Others: Science Fiction, Feminism and Postmodernism*. Hemel Hempstead, UK: Harvester Wheatsheaf, 1994.

Wong, Paul. *The Class of 2000*. http://www.ccca.ca/artists/media_detail.html?languagePref=en&mkey=47724&link_id=744.

———. *Commentary from the Producers of Unite Against Racism: See People for Who They Really Art*. Toronto: Canadian Race Relations Foundation, 2005.

———. *Hungry Ghosts*. http://www.hungryghosts.net/hungryghosts.htm.

———. "Walking the Mountain: Performance Description." In *Feng Shui*, ed. Elspeth Sage, 31–32. Vancouver: On Edge, 1994.

———, ed. *Yellow Peril Reconsidered*. Vancouver: On Edge, 1990.

Wong, Rita. "Market Forces and Powerful Desires: Reading Evelyn Lau's Cultural Labour." *Essays in Canadian Writing* 73 (2001): 122–40.

Wong, Rita, and Larissa Lai. "Sybil Unrest." *West Coast Line* 38, no. 2 (2004): 39–60.

Wong, Sau-ling Cynthia. *Reading Asian American Literature: From Necessity to Extravagance*. Princeton, NJ: Princeton UP, 1993.

Yau, John. *Radiant Silhouette: New and Selected Work, 1974–1988*. Santa Rosa, CA: Black Sparrow Press, 1989.

Yu, Sydnia. "Asian Canadian Theatre Group Looks to Future." *Young People's Press*, February 11, 2003. http://www.ypp.net/fullarticle.asp?ID=154.

Yu, Timothy. "Form and Identity in Language Poetry and Asian American Poetry." *Contemporary Literature* 41, no. 3 (Fall 2000): 422–61.

Yudice, George. Introduction and trans. *Consumers and Citizens: Globalization and Multicultural Conflicts*, by Nestor Garcia Canclini. Minneapolis: U of Minnesota P, 2001.

Young, Judy. "No Longer 'Apart'? Multiculturalism Policy and Canadian Literature." *Canadian Ethnic Studies* 33, no. 2 (2001): 88–116.

Yu, Henry, and Guy Beauregard, guest eds. *Pacific Canada: Beyond the 49th Parallel*. Special Commemorative Issue of *Amerasia Journal* 33, no. 2 (2007).

Žižek, Slavoj. "Multiculturalism; or, The Cultural Logic of Late Capitalism." *New Left Review* 225 (September–October 1997): 44.

[contributors]

Pilar Cuder-Domínguez is Associate Professor of English at the University of Huelva (Spain), where she teaches British and English-Canadian Literature. Her research interests are the intersections of gender, genre, nation, and race. She is the author of *Margaret Atwood: A Beginner's Guide* (2003), and the (co)-editor of five collections of essays (*La mujer del texto al contexto*, 1996; *Exilios femeninos*, 2000; *Sederi XI*, 2002; *Espacios de Género*, 2005; and *The Female Wits*, 2006). She has been visiting scholar at universities in Canada and the United States: McGill (1997), Dalhousie (1999), Northwestern (2002), and Toronto (2004). Her current research deals with Canadian women's transnational poetics.

Smaro Kamboureli is Canada Research Chair in Critical Studies in Canadian Literature at the University of Guelph and the Director of the Trans-Canada Institute. Her publications include *Scandalous Bodies: Diasporic Literature in English Canada* and a new edition of *Making a Difference: Multicultural Literatures in English*.

Eva C. Karpinski teaches women's life writing, cultural studies, and feminist theory in the School of Women's Studies at York University in Toronto. Her research interests include postmodernist fiction, immigrant autobiography, translation studies, and feminist ethics. She has published articles on John Barth, Thomas Pynchon, Raymond Federman, and Eva Hoffman. She is the editor of *Pens of Many Colours*, an anthology of Canadian multicultural writing. Her article on Angela Carter won the best essay award from *Utopian Studies* in 2001.

Christine Kim is Assistant Professor of English at Simon Fraser University. Her teaching and research focus on contemporary Canadian literature, feminist theory, print culture and publishing, and diasporic writing. She has published articles in *Mosaic, Open Letter*, and *Studies in Canadian Literature* and has an essay forthcoming in *Essays on Canadian Writing*.

Kristina Kyser is an instructor of Canadian literature at the University of Toronto, where she completed her doctorate in 2004. Her research and teaching interests include literature and ethics and postcolonial theory. She is also interested in interdisciplinary approaches to Canadian literature from the perspectives of philosophy, religious studies, and political science. She has published or presented papers on Michael Ondaatje, Thomas King, Rohinton Mistry, and Yann Martel. She is currently revising her book-length study, *Swallowed by the Whale: Bible and Nation in English-Canadian Writing*, for publication.

Larissa Lai is Assistant Professor of English at the University of British Columbia. She is the author of two novels, *When Fox Is a Thousand* and *Salt Fish Girl*. Her research interests include race, memory, subjectivity, globalization, sexuality, labour, cyborgs, strategy, and borders.

Paul Lai teaches Asian American literature at the University of St. Thomas in Minnesota. He is researching a project on sound and Asian American cultures. His work considers Asian American Studies as a pedagogical practice, an institutional presence, and a theoretical space for addressing social issues. His work explores how things like anthologies, music websites, and comedy routines link screams, cries, melodies, accents, and other sounds to Asian American identities and politics.

Tara Lee holds a Ph.D. in English Literature from Simon Fraser University. Her teaching interests are in Canadian literature and ethnic minority writing. She has published articles on Asian Canadian literature and identity in journals such as *West Coast Line, Dandelion*, and *Cultural Studies Review*.

Christine Lorre is an Assistant Professor of English at Université Paris III—Sorbonne Nouvelle. Her teaching interests are in American studies, literature in English, and translation. She has published articles in journals edited in France (*Etudes canadiennes / Canadian Studies, Commonwealth, Journal of the Short Story in English / Cahiers de la nouvelle, Lisa*) and as chapters in books published in France (*Lectures d'une œuvre:* The Handmaid's Tale, *Margaret Atwood*, Editions du Temps; *Les Amériques et le Pacifique*, Université Rennes 2) and in Canada (*Vision / Division dans l'œuvre de Nancy Huston*, Presses de l'Université d'Ottawa).

Mariam Pirbhai is an Assistant Professor in the Department of English and Film Studies at Wilfrid Laurier University in Waterloo, Ontario, where she teaches Post-Colonial Literatures and Theory. Her publications include articles on Indo-Caribbean Literature, Post-Colonial Theory, Multicultural Writing in Canada, and on literary figures such as Salman Rushdie. She is presently working on a book-length study of the theoretical and socio-historical intersections between indentured labour and slavery in Caribbean writing.

Joanne Saul teaches English and Canadian Studies at the University of Toronto. She is author of *Writing the Roaming Subject: The Biotext in Canadian Literature* (University of Toronto Press, 2006). She is also co-owner of the independent bookstore TYPE Books in Toronto.

Ming Tiampo is an Assistant Professor of Art History at Carleton University in Ottawa. Her research examines questions of cultural translation and transmission in an international context, concentrating on Japan's relations with the West as well as pluralism in Canada. Her current projects include an exhibition on pluralism in Canada, as well as a book that considers the Japanese avant-garde art movement Gutai in a transnational context. She has published and given papers in Japan, Europe, the United States, and Canada, and in 2004–5 was the curator of the award-winning exhibition "Electrifying Art: Atsuko Tanaka 1954–1968" at the Grey Art Gallery in New York and at the Morris and Helen Belkin Art Gallery in Vancouver. She is a founding member of the Centre for Transnational Cultural Analysis (CTCA) at Carleton.

Eleanor Ty is Professor and Chair of English & Film Studies at Wilfrid Laurier University. Author of *The Politics of the Visible in Asian North American Narratives* (University of Toronto Press, 2004), *Empowering the Feminine: The Narratives of Mary Robinson, Jane West, and Amelia Opie, 1796–1812* (University of Toronto Press, 1998), and *Unsex'd Revolutionaries: Five Women Novelists of the 1790s* (University of Toronto Press, 1993), she has edited *Memoirs of Emma Courtney* (Oxford 1996) and *The Victim of Prejudice* (Broadview 1994) by Mary Hays and has co-edited with Donald Goellnicht a collection of essays, *Asian North American Identities Beyond the Hyphen* (Indiana University Press, 2004). She has published essays on Michael Ondaatje, on Joy Kogawa, on Jamaica Kincaid, on reading romances, on *Exotica*, and on *Miss Saigon*.

Christl Verduyn is Professor of Canadian Studies and Canadian literature at Mount Allison University. She publishes on Canadian and Québécois women's writing and criticism, multiculturalism and minority writing, life writing, and interdisciplinary approaches to literature. Recent books include *Identity, Community, Nation: Essays on Canadian Writing* (with D. Schaub, 2002), *Marian Engel: Life in Letters* (with K. Garay, 2004), and *Must Write: Edna Staebler's Diaries* (2005). Her 1995 study *Lifelines: Marian Engel's Writings* received the Gabrielle Roy Book Prize.

[index]

321